D1715926

POLICE PRACTICES
An International Review

Edited by

DILIP K. DAS

The Scarecrow Press, Inc.
Metuchen, N.J., & London
1994

The Introduction to this book is based to a degree on a 1990 article by Dilip K. Das entitled "Review Essay: The Work of David H. Bayley," which was originally published in *Justice Quarterly* 7(1): 209-221. Portions of that article are reprinted in this volume courtesy and permission of the Academy of Criminal Justice Sciences.

British Library Cataloguing-in-Publication data available

Library of Congress Cataloging-in-Publication Data

Police practices : an international review / edited by Dilip K. Das.
p. cm.
Includes bibliographical references.
ISBN 0-8108-2908-8 (acid-free paper)
1. Police—Cross-cultural studies. 2. Law enforcement—Cross-cultural studies. I. Das, Dilip K., 1941- .
HV7921.P5715 1994
363.2—dc20 94-18256

Manufactured in the United States of America

Printed on acid-free paper

CONTENTS

FOREWORD

This book was completed during my term as a Visiting Scholar at Prison Personnel Training Centre in Finland. I am most grateful to Aimo Myllylä, the Director of this Centre for his kindness, cooperation, and assistance. I am also grateful to other colleagues here, particularly Matti Niiskorpi who gave me excellent technical support with the printing of the entire manuscript. Without Matti's help, it would have been impossible to finish this project. His efforts and generous help are most deeply appreciated. Others who deserve special words of thanks are the Prison Administration Librarian, Tuomo Silenti and the draughtsman, Kalevi Yrjänä for their kind cooperation.

Undertaking a task that called for collaboration of colleagues from five different countries was extremely challenging. Language has been one of the biggest challenges. Two of the collaborators being from non-English speaking countries, the finalization of their chapters took me very long. It has also been tremendously hard to get the manuscript printed in a non-English-speaking country. Luckily, the majority of the collaborators had no problem with the language of the book and, therefore, I could finish the project. At times, the numerous challenges were so daunting that I was indeed frustrated and almost gave it up.

I thank Graeme Dunstall, Steve James, Ahti Laitinen, Haruo Ueno, and S. M. Diaz for their splendid cooperation, patience, and understanding. It is a matter of great joy that living in three different continents we were able to keep in touch with each other through correspondence and telephone.

My research visits to Australia and New Zealand, which enabled me to contact Steve James and Graeme Dunstall, were greatly facilitated by the assistance I received from the Criminology Departments at the University of Melbourne and the Victoria University of Wellington as well as the police departments in New Zealand, particularly the Royal New Zealand Police College, and the Victoria Police Department in Melbourne. I was greatly helped by Professor Sadahiko Takahashi of Toyonaka and the National Police Agency in Tokyo during my visit to Japan which enabled me to contact Haruo Ueno. My visit to Finland was financed by the University of Turku and the Peace Research Council in Tampere. It was during this visit I was able to get Ahti Laitinen to work on the Finnish chapter.

This is the second book project that I finished during the sabbatical granted to me by Western Illinois University. In this connection, I must mention K. J. Lång, the Director General of Prison Administration in Finland for inviting me to spend the entire sabbatical as his Department's guest. This invitation supported by generous financial grants has enabled me to utilize the sabbatical most productively. I thank him profusely. Last but not the least, I wish to thank my wife, Snezana and my children, Mintie and Trideep. Mrs. Ulla Foley and Mrs. Purnakala Gurung also did their best to provide me with loving support in this endeavor, along with my wife and children. I am profoundly indebted to them all.

Dr. Dilip K. Das
Department of Law Enforcement Administration
Western Illinois University
Macomb, Illinois

INTRODUCTION

by Dilip K. Das

This project was conceived in 1986. It has taken several years to complete it. I found it very challenging to assemble a group of writers from vastly different countries in order to work on a set of specific topics. It is easy to lose sight of the commonality of the purpose and the integrity of the theme. Concepts, connotations, understanding, and priorities vary enormously across cultures and academic disciplines causing big problems for a project director. It requires extraordinary efforts to keep the team on track. All this is time-consuming.

A DESCRIPTION OF THE PROJECT

The project involved a new kind of book on international comparative policing covering a few countries with respect to some specfic aspects of policing. These aspects were: mandate and philosophy of the police; functions; personnel practices (selection, training, and promotion); leadership and supervisory calibre; standards used in evaluating individual performance; professionalization; wages, status, subculture, and morale; unions and associations; public police relations, public confidence, trust, and restraints on the police; and, problems of the police. Each country's account was to include an "introduction" containing relevant information about the country with a view to enabling the reader to appreciate the police as the product of a unique culture. Each writer was also to add a "conclusion" to the chapter analyzing and highlighting the major points of his account as well as his thoughts and reflections on the police of his particular country. It will be noted that the chapters vary in size because of varying degrees of the availability of the material, language difficulties, and each writer's style of presentation.

Included in the book are the police of Australia, Finland, India, Japan, and New Zealand. The countries included were chosen for reasons of convenience. To begin with, I approached potential contributors in a large number of countries. But for a variety of reasons, I was unable to find many successful contributors. While scholars from several other countries were initially agreeable, their contributions were not forthcoming. I had to receive the contributions on time. Further, it was my plan to study personally and directly the police of each country included in the book. This was so planned as I wished to acquire a firsthand knowledge of the police covered in the project in order to satisfy myself regarding the objectivity of the accounts included in the book. (See also the book, *Policing in Six Countries Around the World* (Das, 1993), containing my account of policing in India, Australia, Canada, Finland, Germany, and New Zealand. I am working on a book which will include my observations regarding the police in Japan). Not all countries welcome police research. So I could select only some of those countries where I was allowed to study the police according to my plan. Finally, I was successful in making the contributors of the countries included send me their accounts on time.

The aspects selected for discussion, in my opinion, are logically connected with each other. They constitute an important set. It is useful to know what the mandate and philosophy of the police are. Are their "functions" consistent with their mandate and philosophy? If not, why are they not so? In order to carry out the functions they are entrusted with, the police need to have suitable personnel. It is logical, therefore, to enquire as to how personnel are inducted, trained and nurtured. Hence, a section in each chapter is devoted to "Personnel Practices."

How are these personnel led and supervised? In order to understand the practice in this regard, included is a section on "Leadership/Supervisory Calibre." Moreover, a section on the "Standards Used in Evaluating Individual Police Performance" was considered necessary. It is important to know how the police are evaluated in various countries. Related to such an evaluation procedure are police professionalization and the matters of police wages, status, subculture, and morale. A discussion of "Unions and Associations," is included in a section that comes toward the end of each chapter; it also provides information concerning the ways grievances, officers' complaints, and their demands are settled. To enjoy popular trust and confidence is important for the police for their success depends a great deal on public support and goodwill. Therefore, I have included a section on police public relations, public confidence, trust, and restraints on the police. The more trust and confidence of the public the police enjoy, the more likely they are to be free from unnecessary restraints. I was also interested in obtaining each contributor's account of what he considered to be the burning problems of his country's police. Hence, a section on "Problems of the Police."

As mentioned above, each contributor was aware of the unique nature of his country's police. They were encouraged to write their accounts in such a way as to enable one to see the police as the product of their country's culture. In this context culture was defined as every thing that gives a distinct character to a people, a particular society. Apart from tracing the police to their culture, each contributor was urged to highlight the most attractive features of the police of his country. This was important as the book has a pragmatic purpose. This practical objective necessitated an enquiry, an exploration as to what the police from one country could learn from one another. The authors were asked to support their description of the attractive features with details so that those who wanted to experiment with any of the practices could do so based on the elaborate accounts given in the chapters. Depending on the cultural compatibility (Bayley, 1977), certain attractive features of policing from one country can be introduced in another. Finally, in a conclusion of the book entitled "Summary and Overview" I have made some generalized observations on policing based on the police included in the book. Since these observations are based on the police in Australia, Finland, India, Japan, and New Zealand, however, they are likely to be severely limited.

At the back of my mind I always had United States police as the point of reference to compare the police of other countries with. It is hoped that an American reader will be able to recognize the true and unique nature of his police by reading *Police Practices: An*

International Review. Non-American readers, too, will be able to compare the police of their country with their counterparts included in the book. This should enable them to understand their own police better. Indeed, the accounts of the police in Australia, New Zealand, Japan, and Finland have helped me understand my own Indian police experience more clearly.

WHY COMPARATIVE INTERNATIONAL STUDIES? AN AMERICAN PERSPECTIVE AND SURVEY OF RELEVANT LITERATURE

Major comparative police works by U. S. researchers seem to have a number of objectives. They help us recognize "the character" of the police of the U. S. (Bayley, 1977). True, as Punch (1983) says, "we remain fundamentally backward in exploring police organization." International comparative police studies in the United States also present several practices and features of international policing which are generally praised as superior to those found in American police. Implicit in such praise is a message that American police can perhaps benefit from some of these admirable practices. Of course, it is recognized in the international comparative police literature in the United States that unless they are culturally acceptable, police practices imported from a culturally different region will not survive (Bayley, 1977; Mawby, 1990; Das, 1993). Third, international comparative police works also enable us to appreciate that "cultural and national traditions are powerful determinants of police activity" (Bayley, 1983).

International comparative works in the United States mostly are concerned with European police. But some Asian countries, namely, Japan, India, and Israel, have been included in a number of studies. From Bayley's own international comparative works American readers will understand U. S. police better. They can, for example, compare their police with Indian police in *Police and Political Development in India* (Bayley, 1969). Bayley notes attractive Indian police features that are not found in U. S. police. Indian police executives, Indian Police Service (I.P.S.) officers, "display a breadth of interest and knowledge." Bayley does not believe that "an American high school graduate or even many college graduates would show up as well." Here he has in mind the fact that U. S. police chiefs generally have high school education. Educationally, Indians have done better. Bayley also says that India has "half again as many people per policeman as the United States or Great Britain." But crime rates in the "largest cities are only one-third the national rates in the United States, England and Wales." He mentions that "judged by proportionate size of police force, India has done as well as the West, if not somewhat better, in her major cities." Bayley (1977) comments that police behavior is "determined by factors located in the social environment in which police operate" and, so the reasons for the existence of some attractive features are to be sought in Indian history and culture.

Indian police are indeed very rarely a subject of comparative international police studies by U. S. researchers. Another author who includes India and compares it with American police is Shane (1980). He points out that the police in India perform "several tasks" which are broadly connected with "social integration and social control." While Indian police are involved in mediation and arbitration work quite considerably, other "service-related activities" are not performed extensively there. Moreover, Shane finds that support activities are not as well "integrated" into police work in India as in the other countries that he studied. As the police have a poor image and they are generally not trusted by the people (which could be traced to India's colonial past), Shane remarks that the feeling of mistrust "interferes" with "the integrative function" and "preventive activities" of the police. Indian police also reflect "the poverty of a poor nation" and there are even today "some colonial habits and legacies" that are not really democratic. Shane traces the cultural influences on Indian police. My own work (Das, 1993) refers to Indian police as the product of the culture. Obedient and fine personnel have enabled the police to maintain high standards despite enormous problems of human resources, equipment, and other forms of technological support.

In his *Forces of Order* (Bayley, 1991), Bayley says that Japanese "law enforcement is a different world," very different from U. S. law enforcement. There is no "blue power" syndrome, no heroic stand by the police as the "society's last defense against moral decay," and crime and violence against the police occur much less often in Japan. The police show no undue vulnerability to "stress"; they are "proud," confident of public support, and accustomed to being viewed by the public as the demonstrators of exemplary conduct. Japanese police officers were "proud rather than defensive." What's more, they "perceive the public as supportive" who, in turn, expect "exemplary behavior from policemen." Police officers in Japan are "compelling without being coercive." They are "self-effacing," "low key," "undramatic," "inconspicuous" and averse to playing a "visible role in public." They do not use "earthy language" which in the United States acts as "a badge of membership." In Japan police officers are not used to "swearing and crude language."

Bayley then asks: "How can it have happened that a country so similar to the United States can be a heaven for a cop?" In the United States "administration is considered a necessary evil, a fit place for persons without the ability to hold active command." There exists a "profound difference in the evolution" of the police systems in both countries. U. S. police forces "grew haphazardly out of patrol and watch activities." Japanese police were "created from top down by explicit acts of central government initiative." In Japan there are some unique factors like "group oversight" which may extend to the practice of senior officers acting as "marriage brokers" for young police officers. Group norms in Japan stress values that strengthen the police such as the police are the "new Samurai," infused with "Nihon damashi-Japanese spirit." To police officers in Japan, their organization is a "community" and their job "a way of life." Their work in the community emphasizes that "the key to public morality is public respect" to be secured through "responsible self-discipline and identification with the larger community's standards of appropriate behavior." The U. S. public believe more in external checks over the police; public standards are rejected by police officers and the police resist public criticism as "acceptance of outside criticism (that is) equated with disloyalty to the organization." In brief, the Japanese police are "molded" in unique ways and police behavior is a product of "general patterns of value and behavior."

Bayley (1991) discusses whether "Japanese practices" can be fruitfully imported to the United States in view of the excellent record of the police in Japan. He says that "police practices are not interchangeable parts" as not all of them are unlikely to "fit a different social context." To those who may advocate U. S. police reform through "importation" of practices from Japan, Bayley suggests that they must first decide in "practical terms what is to be changed." Second, the advocates of police reform must diagnose "where the impediments to change lie." Such impediments may vary depending on what is to be changed. Over certain matters like direct recruitment at two levels as in Japan, the police may have "total control." In order to change, practices which call for additional funds (upgrading U. S. police training to the Japanese level, for example) will have to be undertaken only with "community support." In certain areas of reform the police do not have to "stand helpless" waiting for community support but can take the initiative themselves. They can "encourage the growth of community spirit" by soliciting greater participation of "private citizens in crime prevention." He indicates that "some reforms will be easy...some will be unthinkable resting on the encrusted reefs of tradition and culture."

Other American researchers have also been impressed by many aspects of Japanese police. In *Police and Community in Japan* (1981) Ames' central argument is that the Japanese society polices itself and the police in Japan adroitly utilize public support in order to achieve great success in their work. This is also stressed by Clifford (1976). According to him, "the substance of public participation in Japan is far more than its form." Ames notes:

> The Japanese police pride themselves on being the world's best. Their confidence is apparently well founded, for Japan has the lowest crime rate in the industrialized world....This stems not only from an efficient and strong police organization, but from general cooperation by the community in fighting crime.

Ames constantly refers to the relationship between the police and culture stating that the Japanese police are themselves "Japanese" and they share a "common humanity with other Japanese." He mentions that he has followed "the anthropological tradition." Pragmatic concerns do not seem to be Ames' motivation. He indicates that it is not possible to import police practices from Japan because of certain unique characteristics of the police there. Ames says that the "western concepts of the right to privacy and self-fulfilment are sometimes abridged in Japan...Japan is politically one of the freest nations on earth, but this does not necessarily equate with social freedom." Another work on Japanese police is Craig

Parker's *Japanese Police System Today* (1984). Parker says that although he is not a "Japanologist," he found great help in Japan "in getting acquainted with the country and its customs." He says that he is not averse to U. S. police learning from Japanese police. He comments that his work shows his "very high regard for the Japanese system...possibilities for learning from this system are rather obvious."

Apart from these studies of India and Japan, there is no major international comparative police work by a U. S. writer in which an Asian country is included. Exceptions are Shane's study of Israel in the book discussed above. Another book with the discussion of Israel's police is Friedmann's *Community Policing: Comparative Perspectives and Prospects* (1992) in which there is a chapter on Israel. According to Shane, Israel's police force "embodies Rowan's concept of prevention." Shane says that the police in Israel are "seen primarily as law enforcement agents." But there "the emphasis is on crime prevention," and along with other social institutions the police are "helpers and service givers." As in the other countries here, too, "the largest element" in police work is "support activities." In Israel support activities of the police consist of "primarily arbitration-mediation of a wide range of conflicts and disputes" but, also, "various services to people in need." One unique phenomenon Shane notes is that "the police have the total cooperation of the public." Therefore, there is no police community relations problem that bedevils the police in the United States. Shane's account of the police in Israel is located within the framework of that country's culture, including its history. Friedmann's work, which includes Israel, is narrow in scope as it is "an examination of the major influences on community policing." According to this author, the greatest contribution the police in Israel are making through community policing is paying "greater attention to the needs of individual citizens."

Fosdick (1915; reprinted 1969) presents some admirable features of European police which he finds missing in the United States. The police in Europe are by and large "under the direct control of the state." He notes that "municipally controlled police forces" operated in some smaller cities. He admires the situation that political considerations play no role in the "management" of the Metropolitan police and as a result, "the policy and discipline of the police cannot be upset as an incidental consequence of the determination of political issues."

He praises the police leaders in Europe for their "strength combined with tact," "keen intelligence," and "incorruptible integrity." They are well-trained jurists, and their tenure is indefinite. He describes in detail the training of higher-level officers remarking that Austria and Italy offer "the most thoroughgoing method" for training of such officers. He also adds that the police schools in Europe were "better equipped" than such schools in Great Britain and the courses offered in the continental schools were more comprehensive.

In the continent there are "multifarious police functions." Fosdick states at the outset that police task varies from community to community. Variability is between countries, different cities in the same countries, and between different periods of time in the same cities. Among the "factors" responsible for variability he lists "alterations in economic conditions," "size and character of its industry," and heterogeneity or otherwise of the population. Fosdick also refers to the impact of "racial or historic reasons, or both." He mentions "national traits and characteristics." Fosdick attributes the "sharp contrasts" between English and German police to the "fundamental differences in race history and national character."

He finds "many points worthy of careful study" in the German police. Fosdick observes that in London police there is an attempt to "harmonize...the democratic spirit with the requirements of effective organization." He sees an "undoubted advantage" in the continental practice of bringing in "new but well-trained material from outside sources" for filling superior positions in police departments. But he also notes that the possibility of "extensive promotions" which exists in the English police departments provides "the incentive to faithful and painstaking work" on the part of the rank and file of the police forces in that country. Compared to that situation, subordinate officers in continental police units are likely to find "few compelling inducements to efficient work." Fosdick admires that in order to avoid being "mechanical" police departments encourage "infusion of new blood in high administrative positions."

In *Continental Police Practice* (1974), Sheldon Glueck presents a "survey of certain European police systems" in 1926. He suggests that policing as a profession made much headway in Europe because of "the excellent calibre of the men in directive and semi-directive posts." There were university graduates and they had special training in police work. Police instructors in professional academies were men with "outstanding contributions." The courses offered were balanced consisting of lectures on the "duties and rights of the policeman, with practical hints as to human nature and how to deal with people." In Europe he found that the police patrol systems were "responsive" to the local needs and proper "control of the men on beats." Glueck praises criminal investigation and detective work of many of the European police departments as "justly famous" due to the unique system of "identificatory records." He takes note of the excellent work done by the police overseas in the area of "preventive (repressive) efforts in the case of known criminals and, more fundamental, preventive efforts with juvenile delinquents and criminals in the making." Glueck states that there are "important lessons" to learn from Europe. The beat system and effective patrol work can be imported from The Hague and Berlin. Most importantly, America should learn from Europe that police work is a profession "practiced by men of education, training and dedication." He mentions that "high respect of the general population" is responsible for the "superiority of the rank and file." According to Mueller (1974), Glueck's work was conceived at a time when New York was looking for "answers to great problems facing the city's law enforcement apparatus." He adds that the city could not find the answers in America because the situation was bad in every city as it was shown in the *Wickersham Commission Report* a few years later.

Berkeley's *The Democratic Policeman* (1969) is a comparative study of American police with some selected countries in Europe. Referring to the police organizations in Sweden, England, Germany, and France, he comments that centralization has not obstructed their pace of democratization. He finds that "internal operations" represented by standardized rules and regulations, job mobility, and employee participation in the police forces in the democratic countries of Europe reflect their concerns for democracy. But the situation in the United States in this regard is far from satisfactory. Berkeley points out that even the FBI which enjoys great "prestige" is not free from favoritism and partiality in its internal administration. He notes that the American police system is "weak" in job mobility and standardization but it is "perhaps the weakest of all in employee participation."

Noting that the nonmilitary character is an important feature of the democratic police departments in countries like Sweden, England, and France, Berkeley mentions that "semimilitary organization" is somewhat more prominent in America today. Unlike many European police forces which are headed by civilian administrators, there is an American police tendency to view themselves as a non-civilian agency. Generally, only professional police officers head the major city police departments. Further, the boards of police commissioners consisting of civilians are disappearing, the percentage of civilian employees in police agencies is low and there have been changes in police uniform to "make the gun more visible and reachable." American police ranks are more militaristic than in European countries under review. It is suggested by Berkeley that slow development of the police union movement in America could be due to the vestiges of the quasi-military culture of the police. He notes that unionism is strong and vital in the police forces of numerous European countries with vigorous democratic culture.

Berkeley discusses a number of "recruitment criteria and educational programs" followed by some European countries which help in "the task of finding and developing democratic policemen." He refers to the prevalence of a great deal of agreement that democratic police agencies need recruits with "a perfect command of temper," "a high level of tolerance," and "friendliness and interest in people." In many countries maturity of "age" is considered critical for the development of patience, social skills, and understanding required in police officers. Berkeley says that these considerations do not play an important role in the area of recruitment and hiring practices of the American police. Berkeley also includes height (apparently, it reduces the need for coercive force) as an important factor in democratization along with geographic, ethnic, racial, and religious representation. He argues that the European system of lateral entry to higher police positions and active recruitment of women are right steps for democratizing police departments. Berkeley castigates American police for the failure to "attract the recruit who wishes to interact with people in a positive and humanely fulfilling manner" through such recruitment drives as seen in England and Germany. According to this author, education is extremely important for democratizing police officers and democracies of Europe, particularly Germany and Sweden, which pay considerable attention to proper police education in psychology, sociology, law, government and citizenship, and public service. In this area the United States show "grievous shortcomings."

Berkeley contends that the "concept of policeman as one who performs positive tasks and directly aids the citizen" has not been popular with city police departments in New York, Chicago, San Francisco, and so on. But in Sweden, Germany, England, or France such a concept is part of police approach to their work. Compared to European police forces (two of them, namely, Norwegian and British, among those he studied do not carry guns), Berkeley argues, the American police were trigger happy. In his discussion of the problems of policing the police, Berkeley mentions that many police agencies in Europe have learned to live with the restrictions imposed on their use of powers. But there is a great deal of "police hostility" in America toward procedural restrictions. The author contends that corruption is a feature of totalitarian police although it has been also a major problem in American police. But the police in the democracies of Europe have a reputation for integrity. In nondemocratic countries the police use "torture and more subtle forms of pressure and duress" in the interrogation of suspects which were practiced by the American police and "it took action by the U. S. Supreme Court to bring" changes in this area. In order for a police department to internalize democratic values, Berkeley thinks that scrupulous internal control over police misconduct must be given as much importance as fairness of internal administration, proper education of all concerned, and ongoing programs for positive work for helping the community in various ways. He comments that the systems of internal controls in the police departments in France, Sweden, Germany and England are thorough, adding that the disciplinary code of the British police is "possibly most highly developed." Berkeley notes that internal control mechanism in American police departments suffers from "the norm of secrecy and mutual protectiveness," milder forms of punishment, tendency to "reject complaints out of hand," and so on.

Apart from internal controls, Berkeley has found three external control agencies in Europe, namely, judiciary, ombudsman, and legislature. He also discusses the Civilian Review Board in connection with the bad experience in New York, noting that none of the European countries included in his study has this device of external control over the police. According to him the police are too near the judiciary and it is realized in many democratic countries that the judiciary alone is not considered as sufficient to oversee potential police excesses. The office of ombudsman has been found an effective means of external control on the police in Sweden. Moreover, the legislatures in England, Germany, Sweden, and France control the police zealously but the American police are left alone by the legislature from the city councils to the congress.

According to Berkeley, public relations strategies of many European police forces are better than those practiced by American police. Police officers in these countries walk the beats in order to build positive relations. Foot patrols help them to become familiar figures, retain "a close link with the public," and remain easily approachable which encourages the people to come to them with their problems. Police participation in active politics, utilization of civilians as auxiliaries, centralization, standardization, civilianization, police unionism, avoidance of repressive approach and, lastly, the strict adherence to the rule of law have been suggested by Berkeley as valuable means of democratizing the police.

Berkeley acknowledges that societal framework is the basis for the development of the police characteristics. Pragmatic considerations play a major role in his study. As a matter of fact, his "Conclusions," particularly the last portion, contains many suggestions for the improvement of American police based on the practices of the police in Europe. He recommends that education of the police should form the central core of the reform strategy as Berkeley considers that police education has received great attention in the countries across the Atlantic. He also advocates centralization for American police as it has been a great boon to some foreign police forces he has studied. He adds to his list many other features of excellence he found in several European police agencies such as civilianization, unionization, positive work, reduction of repressive tactics, elimination of corruption, and enhancement of the police role as a positive social instrument.

Paul Shane's *Police and People* (1980), which includes five countries (besides India and Israel discussed above, he includes the police in the Netherlands, England, and America), seeks "to present facts about what police actually do in these societies." He is also interested in probing "various philosophical approaches to police function," describing "the development and organization of police forces," and looking at "social conditions that might be correlated with the incidences of some of the tasks that police do." He devotes a considerable part of each chapter to the description of the influences of these conditions on the unique characteristics of the police in England, America, India, the Netherlands, and Israel. Shane refers to "many very difficult functional problems" in the United States. He attributes these problems to the fact that the American police powers and responsibilites are "dispersed, fragmental, duplicative, unstandardized and disorganized" but in none of the other countries such a phenomenon is seen. "Scandals that at times rock various American forces" are unheard of elsewhere. According to Shane, this is because unlike the other countries studied America does not have "supervision by higher levels of government" over the police. He feels that there are "certainly viable alternatives in equally democratic countries that could be examined for possible application with the United States."

In *Police Systems of Europe* (1973), Harold Becker demonstrates concerns similar to those of the authors discussed above. He provides "external physical description" of each country included in the book. He acknowledges the importance of "culture" in comparative police work "as a technique of analysis." He admits his attention to pragmatic considerations and says that "the choice of change or no change is the final phenomenon of comparative research."

All the international comparative police authors described above attempt to draw theoretical conclusions about the nature of policing based on their comparative studies. But it is done more thoroughly and systematically by Bayley. This is particularly true of his *Patterns of Policing* (1985). He observes that the "countries that rely on external accountability, like India and the United States, are extremely heterogeneous socially." But those countries "which emphasize more internal regulation, are less so" like Japan and Great Britain. He says that "external control" over the police as seen in America is indicative of the society's lack of confidence in the police ability to exercise self-control. As a result, the police in such society demonstrate a low level of "pride and self-respect" compared to the police in countries, such as Japan, where internal control is given a greater role. He explains that in private policing the democracies of the West have found a "unique way of meeting crime needs while avoiding the authoritarianism of both formal deterrence or pervasive community penetration."

POLICE PRACTICES: AN INTERNATIONAL REVIEW

The present book is an extension of international comparative police research tradition in the United States. The U. S. police are not included in the book. Nevertheless, as mentioned elsewhere, an implicit comparison with the police in America is an objective of this undertaking. It is hoped that police in this country make note of numerous interesting practices, problems, and dilemmas in police organizations of other nations.

Insiders as they are, the authors are fully conversant with their countries' history, culture, and tradition. Two of them, namely, Ueno and Diaz, are also police officers. Contributors have adopted a wise combination of macro and micro perspectives. It is perhaps necessary to explain how I have used the terms. I am using the term "macro" here in the sense Vallier (1973) employs the concept of "macro-structural analysis." He includes within this methodology "problems of structure and change in large-scale, complex units, e.g., societies, international systems, institutions, bureaucracies, or other wide-ranging organizations." Johnson (1983) refers to macro perspective as an examination of "the society as a whole because it is the macroenvironment that gives meaning to the work of the police, courts, and correctional agencies." He adds:

> In other words, the macro control system of the given society must be considered when we try to understand the obligations assigned to criminal justice agencies and the total responses to criminality. In the pursuit of that understanding, we have reason to examine the similarities and differences among societies in the functions assigned to those agencies within that macro social control system.

Terrill (1984) explains the terms micro and macro slightly differently. He does not use "macro" in the context in which Vallier and Johnson apply the term. According to him:

> Macro-comparison compares entire systems (i.e., one country's justice system with another country's system) whereas micro-comparison involves comparing a more detailed issue or problem (i.e., an examination of search and seizure legislation in two countries or the policies of more than one probation department).

He describes his book, *World Criminal Justice System* (1984), as based on "the macro-approach...because of the nature of the text." And, the nature of Terrill's text is that he discusses the entire justice systems of five countries, namely, England, France, Sweden, Japan, and the Soviet Union. I am using the terms in the sense in which they are utilized by Vallier and Johnson. Further, I agree with Vallier that comparative studies may be utilized for policy research. This "involves an identification of either the conditions under which certain outcomes occur, or of underlying causal systems." Policy research can become an "effective basis for relating social science knowledge to collective problems" and "by being comparative...studies of social structure...allow for testing of hypotheses." Bayley's comparative works are based on macro perspective which he uses for the kinds of things Vallier recommends.

Although a conflict between patriotism, organizational loyalty, and scholarly objectivity can arise in the minds of contributors to a book of this kind, I have no doubt that my collaborators have never deflected from scientific objectivity in their accounts. As a matter of fact, four of them are rather critical of their police. I have, as indicated, researched the police as an observer in each of the countries. I was a high-ranking police officer in India. I remained in close touch with the contributors during the production of the chapters sharing with them my views, opinions, and concerns. I am indeed most grateful to them all that they generously conceded to all my requests for revisions, modifications, and additions in the light of the objectives of this volume.

I think this volume differs in one respect from the comparative police works of Fosdick, Glueck, Bayley, Berkeley, Shane, and others. It provides a plethora of details in the course of the analysis of police practices. This has been done primarily with a view to making available adequate and relevant information should any police leader or policy maker feel an urge to experiment with any foreign police practice described in the book. While the important goal of understanding the police in the context of the culture has not been overlooked, this volume lays stress on pragmatic concerns. My collaborators and I hope that police forces who are interested in learning from others will find this book a valuable source.

REFERENCES

Ames, Walter L. *Police and Community in Japan*. Berkeley, California: University of California Press, 1981.

Bayley, David H. *Police and Political Development in India*. Princeton, New Jersey: Princeton University Press, 1969.

__________. *Forces of Order: Police Behavior in Japan and the United States*. Berkeley, California: University of California Press, 1976.

__________. *Police and Society*. Beverly Hills, California: Sage Publications, 1977.

__________. "Knowledge of the Police." In Maurice Punch (ed.) *Control in Police Organization*. Cambridge, Massachusetts: MIT Press, 1983.

__________. *Patterns of Policing: A Comparative International Analysis*. New Brunswick, New Jersey: Rutgers University Press, 1985.

Becker, Harold K. *Police Systems of Europe*. Springfield, Illinois: Charles C. Thomas, Publishers, 1973.

Berkeley, George E. *The Democratic Policeman*. Boston: Beacon Press, 1969.

Clifford, W. *Crime Control in Japan*. Lexington, Massachussets: Lexington Publishing Company, 1976.

Das, Dilip K. *Policing in Six Countries Around the World: Organizational Perspectives*. Chicago: OICI, University of Illinois-Chicago, 1993.

__________. "Image of American Police in Comparative Literature." *Police Studies* 8(2) (1985):74-83.

Fosdick, Raymond B. *European Police Systems*. Montclair, New Jersey: Peterson Smith, 1969 [originally published in 1915].

Friedmann, Robert R. *Community Policing: Comparative Perspectives and Prospects*. New York: St. Martin Press, 1992.

Glueck, Sheldon. *Continental Police Practice in Formative Years*. Springfield, Illinois: Charles C. Thomas, 1974.

Johnson, Elmer H. *International Handbook of Contemporary Developments in Criminology.* Westport, Connecticut: Greenwood Press, 1983.

Mawby, R. I. *Comparative Policing Issues: The British and American Experience in International Perspectives.* London: Unwin Hyman, 1990.

Mueller, Gerhard O. W. "Introduction." In Glueck, Sheldon. *Continental Police Practice in Formative Years.* Springfield, Illinois: Charles C. Thomas, 1974.

Parker, Craig L. *The Japanese Police System Today.* Tokyo and New York: Kodansha International, 1984.

Punch, Maurice (Ed.), *Control in Police Organization.* Cambridge, Massachusetts: MIT Press, 1983.

Shane, Paul. *Police and People.* St. Louis: The C. V. Mosby Company, 1980.

Terrill, Richard J. *World Criminal Justice Systems: A Survey.* Cincinnati, Ohio: Anderson Publishing Co, 1984.

Vallier, Ivan. *Methods in Sociology.* Berkeley, California: University of California Press, 1973.

POLICE IN AUSTRALIA

by Stephen James

INTRODUCTION

Australia is a continental land mass in the southwest Pacific region, and consists of a federation of six states and two internal territories. It was colonized by the British in the eighteenth century, and 1988 saw the bicentenary of the first permanent settlement of white colonists in the now state of New South Wales. Federation of the six previously self-governing states was achieved through the Commonwealth of Australia Constitution Act of 1900. Political authority is shared between the states and the federal government. Each state has its own legislature, and retains those responsibilities and powers not assigned to the federal government under the constitution. Governments at both state and federal level are formed by those parties which secure majority electoral support in the lower houses of parliament (some states and the federal parliament retain upper and lower houses, while other states have abolished the upper or review house). The federal government is headed by the Prime Minister, the parliamentary leader of the majority federal party, who forms a ministry from elected members of that party. The states are headed by their respective Premiers, the parliamentary leaders of the state majority parties, who also form ministries from elected members. Government departments are allocated to ministers and administered by public servants.

Criminal law in Australia is based upon a combination of common and statute law. That is, Australia has followed the British model of both court-made law and legislative statute. English legislation held sway until 1828. As the various colonies became self-governing after that year, they developed their own legislation, which originally complemented, and then effectively superceded English legislation developed before 1828. Thus, current English statutes have no direct bearing upon Australian law. On the other hand, English case law still exerts an influence. Chisholm and Nettheim (1978) explain the circumstances:

> In those areas where there is no relevant statute..., an English decision, particularly in the Court of Appeal or the House of Lords, will often be followed by an Australian court if the matter is not already covered by an Australian decision. Indeed, where there is a House of Lords decision on a point, although it is not strictly "binding" on Australian courts, those courts, even the High Court, will very rarely refuse to follow it.

In general, state-legislated criminal codes have replaced much of the common law in relation to crime, and criminal justice administration is largely the responsibility of the states. Each state generally has a three-tiered system of criminal courts: courts of summary jurisdiction (magistrate's courts, or courts of petty sessions), which hear summary offenses, or indictable offenses triable summarily under the relevant acts, without juries; district, county, or general sessions courts, which try all indictable offenses except the most serious before a judge and jury, and which act as appeal courts from magistrate's courts; and the state supreme courts, which try before judge and jury the most serious offenses, such as homicide, and that hear appeals from intermediate courts. The High Court is a federal court which can hear appeals from state supreme courts in certain prescribed circumstances (see Chisholm and Nettheim, 1978).

Prosecution of criminal cases in the courts of summary jurisdiction, which try the bulk of all criminal cases, is generally conducted by members of the respective state police departments. In the higher courts, criminal cases are prosecuted by barristers, lawyers whose primary role is to act as advocates in court. In recent years, Australia has seen the establishment of Directors of Public Prosecution, both at the federal level and in such states as Victoria, who prosecute cases in court. Each state has its own correctional systems, which are utilized in the case of offenders sentenced under federal legislation.

Policing in Australia is largely the responsibility of the states. Each of the states has its own police department, as does the Northern Territory. The Australian Capital Territory, the seat of the federal government, is policed by the Australian Federal Police, a body formed in 1979 through the amalgamation of the Australian Commonwealth Police and the Australian Capital Territory Police. The Australian Federal Police are responsible for general law enforcement in the Australian Capital Territory, and for the enforcement of federal laws and the protection of federal property and interests across the nation. Figure 1 presents relevant statistical information relating to the various Australian police departments.

In addition to the standard police agencies, there are a number of other organizations whose responsibilities involve some aspect of law enforcement. These include various federal agencies and offices such as the Taxation Office and the Customs Department. There is an internal security agency, the Australian Security Intelligence Organization, which was created in 1949. In 1981, the Australian Bureau of Criminal Intelligence, an intelligence-gathering body, was formed under the auspices of the various state territory and federal police commissioners. In 1984, the National Crimes Authority was set up under federal legislation to pursue and prosecute organized crime. It is staffed by lawyers and seconded state and federal police officers. In all these organizations, the law enforcement powers of the state police departments are generally required for dealing with breaches of state criminal law.

Before the substantive matters of the chapter are discussed, it is useful to outline briefly the major sources of information on Australian police and policing. Detailed scholarship in the area can be described as limited. Nevertheless, over the past two decades or so, academic interest in policing has burgeoned, and there is now a nucleus of what will undoubtedly be a substantial corpus of reference and analytical work in the near future. A formidable beginning has been made in the former category with the publication of the two editions of the *Police Source Book* by the Australian Institute of Criminology. Under the principal editorship of Bruce Swanton, these two volumes (Swanton, Hannigan and Biles, 1983; Swanton, Hannigan and Psaila, 1985) bring together a prodigious compendium of facts and figures about Australian policing. The

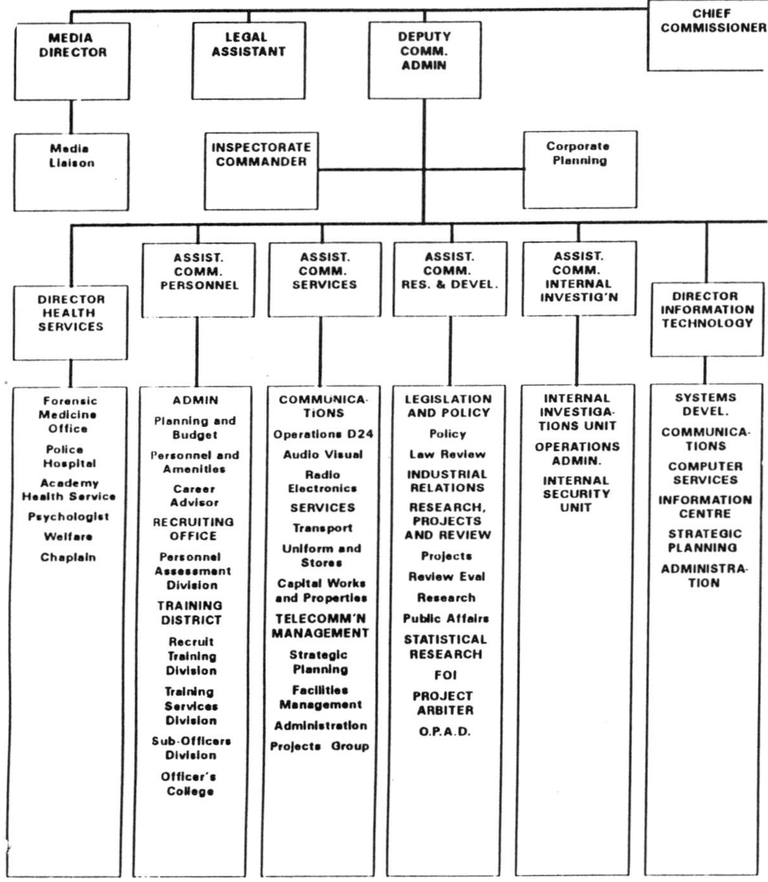

Fig. 1: Organizational Structure of the Victoria Police (*Source:* Victoria Police, *Annual Report 1989/1990*).

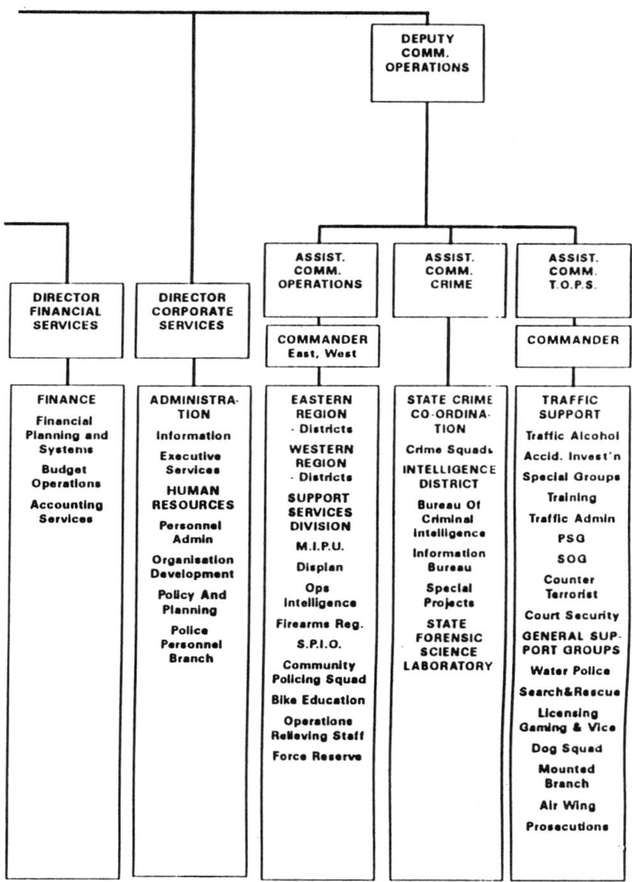

Fig. 1: Organizational Structure of the Victoria Police (continued).

1985 edition makes an especially marked contribution to the literature. Within its 756 pages lie summaries of police histories, chapters on police demography, conditions of service, legal powers, administration, industrial relations, as well as detailed bibliographies of related literature and resources. The present writer owes an enormous debt to this volume for much of the descriptive material in the following sections. Indeed, a major challenge facing the writer has been to render digestible in a relatively small number of words material it has taken the *Source Book* so many to outline. At the same time, it is fair to describe the *Source Book* as a reference rather than an analytical work, and the present chapter sets out to be both.

Historical perspectives on police have been appearing in press at an increasing rate, although a comprehensive history of Australian policing has yet to be written. Haldane (1986) has produced a detailed and thorough account of the Victoria Police from its origins, and a recent edited book on a variety of historical aspects of policing has proved invaluable (Finnane, 1987). Somewhat less comprehensive accounts appear embedded in works with a broader police focus (Chappell and Wilson, 1969; Milte and Weber, 1977; O'Brien, 1960; O'Malley, 1983). These works, along with more specialized scholarship which deals with police as parts of wider perspectives on Australian history (Clark, 1978; Inglis, 1974; Ward, 1970), provide an adequate coverage of early colonial policing. Finnane (1987) is not alone, however, in lamenting the paucity of postcolonial accounts which analyze policing developments within the context of the social and political life of Australia to the present day.

Contemporary accounts of police organizations, principles and practices have not yet demonstrated the breadth of the *Police Source Book*. But several works offer rather more analytical approaches to the topic. Valuable (although increasingly dated) publications include Chappell and Wilson (1969), Milte and Weber (1977), Swanton (1977), and Wilson and Western (1972). Avery's (1981) work is also valuable, although slim; he is currently commissioner of the New South Wales police. Swanton's (1983) book on police unions ranges widely across Australian policing, and is required reading in the area. Two recent edited books provide more contemporary analyses of Australian policing (Chappell and Wilson, 1988; McKillop and Vernon, 1991). There are, in addition, a variety of specialized contributions which tackle aspects of policing in a scholarly fashion; these are cited in the following sections.

A particularly rich source of material on Australian policing is represented by a number of Royal Commissions and other commissions of inquiry which examined police directly or indirectly during the course of their deliberations. Prominent examples include the Beach Inquiry into Allegations of Corruption Against Members of the Victoria Police (1976); the Moffitt Royal Commission of Inquiry in Respect of Certain Matters relating to Allegations of Organised Crime in Clubs (New South Wales, 1974); the Lusher Royal Commission of Inquiry into the New South Wales Police Force (1981); the Williams Royal Commission into Drugs (1979); the Stewart Royal Commission into Drug Trafficking (1983); and the Fitzgerald Inquiry into Corruption in the Queensland Police (1990). These commissions are often painstaking and detailed, and include a wealth of data on police administrative arrangements and operational practices. Another inquiry into the Victoria Police, the Neesham Inquiry (1985) exhaustively addresses that department, and provides the additional worth of contracted attitude surveys which have increased substantially our knowledge of policing in that state.

Further useful sources of material can be found in police department annual reports, accessible research work conducted by police departments themselves, monographs from the Australian Institute of Criminology and the National Police Research Unit, and from state Bureaus of Crime Statistics.

This brief listing is of course by no means exhaustive; rather it is illustrative of relevant sources on Australian policing. Swanton et al. (1985) should be consulted for more comprehensive details. The point also needs to be made that the inclusion of a source either here or later in the narrative ought not be construed as an uncritical endorsement of its worth. In addition, it is obvious that in work of this nature, a writer's perspective is borne of many diverse sources, not just those of the printed and accessible word. While an attempt has been made to keep unsourced assertions to a minimum, the eclectic nature of scholarship in this area invariably and legitimately involves a degree of opinion and speculation.

A chronological account of the development of Australian policing offers a number of anticipated parallels with the emergence of centralized and bureaucratized policing in Britain in the nineteenth century following Peel's reforms in 1829 (see Silver, 1967). At the same time, there were clear differences in the social, economic, and political circumstances of Australia's early history compared with Britain, and it is important that the parellels not be overextended. The history of Australian policing occupies a crucial analytical place in understanding contemporary policing; in both the public imagination and in practice, the legacies of the past are to some extent with us today.

Australia was originally settled as a penal colony, an origin which helped modify the direct transplanting of prevailing British models of policing. There were more convicts than free settlers, administrators, or military personnel among the first arrivals at Sydney Cove in 1788. Law enforcement was initially carried out by military detachments primarily detailed for convict supervision, but this quickly proved unsatisfactory. In New South Wales, until the end of the eighteenth century, various combinations of appointed and elected freemen and "best behaved" convicts acted as constables under arrangements similar to those prevailing in London (Milte and Weber, 1977). Similar arrangements existed in Tasmania, the second earliest settlement, until 1806. In most cases, these constables, who operated on temporary or part-time bases in return for board and lodging, were under the authority of local magistrates. The beginning of the nineteenth century ushered in the development of full-time and paid constables, often ex-convicts. As urban centers grew larger, separate and independent constabularies under district magistrates and justices also grew. By 1812, while the Sydney constabulary had been brought under a single police magistrate, rural constabularies were created autonomously under appointment from local justices. These rural forces were more military in formation and practice than the urban forces, partly as a function of increasingly violent conflict between settlers and aborigines. Military Mounted Police operated in rural New South Wales between 1826 and 1850; this force comprised military volunteers, and was, according to O'Malley (1983) modelled on the Royal Irish Constabulary, a model "which had been rejected for Britain by an English Royal Commission on the grounds of its military and repressive character."

In 1833, New South Wales saw the passing of the Sydney Police Act which was based largely upon the London Metropolitan Police Act of 1829. It placed the Sydney constabulary on a statutory basis, but did not abolish police accountability to the magistracy. Although the Act was extended to Victoria in 1838, constables in that colony still operated on the fragmented basis of local magistracy hegemony. In 1839 Victoria saw the establishment of a Border Police, charged largely with controlling conflict between settlers and aborigines (Haldane, 1985). Western Australia established Mounted Police in 1834 for the same purpose (Doherty, 1985). South Australia experienced similar conflict by 1841 (Clyne, 1985).

South Australia led the development to a colony-wide, centralized police force under its own administrative arrangements in 1838 (Clyne, 1985). South Australia had never been a convict settlement, and had rejected military or quasi-military formations evident in other colonies. The 1838 establishment was modelled closely on Peel's Act. Victoria was next. The decentralized and independent constabularies and rural militias were unable to cope with the social and economic consequences of the gold strikes in the colonies from 1851, and the Police Regulation Act of 1853 established a centralized and colony-wide force (Haldane, 1985). Western Australia had severed the nexus between its constabularies and the magistracy in 1853, and it proclaimed the Police Ordinance Act in 1861 which brought uniformity and centralization (Doherty, 1985). Under similar gold field unrest to that which took place in Victoria, New South Wales proclaimed its Police Regulation Act in 1862. Queensland had relied upon military forces for much longer than the other colonies, until 1844, when rural and urban constabularies took over under the authority of magistrates. After separation from New South Wales in 1859, Queensland proclaimed its Police Act in 1863 (Hannigan, 1985). In many regards, Tasmania was the odd state out. Under the Municipal Police Act of 1857, constabularies were placed under the control of and administered by municipalities. It was not until 1896 that the Police Regulation Act brought Tasmanian policing into line with the other colonies (Erwin, 1985). The Northern Territory Police, the Australian Capital Territory Police and the Commonwealth Police were all formed in the twentieth century. While many of the Acts under which the various colony (and now state) police departments were established have been significantly amended or repealed and replaced, they collectively represent the creation of centralized, statute-based police bureaucracies with clear separations in terms of authority and accountability from the judiciary. These acts generated all modern police departments in Australia.

While the histories of the police departments between the second half of the nineteenth century and the present day deserve detailed scrutiny, such is not possible here. However, several themes in that more recent history will be touched upon. Before this is done, it is useful to briefly highlight some of the salient features of the earlier history which have, arguably, ramifications for contemporary Australian policing. These features relate to the "image" (Das, 1985) of police generated by their historical development.

The transitions in modes of law enforcement and social control reflected by the emergence of professionalized police bureaucracies in Australia have clear resonances with developments in Britain in the nineteenth century (O'Malley, 1983) and, to perhaps a lesser extent, in the United States (Lundman, 1980). At the same time, there are a number of sharp or subtle distinctions. Foremost amongst these is the penal nature of Australia's early colonization. The initial use of military forces in law enforcement, and later of convicts in the same role, established a climate of significant coercion and repression. Rural militias amplified this climate, and the effects were undoubtedly most acutely felt amongst the indigenous population of Australia, the Aborigines. Hughes (1987) has chronicled the extremely hostile relationships between convicts, early settlers, and Aborigines. And as Sturma (1987) notes, control and law enforcement amongst Aborigines was predominantly conducted by police, rather than by the formal military arrangements adopted in the United States at the same time. That police acted repressively in this regard, and often brutally, is not in dispute. In some states, police later had formal global authority over Aboriginal reserves, which meant that they dispensed both law enforcement and welfare (Ronalds, Chapman and Kitchener, 1983). The historical impact of policing services upon Aborigines is almost certainly responsible in part for the enduring problems between contemporary police and Aborigines (Wilson, 1988).

A further factor which has undoubtedly affected traditional images of Australian police has been the poor calibre of early recruits to police service, and the poor conditions with which police were rewarded. High resignation and dismissal rates, limited or nonexistent training, low remuneration, and appalling conditions of service, as well as crude or negligible recruiting standards, did little to foster a confident and professional image amongst police (Haldane, 1986); this situation apparently differed little from that which prevailed in England during the later part of the nineteenth century (Critchley, 1967).

Despite attempts to professionalize policing following the rush of statutory establishments in the middle of the nineteenth century, Australian police continued to suffer poor images, through both the conditions under which they labored, and those labors themselves. The discovery of gold in the 1850s contributed markedly to the police problems. Besides the normal problems of policing instant tent-cities of thousands of entrepreneurial gold diggers, police were used as revenue collectors on the gold fields. Police in Victoria were responsible for checking the currency of mining licences, and received a half-share of fines levied upon defaulting miners. Their heavy-handed approach to this task, in combination with other disenchantments felt by miners treated badly by government administration and large mine owners, led to the infamous "Eureka Stockade" incident in Ballarat in rural Victoria, where miners gathered and publically burned their licences. A pitched battle between the miners and a force of soldiers and police left an estimated 30 miners and four soldiers dead. Haldane (1986) comments:

> ...some of the hopes the Victoria Police had of throwing off the yoke of public emnity died at Eureka. Just as the police were gradually improving in organization and efficiency and gaining limited public recognition for their work, they became embroiled in the events of Ballarat.

Later in the nineteenth century, police involvement in the outbreak of bushranging (single or organized gang highway robbery) did little to enhance their image. In New South Wales, police were castigated for their ineptitude in dealing with bushrangers. In Victoria, the sage of the Kelly gang produced similar results. Perhaps the most famous criminal in Australian history, Ned Kelly and his gang killed three policemen who were hunting him in the 1870s. For nearly two years following the killings, Kelly managed to evade his pursuers, until caught and hanged in late 1880. Haldane (1986) notes: "It was both a tragic and humiliating time for the police; they were pilloried in the newspapers, criticized in parliament and made antagonistic to each other in the field."

Queensland police also experienced gold field troubles during the same periods. But perhaps more important were the conflicts between police and organized labor in other industries which established a long enduring hostility towards police from many members of the working class. Queensland labor was in the forefront of Australian (and international) emergence of democratic socialism, and police involvement in strikes and lockouts generally favored owners and strikebreakers (Hannigan, 1985). Further involvement of police, especially in Victoria and New South Wales, in relief measures and tenant evictions during the 1930s created anti-police feelings. Depression years further antagonized the working class and labor movement (Finnane, 1987). The extent to which the early and middle years of police development in Australia have affected both the contemporary images and practices of police cannot be established with any certainty, of course. Rather than suggest the links at this stage, it is better to leave it to the reader to test the information in the following sections on contemporary issues against the images generated by this brief early history of policing. That there are continuities will be evident; at the same time, the pace of change and development, especially in the last decade or so, has been such that modern Australian police departments often bear little or no resemblance to their ancestors in at least some aspects of their enterprise.

MANDATE AND PHILOSOPHY

In this, as in the following sections, definitive and succinct descriptions of Australian police are difficult. Policing is essentially a state responsibility, and the historical, geographical and demographic diversities between the states render global assessments and statements about Australian police somewhat tenuous. At the same time, there are communalities between the states in some aspects that enable some degree of confidence in broad statements. The task in the remaining sections of this chapter is to identify those communalities. Considerable use is made of material relating to police in Victoria, the writer's home state. Victoria has the second largest state population in Australia, and the second smallest state land mass. It is situated in the southeast of the country, and its capital city is Melbourne. Together with New South Wales, it dominates Australia's business, finance, and nonmining heavy industry sectors. Its relatively small land mass and its high degree of urbanization make it somewhat untypical of all Australian states. Nevertheless, there are many aspects of its police agency and policing arrangements which can be readily generalized to other parts of the country. Where critical differences arise, these are noted.

Australian police departments derive their mandate primarily from direct legislative authority. That is, their organizational existence and continuity is mandated by the various state legislative acts and their descendants which have already been briefly touched upon. Each state has a Police Regulation/ Administration Act, as well as procedural guidelines in the form of Police Rules/Regulations. In addition, there are various ancillary acts, either directly relating to police service (for instance, legislation covering superannuation and pension benefits) or impinging upon police service (for example, industry regulation acts).

The critical issue in any discussion of the mandate of police is the question of accountability: to whom and for what are the police accountable? There is no simple answer to this question in the Australian context. Australia hypothetically adheres to the British philosophy of the separation of powers, where the three distinctive elements of government, the legislature, the executive, and the judiciary, are seen as independent (see Chisholm and Nettheim, 1978). There are senses in which police agencies are at various stages accountable to all three: to the parliament or legislature for the enforcement of law; to the executive government for the carrying out of government policy; and to the judiciary for the ways in which police enforce the law and carry out policy. Avery (1981) puts it slightly differently:

> ...the police organization is a discrete unit functioning within the social fabric of the state, with much autonomy in the areas of tactical operation and logistical function, answerable to parliament in policy matters and having its performances monitored by the courts.

In order to clarify the issue of accountability in Australian police departments it is useful first to describe briefly the organizational command structure of the departments. The chief officer of all Australian police departments is known as the Commissioner (with the one exception being Victoria, where the chief officer has the title Chief Commissioner). Assisting the Commissioner are one or two Deputy Commissioners and a number of Assistant Commissioners. The responsibilities of the Deputies and Assistants are divided between the major organizational divisions with a department, such as crime, traffic, services, personnel, internal investigations and so forth. Commissioners are executive government appointments, formally made by the state Governor (the British monarch's representative) on the advice of the Executive Council (the state government's cabinet, the senior ministry) (see Chisholm and Nettheim, 1978). According to Milte and Weber (1977): "In practice this means that the Minister responsible for the police department will make a recommendation to cabinet and if adopted the appointment...will be ratified by the Governor." While Deputy and Assistant Commissioners, to the writer's knowledge, have come from the ranks of the particular police department, Commissioners are often appointed from other police departments, or even from non-police (but usually military) backgrounds. However, the practice in recent years at least within the state police departments is to appoint experienced police officers.

The Commissioner of Police is responsible in most states to either the Minister or to the Executive Council. While some state acts are vague on the point, Commissioners appear to be subject to removal only on the grounds of misbehavior, incompetence, or incapacity by the appropriate Minister or Executive Council (Milte and Weber, 1977). Avery (1981) holds the view that Commissioners can be suspended by Ministers or Executive Councils, but can only be removed by resolution of parliament. The nature and extent of the responsibility of the Commissioner to the government and parliament has received considerable attention in Australia over the last two decades, largely as a result of conflicts between police administration and the government of the day (although in one case it has arisen from critiques of the extent to which one state police department has slavishly followed the political dictates of its state government (Brennan, 1983).

In practice the issue of executive police accountability has hinged upon the extent to which police Commissioners are obliged to take instructions from government. In a critical test of this issue, a Royal Commission of Inquiry was set up by the South Australian government in 1971 in order to assess the Commissioner's accountability. The then Commissioner had refused a request by the government to allow anti-Vietnam War demonstrators to occupy a public place. In effect, the government requested the police not to enforce the law. The Royal Commissioner argued for the legitimate direction of police by government, especially in situations with a political flavor, and subject to certain guidelines (cited in Milte and Weber, 1977):

> In a system of responsible government there must ultimately be a Minister of State answerable in Parliament and to the Parliament for any executive operation. This does not mean that no senior servant or other officer of State has independent discretion. Nor does it mean that the responsible Minister can at his pleasure substitute his own will for that of the officer responsible to him.

A significant part of the rationale for this perspective was the view that police ought not be put in the position of having to take sole responsibility for operational (and policy) issues which could be construed as politically-laden. The mechanism for guarding against arbitrary interference by the government in circumstances of direction to the Police Commissioner was the tendering of the direction publicly in parliament, where it could be subject to justification.

A later case in South Australia again touched on these issues. The government of the day sacked the then Commissioner for allegedly misleading parliament over the files collated and held by the Special Branch, the unit within the police department charged with surveillance of potentially subversive political activity (Victoria's Special Branch was disbanded with a change of government in 1982). It appears that the South Australian Commissioner believed that Special Branch files should be free of scrutiny by politicians because of their security implications; the government felt that it had a legitimate interest in the contents of such files. A subsequent Royal Commission found: "...(that) the Governor, and hence the government, has power to make binding regulations for the administration and regulation of the force and thus is able to posit legally enforceable guidelines as to the activities of the Special Branch" (Avery, 1981).

While states such as South Australia have experienced a number of detailed Royal Commissions on the issue of the accountability of the executive of the police department, such has not occurred in all states, and it remains an area of contention that is most often raised and resolved in the context of particular state-based crises and controversies. It is, consequently, difficult to render an Australian-wide maxim which adequately captures the legal status of executive accountability. But it appears that a reasonably strong convention, with all the caveats that such a term implies, exists across Australia. That is, police commissioners are granted considerable autonomy over the day-to-day administration, organization and policy-setting operations of the police department, free from arbitrary and intrusive interference by government. On the other hand, the performance of these operations is subject to scrutiny by government, which may from time to time advise and occasionally direct the police executive to implement particular policies. And, of course, governments can effect, through legislation passed by parliament, any amount of formal statutory obligation on police departments. Avery (1981) makes the important distinction between statutory authorities in Australia and ministerial departments. The latter are generally established by order of a state Executive Council, while the former come into being through parliamentary statute. Avery (1981) explains the functional differences:

> The statutory authority has a degree of autonomy in making decisions which is different from the set of discretions and relationships of ministerial departments, where the minister accepts full responsibility for decisions taken by the department. The statutory authorities recruit their staffs outside the public service system and often have separate budgetary arrangements.
>
> In the case of police departments, the ordinary management is not vested in a minister, but the minister does accept an ultimate reponsibility for the function of the police department in the parliament and tables the report of the commissioner to parliament. There is a clear statutory mandate for ministerial direction, (but as it has been indicated), ministers have shown reluctance to assume responsibility for police policies and practices. In reply to questions in parliament they have stressed that police are independent and that ministers should not interfere with police decisions. (parenthesis added)

A second critical aspect of the issue of police accountability is that which concerns the individual officer as opposed to the chief executive. To whom is the individual officer accountable? An answer to this question raises an interesting paradox. For like most police departments, Australian police organizations are hierarchically structured with a quasi-military rank and command apparatus, and officers are expected to obey the commands of superior officers. Yet, as a number of court cases have demonstrated, individual police officers in Australia are held accountable primarily to the law for their actions rather than to the police organization. This accountability derives from English common law principles, which have held that a constable of police exercises original rather than delegated authority, and is consequently responsible personally for the execution of that authority. This means in practice that there is no master-servant relationship between an officer and the employing body, the police department, and that the officer is liable under law to criminal or tortious action for impropriety while conducting police duties. Milte and Weber (1977) speculate that:

> This notion appears to have evolved from the peculiar status accorded to the constable by the common law which can only be explained in terms of judicial authorities forming the belief that the police, like the courts, occupy a special position in human affairs and in the interests of liberty, and ought not to be subject to arbitrary interference by executive and local authorities.

Thus the individual constable is granted theoretically considerable independence in decision-making and performance. Yet, as Milte and Weber (1977) claim, the officer is subject to a chain of command which entails disciplinary proceedings for failing to obey lawful commands of superior officers. Avery (1981) suggests that the operational police officer solves this dilemma by a sharp awareness of the boundaries of individual decision making and the need for lawful obedience:

> A constable is aware that his independence is only related to his actions to enforce laws and to keep the peace. He is obedient to administrative instructions designed to allow him to perform the function of an "officer of justice" in a structured and organized way but he is well aware that when he is in action on the street or out in the community somewhere, his

> decision to act, whether to arrest or not arrest, to detain or to allow to leave or his decision to use his firearm is his own.

However it can be argued that the operational reality of the constable's independence is not so simply comprehended. An officer's actions or inactions are subject to a good deal more scrutiny, especially in crisis situations, than those of more traditional professionals, such as lawyers and medical doctors. The command and supervision structure of police departments, and the existence of internal complaints investigations and disciplinary procedures, render the officer's decision making subject to extensive (although by no means necessarily effective) review. Avery (1981) argues that: "Police may be forgiven for sometimes feeling that the rewards of being correct in their actions are small." The accountability of the individual officer is, even in legal or regulatory terms, complicated; it becomes even more so if one considers the more abstract notion of accountability to the community which the officer serves. While the notion of community accountability has no legal connotation in Australia, given that no police department is directly governed at a local community level under statute, it has become a crucial philosophical issue in Australian police circles.

A philosophy of policing implies a particular or distinctive approach to the discharge of the police role, a framework within which the disparate components of the police enterprise are to be interpreted and executed. It is, of necessity, an abstraction in a complex organization such as policing, and in many cases would have to be inferred from global assessments of operational practice. Nevertheless, in recent years in Australia, attempts have been made to both reflect upon and posit appropriate philosophies for policing. In large measure, these attempts have arisen from assessments that the directions of Australian policing that have evolved over the years have not borne the fruits expected of them.

If there is a key word in the rhetoric of policing philosophy in Australia, it is community, or one of its surrogates, such as people. The tenor of recent writings on the Australian police, at least from liberal police scholars, has been one that emphasizes the essential reciprocality between the police and the policed.

Haldane's history of the Victoria Police is emphatically called "The People's Force"; Milte and Weber (1977) argue that: "The Police are the people's police." Whether arguing for how policing ought to be construed and conducted, or how it has in fact been construed and conducted, these writers are returning to the fundamental tenets of policing advanced by Sir Robert Peel in 1829. In the Instructions to the new Metropolitan Police, we find the following expression of that nexus between police and the community (cited in Milte and Weber, 1977):

> Therefore every member of the Force must remember that it is his duty to protect and help members of the public, no less than to bring offenders to justice. Consequently, while prompt to prevent crime and arrest criminals, he must look upon himself as the servant and guardian of the general public and treat all law-abiding citizens, irrespective of their race, colour, creed or social position, with unfailing patience and courtesy.

The British Royal Commission on the Police in 1967 went further in its understanding of the fundamental relationship between police and the public (Avery, 1981):

> The prevention of crime and the detection and punishment of offenders, the protection of life and property and the preservation of public tranquility are the direct responsibilities of ordinary citizens.

These are obligations and duties of the public, aided by the police and not the police, occasionally aided by some public-spirited citizens.

Thus the police are construed as part of the people, sharing their requirements and obligations, and enjoying only such additional authority and resources above those of ordinary citizens so that they can assist the public in the discharge of social control. Unfortunately, such propositions are rather more rhetoric than reality, when tested against the accounts of history and the parade of inquiries and Royal Commissions which seek to establish just how and why it is that police are not one with the community. In Australia particularly, the conclusions already touched upon in the early section on history that policing has enjoyed at best a fluctuating and fragile rapport with the community are echoed by other police writers (Avery, 1981; Milte and Weber, 1977; Whitrod, 1977). Some, like Haldane (1986) would argue that problems and difficulties in both police organizations and in the practice of policing the public only mirror the social and political realities of a polity at any one time. Nevertheless, the proposition remains very tenable: the nexus between the police and the public rarely demonstrates the functional utility and effectiveness envisaged by Sir Robert Peel. This is not the place to debate in detail why this is so. Whether it be derived from the historical sociopolitical realities of police development in this country (Finnane, 1987) or from the inherent contradictions of law enforcement and social control within capitalist economies (O'Malley, 1983) cannot be addressed here. On the other hand, arguments used by the police themselves about the need to reorient, or at least reemphasize, the association between the police and the public are very relevant, because it is these arguments which give rise to those public expressions of appropriate policing philosophies which are available.

John Avery is a useful representative of the progressive police position. In his *Police: Force or Service?* (1981), he argues strongly that for historical reasons, already adumbrated, processes of increasing urbanization with the attendant growth of crime rates and alienation, and the various technological changes that have impacted upon the delivery of police services, such as radio communication and mobile patrol, have served to distance the police from the community they seek to serve. The thrust of his thesis is that the typical title for an Australian police department—a police force—is indicative of attempts to achieve social control by the imposition of coercive power. The evolving hegemony of police over a range of social control functions once expected of the ordinary citizen has, in his terms, eroded the role of the citizen. The increasing specialized nature of police work has isolated the police officer from his or her constituency. Avery favors a reaffirmation of the interconnectedness of the police and the policed, symbolized by a change from the nomenclature of "force" to "service." He advances a number of strategies to implicate the public more directly into the business of social control and law enforcement, and suggests complementary changes in police attitudes and practices. There is much which is laudable about Avery's thesis, although many of his assumptions and interpretations can fairly be critiqued. The point about his work is not whether it is historically accurate or philosophically sound, but rather that it reflects an important shift in the rhetoric of police about their relationship with the community. Whether that rhetoric is reflected in practice can be vigorously debated. The shift is most evident in the formal expressions of policing philosophy; it is a shift which acknowledges that the traditional implicit assumption about the oneness of the police and the community must be rendered more explicit. The Victoria Police have, for the last decade or so, been attempting just that.

For some time now the Victoria Police have been publishing in their Annual Reports an organizational philosophy. That philosophy has evolved considerably while the department has struggled to find the right words to express its intentions. The *Victoria Police Annual Report* (1981) states:

> The foundations of modern police forces in the English speaking world were laid by Rowan and Mayne, joint Commissioners of Sir Robert Peel's New Police in London in 1829. At that time, they expressed the objectives of the new police service. Simply stated, those objectives were:
>
> - Preservation of the peace
> - Protection of life and property
> - Prevention and detection of crime
>
> Those objectives still provide an effective statement of organizational aims for modern police forces. The purpose of the organizational philosophy is to indicate the means by which we seek to achieve our objectives and to ensure that individual tasks are goal orientated. The organizational philosophy is, therefore, expressed in the policies and practices adopted by an organization in an effort to achieve its aims. The following are examples of the organizational philosophy of the Victoria Police Force:
>
> Professionalism through a total committment to unconditional police service.
>
> Optimisation of existing resources by ensuring the most advantageous utilisation of manpower, mobility, communications and equipment.
>
> Emphasis of the visible police presence by patrol strategies involving maximisation of foot patrols and conspicuous, marked vehicles to inspire public confidence.
>
> Improvement of existing performance or maintenance of superior performance through in-service training and self-development.

> Police involvement in community affairs, ranging from participation in local government to involvement in ethnic community interests and conducting local dances.
>
> Innovation in operational and administrative practices, designed to simplify police problems and to promote organizational effectiveness.
>
> Planned development in the short term and long term through the development of 5 year plans progressively updated annually.
>
> Involvement of every member or the force in practical public relations projecting a professional image at all times.
>
> Sensitivity to public opinion and responsiveness to change in providing the service which the community needs.
>
> Willingness to accept public accountability for our actions and performance.
>
> Recognition of the sense of security of the public—in their homes and on the streets—as the true measure of police effectiveness.

Contrast the implications for the primacy of organizational effectiveness and efficiency reflected by the rank order of these principles with those which appeared in the 1986 *Annual Report:*

> The police are part of the community and act for the community in maintaining law and order. Each member of the Victoria Police carries the responsibility and privileges attached to the office of constable, which is one of honour and dignity. Its origin dates from antiquity and its history is bound up with the historical development of peace, order and good government in England. The functions of the Victoria Police Force are to:
>
> (i) protect life and property
> (ii) preserve the peace
> (iii) prevent crime
> (iv) enforce legislation
> (v) help those in need of assistance
>
> These are responsibilities of all police, but modern policing also requires a social contract between police and the community and the active co-operation and support of the public. Police must be aware of the changing nature of society, so that

Force goals are consistent with society's goals. Police should contribute their expertise to debate on social change, to ensure that debate serves the public interest. A police force is drawn from the community, so its members should be representative of that community...

The philosophy of the Victoria Police is based on principles designed to ensure that the public is well served by a Police Force that it respects. These principles are that:

(a) it is preferable to prevent an offense rather than to detect the offender after someone has become a victim. This requires:

(i) close community involvement
ii) maintaining a visible police presence
iii) a certainty that offenders will be caught;

(b) disorder in the community is prevented by consultation and peaceful means, rather than by repression and force;

(c) the use of force should be reserved for situations where peaceful means have failed or are inappropriate. If force is used, it should be limited to the degree of force necessary and legally permissible;

(d) the ability to fulfil the functions and responsibilities of policing depends on the esteem in which the Force is held by the public;

(e) public co-operation in fighting crime is dependent on its confidence in police performance;

(f) public confidence is enhanced by police carrying out their duties with courtesy, care and compassion;

(g) police discretion must be exercised in the public interest to avoid harsh or unreasonable consequences of police action;

(h) police must strive to maintain a cooperative relationship with the public which continues the tradition that the police and the public are one, and each supports the other;

(i) the Force must respond to changes in the community and be sensitive to public opinion so that it is seen to act in the public interest;

(j) police are often the first to be contacted by people in trouble, however the expertise of other community service organizations is acknowledged and used where appropriate;

(k) it is our members' duty to uphold the law and they must scrupulously obey it, even when powers seem inadequate;

(l) in the public interest, the Force must aim to improve existing performance or to maintain superior performance; and

(m) individual police are entitled to hold political or religious beliefs like any other member of the community. However, the public interest demands that members of the Force act with complete impartiality in all circumstances.

The juxtaposition of these expressions provides a fascinating insight to the changes wrought in only a short number of years to the expressed orientation of the Victoria Police. From a concern in 1981 primarily related to organizational efficiency and effectiveness, we see the considerable shift by 1986 to a model of policing which embraces and keeps reiterating the importance of the police-community nexus. Of the eleven principles advanced in 1981 and the thirteen advanced in 1986, only two are common. Whatever the practical consequences of this crucial shift in rhetoric towards a "people's police," the Victoria Police philosophy clearly signals a public concern to be more accountable to the community it serves.

FUNCTIONS

The broad functions of Australian police have already been touched upon in the previous discussion of the organizational philosophy of the Victoria Police. The general imperatives of preserving the peace, protection of life and property, and the prevention of crime appears in various guises in either police regulations acts or in annual reports. The prescriptive paucity of these imperatives is attested by the recent *Report of the Committee of Inquiry into the Victoria Police Force* (1985; the "Neesham Inquiry," named after the chairman of the committee). That Inquiry went to considerable pains to formulate a realistic and legally-defensible set of functional parameters for the Victoria Police, and it addressed a wide range of previous material which had discussed the issue in the Australian context. Particularly, the Committee looked to the discourse provided by what is known as the "Lusher Inquiry," a Commission to inquire into New South Wales Police Administration (1981). That inquiry inferred from amendments to the enabling

Act (the Police Regulation Act 1899 [NSW]) that the functions of police were:

> (i) prevention of crime;
> (ii) detection and apprehension of offenders;
> (iii) preservation of good order;
> (iv) protection of people from injury or death and property from damage.

The Neesham Inquiry then went on to cite the British Royal Commission on the Police (1962), which stated that the functions of police were:

> (a) a duty to maintain law and order and to protect persons and property;
>
> (b) a duty to prevent crime;
>
> (c) responsibility for the detection of criminals and, in the course of interrogating suspected persons, the police have parts to play in the early stages of the judicial process acting under judicial restraint;
>
> (d) ...the police have the responsibility of deciding whether or not to prosecute persons suspected of crime;
>
> (e) ...the police themselves conduct many prosecutions for the less serious offenses;
>
> (f) a duty to patrol road traffic and advise local authorities on traffic questions;
>
> (g) the police carry out certain duties on behalf of government departments, for example, the conduct of inquiries into applications made by persons who wish to be granted British nationality; and
>
> (h) the police have a long tradition to befriend anyone who needs their help and they may be called upon to cope with minor or major emergencies.

The Inquiry, like other Australian authorities (Milte and Weber, 1977), also cited the major responsibilities of police identified by the American Bar Association in its Projects on Standards for Criminal Justice (1973).

The Inquiry then adopted the approach of extracting an idea of the police function from the range of police activities that could be demonstrated. While not an exhaustive list, it felt able to enumerate the following:

- crime prevention;
- detecting offenders;
- prosecution duties;
- protection of persons and property;
- property recovery;
- conflict resolution;
- the assistance of those in special need of care;
- the safety and orderly movement of traffic;
- the investigation of sudden deaths;
- enforcement of court orders;
- protection of fundamental freedoms;
- statutory duties (such as supervision of the provisions of the Liquor Control Act;
- miscellaneous services, such as search and rescue work.

The Neesham Inquiry also examined thoroughly the historical and legislative basis for the range of activities currently undertaken by the Victoria Police. It argued that the original set of three imperative functions which began this section are well-anchored in historical terms and in terms of the provision of police regulations. However it goes on to argue that the reality of contemporary policing is such that (Neesham Inquiry, 1985):

> We are therefore of the opinion that it has become a police function where there is no other responsible agency available, or where such responsible agencies are inadequate, to provide reasonable help to those persons who are in need of help (whether for their protection or the protection of their property) who reasonably look to the police to provide it. In our opinion it is not desirable to attempt a catalogue of all police activity. In the first place such an attempt would be unlikely to succeed. In the second, if it was set down, flexibility might be lost and initiative and progress inhibited. Having said that, we are of the opinion that the function of the Victoria Police is:
>
> (i) the preservation of the peace;
> (ii) the prevention and detection of crime;

(iii) the protection of life and property endangered by an actual or apprehended breach of the peace or criminal act;
(iv) the control of road traffic;
(v) the performance of duties allocated pursuant to the overall coordination of land, sea and air searches in respect of persons, land vehicles and small craft in "in shore" and inland waters;
(vi) the provision of reasonable help to those persons who are in need of help and who reasonably look to the police to provide it.

The Neesham Inquiry's deliberations and conclusions cannot be considered perfectly representative of all Australian police departments; yet, given its attempt to canvass relevant Australian legislation and scholarship regarding the functions of the police, it stands as indicative of the general thrust of established thinking on this topic.

A list of functions, of course, tell us little or nothing about how it is that police discharge them. One gauge of the operationalization of departmental functions and objectives is the manner in which police departments are formally organized to fulfill those functions. The details of organizational structures differ, naturally, between the state police departments. Nevertheless, Victoria's police structure is sufficiently typical in its broad aspects to be worth reproducing here. One important qualification, however, is that as a large department within the context of Australian policing, it offers a more diverse and specialized set of operations than is possible by some of the smaller departments. The present structure is reproduced in Figure 1 on pages 4-5.

The respective weight given to the different operational and support areas can be gained by looking at the personnel distributions across the areas. Figure 2 presents that distribution. A recent innovation in the Victoria Police *Annual Report* is the attempt to set corporate and divisional objectives, and to specify the means by which they are best effected. While the massed presentation of these details is rather overwhelming, it in fact describes more succinctly the current objectives, strategies, and tactics of one large Australian police department than would be possible in a narrative account. Figure 3 presents the overall corporate plan of the Victoria Police for the period 1989-1990, while Figure 4 presents the corporate objectives. The reader can be confident that there are no radical divergences between these details and those which would apply to other police departments in Australia. However it should be

FIG. 2: VICTORIA POLICE ACTUAL STRENGTH BY DEPARTMENT AS AT 30 JUNE 1990

Ranks	CCO	Operations	Crime	Traffic	Services	Personnel	R&D	IID	ITD	Health	Admin	Other*	Male	Female	Total
Chief Commissioner	1												1		1
Deputy Commissioner	2												2		2
Assistant Commissioner		1	1	1	1	1	1	1					6	1	7
Commander		2		1									3		3
Chief Superintendent	1	15	4	3	2	4							29		29
Superintendent		28	4	2	1	2	3	4					44		44
Chief Inspector	4	29	14	11	6	13	3	5	1			22	107	1	108
Inspector	5	120	26	23	17	14	9	13				4	225	6	231
Senior Sergeant	3	336	65	40	26	23	9	8	1	1		3	502	13	515
Sergeant	1	1,125	192	143	121	50	10	7	3	2		4	1,603	55	1,658
Senior Constable	7	2,249	318	352	121	39	15	7	4	4		2	2,648	470	3,118
Constable	9	2,467	84	128	112	11	56						2,222	647	2,869
Constable PCETS						792							655	137	792
Recruits						505							403	102	505
At Force Reserve		66											48	18	66
TOTAL FORCE		6,438	708	704	407	1,454	106	47	9	7		35	8,489	1,450	9,948
Reservists		85	5	4	1	7	3			1			78	28	106
PSO				97									83	14	97
PSO-Trainees													2	2	4
Public Servants	10	567	300	153	228	68	40	14	84	40	254				1,758
FORCE TOTAL	43	7,090	1,013	958	636	1,529	149	61	93	48	254	35			11,913

* - Surplus positions due to Operations Department reorganization under Project Arbiter.
The average number of police personnel in the Force this financial year was 9,942. This compares to an average of 9,564 last year. The average number of public service personnel employed by the Force this year was 1,789 (compared to 1,765 last financial year).

Source: Victoria Police, *Annual Report, 1989/1990.*

Corporate Plan

The Mission Statement of the Victoria Police was redefined in March 1990 and is now:

"To provide a safe orderly society by serving the community and the law".

The functions of the Victoria Police are to:

- protect life and property;
- preserve peace;
- prevent and detect crime;
- perform duties prescribed by law; and
- provide help and assistance to those in need of it, in accordance with community expectations and the law.

In 1989/90, the Victoria Police Force issued its second Corporate Plan. The publication of this second Plan was the first step in a new "Annual Planning and Budgeting Cycle" (a sequence of activities designed to base the Force's budget estimates on pre-determined Force-wide initiatives and plans developed by Command), which was implemented in 1989/90. The Corporate Plan was distributed throughout the Force and to interested individuals and organisations, to help publicise the future directions, long-term aims and immediate targets of the Victoria Police Force.

Key elements of the Plan include:

- the Mission Statement (this was redefined in March 1990);
- the Force's Corporate Goals which outline the long-term aims of the Force and provide the organisation with clear directions to pursue; and
- the Corporate Objectives for 1989/90 (the specific targets that the Force had to achieve during the year).

Corporate Goals

The Corporate Goals of the Victoria Police are in the areas of:

- public order and community service;
- traffic control;
- crime reduction; and
- resource management.

Fig. 3: Corporate Plan of the Victoria Police (*Source:* Victoria Police, *Annual Report 1989/1990).*

Corporate Objectives

In 1989/90, nine specific objectives were pursued by the Force. These were to:

1 **Create a public awareness of, and support for, a multi-faceted, integrated anti-crime strategy.**

The success of programs such as Neighbourhood Watch, Crime Stoppers, Operation Noah and the "Look-Lock-Leave" campaign indicate that this objective has been met.

2 **Increase the level of police visibility by 5%.**

Through a variety of activities, the Force increased its visibility by an average of 20%.

3 **Reduce the ratio of vehicular collisions (per number of vehicles registered by 3%.**

A reduction of 9.4% (below the 1988/89 level) in vehicle collisions was achieved. When this result is compared to the growth in the number of vehicles registered, the real reduction was 14.9%.

4 **Maintain the clearance rate of Major Crime Index Offences above 25%.**

As at 30 June 1990, the Force had cleared 27% of all Major Crime Index Offences reported.

5 **Acquire, develop and deploy sufficient resources to adequately allow for ongoing operations, natural growth and new initiatives in the Force.**

Funding for the year was insufficient to sustain all the planned activities. Factors contributing to this included a 4.9% growth in the Force and a 4% increase in the demand for Force services.

6 **Conduct a survey to determine public attitudes towards policing in Victoria.**

There was insufficient funding to undertake a public attitude survey.

7 **Commence implementing the improvements to the budget programs, organisational structure and systems of the Force.**

Significant progress was made in the overall program of change throughout the Force, including the new district structures, the new budget structures and the devolution of decision-making authorities.

8 **Improve police operational and resource management efficiency by upgrading the Force's corporate computer systems, including linked micro-computers.**

A long term information technology strategic plan titled "Information 2000" was developed. While the delivery of some new systems during the year may be said to constitute an improvement, insufficient funding prevented the Force achieving all its planned developments.

9 **Increase public confidence in the integrity, accountability and professionalism of the Force.**

Complaint data collection has been enhanced.
The average time taken to complete complaints has been reduced.
The Internal Security Unit has been formalised and upgraded.

Fig. 4: Corporate Objectives of the Victoria Police (*Source:* Victoria Police, *Annual Report 1989/1990*).

reiterated that Victoria's police department is large, the state is geographically compact and highly urbanized, and that particular initiatives and innovations reflected in Figures 3 and 4 may be functions of these characteristics, and may not be as feasible in other states with larger land masses and more diversely located populations.

A last perspective on the functions of Australian police relates to the enabling powers that police hold to execute their duties. Hannigan (1985) outlines what he considers to be the significant powers police have available to them: powers of arrest, search and seizure, and prosecution. With regard to the first of these, Hannigan (1985) states:

> Police powers of arrest (which are much greater than those of ordinary citizens) are prescribed in specific statutes. The common law, so influential in the development of the law of arrest, no longer possesses its former significance. Indeed, in some states at least, e.g., Victoria, powers of arrest are now exclusively defined by statute.

In practical terms, arrest powers can be divided into those which allow arrest without warrant, and those which require a warrant. Statutes have enlarged the range of circumstances where a warrant is not required; the New South Wales legislation is reasonably typical, in that it allows arrest without warrant when persons fall into any of the following categories (Hannigan, 1985):

- caught committing an offense against any Act
- caught and have committed an offense
- loitering at night and are suspected with reasonable cause of having committed an offense
- found on premises which have been searched under a search warrant and the persons are linked to seized objects
- believed to be subject to a warrant that has been issued for their arrest

Many statutes contain provisions which require police to exercise the discretion to arrest only when it is believed that a charge on summons will not be sufficient. Such provisions as found in the Victorian Crimes Act illustrate the possible circumstances where an arrest is considered necessary (Hannigan, 1985):

- to ensure the appearance of the offender before court
- to preserve public order
- to prevent the continuation or repetition of the offense or the commission of a further offense
- for the safety or welfare of the public or the offender

Hannigan (1985) makes the following important point:

> When making an arrest without warrant, it is not necessary for police officers to explain in detail to their prisoners reasons for their arrest. However, suspects are entitled to know in broad terms what their offenses are and, if police officers refuse to tell them or deliberately mislead them, such arrests are tainted with illegality.

There are no provisions under the various state laws for police officers to legally detain suspects against their will without first arresting them. Upon arrest, an accused person must be brought before a court as soon as is reasonably possible. Victoria has recently experimented with and abandoned a legislative provision that allowed police to question an arrested person for six hours before bringing that person before a court or applying for an extension of the questioning time, with the consent of the accused.

The searching of persons and the seizure of personal property is generally governed by arrest legislation. While some statutes allow searches of unarrested persons under circumstances where there are reasonable suspicions of drug or illegal firearm possession, police do not in general have the power to stop and search people on suspicion. Once arrested, accused persons can be searched. The taking of fingerprints from and medical examinations of accused persons is differently covered in the various state legislations. Some states allow fingerprinting in general circumstances; others allow it only when questions of the prisoner's identity are raised. Medical examinations must normally be conducted only under specific statute. All states have legislation which allows the taking of blood or breath samples from motor vehicle drivers under the influence of intoxicating liquor.

The search of premises and the seizure of property is usually conducted under warrant, although specific statutes allow searches without warrant under some circumstances, especially in the case of drugs. South Australia and Tasmania are unusual in that their respective state legislations allow the issue of general warrants to police which remain in force for some time, and which allow general seizure of illegal goods. Warrants in other states usually specify particular premises and kinds of goods.

It has already been noted that police prosecute in the courts of summary jurisdiction, the magistrate's courts. All police departments have a prosecution section or division, staffed by police officers specially trained in prosecution. An increasing (but nevertheless very small) number of these officers have formal tertiary legal qualifications.

The police carriage of firearms in Australia has increased significantly in recent years. According to Swanton et al. (1983): "Less than a decade ago, the majority of operational police in Australia did not carry firearms. Now, a majority carry them." The use of deadly force by police officers is generally governed by the common law principle of minimum force; that is, police officers are entitled to use only such force as is necessary to obtain an arrest. In violent confrontations, this in practice means that an officer must reasonably believe that his or her life is in danger. In fugitive arrests, deadly force must be confined to those circumstances where no other means of arrest are possible, and where the arrest is for a very serious crime; in some states, those crimes must be punishable by death or life imprisonment (see Swanton et al., 1983).

PERSONNEL PRACTICES

Recruitment can be considered that process whereby people with appropriate qualifications and qualities are attracted to apply for police service. Each Australian police department has a recruitment section or division, which coordinates recruitment programs, selection procedures, and in some cases departmental careers programs. Such sections avail themselves of standard advertising media, such as newspapers, television, and cinema. Careers presentations at public festivals and secondary schools play a prominent part in recruitment.

Nonacceptance rates for applicants to Australian police departments is generally high. A study commissioned for the Neesham Inquiry (Victorian Ministry for Police and Emergency Services, 1985) revealed that in 1982 the following percentages of applicants were rejected before they sat for the selection examinations: Victoria (79 percent); New South Wales (48 percent); Tasmania (68 percent); Western Australia (88 percent); Queensland (41 percent); Northern Territory (16 percent); and Australian Federal Police (33 percent) (no data were available from the survey on South Australian police applicant rates). Of all applicants, the following percentages were accepted after successfully completing the selection tests: Victoria (17 percent); New South Wales (26 percent); Tasmania (32 percent); Queensland (24 percent); and Northern Territory (11 percent) (relevant data unavailable from South Australia, Western Australia and Australian Federal Police).

The minimum standards for eligibility for the respective Australian police departments are generally set by state legislation. The degree of precision within these legislative (or in some cases regulatory) provisions differs considerably. Some states, such as New South Wales, prescribe rather precise standards, while others rely upon archaic expressions, such as: "that the applicant be healthy, physically fit and of good character" (Victorian Ministry, 1984).

The lower and the upper age of entry for most Australian police departments are specifically stated. Commissioners of police generally have discretion to waive these (and other) requirements in special circumstances. Minimum height is generally specified separately for men and for women although Victoria has recently abolished its height requirement, following the recommendations of the Neesham Inquiry (1985). Weight minima for males and for females are also specified. Most states require a high standard of unaided vision and normal color vision. South Wales allows corrected vision. Three state police departments—Victoria, New South Wales, and South Australia—require the ability to pass specific physical agility tests.

Psychological testing does not in general have a high selection test profile. When tests are used—as in the Northern Territory, Tasmania, South Australia, and Victoria—they tend to be personality inventories such as the California Psychological Inventory, the Minnesota Multiphasic Personality Inventory, the 16 PF and the Maudsley Personality Inventory, and they are used primarily as an aid to the selection interview panel rather than as stand-alone elimination tests. All departments, except the Northern Territory and the A.F.P. departments, administer general ability or intelligence tests. Victoria is probably typical in that its general abilities test is pitched around the fourth year of secondary schooling.

While educational qualifications have historically been set quite low (around four years of secondary school), recent developments have seen a marked increase in the minimum educational standard. The Australian Federal Police, for example, are moving toward a tertiary qualification as a minimum standard; while state police departments have not yet followed suit, the completion or near completion of secondary schooling (twelve years) is becoming the standard.

Applicants for Australian police departments must, in general, be Australian citizens or British subjects. Applicants must not usually have been convicted of a criminal offense. Victoria distinguishes between serious and less serious offenses, while the Northern Territory takes into account the nature of the offense, the age at which it was committed, and the sentence of the court.

All Australian recruits undergo constabulary training and generally begin their careers as junior constables. There have been some exercises of discretion by commissioners with regard to lateral entry, whereby an applicant with particular qualifications is inducted and bypasses traditional extended periods at junior rank. Pilots, for instance, and in one case in Victoria, a psychologist, have been inducted and then rapidly given brevet rank as commissioned officers. However these are relatively isolated cases, and graduates and others with professional qualification are advantaged at selection only in the sense that they are more likely to pass the educational components of the selection tests. Accelerated career paths after induction as basic recruits for those with specialized qualifications is at this stage largely informal where it does exist; as we shall see, however, the possession of specialized qualifications is becoming increasingly important in the later years of service promotion.

Selection testing in Australian police departments can be described as thorough and exacting if the proportion of rejections and the number of selection hurdles are taken into account (although the quality of selection criteria and the conceptual approach taken with selection paradigms have been criticized; see James, 1985; Rowe, 1985). Complete testing usually takes between two and three days, and involves comprehensive checks on past employment, character references and offense history. All departments, except New South Wales, require appearance before an interview panel normally composed of senior officers. Besides the orthodox specification of criteria regarding height, vision, fitness, educational standards and so forth, most Australian police departments also prescribe less quantifiable standards of personal functioning, such as "communication skills, demeanour, maturity and motivation" (Victorian Ministry, 1984). These dimensions are probed most usually at the interview stage, although there is relatively little use made of developments elsewhere in personnel selection, such as behaviorally-anchored rating scales. Indeed, the Victorian Ministry survey report (1984) said: "It is notable that most of the criteria appeared to require arbitrary judgements from interviewers and that the variation in methods and criteria used reflects the lack of definition as to the optimum qualities necessary for operational police work."

Training: The Victorian Ministry survey report (1984) divides Australian police training into four categories: recruit, sub-officers (generally sergeants and senior sergeants), commissioned officers, and specialist (especially criminal investigation).

Recruit training in every Australian police department takes place initially in police academies. As Fogarty (1985) points out: "the subject of police training is dynamic, with curricula being refined and enlarged almost weekly." Hence it is difficult to both succinctly describe and keep current an account of training dimensions. Nevertheless, it is possible to outline the major features of training in recent years. Recruit training typically involves a period of classroom and drill instruction at an academy, followed by an extended period in the field as probationary constables under training supervision, with follow-up refresher courses. Fogarty (1985) provides some examples:

New South Wales:	12 weeks academy course 9 months field experience 6 weeks academy refresher course
Victoria:	18 weeks academy course 53 weeks field experience 4 weeks academy refresher course
Tasmania:	29 weeks academy course 12 weeks field experience

Northern Territory: 15 weeks academy course
22 weeks field experience
9 weeks academy refresher course

Recruit training is primarily vocational in its curricula; that is, recruits concentrate upon instrumental topics such as law, first aid, drill, firearms, restraint and control, the preparation of charge sheets and court briefs, and so forth. A softening of the traditional vocational orientation is apparent in recent years. Behavioral studies, police studies, management courses, and such academic subjects as English have appeared on the curricula of most departments (Fogarty, 1985); their penetration rate remains low, however, in proportion to the more orthodox courses.

Subofficer and Commissioned Officer Training: Most departments provide a number of what Fogarty (1985) calls "development" courses, which refer to courses necessary for promotion to higher rank. New South Wales, for instance, requires a four-week course for aspirants to Constable First Class, a four-week course for Sergeant 3rd Class, a seven-week course for Senior Sergeant, a three-week course for Inspector, and a two-week class for senior executives (see below for a description of the rank structures of Australian police departments). Victoria has less diversity of courses, but of longer duration: 15 weeks sub-officer course (for those senior constables aspiring to sergeant rank); 15 weeks officer's course (for senior sergeants) and a three-week senior executive course (for chief inspectors). Other departments employ similar courses for promotional purposes. The curricula of these courses differ considerably from state to state, as do their durations. As the courses apply to more senior rank, they naturally become more concerned with administrative and managerial topics. It is fair to describe Australian police departments as relying extensively upon in-service development courses, although, as we shall see, that pattern is slowly changing.

Specialist Training: All police departments offer a broad range of police-related specialist courses. Of these, the most extensive is usually the detective training courses for criminal investigation (Fogarty, 1985): New South Wales (13 weeks); Victoria (12 weeks); Queensland (three weeks); and Tasmania (six weeks). Other courses available within or across the police departments include: traffic control, driver training, juvenile bureaus, breath analysis operators, accident investigation, prosecution, search and rescue, sexual offenses investigation, crisis intervention, and communication operations. All departments maintain in-service firearm refresher and advanced training, while those states which have formed tactical operations groups generally train their own personnel. There is some interchange between departments in terms of specialist training courses and advanced development courses, although this appears to take place largely amongst the smaller departments without the personnel to mount extensive arrays of their own specialist courses.

Promotion: Australian police departments endure a broad rank structure, with some differences in nomenclature and range between them. The basic rank structure common to all departments is, in ascending order: constable, senior constable, sergeant, inspector, superintendent, and then the commissioner ranks, already detailed. All departments, with the exception of Victoria, have grades or classes of constable, and all have either two or three grades of sergeant, with senior sergeant usually the designation for the top grade. All departments except Tasmania have three (or more usually two) grades of inspector, with the senior grade designated chief inspector. All departments except the Northern Territory have two (and in one case three) grades of superintendent, with the senior grade usually designated chief superintendent. Four departments (New South Wales, Victoria, Western Australia and South Australia) have a higher rank before commissioner rank is reached; this rank is known as executive/senior chief superintendent or commander. The minimum number of ranks in any department is nine, while the maximum is thirteen, before the ranks of commissioner. This enormous range of ranks probably partly explains why Australian police departments require so many in-service development and promotional courses.

There are moves to reduce the array of ranks and grades, led by the A.F.P. which has essentially reduced the structure to the four basic ranks, with salary bands within each rank; some departments, such as Queensland and Western Australia, have retained up to ten or more rank/grade structures.

Promotion in Australian police departments generally comprises a mixture of seniority (period spent in the department) and merit (in terms of various degrees of promotional examination success, other relevant qualifications and experience, and appearance before a promotions board), which are weighted differently at different rank levels. It is fair to say, nevertheless that current directions in promotional policy, particularly at a senior level, indicate an increasing emphasis on merit-promotion. There is, naturally, a good deal of diversity between the departments regarding the mix of promotional techniques. The average length of service between sequential promotions also differs. Foremen and Allan (1985) provide an overview of the patterns across the departments although this is quite dated by now.

Many police officers do not, of course, consistently apply for promotion, and many of those do stay for longer periods in any one rank before promotion. At the junior ranks, until commissioned officer stage, promotions can be considered largely seniority-based, with noncompetitive examination completion and subject to vacancies. At the commissioned officer levels, examinations tend to become more competitive and merit considerations play a greater role in promotion. However, it is very difficult to describe an acceptable general rule for promotions across the various departments.

The possession of external educational or professional qualifications by police officers is increasing in importance in Australian police departments. According to the Victorian Ministry survey report (1984), three departments (Victoria, South Australia, and Queensland) offer salary incentive schemes for officers with approved external qualifications, especially in the fields of science (electronic, engineering, computer), law, psychology, and accountancy. Most departments recognize the possession of external qualifications for consideration in promotions or transfers, and all departments encourage the use of study leave for the undertaking of approved external courses. The Ministry's survey, which is now quite dated, revealed that 1.4% of Victoria police, 1.3% of Tasmanian police, 13% of South Australian police, 8% of Western Australian police, 9% of Queensland police, and 5.8% of Northern Territory police held external higher educational qualifications (the high figure for South Australia was due to the in-service training requirement to complete several external subjects in Police Studies). These figures represent a major change over the situation twenty years ago, when there were few if any tertiary educational qualifications amongst Australian police; and current figures can be expected to be considerably higher again. Nevertheless, despite these changes, the percentage rates must be considered to be rather low in an absolute sense, compared with many overseas police departments.

LEADERSHIP/SUPERVISORY CALIBRE

Various aspects of leadership and supervision have been touched upon in the previous sections relating to accountability, command structure, training, and promotions. However, it is very difficult to make definitive statements about the calibre of leadership and supervision in Australian police departments. Not only are there wide divergences between the states upon range of matters which impact and reflect leadership calibre, there is also the crucial question of from which perspective is the issue of leadership to be viewed. Legitimate perspectives arise from quite disparate groups: parliamentarians, interfacing organizations within the criminal justice system, members of the community and the community as a whole, and most importantly, members of the police departments themselves. These groups do not, of course, always share the same set of criteria concerning the calibre of leadership. There have been several circumstances in recent Australian police history where explicit conflict and hostility has broken out between politicians, commissioners of police, and police unions, where it is clear that the parameters of appropriate leadership were not held in common by the contesting groups. Swanton (1983) provides a number of examples where commissioners have acted to reform various aspects of police administration with the support of some sectors of the department and wider groups in the community, only to be castigated and ultimately thwarted by the membership of the department acting concertedly through its union, with the support of other outside groups. The role of police unions in Australia will receive attention in a later section; the point here is that the assessment of the calibre of leadership, even if only that of the chief executive officer of a department, is dependent upon the perspectives, vested or otherwise, of relevant groups. The issue becomes considerably more complicated when leadership is taken to embrace superior/subordinate supervision through the various ranks. Perhaps the best way to address the issue of leadership is discuss those attempts made by Australian police to upgrade the capacities of their executive officers to discharge their duties. In addition, it is useful to discuss briefly the broader issue of rank supervision. These topics require a reiteration of information presented in earlier sections, but they also make use of other material not yet addressed. At the highest level of police leadership, only one state police department has attempted to radically reform the traditional arrangements whereby commissioners are vested with a functional autonomy over the administration of their department. In 1984, the New South Wales government created a Police Board, on the recommendation of the Lusher Inquiry (1981). The creation of the Board cannot be directly related to assessments of the lack of leadership provided by previous and contemporary New South Wales commissioners, but it does have the clear implication that in the view of one state government, the governance of the police department could be improved by interposing a new body between the traditional arrangements of commissioner-minister-parliament. The Board comprises the commissioner of police and two part-time, non-police members, one of whom is chairman. The functions of the Board are as follows: (Police Board of New South Wales, *Annual Report*, 1984)

> (1) The overriding function of the Board is to promote the improvement of the Police Service and to ensure the maintenance of an efficient and effective Police Service. By Police Service is meant the Police Force and its support services.
>
> (2) Without affecting the generality of this overriding function, the Board is also required to:
>
> (a) formulate plans for the provision of a comprehensive, balanced co-ordinated Police Service;
>
> (b) make recommendations to the Minister on policy matters relating to the Police Service;
>
> (c) ensure the development of modern personnel practices within the Police Service;
>
> (d) make, in relation to the Police Service, recommendations to the Minister as to financial resources, property management, priorities and allocation of finances;
>
> (e) initiate research into new police methods and other research related to law enforcement generally;

> (f) consider applications and make recommendations to the Minister in relation to all appointments of persons to the rank of superintendent and higher ranks;
>
> (g) make a recommendation to the Minister in relation to each appointment to the rank of inspector of any grade, after considering
>
> (i) such information in relation to the applications for the appointment as the Board requires to be provided by the Commissioner; and
>
> (ii) the advice of the Commissioner;
>
> (h) make recommendation in relation to all transfers at the rank of superintendent and higher ranks; and
>
> (i) make reports or recommendations to the Minister on any matter referred to the Board by the Minister.

In effect, the commissioner retains the governance of the department in terms of operational command and day-to-day management, but is required to implement the decisions of the Board. Many of the above functions are similar to those found in various police acts and regulations regarding the duties of the commissioners of other police departments. The important difference lies in the Board's creation as an advisory or oversighting body, especially in terms of forward planning and policy development. It is, in fact, a reflection of the view in New South Wales that the commissioner of police requires such advice and oversight.

The Neesham Inquiry (1985) examined the concept and functions of the New South Wales Board in its deliberations on the Victoria Police. The Inquiry saw the major advantage of a Board as its provision of "broader avenues for advice to the Chief Commissioner (especially in high level management expertise)...." On the other hand, the Inquiry saw a Board's potential for interference with the chief commissioner's responsibility for the management of the department. In a telling statement, the Inquiry said:

> A Board with executive authority to direct the Chief Commissioner was we believed undesirable because of the inevitable inroad into the Chief Commissioner's independence. The appointment of such a Board could, we thought, only be justified by evidence of serious mismanagement in the force, and that is contrary to the situation as we found it.

Thus, with the exception of New South Wales, no structural changes have been wrought in the arrangements for the operation of the chief executives of Australian police departments. It is worth noting that the current commissioner in New South Wales, John Avery, has had this said about him (*The Bulletin*, 31 May, 1988):

> He is regarded by Duncan Chappell, director of the (Australian) Institute of Criminology, as "one of the most significant police leaders not just in this country, but in the whole of western democracy." He is regarded by many senior NSW policemen as a pain in the butt. He has been regarded by a succession of Police Ministers as the most able and astute man to have held the job.

This is a nice illustration of the variety of leadership perspectives which can be brought to bear upon police executives. In any case, it is apparent that at the government level in most states, assessments of the calibre of respective commissioners have not brought forth radical reforms for altering the traditional governance of police departments. This, of course, does not reflect a blanket endorsement of current or past commissioners. Haldane (1986) comments quite critically on many of the past commissioners of the Victorian Police, while the dismissal and consequent criminal conviction of the current commissioner of the Queensland Police, Sir Terry Lewis, because of revelations arising out of the Fitzgerald Inquiry into Corruption in the Queensland Police (*The Age*, 24 April, 1988) is not the first time that Australian police commissioners have been (allegedly) found to be lacking in appropriate qualities for the position. On the other hand, a number of current and immediately past commissioners have enjoyed good public standing, and have come to reflect a more highly educated, professionally management-oriented group of executives. Miller, the immediate past commissioner of the Victoria Police, who had been to the British National Police College, Bramshill, (Haldane, 1986) claimed that he would be the last chief commissioner in Victoria without tertiary qualifications. He was proved right when Glare succeeded him in 1987; Glare possesses an honors law degree, as does Horman, an ex-Victoria assistant commissioner who was appointed commissioner of the Tasmanian Police in 1988. John Avery possesses a Master of Arts degree.

While there have not been profound structural changes in the ways in which the chief executives of Australian police departments are allowed to exert leadership within their departments, attempts have been made at the training level to equip potential commissioners and other senior executives with advanced management training. Perhaps the most prominent of these was the establishment of an Australian Police College in New South Wales in 1960. According to Milte and Weber (1977), the College was established because the 1957 Conference of Commissioners of Police "resolved that there was a need for a national college for the training of executives and potential executive police officers from the Australian States and territories and New Zealand." Amongst the range of courses taught at the College is the Senior Executives' Course, designed to "inform senior police executives concerning the duties of a Police Commissioner" (Milte and Weber, 1977). Chappell and Wilson (1969) describe the course thus:

> A six months residential course is now provided by the Australian Police College for Australian and New Zealand police force officers, and also for selected officers of various South East Asian police forces. The syllabus for the course is an extensive one, involving an in-depth consideration of police administration and procedure, together with a survey of various topics such as criminology, psychology, psychiatry and sociology. Members of these forces are exposed not only to internal police lecturers but also to external lecturers from a wide range of institutions. They are required to prepare a substantial thesis during the course and this is a major factor in assessing the potential capabilities of the particular course member.

However, no police department makes attendance at the College a mandatory requirement for its senior officers. It is interesting to note that in his listing of all the provisions for the training of senior officers in Australian police departments, Fogarty (1985) indicates that only the Australian Federal Police explicitly acknowledge that the College is utilized in senior police officers' training. It would appear that while many senior police officers do attend the College, it faces a degree of competition, both from each state department's training facilities and from a range of other national and overseas training institutions. Swanton et al. (1983) list some of the overseas courses attended by a (small) number of Australian officers, such as the Federal Bureau of Investigation National Academy in Virginia, Bramshill in England, and the School of Justice Administration at the University of Louisville, Kentucky. Within Australia, police also attend the Australian Administrative Staff College, the Australian Institute of Management, the Australian Counter Disaster College (which was once burned down in a bush fire!), and various defense training institutes, such as the Joint Services Staff College (Fogarty, 1985). The Victoria Police have recently developed an Executive Development Program, which involves the secondment of senior police executives to organizations in the private and public sectors (Victoria Police, *Annual Report*, 1986/87).

The existence of a number of senior level management and administration courses and institutes, both within police departments and in other public sectors, does not necessarily indicate the quality of either the courses themselves or of the police officers who attend. Chappell and Wilson (1969) make the comment about the Senior Executives course at the Australian Police Academy:

> ...there is reason to doubt the wisdom of the policies of individual forces with regard to the personnel they send to the College for instruction....Those who attend the executive course are in the main officers of some thirty years' or more service within the police force. They are men approaching the end of their police careers, men whose views and ideas about police work in particular, and life in general are firmly fixed.

Nevertheless, efforts made to mount such courses and to encourage senior officers to attend them reflect an increasing concern to match the skills required of police executives to the demands and complexities of modern police management. In a global sense, then, it can be said that the calibre of leadership in Australian policing is, if by no means unequivocally established, at least subject to some attempts at upgrading.

Comparable efforts have been made at the middle management level, although as we have noted there is some disparity between the states in terms of the extent of their formal training of commissioned officers. It is instructive to comment briefly on one inspectors' course, that taught by the Victoria Police at its Police College. The course is residential, currently takes 16 weeks, and is for those senior sergeants eligible for promotion to inspector (that, is, when they have passed the relevant examinations). In their review of the Victoria Police, Wilson and Western (1972) describe it thus:

> The aim of the course is to train officers and potential officers in matters relating to the organization, role, command, control, administration, and techniques of the police force in Victoria. Within this general proposition the course is designed to broaden the participants' outlook, improve professional knowledge, stimulate the energies of men who are reaching the higher ranks of the service, and increase the efficiency of the police force.

The authors also note that (at that stage), the Victoria Police did not send their potential executive officers to the Australian Police College because the Victorian course was considered as good as, if not superior to, the national course. Wilson and Western (1972) appeared to share that view; they describe what they felt to be the following characteristics of the course:

> ...it is non-doctrinaire, students at all times being encouraged to think for themselves; instruction and material taught at the college are of a high quality; there is a strong emphasis on teaching administrative skills so necessary for police executives; there is a real attempt to have students come to grips with problems in contemporary society; there is a diligent and effective use of non-police professional lecturers; and finally, there is a keen awareness on the part of personnel at the college of the need to keep abreast of the latest developments in education—particularly education aimed at producing professional police administrators.

Yet the course has not been without its critics. In a report handed down by the Police Service Board (the Victorian Board which, amongst other functions, hears claims for improved salaries and allowances in the Victoria Police) in 1980, the effects of the officers' course upon its students was commented upon. The 1980 report barred a finding and reduced a claim that would have compensated police officers on the basis of the stress they incurred in their occupations, in which the extensive demands made upon Victoria police to complete almost continuous in-service training courses was argued to be a stress factor. In evidence before the Board (Police Service Board Determination 308, 1980), a psychiatrist with experience of members who had attended the course argued that the course was in many ways too demanding and not sufficiently appropriate for advanced executive training. In the period of which the witness was talking, the course was of six months duration, and the students on average were aged over 40 years with around 20 years of service. The psychiatrist argued that this was a later age bracket for executive training than occurred in other occupational sectors, and that the police students were less able to withstand the rigors of a long residential course at this age. Echoing the comments made by Chappell and Wilson about the Senior Executives' Course at the Australian Police College, the psychiatrist claimed that officers had had "...too little advanced training, generally speaking, too late in the piece to benefit them greatly." The report went on to say of the expert witness's evidence: "He indicated that the officers' attitudes had become set before they commenced this form of advanced training, their aptitude for its proper absorption had lessened, and that this increased their frustration."

Since the period of which the witness spoke, the average age of students at the course has been reduced somewhat, but not to the bracket of 30- to 35-years that the psychiatrist thought appropriate for extended executive training. As we saw earlier, the average age of promotion to inspector rank in other departments is in many cases considerably higher than in Victoria. This sort of problem would thus be exacerbated even further in those departments. The clear implication from these observations is that training for leadership needs to take place earlier than is currently the norm in Australian police departments.

Since the above report was written, the Victorian officers' course has been shortened to 16 weeks. Nevertheless, it has not remained free of other criticisms. During the Neesham Inquiry (1985), the Victorian Police Association, the police union, made a critical submission about aspects of the course. Prominent amongst these, and contrary to the view formed by Wilson and Western, was that the instructional staff were ill-equipped for their tasks (Neesham Inquiry, 1985):

> ...members who achieve good results at the Officers College are invited to return to the directing staff because the criteria is that they are good students. It does not necessarily follow that they become good members of the directing staff. It is our belief that the operational members who are obtaining Senior Executive level, should be exposed to full-time external management courses and a number of selected individuals with the necessary aptitude should be exposed to personnel management external courses and attachments.

The Inquiry later reported that a number of other submissions, including that of the Chief Commissioner "...urged upon us the need to expose police, particularly those involved in training, to interstate and overseas courses."

It is possible to detect in these descriptions of aspects of the training of officers and senior executives an interesting reflection upon the notion of leadership training. From previous sections, it is clear that Australian policing has traditionally attempted to train itself throughout the spectrum of ranks and command levels. Even initiatives such as the Australian Police College were in keeping with an essential belief in the need to hegemonize police training within the police occupation. Other reflections upon this proposition can be found in the general absence of lateral entry for specialists, especially with middle-management qualifications, and in the very slow penetration rates of professional and higher degree qualifications both at recruit level and amongst serving personnel. But in the last decade or so, it is clear that police administration is looking increasingly beyond the avenues for training offered from within police departments. While this movement cannot yet be described as either profound or radical, it is now firmly in place, as evidenced by descriptions in previous sections of the array of courses external to police departments undertaken by police officers. This issue will be examined further in the section on professionalism. At this stage, it is appropriate to repeat the observation made previously: from the attempts made by police departments themselves to render more comprehensive and sophisticated their training of executive officers, it is apparent that the issue of the calibre of leadership within the departments has been of some considerable concern.

The last issue to be discussed in this section on leadership is that of supervision. As was noted previously, the assessment of the calibre of leadership is ultimately a matter of perspective and judgment. While the calibre of supervision falls into this same general category, it is useful to concentrate on a specific aspect of supervision which lends itself to more concrete discussion. That aspect is the span of control, or the rank ratios which reflect a police department's organizational structure and its levels of formal supervisory capacity. This aspect is, it can be argued, a very important reflection of the broad ways in which the work of police can be typified, because it identifies the relative degrees of autonomy and control that exist among police officers. From a knowledge of formal supervisory capacity, we can assess the extent to which police are monitored in their duties, if not the quality of that supervision. The rank ratios in the Victoria Police are: officers to all other ranks, 1:22; officers to subofficers, 1:5; and subofficers to senior constables, 1:3. It is necessary to note that broad ratios such as the above obscure considerable deviation within the divisions of a department. In Victoria, the Traffic Department has a lower ratio of sergeants to other ranks than the average, while policy areas, such as the Research and Development department have a higher ratio of officers to other ranks. Additionally, the nature of supervision clearly differs with the nature of the duty assignment. Operational police (uniformed patrol, traffic, detectives and so forth) would tend to be less regularly supervised by their superiors than those police deployed primarily in sedentary duties. Nevertheless, the ratios provide a general reflection of the supervisory capacity of one Australian police department; its generality to the other departments can broadly be assumed.

There can be no suggestion of an ideal set of rank ratios; particular functions, differences in the nature of the communities being policed (especially metropolitan versus rural communities) and a range of other factors will dictate various ratios. With these qualifications in mind, a consultant review body to the Neesham Inquiry (1985) suggested that a reasonable yardstick for ratios was one officer to three to four subofficers, and one subofficer to five to six junior ranks. Against that yardstick, the current Victorian ratios indicate that there are proportionately rather more subofficers than there are officers. However, the Police Service Board (Determination 308, 1980) argued that the ratio of officers to junior ranks has steadily been improving, while that of subofficers to junior ranks had been declining. The Board saw this as a significant problem, because it felt that junior rank supervision by experienced subofficers was the critical focus of supervision. It argued that the increasing office work-load of senior sergeants removed them from direct field supervision, and that the administrative load on sergeants had also increased to the point where they too were less able to exercise field supervision. On the premise (shared by this writer) that service delivery by junior ranks, especially uniformed general duties constables and senior constables (that is, patrol officers) is the most important aspect of policing, the Board believed that consistent and adequate field supervision was lacking.

In relation to this last point, it is worth pointing out that the whole issue of the calibre of leadership and supervision in policing is inextricably bound up in an enduring paradox in Western policing, or rather those Western forms of policing which adhere to the quasi-military style of policing based on a pyramidal hierarchy with rigid rank structures and the expectation of discipline based on obedience of subordinates to superiors. That paradox is that within this traditional formal command and control structure, junior police are expected to exercise considerable degrees of discretion, autonomy, initiative, and sensitivity. And as we have seen, in Australia the legal position of the constable is that he or she is held legally accountable for actions conducted in the performance of duty. There is nothing incomprehensible about the dual imperatives of a formal military-style command structure and the autonomy necessarily exercised by junior ranks. The structure of policing can be readily traced back to the origins of the police role, especially in Peel's London, but also in Australia's emerging models of formal centralized policing. At the same time, the reality of police work on the street and in the community calls for significant reserves of a most unmilitary set of skills and capacities amongst junior ranks. While hardly incomprehensible, this paradox does, however, have important implications for the development of leadership skills. We have seen how the senority system of promotion still holds considerable sway at the junior ranks of Australian policing, although it is now being eroded slowly at more senior ranks. The seniority promotional system is a classic reflection of the leadership paradox. It implies that the necessary learning of the skills required to operate autonomously, creatively, and effectively at junior rank level are not readily rewarded by the promotion system. Leadership capacity under such a system is impliedly generated by years of experience within a rigid rank structure rather than by demonstrated aptitude on the ground. One of its possible negative effects is that able junior ranks with leadership potential are subordinated to higher ranks whose only essential qualification for command is longevity in the job. The traditional in-service training parameters in Australian policing, it can be argued, are likely to perpetuate some of the problems thrown up by a system which demands the development of leadership skills within a framework which emphasizes years of service as an important criterion for promotion. It is undoubtedly for this reason (amongst others) that a movement away from exclusive reliance upon in-service leadership training is evident. Whether this movement will solve the problems of generating leadership of sufficient calibre amongst officers who are simultaneously faced with a slow and lengthy promotional system and the demand to in fact exercise many facets of leadership at quite junior ranks, remains to be seen.

STANDARDS USED IN EVALUATING INDIVIDUAL POLICE PERFORMANCE

A variety of objective and subjective measures of police performance are utilized by Australian police departments. Objective measures are usually considered to be those which are readily quantified and observable, and which arise directly out of an officer's duties. Examples include arrest and conviction rates, number of citizen complaints, letters of commendation and departmental awards, disciplinary charges, rates of sick leave and so forth. Subjective measures are usually considered to be those which depend upon judgments of the officer's actions, capacities, and capabilities (see Froemel, 1979, for a comprehensive discussion of performance measures).

The typical Australian police department keeps a detailed file history of an officer's service, and on it are noted the range of performance measures obtained upon the individual. There is, however, a clear distinction between objective and subjective measures. While the former can be and are taken into account in promotional and counselling/disciplining situations, they are often statistically rare events, heavily dependent for their incidence upon factors such as rank, seniority, duty assignment, duty location, and so forth. It is virtually impossible to extract from them any sense of a standard at which an officer ought to be performing without noting these particular influences. For instance, while all citizen complaints are to be regretted, operational police at the more junior ranks can be expected to be considerably more exposed to those circumstances where they are likely to arise than are administrative police officers; levels at which the number of complaints become intolerable clearly differ between the two groups.

Similarly, arrest rates differ between police duties and locations; effectiveness amongst detectives can at least partially be reflected in high arrest rates (although conviction rates are undoubtedly superior measures), while the efficiency of the police officer servicing an isolated and close-knit community in the country is probably best reflected by a low arrest rate. Thus, there is little point in trying to establish standards of police performance from the range of objective measures.

On the other hand, subjective measures at least theoretically offer the possibility of establishing standards. A typical subjective measure is the supervisor rating, where on a regular basis individual officers have a range of their performances assessed on a standardized rating schedule. Such a system offers comparability between officers and is able to tap more comprehensive performance dimensions. There have been, of course, many criticisms levelled at performance rating systems (see, for instance, McIver and Parks, 1983). Nevertheless, they remain pervasive in policing circles, and can be a crude guide to the criteria by which police management judges the performance of its members.

Most Australian police departments utilize supervisor rating systems. However, the forms these systems take differ considerably between departments, and it is impossible to generalize. In addition, no department has, to the writer's knowledge, developed a proper behaviorally-anchored rating scale based upon a thorough job analysis (see Bradley and Pursley, 1987). The derivation of Victoria's recently abandoned rating system is probably quite typical. It was introduced following an inquiry into the Victoria Police by a senior English police officer in 1971 (Brown and MacNeill, 1978):

> Inquiries were made about the assessment systems in use in other services; and a system which was...in use in the Tasmania Police was considered to be the most attractive. This scheme was adopted in 1970 by the Tasmania Police from the New Zealand Police, who had begun using the scheme in 1964, reputedly after "borrowing" it from the Metropolitan Police in London.

That system was extensively reviewed by Brown and MacNeill (1978), and found wanting. Typical of many of the problems in rating forms, the reviewers found that the system suffered from the collapsing of the various performance dimensions into a much smaller number of overall judgments which did little to systematically differentiate between ratees. A new system was introduced in 1986 and has, since, typically been abandoned. It captures, in general terms, the sorts of procedures used to rate performance in Australian police departments. Eight performance dimensions are rated on five-point scales (5= excellent to 1= well below job requirement). The dimensions are: job knowledge; work performance; initiative; energy and drive; mental alertness; judgment; impact; and communication skills (oral and written). There is provision for three raters (normally the ratee's immediate supervisors) to complete the form. In addition, ratees also contribute to the assessment by noting details of their current job, any training they have engaged in since their last rating, and their own assessment of their performance. Individuals are rated regularly, about every second year.

The difficulty of generalizing across Australian police departments in regard to standards of performance assessment is evidenced by scheme implemented in 1980s by the Northern Territory Police. Unlike the Victorian system, that scheme involves a numerical grading, summed across a broad range of performance dimensions which are assessed by checking one of a number of descriptive statements. The dimensions are these (*Northern Territory Police Staff Development and Appraisal Scheme Manual*, undated):

- Community involvement
- General knowledge of force
- Comprehension and expression (verbal and written expression, and intelligence and comprehension)
- Job proficiency (effective output, accuracy, and reliability and reaction to pressure)
- Attitude (attitude to public, loyalty to peers, subordinates, superiors and Force, attitude toward change, and mobility to serve anywhere)
- Personal characteristics (team work, ability to work independently, initiative, moral courage, dependability, application to the job in hand, ambition, temperament, punctuality, attendance, personal appearance and dress, personal conduct)

- Leadership (for senior constables and above: ability to motivate staff, ability to impart knowledge, ability to control staff, and ability to make logical decisions)
- Management (for sergeants first class and above: ability to identify issues and program work, ability to delegate, knowledge of management techniques, and responsibility)

Like the Victorian system, the Northern Territory scheme requires the ratee to contribute to the assessment, but again in considerably more detail than that required in Victoria. The ratee must answer the following questions:

- Resume of service history
- Present role in the police force
- Satisfaction with present role
- Most interesting aspects of present role.
- Consideration of whether the ratee has received adequate training
- Most irksome or distasteful aspects of present role.
- Changes in procedure or equipment which would benefit present role.
- Satisfaction of spouse with ratee's job
- Preferred role in twelve months time
- Additional training required for preferred role
- Preferred role five years hence
- Training required for preferred role
- Likely career path
- Preferred career path
- Attitude towards serving outside a main center
- Spouse's attitude to moving outside a main center
- Major benefits of being a police officer
- Major disadvantages of being a police officer
- Prospect of further academic studies
- Any reasons for not serving anywhere in the Northern territory

Individuals are rated annually, with a separate triennial rating as well.

The difference in approaches taken by the Victorian and Northern Territory police departments in performance assessment are obvious. Those differences are repeated between the other departments. It is, consequently, difficult to argue that there is a recognizable standard by which Australian police officers are assessed in their performance. Australian police administrations are faced with the same dilemmas that all police departments face in terms of providing accurate, reliable, and comprehensive performance assessment. Schemes in place, either in the guise of formal rating systems or the less structured collation of material related to critical incidents, are flawed. There has been, to the writer's knowledge, no attempt made anywhere to implement innovative assessment schemes which move beyond traditional intradepartmental evaluation, such as those suggested by Jones (1986) and Marx (1978). It can be argued that performance assessment of individual officers in Australian policing has made little progress and has not made significant use of management techniques in place in other areas. Adequately capturing the performance parameters of police work, that most complex and diverse set of roles, remains a considerable problem.

PROFESSIONALIZATION

Aspects of Australian policing discussed in previous sections of this chapter have a clear bearing upon the concept of professionalization, such as the discussion of leadership. However, there has been little scholarly work on police professionalization published in Australia. Most commentary on the subject simply aligns progress in the use of technology and the development of more sophisticated training regimes and management structures and planning (such as Victoria's corporate planning) with a largely undefined and unexplained notion of professionalism. One of the few scholars to address the issue systematically has been Bruce Swanton (1983). In the context of his discussion of the present and future nature of police occupational development, Swanton has looked closely at the components of professionalism, and the extent to which Australian police can be argued to possess some of those components.

Swanton (1983) draws an initial contrast between what he calls the classic professional model and the modified classical model. The first model embraces traditional professions like medicine and law, and is defined by a set of characteristics, such as that proposed by Niederhoffer: high admission standards; specific body of knowledge and theory; dedication to a service ideal; lengthy training; code of ethics; licensing of members; autonomous control; pride in profession; and public acceptance. The modified classical model arises from more recently emerging occupations aspiring to professional status, which do not conform fully to the classical criteria:

> Modern occupations matching these conditions are sometimes referred to as modified classical professions. These modified criteria may be applied, inter alia to police, an occupation widely agreed not to have achieved professional or even advanced status as yet, but which has the potential. (italics and footnotes omitted)

Swanton argues that there are in fact several other varieties of professional development which are hypothetically relevant to policing. These are all necessarily departures from the classical model, and they emphasize different modes of professionalization, and different outcomes in terms of which members within the police occupation can legitimately aspire to professional status. Swanton (1983) suggests that police occupational development can proceed along any of three paths: (1) the modified military model, which represents a continuation of traditional police management structure, but which emphasizes improved administrative performance, as a result of which top management positions can assume professional status; (2) the modified bureaucratic model, in which senior management and specialists within the police organization assume professional status, while the whole organization is oriented towards professional service; and (3) the modified classical model, in which all members of the organization assume professional status.

The dilemma facing police departments in their attempts to professionalize their occupation is that many of the intrinsic features of their organizational structure are antithetical to the classical parameters of a profession. Reflected against the Niederhoffer characteristics, the police occupation places a premium upon experiential learning rather than formal training, admission standards are not traditionally high, required learning has emphasized procedure and regulations rather than a coherent body of theoretical knowledge, and autonomy has been trammelled by the constraints of a rigid, quasi-military command and disciplinary structure. On the other hand, aspects such as an assumed dedication to a service ideal, a burgeoning body of technical and managerial sophistication necessary for service delivery, and the paradoxical reality of the need for quite junior members to exercise decision making, responsibility, and autonomy of considerable gravity, illustrate the reasons why many police and police commentators argue the case for police professionalism. Swanton's taxonomy of potential occupational developments reflects a concern to encompass these aspirations within a flexible framework which does not founder against the tight criteria set for classical professions.

In his attempt to fit current policing developments into his taxonomy of professional models, Swanton (1983) notes the retarding influence of the multiplicity of rank structures in Australian police. He argues that union opposition to the industrial implications of a reduction in ranks makes such reduction unlikely in the near future; at the same time he points out that the proliferation of complex rank structures aligns future police development to a modified military model which probably has the least potential for a fully developed professional occupation. He also argues that an implied hallmark of a professional occupation, organizational leadership, has been largely missing in the Australian police context. From a perspective of protecting the interests of the occupational membership, Swanton (1983) claims that leadership has been most obvious from the various police unions rather than from the chief executive officers of the police departments themselves. He cites examples where on matters of crucial importance to the membership, commissioners have taken a less obvious stand than union officials. This is, however, at best a crude reflection of professionalism, given that in many cases union leadership has been exercised against initiatives from government or police administration that many would argue have been governed by considerations of upgrading police practice and service delivery. At the very least, it can be argued that assessments of leadership calibre from either unions or police executives require value judgments that are difficult to characterize unequivocally as professional in orientation.

On a considerably more critical point, Swanton raises the issue of police control over the directions that police departments are able to pursue. On the one hand, there is the reality that a significant part of policing is directed from outside the organization, by means of government policy, legislative directive, and the pressure on both from various Royal Commissions and committees of inquiry, upon none of which, according to Swanton, have the police managed to exert much influence. On the other hand, attempts to provide for more police control over their occupational environment, in both policy and practice terms, have met with resistance from those who argue that the nature of police power in society is such that police must be directed or at least supervised in their occupational development from outside the organization. Such a perspective comes from those who believe that police attempts to regulate themselves in matters such as investigating complaints against police have a history of at least controversy, if not outright failure. Swanton (1983) disputes the proposition that police have proven conclusively to be incapable of regulating themselves, but his point is well-taken: the hallmarks of classic professional development, the autonomy traditionally vested in occupational membership for accountability and regulation, are missing in broad terms in Australian policing.

Another aspect of Australian policing Swanton (1983) sees as indicative of a movement towards a modified military model of professionalism is what he sees as the emphasis placed upon obtaining a result, an outcome, rather than upon the processes by which those results are achieved. By process, Swanton means the principles and ethics by which police operate, the legal and social frameworks within which they function. He seems to be referring to what Goldstein (1977) argues is the need for police to reassert their commitment to a democratic ideal, or what Skolnick (1966) writes about in relation to police adherence to the rule of law in the manner in which they fulfil their duties. Swanton may be right, but it is instructive to reiterate the interesting shift in the published philosophy of the Victoria Police discussed previously in this chapter. That shift in the recent years reflected a movement away from a primary concern with aspects of the efficiency and effectiveness of police service towards one which was considerably more cognizant of the need to operate within the context of a community constituency; that is, a shift from an emphasis upon product to one of process within a community framework. It is too early to determine whether this shift is one of rhetoric or substance, but the public recognition accorded to the process implied by the present Victoria Police philosophy indicates some movement away from Swanton's proposition.

A further stumbling block to professional development which embraces all members of an occupation is the diversity of actual job functions within a police organization. Swanton (1983) makes the point:

> Reception, process serving, guarding, traffic controlling, despatching, chauffeuring and piloting, offer no potential for professionalization in the traditional mould whatever. Such positions however, are consistent with the modified military model of professionalization and to a lesser extent, with the modified bureaucratic model. The present organizational solidarity of police officers in Australia indicates the shedding of positions lacking professional potential could not be easily achieved, especially should discarded positions be civilianised.

Along with the difficulties of according professional status to these such jobs, there is the other problem of according general professional status to the range of quite distinctive specialities within police organizations. There need be little in common in the training and duties of specialists in communications and electronics on the one hand, and forensic science technicians on the other, or between criminal investigators and specialists in traffic patrol or community policing.

Swanton (1983) also turns his attention to traditional modes of induction and training within Australian police departments. He argues, for instance, that training in policing is more of an organizational procedure rather than an occupational one. By this he means that training has emphasized the administrative procedures necessary to function as part of a complex bureaucracy rather than the substantive procedures of the delivery of a professional police service. The outcome of this emphasis has been the development of a considerable body of information about police procedure, but little knowledge about policing as an occupation. Swanton points to the recent encouragement of tertiary-based police studies courses in a number of states as a possible reversal of this situation. To this can be added the previously discussed movement toward police pursuing specialist and general qualifications beyond those offered in service. Swanton (1983), in fact, argues that the retention of police within the service who have completed tertiary courses such as law and accountancy "must favour the broad professionalisation process regardless of model."

In a later work, Swanton (Swanton et al., 1985) has argued a rather more unorthodox point in relation to police professionalization. Swanton is a vehement critic of what he sees as the federalization of Australian policing. He argues that policing has traditionally been the province of the states, and that the intrusion of the federal government into this province has been bad for Australian policing. He cites as intrusion such developments as the amalgamation of the Commonwealth Police and the Australian Capital Territory Police into the Federal Police, and the establishment of the National Crimes Authority. He argues (Swanton et al., 1985):

> One problem associated with these recent innovations, in the long term, concerns possible weakening of police agencies, which would militate against professional development by eroding police function and credibility. Within the federation, only Victoria Police and South Australia Police show significant professional development at the present time as evidenced by their organizational and operational sophistication; but the current emphasis on centralisation could have the effect of offsetting the advantages presently enjoyed by these two agencies.

It is difficult to assess the likelihood of Swanton's prediction. Certainly his rejection of the right of the federal government to involve itself in policing has received strong criticism (Harding, in the Preface to Swanton et al., 1985). To this writer, the paramount dangers to and difficulties of police professionalization would seem to lie in areas more prominent than those advanced by Swanton above. Rather, Swanton's previous work cited in this section seems to adequately capture the essence of those difficulties.

One final work on Australian police professionalism is discussed here. The Victorian Police Service Board (Determination 308, 1980) turned its attention to the issue of professionalism in the context of its hearing a claim for increased salary by the Victoria Police union. The Board argued, inter alia, for the following criteria to be used in assessing the professional status of an occupation:

> (a) conformity to a code of ethics and occupational practice commonly established, controlled and supervised amongst the members by authorities developed and established within the occupational group itself. However, such matters may be subject to modification and control, in part at least, by external authority—sometimes through legislation and other forms of regulations;
>
> (b) The exercise of discretion and judgement in the application of their skills and responsibilities in regard to those occupational relationships to other persons including, in some cases, the community at large;
>
> (c) Acceptance of responsibility for the training, development and, where appropriate direction of those junior to them in the occupational group...;
>
> (d) The degree of personal responsibility for their actions required to be accepted by members and the degree and nature of their accountability for such actions taken.

The Board made much use of a 1971 committee which inquired into the salary and conditions of members of the Australian Regular Armed Forces, which concluded that commissioned officers of those forces could properly be considered members of a professional class. The Victoria Police Service Board stated that members of the Victoria Police fully met the conditions set out in point (a) above, by virtue of the disciplinary requirements of the department, and the control and supervision exercised upon police by the courts and by legislation. The Board also found that all members exhibited the characteristics noted in point (b).

With regard to point (c), the Board stated that commissioned officers fully conformed, and that junior ranks, from senior constable upwards, were increasingly required to exhibit conformity. The Board found that the criterion described in point (d) was met by all members of the department. The Board summarized its considerations thus:

> Having regard to the matters discussed...above, and having regard also to the policeman's progressive subjection to formal and informal training required to enable him to pass his successive promotional examinations, it is apparent that the further he proceeds in the Force the greater the degree of professionalism he is required to, and does, achieve. The emphasis placed upon improvement in such aspects of the

> work of members in the Force has progressively increased the standard of professionalism in the Force in the last decade.

However, the Board finally equivocated on granting professional status to all members of the department. It felt comfortable with regard to commissioned officers:

> Consideration of all the above factors satisfies the Board that (commissioned) Officers of the Force fall into a similar category to Officers promoted from the ranks in the Defence Services....They have professional status in what may now properly be referred to as the "Profession of Police" or the "Police Profession."

But across all the ranks, it could only bring itself to state:

> The general advances in professionalism throughout the rank structure of the Force reflect the increases in the standard of skills and responsibility demanded and attained over the last decade.

The Board's function as an industrial tribunal adds a certain weight and a certain circumscription to its published determinations. These factors ought to be taken into account in assessing the scholarly worth of its conclusions. At the same time, it is interesting to note that without the benefits of Swanton's later taxonomy of possible developmental models for policing, the Board pursues a "modified military model" to its extreme.

WAGES, STATUS, SUBCULTURE, AND MORALE

Police wages are set by the various industrial awards and agreements which pertain to each state and territory. While salaries are comparable between departments, they are by no means identical, especially given different rank structures and increment levels within ranks. The most current salary figures (in Australian dollars) at the time of writing are presented in Figure 5.

The salaries shown in Figure 5 do not include a range of shift, penalty, and incidental allowances generally appropriate to the ranks below commissioned officer. At the time of writing, the Australian dollar is worth approximately 80 U.S. cents. By way of comparision, the average Australian wage is approximately

FIG. 5: BASE SALARIES OF AUSTRALIAN POLICE OFFICERS (Australian Dollars)

Police Department	Constable	Sergeant	Inspector	Superintendent
Federal Police (1)	25,100	35,882	N/A	46,809
New South Wales (2)	24,056	33,366	53,191	67,219
Victoria (3)	23,217	32,938	43,032	48,568
Queensland (4)	24,362	30,352	48,048	54,199
South Australia (5)	23,120	32,137	48,006	53,819
Northern Territory (6)	24,885	33,796	41,499	47,991
Western Australia (7)	23,611	31,740	49,463	56,070
Tasmania (8)	21,895	30,612	43,310	50,913

1. November 1990
2. December 1990
3. April 1991
4. March 1991
5. August 1990
6. July 1990
7. October 1990
8. July 1990

Most junior ranks have annual increments above base salary.

Source: Police Federation of Australia, 14 February 1991.

$23,500; the award for a junior academic lecturer (assistant professor) is approximately $30,000. Historically, police have been considered (and have considered themselves) to be poorly paid (see Haldane, 1986, for some illuminating examples of the treatment of Victorian police in terms of salary by early successive governments). A 1974 survey of South Australian police revealed that inadequate pay and/or allowances was ranked first as a major problem amongst nine crucial issues seen to affect police officers (Swanton et al., 1985). However, the last decade or so has seen a number of successful wage claims by police unions which have brought a good deal of parity to police officers in terms of salaries (Swanton, 1983). In a recent attitude survey of members of the Victoria Police, salary was considered as the first, second, or third most important factor affecting morale (from amongst 34 factors) by only 3 percent of the sample (Neesham Inquiry, 1985). It is fair to describe Australian police officers as currently relatively well-paid.

A prominent method to assess the status of an occupation is to conduct public opinion polls which require the ranking of a number of occupations. Daniels (Swanton et al., 1985) found in her 1981 survey that "policemen" were classified as "lower middle class" in a five-point taxonomy of social class (upper, upper middle, middle, lower middle, and lower). Swanton and Wilson (Swanton et al., 1985) adopted Niederhoffer's proposition that "policeman" was too broad an occupational category, and categorized police into five (superintendent, inspector, sergeant, detective, and constable) in their 1974 survey. Out of 23 occupations, the police categories were ranked as follows in terms of prestige: superintendent (5); inspector (8); detective (10); sergeant (14); and constable (17). In terms of benefit to society, they were ranked as follows: superintendent (11); inspector (13); constable (14); detective (15); and sergeant (16). In a 1979 survey conducted by the writer (James, 1979), a sample of Victorian police officers was asked (a) whether they thought that the general public considers police work to be an occupation requiring skill and expertise; and (b) whether they thought that the police occupation has the job status that it deserves in the community. Around 60 percent of respondents answered "no" to both questions.

Unfortunately these are all dated results, and it is uncertain about the effects upon public standing of those recent efforts made to upgrade police salaries and to present a more professional image. It is this writer's belief that some improvement is likely to have taken place in that public standing because of these factors, but it is unlikely to have been dramatic. The legacy of the past in Australian policing, where the calibre and performance of early police were universally considered to be poor, has undoubtedly left its mark on the occupational image of policing. Further data on public attitudes towards and confidence in the police is discussed in the section on public relations and should be considered when assessing the status of Australian police.

Little research attention has been paid in Australia to the existence and nature of an occupational subculture which might reflect an identifiable behavioral and attitude set among police which places them significantly apart from members of other occupations. There is considerable anecdotal evidence around that would indicate that police officers form or bring to the occupation distinctive political and social beliefs, and that they tend to view the world through what Skolnick (1966) describes as a "cognitive lens" unique to police officers. Indeed, many of Skolnick's propositions regarding police culture—social isolation, police solidarity, exposure to danger and the effects of exercising authority—appear to be readily accepted by police observers. However, the empirical evidence for such propositions is at the best slim, and sometimes contrary.

In an approximate test of social isolation, the writer (James, 1979) asked a number of questions of his sample of Victoria police officers: (a) Do you regularly see many of the friends you made before you joined the force? (b) When you want to entertain at home, or go out to parties and other social gatherings, do you find that your companions are mostly fellow police, mostly non-police, or roughly an even mix of the two? (c) Do your non-police friends generally mix socially with your police friends? With regard to the first question, 40 percent of the sample said they continued to mix with their old friends, and only 12 percent said they no longer did so because of their status as police officers. In response to the second question, 36 percent said they mixed mostly with police, 25 percent said they mixed evenly, and 32 percent said non-police. Over 50 percent of the sample said that their non-police friends mixed socially with their police friends. The tendency in all responses was for younger respondents to express more social isolation. In general, it was not possible to conclude that this sample of police demonstrated dramatic levels of social isolation.

In a comparison between samples of Queensland and New Jersey police officers, Lester, Lewis, and Swanton (1985) tested, inter alia, levels of cynicism on the Niederhoffer cynicism questionnaire. Compared with the American police officers, the Queensland police demonstrated significantly less cynicism, and could not be considered too highly cynical, one of Niederhoffer's precursor conditions for at least one version of a distinctive subculture. In another test of a large number of applicants for the Victoria Police in 1978, California Psychological Inventories were administered. The total sample of applicants scored around the American norm scores on all scales, and successful applicants demonstrated slightly elevated scores over failed applicants on most scales (James, Campbell, and Lovegrove, 1984). There was no evidence of a distinctive personality pattern either amongst applicants in general or among inducted recruits; in other words, there was no confirmation of the proposition sometimes put forward that certain people with distinctive characteristics are attracted to and selected by police departments (see Lefkowitz, 1977 for a general review of this area).

The limitations of these data are obvious in terms of proving or disproving the existence of a police subculture. It is doubtful, in fact, whether the sorts of quantitative data represented in survey research is adequate to such a task. Detailed observational studies such as those undertaken by Skolnick (1966) and Van Maanen (1975) on the socialization processes in policing are largely absent in Australia, and it is impossible to draw upon any coherent and comprehensive body of data on police subcultures in Australia. In addition, there are a number of other qualifications one must make even in terms of speculation. First, diversities in operational practice and community contexts both within and between Australian police departments are such that a generalized perspective on police subculture is likely to be misleading. Second, it is obvious that the term subculture is vague and undefined as it stands; one can posit a variety of possible subcultural forms which might be equally relevant in discourse, but which share few if any features of significance in common. Nevertheless, it is useful to suggest two observations about Australian police subcultures which may contribute to the debate.

It can be argued that a number of changes in recent years in Australian policing may have the combined effect of moderating or eliminating the conditions which have been alleged to generate and maintain a police occupational subculture. Those changes include: the shift already noted towards external training opportunities for police officers, and the increasing encouragement by departments for members to upgrade their general and specialist qualifications; the improvement in police salaries over the last decade or so; departmental attempts to improve the community context in which police operate, and to moderate the effects of decades of isolation from those communities; and the movement in police recruiting for more highly educated applicants applying for service. At least some of these factors are, of course, those that Niederhoffer argued actually generated cynicism amongst traditional police officers. But it can be argued that if the movements, especially those related to upgrading of qualifications, is pervasive enough throughout the police department, and if it coincides with a significant change in the demographic profile of applicants for police service, then it is possible that the shifts in combination might well positively influence sentiments of social isolation, lack of public status, and low occupational esteem. To these factors ought to be added another which may have even more profound consequences upon the dissolution of traditional subcultures. Police service has historically been considered a "calling," a vocation which, in common with other occupations in the past, has been considered one to be taken up for life. It is clear that occupational subcultures can only flourish in organizations which entail a relatively high degree of service continuity. However, it is possible to detect a shift in this traditional sentiment towards a lifelong police career. One of the outcomes of the improvements in police salaries and conditions in recent years has been a corresponding improvement in pension and superannuation benefits (see Remfrey, 1985). A past impediment to early retirement or resignation from police departments has been the relatively low rate of benefits accruing from premature departure. However, generally improving conditions have made it more financially acceptable to retire early, and, more importantly, to resign early. Estimates of early retirement and resignation in the Victoria Police as a result of an improved superannuation scheme introduced in 1987 are that at least two times the number of officers who annually resign and prematurely retire are taking advantage of the scheme (see Hendry, 1988; James and Hendry, 1991). In conjunction with the movement for serving officers to either enter the department with, or to acquire, higher qualifications, it is possible that Australian policing is entering a period where the occupation is only one that an increasing number of officers are going to experience during their working life. In other words, policing may well experience much more personnel mobility, not just on the grounds of unsuitability, but in terms of career expectations. Under these circumstances, the generation and maintenance of distinctive traditional subcultures is likely to diminish.

The second observation relies upon the same basic movements and shifts in the police occupation, but paradoxically suggests the development of a new form of subculture. This subculture, if it can be so named, reflects the opposite to the traditional variations, with their characteristics of a solidarity built upon shared senses of alienation and isolation. Rather, this new form reflects a much more dynamic solidarity concerned with aggressively putting forward a police perspective on matters considered relevant to police interests. By another name, it can be considered a new form of professional lobby. It was mentioned previously that police in the past have had relatively little formal input in the control and policy arrangement made by government, the courts, and various inquiries. It can be confidently stated that the general proposition is no longer true.

A combination of articulate and well-reputed chief executive officers in recent years, increasing examples of senior executives with formal university training (five of the ten deputy and assistant commissioners of the Victoria Police have postgraduate diplomas in criminology taught by the University of Melbourne and three others have other tertiary qualifications), and increasing membership of and formal submissions to government inquiries into matters affecting police, has brought forth the capability of police departments to act upon and present a formidable occupational presence in political and social affairs. In addition, as we shall see in the next section, the police union movement has begun in no uncertain way to flex its industrial and occupational muscle in Australia. Such movements are nicely reflected by the Victoria Police Department's Media Director's Office, staffed by professional journalists, which professionally presents police perspectives to the general community. This writer argues that the very forces which are likely to diminish the development of traditional and negative subcultures are also likely to foster the development of a much more confident, aggressive, and publicly-located police solidarity, which in large measure reflects a new form of collective occupational identity. The extent and consequences of such a movement are uncertain at this stage, and there are likely to be considerable differences between departments. And the robustness of the movement may well be limited. Swanton (Swanton et al., 1985), for instance, has argued that as a result of factors such as "federalization" of Australian policing, police occupational development and identity has been hindered. At the same time, highly critical public inquiries into police malpractice, such as that conducted in Queensland by the Fitzgerald Inquiry, are likely to reduce the capacity of police departments to both share a strong collective identity and to argue on the strength of that identity in the public forum. Nevertheless, balanced against these qualifications are those factors raised above which indicate to this writer at least that the signs and potential for a form of powerful occupational solidarity in Australian policing not recognized in the writings of scholars such as Skolnick and Niederhoffer are present.

In his book on Australian police unions, Swanton (1983) devotes a considerable amount of attention to the issue of police worker morale. He notes that the term is generally ill-defined, and its alleged expressions diverse and complicated. He strikes his own definition, which seems acceptable (Swanton, 1983):

> In all organizations there is an ongoing, permanent and complex corporate-psychic state known popularly as morale. Morale varies across time, across individuals and groups of individuals. There is no agreement among theorists as to the concept's validity but in the sense employed here, it comprises the aggregate of those factors determining workers' overall contentedness with their employment. (footnotes omitted)

Swanton goes on to suggest that at a practical level, morale can be considered to be a point somewhere on a continuum of satisfaction-dissatisfaction. He argues that all organizations experience a baseline of worker dissatisfaction, the consequence of the reality of imperfect fit between occupations and their workers. On top of this baseline exist levels of dissatisfaction which arise more specifically from the particular nature of the occupation and the nature of the personnel who service the occupation. Swanton argues that this type of satisfaction is relatively stable and consistent, although it is capable of fundamental shifts if significant factors in the dissatisfaction matrix also shift. The dissatisfaction hypothesized by Niederhoffer to result from uneven movements to professionalize American police departments is an example of such a type. A third component of dissatisfaction suggested by Swanton is that derived from relatively short-term and topical influences upon the police officer's roles and duties. Such influences include new legislation that police find onerous or hindering, industrial developments seen to disadvantage police, and public scandals generated by the adverse findings of committees of inquiries. It is this last category of dissatisfaction that Swanton argues gives rise to examples of police worker militance, the major focus of his concerns with police morale.

Swanton's description of the broad framework of morale is quite reasonable. It captures well the variety of potential sources of and changes to levels of morale and worker satisfaction. Nevertheless it raises the problem of establishing at any one time which components of morale are functions of long-term residual sentiments towards policing and which are situational and likely to dissipate with time. While it is possible to monitor gross and obvious situational influences, the extent to which these forge new dimensions in morale, or alternatively build upon or are absorbed by existing levels of morale is likely to remain uncertain. This point is raised because the measurement of morale can take a variety of different forms, all of which tend to be affected by a range of complicating and/or extraneous factors. For instance, broad personnel statistics are often used as an indication of levels of morale or worker satisfaction. Sick leave, absenteeism, resignations, and early retirements are examples of personnel data used in this way. As was noted in the previous discussion, factors such as improved superannuation benefits accruing for early leavers are likely to generate an increase in resignations which need not be directly linked to morale factors. Potentially more sensitive indicators of morale, such as sample surveys, have obvious limitations in that they are rarely conducted across police departments, nor are they conducted with sufficient standardization or regularity to be able to distinguish between short- and long-term trends in the level of morale. In all, the capturing of Australian police morale represents a most difficult and complex task, and it has not been accomplished to date.

Nevertheless, there are data which bring some relevance to the issue. In the next section on unions, some pertinent examples are noted. Here, it is useful to describe the results of those few surveys which have been conducted in relation to morale. In an early morale survey of members from the Queensland, Tasmanian,and South Australian police departments, Chappell and Wilson (1969) reported that 25 percent, 29 percent, and 11 percent respectively of the respondents in the three departments claimed that morale in their department was poor. The factors claimed by at least 25 percent of the respondents in each department that weakened morale were: Queensland—too much red-tape, lack of effective leadership, adverse media publicity, inadequate pay, system of promotion, substandard police stations and political intervention; Tasmania—lack of leadership, inadequate pay, promotion, substandard stations, political intervention; South Australia—inadequate pay, promotion. In the previously cited study by Lester et al. (1985), it was found that in satisfaction-related issues concerned with work, pay, promotion, and supervisor quality, the sample of Queensland police scored as significantly more satisfied than the New Jersey police officers (this is, to the writer's knowledge, the only study conducted which has directly compared Australian and overseas police officers on dimensions such as these).

The most comprehensive survey conducted to date on morale in Australia is unfortunately confined to Victorian police. That survey was commissioned by the Neesham Committee of Inquiry into the Victoria Police, and it took place in 1984 amongst some 460 members of the department from all ranks and duty assignments. When asked how they viewed the level of morale in the department, 11 percent considered it to be high or very high, 43 percent considered it to be medium, 35 percent considered it to be low, and 10 percent considered it to be very low. That 45 percent of respondents considered morale to be low or very low can be compared unfavorably with the results of the earlier Chappell and Wilson survey. Morale was generally higher as respondents increased in rank, were deployed in areas other than operations or criminal investigation, were stationed in the country rather than the metropolitan area, and were stationed in the smaller country areas. Poor morale appeared to peak at between six and 20 years of service.

When asked which of a number of factors significantly lowered morale in the department, the following were the first ten to be listed (in rank order of respondents who considered them to significantly lower morale): police powers (that is, a perceived lack of adequate powers—87 percent); political decisions (74 percent); paperwork (74 percent); complaints investigation (74 percent); court delays (61 percent); workload (61 percent); clerical/typing support (55 percent); nonvehicular equipment (50 percent); disciplinary practices (43 percent); departmental administration (42 percent). It is interesting to note that few of these factors overlap with those noted in the Chappell and Wilson study, nor with a study on South Australian police conducted by Swanton in 1974 (Swanton et al., 1985), which revealed that inadequate pay, excessive paperwork, incompetent commissioned officers, inadequate equipment, examination system, lack of communication, excessive control, substandard residential accommodation, and pinpricking by subordinates were ranked in that order as problems facing the respondents. The relative lack of consistency between the results of surveys described above reinforces the position stated earlier that both the nature of morale and the adequacy of the instruments designed to measure it render it difficult to make accurate assessments of the work sentiments of Australian police officers.

UNIONS AND ASSOCIATIONS

Police unions and associations occupy an increasingly dynamic role in Australian policing. In common with developments in America and Europe (Reiner, 1978), the 1970s and 1980s have seen the emergence of unions as an influential variable in the context of Australian police organization and development. The consequences of that influence have yet to be fully charted in a scholarly manner, and there is clearly a good deal of unevenness about both the developments and impacts of the various police unions across the country. Nevertheless, it is incontestable that collective police worker movements have exerted such an influence upon the directions of policing in the last decade or so that they must truly be considered a vital element in any understanding of Australian policing. It is necessary to briefly trace the origins of police unions in Australia, and to identify the parameters of current union activity and impact.

Early association between the police and the trade union movement in Australia was characterized by antagonism and conflict. As Swanton (1983) describes it, the depression years of the late nineteenth century saw a decade of industrial strife in which the police played a prominent role in the protection of government and employer interests. Swanton (1983) argues that the legacy of that role remains critical:

> Although police have always been seen as somewhat unloved symbols of authority in the various states of Australia, the antipathy that has existed between organized labor and police can be said essentially to stem from the industrial conflict of the 1890s. As maintaining public order frequently consisted of activities such as protecting employers' property and strike breakers, and locking up union activists, police became understandably viewed by militant unionists as class traitors. On the other hand, sworn to uphold public tranquility and the rights of the Crown (which usually seemed to be closely associated with the interests of employers) and steeped in an ethos of control and commitment, police disapproved of the violations of public order committed by angry workers and their sympathisers. The disloyal sentiments expressed by international socialists and other extremists in the workers' ranks further served to harden police employee attitudes.

Partly as a consequence of the antagonism generated between police and organized labor, police themselves were relatively slow to organize collectively. The prosperity which followed economic recovery at the turn of the century to some extent favored those industrial workers, such as shearers and miners, whose poor working conditions had forced them to organize and take militant action in the 1890s. White-collar groups, especially those in the public sector, had hitherto enjoyed better working conditions and a degree of job tenure, and were industrially more conservative than blue-collar workers. They had felt little need to organize, and less ideological compunction. Thus, while the established worker groups were able to take advantage of the industrial arbitration mechanisms developed to handle conflict over wages and conditions in the 1980s, the white-collar workers were in a poor position to do likewise. Their relative position in terms of conditions and wages consequently eroded, forcing them, often reluctantly, to organize in the first decades of the twentieth century. Police were even more reluctant to organize, as indeed were police administrations and governments to let them. Yet profound industrial neglect and adverse conditions of employment and remuneration forced even police to organize. Haldane (1986) describes the working conditions of Victorian police in the early years of the century:

> In 1913...policemen in Victoria still worked a seven-day week and each day-shift was divided into two four-hour reliefs spread over twelve hours. Men who went on duty at 5.00 a.m. did not go off duty until 5.00 p.m. There were no rest days or public holidays, and the annual leave of seventeen days could not be taken at Christmas or Easter. Ordinary workers subject to Wages Board determinations were paid double for Sunday work, time-and-half for overtime and holiday work, and an allowance for working certain night shifts. None of this was paid to policemen: the starting pay of constables was 7s 6d a day, plus sixpence a day for rent or quarters...junior constables were paid less than tram conductors and a sum equivalent to the minimum wage paid to laborers.

Governments and police administrations looked askance upon attempts to unionize, believing that unions had no place in a disciplined and "loyal" service (Haldane, 1986). Indeed, police who agitated for better pay, or for the right to form a union, were routinely accused of being disloyal. Governments relied upon the conservative nature of police, their commitment to the service, and their conflicting role with the union movement in general to both resist the formation of unions and to maintain substandard conditions and wages. Yet, in common with white-collar public sector workers, neglect proved intolerable even for police, and all state police were unionized in a twelve-year period between 1911 and 1923 (Hannigan, 1985).

The Western Australian Union of Police Workers (established in 1912), the Police Association of Victoria (1917; abolished in 1932 and resurrected in 1933) and the Police Association of Tasmania (1923) each encompasses all sworn personnel within their departments. In the other states and territory, there are separate unions for commissioned officers and all other ranks: the Police Association of South Australia (1911) and the Commissioned/Officer's Association of South Australia (1950); the Queensland Police Union of Employees (1912) and the Queensland Police Officers' Union of Employees (1925); the Police Association of New South

Wales (1920) and the Commissioned Police Officers' Association of New South Wales (1920); the Police Association of Northern Territory (1945) and the Northern Territory Police Officers' Association (1967). From the 1920s, there were moves to form a federation of police unions, but it was not until 1947 that the respective unions and associations were able to agree on an appropriate form of federal organization and sort out several legal problems (for instance, the Victoria Police Regulation Act of 1928 forbade the Victorian association from joining other organizations, and that prohibition had to be lifted by the state government). The federal grouping was initially known as the Australian Federation of Police Associations and Unions, but the title was changed to the Police Federation of Australia in 1978 (Swanton, 1983).

The formal roles and functions of the various associations and unions are set out in their respective rules, generally registered with the industrial commissions of each state. The Rules of the New South Wales Police Association provide a typical list of duties, functions and responsibilities (Swanton, 1983):

> 1. To conduct negotiations and enter into agreements with the relevant authority or lodge applications with industrial tribunals respecting rates of pay, allowances and conditions of service of members;
>
> 2. to secure preference to members of the association;
>
> 3. to inquire into and secure fair and reasonable adjustment on behalf of members in cases of any charge, suspension, reduction in rank, position or rank and pay, dismissal or retirement;
>
> 4. to secure redress for any grievance to which members may become subject;
>
> 5. to afford opportunity for full discussion of any subject relating to the general welfare of the police association, and to use all reasonable and constitutional means in dealing with any matter;
>
> 6. to provide means for combined action in matters affecting the welfare of members;
>
> 7. to advise and assist members in preparing and placing cases before any departmental inquiry or appeal tribunal and to

> provide financial assistance and legal aid in accordance with these rules;
>
> 8. to establish welfare schemes approved by annual conference for the benefit of members, their families or nominees; and
>
> 9. to promote the interest of the police service by every means consistent with its rules, and with loyalty to the government of New South Wales.

According to Hannigan (1985), the role of the Australian Police Federation is somewhat more circumscribed:

> Within Australia, the Federation provides a focus for periodic discussion by employees of mutual problems but, with the exception of lobbying in respect of certain federal domains such as taxation, exercises little industrial influence. Police industrial relations are solidly based in their respective polities.

Since Hannigan wrote this, there have been discussions within the Federation concerning the wisdom of registering industrially with the Federal Industrial Relations Commission; that has since occurred, and it is fair to say that the Federation has been exercising a more prominent role in industrial issues.

Swanton (1983) summarizes the formal roles of Australian police into six broad spheres of activity: economic, welfare, discipline/legal, resolution of grievances, defence of service, and information. In the economic sphere, unions represent their respective membership before the various commissions which set police wages within each state and territory. Disputes arising from state industrial awards and wage determinations are handled in the first instance generally by collective bargaining between unions and employers (often nominally the chief executive officer of the police department, but in reality the state or territory government) in all states and the Northern Territory except in Victoria (which has its own wages and conditions board, the Police Service Board) and Tasmania (where disputes are referred to the state Public Service Board). The failure of collective bargaining is referred to state industrial commissions (or, in the case of the Northern Territory, to a commissioner of the Industrial Relations Commission).

In the welfare sphere, a variety of mortality, sickness, and incapacity benefit funds are run by the unions, although there appears to be little consistency or uniformity in the services offered across the different unions (Swanton, 1983). Tasmania alone runs a credit union through its association, although, as Swanton (1983) points out, all other police departments run credit unions in close association with their respective unions. All police unions make some provision for financial assistance to their members in matters relating to legal costs incurred by members as a result of their on-duty police work. This continues to be a vexed issue, as some police object to their subscriptions being used to fund the costs of members caught acting improperly or corruptly. The difficulty is that court decisions about the propriety or otherwise of members' actions occur after the often considerable expense of securing legal assistance. Most associations have laid down extensive guidelines covering the circumstances where the provision of legal expense support is considered warranted. In some cases these guidelines permit general across-the-board support, where in other circumstances, tightly-prescribed criteria have to be met. The issue of legal defense funding is likely to become more prominent in the near future. Swanton (1983) notes that for the year 1977, the Police Association of New South Wales spent $40,000 on such funds. In current terms, such a figure would hardly cover the costs of one two-week trial defended by a senior barrister. Some unions are increasingly turning to governments for assistance in meeting these costs, but there is still relatively little provision for "vicarious liability," in which government assumes the responsibility for defending the actions of its police employees.

Police unions spend a considerable proportion of their time tackling grievance issues on behalf of their memberships. Swanton (1983) classifies typical employee grievances into six categories relating to:

1. departmental administration (in matters such as transfers and postings, disciplinary proceedings, examinations and position selection, shifts and rosters, health and welfare).
2. supply (personal and work accommodation, vehicles and transport, clothing, and personal issue).
3. economic issues (pay, leave, allowances, retirement benefits).

4. operations (patrol crewing arrangements, operational resources, command structures and lines of control, coordination and cooperation).
5. public affairs (adverse publicity and media criticism).
6. legal issues (as discussed above).

Swanton (1983) notes that: "The great majority of grievances relate to employee criticisms of departments, suggestions for departmental reform and dissatisfaction with union functioning." Typical union grievance action consists of formal or informal contact with relevant executive officers within the police department where the matter is departmentally-generated, or beyond to police ministers or state bodies such as public service boards when the grievance arises extra-departmentally. Each state has a number of formal employee dispute resolution mechanisms, although given that the bulk of police employee grievances stem from departmental action or inaction, the first recourse is usually through the department's own official channels. Supplementary mechanisms within police departments are beginning to emerge, given, as Swanton (1983) points out, members often have little faith in official departmental mechanisms. Swanton cites the example of the growth of departmental welfare schemes and offices, which play a role of sorts in resolving personal and other forms of grievance. The Victoria Police have for some years appointed a senior officer as an Industrial Relations Officer.

The function of "defending the service" is attempted in a number of guises, usually through the union or association rules concerning the "promotion of the service." In practice this means both formal representations to relevant committees of inquiry and government policy bodies on matters seen to affect the interests of members, and more informal propagation of police member interests through the mass media and at lectures, seminars and so forth. Australia is seeing a more aggressive police union posture on a variety of matters seen to directly or indirectly affect members' interests than has been obvious in the past. This very significant development is taken up in a later part of this section. The provision of information services by police unions has also become more prominent in recent years. All unions regularly publish journals or magazines (some of which, according to Swanton, are amongst the oldest serials published in Australia); increasingly, unions are turning to frequent newsletters to keep members abreast of current industrial matters. And unions are, of course, expected to service members' requests for information concerning matters of pay, benefit entitlements, and so forth; many specifically employ officers who spend their days with their ears deformed by a telephone handset.

Australian police unions generally are governed by an executive committee, elected by the membership, one of whom is elected as president either by the membership as a whole or by the executive for, usually, a one- or two-year period. Executive committee members are serving police officers. Unions are run on a day-to-day basis by a secretariat, headed by a secretary (or a number of secretaries as in the largest union, that of New South Wales) and support staff. In some the secretary is a police officer; in others secretaries have come from outside the department, and appointed on the basis of general union and industrial experience. Swanton (1983) argues that traditionally the balance of power within police unions has resided in the secretary, although he is subject to direction in every case by the executive committee. Secretaries tend to have the highest public profile, being usually the union spokesperson. However, the tradition of secretary domination has not always been observed, and there have been in some unions both personality dynamics and formal structural features which have rendered the secretary subordinate in practice to the president. The larger unions have relatively large support staff numbers, including field officers, industrial officers, accountants and so forth. The unions' supreme bodies are generally their annual conferences, some of which are open to all members, while others are attended by delegates elected at branch level.

Australian police unions and associations perform virtually all of the duties and functions of the union movement in general, and thus exert a range of impacts upon the occupation, both subtle and obvious. In matters such as representing the membership before industrial tribunals, in the provision of welfare and financial services to members, and in terms of negotiating individual dispute resolution with police departments, police unions have little visibility outside the respective police services. In terms of the public's perception of the impact of unions upon policing, these activities are rarely prominent; neverthless, they constitute the bulk of union activities, and they clearly have a role in fostering what Swanton calls "police occupational development." It is impossible to provide a generalization concerning the extent of the effectiveness of unions in this sphere. The various unions have, historically and geographically, performed with different degrees of success in fulfilling the roles expected of them by their membership. Hannigan (1985) suggests that in general, police industrial relations can be considered "satisfactory" in Australia, given the improving degrees of expertise amongst both employee and employer groups evident in recent decades.

On the other hand, there have been examples in recent times where industrial relations cannot be described as satisfactory, and it is these examples by which the public impact of police unions is probably most readily gauged. A significant degree of militancy by police unions and their memberships have been evident in these disputes, and it is this militancy which receives prominent media attention. Militant union activity is, of course, an imperfect measure of impact and effectiveness. It is often generated by situational factors that do not necessarily reflect the conditions under which unions and employers conduct much of their mutual business. Nevertheless, the nature and extent of police union militancy provides a useful indication of the kinds of issues that bring forth the most forceful employee response. In addition, the outcomes of disputes invested with a good deal of militancy reflects the extent of the "muscle" that unions are able to bring to bear.

There are two broad categories of dispute which have generated considerable heat between unions and their antagonists in the last two decades: (1) disputes derived from actions or inactions by police administrations; and (2) those derived from actions or inaction by governments. While the former are the most common, it is in the latter that in recent years we have seen the most militant counteractions taken by unions. It is instructive to describe briefly several examples in both categories, which capture well the range of disputes that are perceived by police employees to most affect them.

The most outstanding confrontation between a police union and the police department administration occurred in the early and middle 1970s in Queensland. As Swanton (1983) records, the relationship between the union and the then commissioner was fragile ever since the latter's appointment in 1969. But a number of issues in the early 1970s precipitated a head-on confrontation. The commissioner had a reputation for reform, one aspect of which was his attempt to introduce widespread completion of a tertiary institution-based Police Arts and Sciences Course Certificate amongst police officers. While initially not directly connected to promotional prospects, the certificate (which involved three years part-time study) emerged in practice (and later in regulations) as an important prerequisite for promotion. Many police felt disenfranchised by this development, and membership resistance to both the course and to the commissioner began to heat up. Votes of no confidence in the commissioner were taken at branch level, and only just defeated on a unionwide level. The Police Minister had been forced by public attention on the dispute to support the commissioner, and became a target for union hostility. On another matter in 1975, the union secretary publicly called for the resignation of the Police Minister. In 1976, the union began to attract significant support from the state Premier and his cabinet, which reduced the capacity of the studies course to affect promotional opportunities. The union membership began what Swanton describes as a very effective campaign to reveal their grievances outside the police service. In 1976 also, the State Industrial Commission rejected a union application for a pay rise, which fostered considerable concern amongst employees. After some informal but apparently effective "go-slow" actions, the Police Minister invited the union to resubmit the application. In mid-1976, the union formally requested the Premier to dismiss the Police Minister. Later in the year, the commissioner backed by the Minister, had attempted to instigate an investigation into the alleged assault by a police officer on a student demonstrator; the Premier disallowed the inquiry, and amid calls for the resignations of both commissioner and minister by police employees, the Minister was sacked in August 1976. In November of that year, the commissioner resigned after a junior officer was appointed to the rank of assistant commissioner over his objections. Incidentally, that officer went on to become commissioner, and was stood down from his position early in 1988 pending the results of the Fitzgerald Inquiry into police corruption. The Premier denied that he had been influenced by union pressure in his decisions, claiming instead that he thought the commissioner and minister were "ahead of their time" (Swanton, 1983). The general consensus of opinion at the time, however, was that the union was largely responsible for both the dismissal and the resignation.

A confrontation in Victoria between the union and the chief commissioner a little later had a somewhat different outcome. In 1978, the then Chief Commissioner made an executive instruction that appointments to the CIB be made only from constables or senior constables with less than two years of service in the rank. The intention was to stop the situation where officers applied for the CIB and after a short time transferred out to gain rapid promotion. This instruction was hostilely received, as many aspirants to the CIB felt themselves unfairly excluded by the order. The union called upon the commissioner to revoke the instruction, but he refused to negotiate. A special general meeting of members voted by a wide majority to conduct a "work-to-rule" campaign. However, despite the vote the issue in reality directly affected only a small number of officers and the work-to-rule campaign appeared to have only limited endorsement by the union. It was not particularly effective, and the commissioner refused to resile from his position. The following year saw a number of issues with which the membership was dissatisfied added to the CIB instruction, culminating in an effective vote of no confidence in the administration of the department. The government supported the commissioner, and the issue was decided essentially in the administration's favor.

It is clear from these and other examples of confrontations between unions and police administrations that employees will take some action against their own department. Nevertheless, there are several obvious constraints upon members taking militant actions against antagonists from within their organization. With the exception of the usually small number of personnel in the union secretariats, most of whom are not police officers in any case, union officials retain their normal roles within the police department. Consequently, they must simultaneously balance their positions as police officers and union officials within an organization which demands expressions of loyalty and which is generally characterized by high levels of occupational solidarity. Unionists continue to depend upon their performance as officers to secure promotion and preferred career paths, and it must generate a degree of ambivalence at times amongst unionists with regard to which role they ought to give priority in times of confrontation. In addition, as the Victorian example demonstrates, effective militant action requires considerable unanimity amongst employees regarding both the principles at stake and the directly perceived consequences of administration actions. If these are missing, the opportunities for effective and militant action are diminished.

On the other hand, actions by government can generate more aggressive responses from police unionists. In the first instance, actions by governments, in terms of economic considerations, conditions of service, legislative matters, and so forth, tend to affect many more police members because they are related to broad policy or financial issues which encompass the police department as a whole. Second, the government is often perceived as a more comfortable target, because confrontations with the government do not so directly impact upon the duality of unionists' roles as both professional police service providers and employee representatives. Confrontations with governments can provide the appearance (and the reality) of a united front by employees, a matter of considerable importance in winning public sympathy and support. It can also, in some cases, involve the specific support of the police administration, thus presenting a solid block of police sentiment over a particular issue. There have been a number of recent examples in Australia which capture these points well.

A bitter dispute arose in Victoria following the findings and recommendations of an inquiry into police malpractice (the "Beach Inquiry") in 1976. As a result of the inquiry, the government announced that 55 police officers were to be charged with criminal offenses or breaches against standing orders. Police had already been resentful of the ways in which the inquiry had been conducted, believing that it was run by lawyers with a strong anti-police bias. Members were particularly bitter that the 55 police might be presented for trial without committal hearings. According to Swanton (1983), "Staffs of two large suburban police stations were reported to have voted to walk off the job, although in fact after receiving advice from the Association, they did not do so." Later, the Association's secretary said this in a public letter: "If they (the Government) seek a confrontation they shall have one. The threat of a strike is now once again a very real possibility" (Swanton, 1983) (Australia's only other police strike occurred in Victoria in 1923; the strike, which in fact was not authorized by the Association at the time, led to a period of considerable repression of police union activity, including a legal prohibition on the right to strike, and a prohibition on the capacity of the Victoria Association to affiliate with any other group). An extraordinary general meeting of the Association was held, attended reportedly by over half of the members of the Victoria Police department. A vote of no confidence was held against the Chief Secretary (the then portfolio in charge of police), while the administration of the department received a vote of confidence. This was a battle in which the union and the administration were largely in agreement. The meeting voted to work strictly to rule until the government agreed to a package of demands. The package included demands for formal due process for charged police officers, prosecutorial reviews of the evidence against the police, costs incurred by police to be met by the government, and total vicarious liability to be accepted by the government in the future. The work-to-rule action lasted two days; Swanton (1983) rightly argues that the effects of such action cannot be reliably measured in empirical terms, given its brevity. Nevertheless, the publicity generated by the action undoubtedly had significant public impact. In any case, the government met with the Association, and agreed to most of the package of demands; the Association called off the action. The government later claimed that the action was unnecessary and they would have agreed to the demands anyway. Association personnel, however, continue to insist over ten years later that it was the vehemence of the membership's response which forced concessions from the government. Incidentally, while the government appeared to accept the notion of vicarious liability, it managed to insert criteria concerning good faith and actions taken within stipulated standing orders. To this date, the Association continues to negotiate (and battle) with the government concerning total liability funding.

In New South Wales, a dispute arose in 1979 over matters of a different hue. In that year, the government replaced the old Summary Offences Act with a new piece of legislation which liberalized the range of behaviors which hitherto had been considered offensive. Police universally use summary or street offense legislation for order maintenance functions, and the New South Wales police and their association argued that their capacity to "keep the streets clean" was considerably hindered by the new legislation. Proposals for modification by the association were rejected by the government; in reply, the association advertised widely in the media concerning their beliefs of the impending lack of control, if not chaos, likely to appear on New South Wales streets. Some support from the commissioner of police for the association's stand was evident; he "issued a statement to the effect that all police taking action under the Act would be fully supported by the department" (Swanton, 1983). The government did not resile. Swanton claims that the number of charges for offensive behavior in 1980 was one-third that of 1978.

The last union-government dispute to be described here is of recent origin. Once again it relates to Victoria, and concerns union agitation, in concert with the police administration, for the granting by government of more resources and powers to police. The issue has been simmering for years, but it first received detailed and prolonged media attention during 1983 and 1984. The attention was generated by police reaction to a Supreme Court ruling in 1982 that police must bring a charged person before a court as soon as possible after enough evidence is gained to lay charges for one offense. Hitherto, police had interpreted the relevant legislation to allow a "sufficient" time for interrogation and questioning in relation to as many matters as thought relevant by police. In other words, police believed that their capacity to thoroughly investigate complicated criminal matters, such as multiple armed robberies and fraud cases, was severely hindered. Requests to amend legislation to allow police further time for investigatory detention by police administration and the union were rejected initially, while the government set up an inquiry on detention powers. By early 1984, police agitation was such that the government made moves to restrict the right of senior administration officers from making public comment. In response to this, the union called an extraordinary general meeting and a vote of no confidence was held against the government (*The Age*, 2 February, 1984). At the same time, the union and police administration broadened the debate to include a range of other issues concerning the adequacy of their powers. The Victoria police wanted the additional powers to take fingerprints from suspected persons, to demand names and addresses of people acting suspiciously, to conduct compulsory identity parades, to take compulsory samples and specimens, and to search suspects. Many of these powers were available to police in other states, and in Britain and the U.S. The union was prominent in the media debating the issue, with headlines such as "Double standards on police powers" (*The Age*, 26 January, 1984) and "Let the community decide on police powers" (*The Age*, 20 January, 1984). The government did amend detention legislation, to allow six hours of detention for questioning before a charged person had to be brought before court; it did not act on the other issues immediately. The union and the administration were unsatisfied by both the action and inaction.

The issue continued to receive some media attention, but it was resurrected as a prominent and topical debate in 1988 before the state government went to the polls that year. The Victoria Police Association decided to take advantage of this likelihood, and threatened to lobby voters directly in marginal seats in the electorate. In a revealing statement replying to an attack upon the union's threat by a civil libertarian, Ron Castan, the secretary of the Association (Bryan Harding) wrote this (*The Age*, 24 February, 1988):

> If the Police Association does circulate material in marginal electorates, our intention is to state the facts, advise the position of the major parties on the issues, and then allow voters to make up their minds accordingly...Mr. Castan's concern is even harder to understand given that we do not, and will not strike, or threaten industrial reaction. We are simply giving the people of Victoria our perspective on the issues which politicians, of all persuasions, have been unwilling to resolve. Contrary to what Mr. Castan asserted, the issue is very much one coming within the mandate of the association....The association has reacted as any other legitimate union in representing the very real concerns of its members.

While the government introduced some legislation which moved part of the way towards the meeting of police demands, the Association was not satisfied and campaigned in the election. The government was subsequently returned, and none of the marginal seats targeted by the police changed hands.

The examples described above indicate a range of impacts of varying gravity of union agitation upon the processes of both police administration and government administration. The dynamics are fluid, and include at any one time the capabilities and personalities of key actors, such as union and police executives, government ministers, cabinets, and premiers. Increasingly, it appears that perceived public support and sympathy are critical factors in the nature and degrees of confrontation. It is also possible to detect increasing sophistication in union tactics and strategies, especially in disputes with governments. From the attempts at industrial action, mostly in the form of work-to-rule campaigns in the 1970s, we have seen a movement towards direct public lobbying, in which police are committing themselves as (potentially) important players in electoral dynamics.

The record to date of the influence of police unions on Australian policing continues to indicate an unevenness and inconsistency. Nevertheless the signs are there clearly that police unions intend to capitalize upon the "muscle-flexing" experiences of the 1970s. That intention is captured very well in a statement by the immediate past secretary of the Victoria Police Association (Rippon, 1982):

> The police associations are now becoming financially and politically strong. Financially strong enough to defend themselves and their members in any court in the land and politically strong enough not to be pushed around by anyone of whatever political philosophy. I believe that the associations and unions can and will in the future make themselves heard more often on major items which affect themselves and the community.

POLICE PUBLIC RELATIONS, PUBLIC CONFIDENCE, TRUST, AND RESTRAINTS ON THE POLICE

It was argued in earlier sections of this chapter that for a variety of historical reasons, police in Australia have not enjoyed a conspicuously high degree of respect in the community, at least in the early part of their modern development. The calibre of the early police officers, the repressive tasks they were set to perform, and an often cited (but rather unsubstantiated) anti-authority streak in the Australian public, have all been noted as determinants of a relatively unfavorable image of police. Certainly police themselves are prone to believing that they are not held in particularly high regard by the public. Nevertheless, it is only relatively recently that reliable empirical data derived from surveys have provided a more sound basis for the analysis of public image. Before selected data from such surveys is discussed, it is necessary to say a little about police attempts to maintain or enhance their public image.

Police acknowledgment of the importance of negotiating a favorable public image has emerged recently in a number of guises. Taking the Victoria Police as a prominent example, we have already noted the significant shift in the orientation of its organizational philosophy over the last decade or so. From an articulated concern with issues of efficiency and general effectiveness in the early 1980s, the department is becoming much more concerned with effecting these goals in the context of community recognition and support. This shift is in part a reflection of the realization that the effective abandonment of foot patrol with the advent of mobile patrol earlier this century led to increasing isolation of police from the community it serviced. It also reflects the increasing exposure of senior executive officers to trends overseas, gathered firsthand from interchange, training, and study scholarship opportunities which began to develop in the 1970s. The Victoria police have attempted to match its organizational rhetoric with a range of programs and stategies designed to bring it closer to the community. Like other Australian police departments, the Victoria police have implemented Neighborhood Watch schemes on a wide basis throughout the major metropolitan areas, and have extended the scheme into country areas (Victoria Police, 1986/87). The department has also implemented what it calls Police/Community Involvement Programs in two metropolitan areas; these programs call for interactive problem solving between police and the local community, and are concerned with such issues as youth crime, the safety of school children, and the setting up of "shop-front" police stations. A large number of Community Policing Squads (successors to the now abolished women police districts) operate in a range of spheres designed to maximize services to families in trouble—in matters such as domestic violence, crisis care, child maltreatment, and sexual assault (Victoria Police, 1986/87). Smith (1985) sums up the general approach of police to these issues.

Programs such as the above are designed both to improve the level of services provided to the community and to foster a better understanding in general between police and the public. Besides these programs, the department has a special Public Affairs Department, the central tasks of which are: to provide better communication with particular groups in the community (Ethnic Adviser's Office and Aboriginal Adviser's Office); to offer crime prevention advice to the community; and to improve public relations by negotiating the most favorable image of police (Public Relations Office, Police History Unit, Media Liaison Bureau, and Media Director's Office) (Victoria Police, 1986/87). The Department also puts out a monthly glossy magazine, *Police Life,* which is widely distributed to libraries, schools, and the media.

Other Australian police departments conduct similar programs and have established similar public relations offices. Efforts such as these by police have not been without their critics. There have been allegations that much of the public relations exercises have been directed not at genuine concern for public inputs into policing and a consequent receptivity to alter policies and procedures, but rather to present to the public the best possible face of policing without any significant changes taking place (See, for example, Hogg and Findlay, 1988). Neighborhood Watch particularly has been alleged to be a stategy primarily designed to generate a new lobby group within the community which will agitate for increased police resources and powers. Certainly, to the writer's knowledge, there have been examples where Neighborhood Watch zone committees have lobbied community members to sign petitions calling on the government to improve police powers. Some observers also argue that "community-based" policing strategies are ultimately designed to provide police with greater powers of surveillance and infiltration in order to more effectively pursue traditional law enforcement and criminal investigation roles (see O'Malley, 1983). Victoria's Media Director's Office has come under attack for overtly manipulating official crime statistics in order to forge the conditions for public acceptance of increased police powers (Freckleton, 1988). The present writer here makes no comment on these criticisms, other than to suggest that no one should be too surprised that police are attempting by diverse means to negotiate a more positive image; that is, after all, what public relations is all about. It is difficult to imagine police not taking advantage of the opportunities for such image-making generated through programs established for more susbtantive reasons; it is also difficult to hold them blameworthy for taking such advantage. The crucial issue is whether such opportunities are grasped through distortion or deceit in terms of the aims and procedures of the programs and the public relations exercises. This writer does not doubt that examples of distortion and deceit have occurred; they have also occurred amongst the critics of police. At times, the critics imply that there is a concerted conspiracy by police to "con" the public in terms of their true agendas. Like O'Malley (1983), this writer takes comfort in the observation that research has consistently shown there to be at times remarkable diversity in both police practices and in the attitudes of police personnel within and between police departments. It seems improbable that every police-community initiative is generated by the hidden agenda of securing public support at the expense of the truth or the facts of the circumstances. The reality is, of course, that the facts of crime, criminality, public order, crime prevention, and so forth which normally form the basis for controversy over police attempts to present themselves sympathetically to the public are nebulous; they need to be rigorously debated in public. That police are increasingly taking part in that debate ought not in itself be cause for alarm.

There have been a number of public opinion polls regarding attitude towards Australian police in the last two decades or so. Swanton et al. (1985) present a useful summary of such polls between 1973 and 1984 on a number of relevant issues. Ratings of a number of occupations in terms of honesty and ethical standards have been taken in 1976, 1979, 1981, 1983, and 1984. Across that period, the following range of percentages of respondents who held police in the various states to be either "very high" or "high" on those dimensions was revealed: New South Wales police (42-50 percent); Victoria police (57-60 percent); Queensland (40-50 percent); Western Australia police (50-64 percent); South Australia police (55-76 percent); and Tasmania police (42-67 percent). The fluctuations followed no consistent patterns. Victorian, South Australian and Western Australian police were consistently rated "high" or better by at least 50 percent of the samples; both New South Wales and Queensland police achieve 50 percent in only one of the poll years. There were ten occupations rated in the polls: bank manager, doctor, dentist, teacher, police, university lecturer, lawyer, politician, journalist, and union leader. In the 1984 poll, the respective state police were ranked amongst the occupations in terms of the percentage of respondents who believed their ethical standards to be high or very high thus: New South Wales (6); Victoria (3); Queensland (5); Western Australia (3); South Australia (4); Tasmania (equal 2). In every state in all poll years, police were ranked ahead of lawyers with the exception of Queensland in 1979.

Swanton et al. (1985) also present comparative opinion poll data across the state police departments between two poll dates, 1967 and 1978, on the question of public respect for police. The percentages of respondents holding "a great deal of respect" for police on those two dates respectively were: New South Wales (68%-47%); Victoria (74%-59%); Queensland (70%-50%); Western Australia (80%-51%); South Australia (81-64%); and Tasmania (76-57%). Swanton et al. (1985) discuss the data thus:

> The extent of the decreases on respect of all states indicates a long term trend rather than perhaps a temporary phenomenon. Some observers of the police scene suggest that in addition to a possible perception of police agencies being increasingly unable to cope with certain social conditions, there is an erosion of middle class support for police as the criminal justice spotlight expands to include a social class not previously subjected to sustained police attention.

A more recent publication updates and adds to the data on public respect for police. Swanton, Wilson, Walker and Mukherjee (1988) compared the results of a 1969 survey and one conducted in 1987 which asked the question about respect in a slightly different manner. Australia-wide, the percentage of respondents who held "great respect" for police dropped from 64 percent in 1969 to 55 percent in 1987. On a state basis, the following percentages of respondents held great respect for police in 1987: New South Wales (51 percent); Victoria (63 percent); Queensland (38 percent); Western Australia (60 percent); South Australia (67 percent); and Tasmania (56 percent). The authors of the report noted that the Fitzgerald inquiry into corruption in the Queensland police had been announced at the time of the survey; they nevertheless argue on the basis of previous polls that Queensland police respect has traditionally been lower than that of the other states. The authors also note that females were more likely than males to hold police in great respect, and that respect generally increased with the age of the respondent. In addition, socioeconomic status was inversely related to respect.

The 1987 survey also included a question concerning honesty. Respondents were asked whether they thought police are more honest than most people, or about the same as most people, or less honest than most people. The percentages of respondents who respectively answered "yes" to those alternatives were: New South

Wales (9%/80%/8%); Victoria (11%/80%/5%); Queensland (6%/79%/10%); Western Australia (9%/80%/4%); South Australia (12%/79%/5%); and Tasmania (7%/80%/10%). The authors comment that the consistency of these responses between the states suggests that the situational effects of prominent inquiries into police such as royal commissions appear to be minimal given that some state police departments have endured considerably more of them in recent years than others.

The last of the 1987 survey results to be described here concerns the question of politeness. Respondents were asked whether they had always found police to be polite and helpful, or had they found police to be sometimes impolite and unhelpful. The percentages of respondents who answered "yes" to the first alternative were: New South Wales (67 percent); Victoria (64 percent); Queensland (62 percent); Western Australia (75 percent); South Australia (71 percent); and Tasmania (68 percent).

Swanton et al. (1988) sum up the implications of the 1987 survey:

> A study of the way in which citizens view their police often provides a revealing glimpse of a nation's commitment to democracy, and respect for authority. Among Australians, commentators have long identified a strong anti-authoritarian trait which has been said to account for the average citizen's view of the "police as enemies, army officers as traitors to democracy...the boss as a barely necessary evil and anyone who gives an order as deeply suspect." The results of a national survey of public attitudes to police and police services reported here indicate that Australians are more respectful of their police, and pleased with the assistance they provide, than some observers have suggested. At a time of major controversy and change among many of the nation's law enforcement agencies, a majority of survey respondents indicated that they still possessed great respect for police. But the report also shows that the level and degree of this public respect varied widely between jurisdictions....

It is of course difficult to be sure of the relativity of the findings described above in the international context. Nevertheless, it should be acknowledged that opinion polls cannot successfully tap all relevant aspects of community respect for police. Police often underestimate the extent of respect expressed in such polls (see Chappell and Wilson, 1969); but it can be argued that their direct exposure to the public in the course of their duties provides them with a more accurate and reliable picture of police-community relations than do the results of surveys which probe the issues in far more abstract terms. Demographic breakdowns of respondent samples often show, as indeed does the 1987 survey, that groups which police believe constitute the most problematic sections of the community, such as young males and aboriginals, express the most disrespect of them (see also Wilson, 1988). In addition, we remain ignorant of the critical parameters of respect in which the police are held by other agencies and practitioners in the criminal justice system and by policymakers in government. These entities exert considerable influence, both positive and negative, upon policing; in some regards, it might be argued that those influences are more crucial in the political arena than that exerted by a community with diverse views. In any case, it remains true that a fully comprehensive capturing of the nature and relevance of public opinion of police has yet to be successfully effected.

Formal restraints upon police can be divided into those which legally prescribe police procedure and performance, those which administratively prescribe procedure and performance, and those which either legally or administratively hold police accountable for their procedures and performance. The distinction is thus made between restraints which formally guide police in their duties and those which formally ensure compliance. Legal prescriptions include: the criminal law, which defines certain behaviors as criminal; those laws which establish the conditions under which various police powers may be legitimately exercised, such as the powers of arrest, search and seizure, deadly force, and detention; and associated legislation, case law, and judge's rules, which define acceptable criminal investigation practices and the criteria for the admissibility of evidence in criminal trials. Administrative prescriptions include police standing orders which regulate police procedure and the guidelines established by government policy in matters of criminal or social justice policy.

The enforcement of legal and administrative compliance operates through the criminal courts, departmental disciplinary tribunals, and the civil courts in cases of torts. In most cases in Australia, the first two of these enforcement mechanisms are enacted by internal investigation divisions within police departments, which either prosecutes cases themselves before disciplinary tribunals, or make recommendations to crown prosecutors or directors of public prosecutions in cases of criminal misconduct. Some states have established police complaints authorities or tribunals which operate outside the formal police organizational structure; most states have mechanisms for the review of complaints investigation by ombudsmen, and so forth. These mechanisms are discussed in more detail in the next section.

An additional formal restraint of another dimension upon police comes from government budgetary allocations to police departments. Police depend upon government for salaries, equipment, vehicles, accommodation, maintenance and so forth, and the level at which the government is prepared to fund these items clearly exercises a variety of restraints upon police organizational structure and operational capacity. Police regulations prescribe levels of personnel at any one time, and also generally prescribe important aspects such as recruiting standards and promotional criteria; all of these facets restrain the discretion of police departments.

Less formal but equally important restraints upon police operate in a variety of guises. Policing can fairly be described as an open systems organization, in that it both influences and is influenced by its environmental context. That is, there is a rich dynamism in policing which takes in formal and informal inputs from a range of agencies and groups, such as police unions, the other agencies of the criminal and social justice systems, and the community. Levels of public support, cooperation with other agencies, industrial harmony or disharmony, all offer the potential to restrain aspects of police practice and initiative (and, of course, at times to enhance these aspects). Broader aspects of the environmental context of police work also exert obvious influence, and hence potential restraint, upon police. Levels of crime in the community—and perhaps more importantly—the types of prevalent crime in the community, public disorder, circumstances of widespread social dislocation and trauma through environmental disaster or crises, or economic recession, all require allocation decisions by police, as well as some structural changes; such decisions restrain the capacity of police to fulfill all aspects of their broad charter.

Finally, treating policing for the moment as a closed system organization, there are historical, functional, and structural restraints upon police. The legacy of traditional procedures, such as recruiting and training methods, promotional systems, and performance evaluation schemes, fetter a police department in its capacity to be innovative and progressive. Traditional functions which span law enforcement, order maintenance, and welfare roles potentially restrict police from either divesting themselves of unwanted aspects of some of these roles or expanding into other aspects they see as relevant to their mandate. Police organizational structures, such as high degrees of centralization, rigid rank structures, and a quasi-military outlook and orientation, hinder the sorts of bureaucratic flexibilities evident in other public and private sector enterprises.

The number and scope of potential and actual restraints upon police are enormous. In addition, their respective gravities are in large measure matters of the perspective from which they are viewed. For instance, some restraints upon the capacity of police departments to be creative and reforming are likely to be viewed by some within the organization as valuable and positive impediments to rash and unnecessary innovation. On the other hand, police attempts to remove those restraints which they believe impede their capacity to fight crime, such as restrictions on suspect detention and fingerprinting provisions, are likely to be viewed by many outside the organization as intolerable interference in restraints justly and wisely put in place. Given this complexity of restraints and the perspectives from which they might be viewed, it is not feasible in this short chapter to explore all of the ramifications of restraints upon police. Rather, it is useful to recast this issue of restraint into the issue of police problems. For it is a sensible consideration of which of these aspects of restraint constitute substantive problems for police and the community that provides the most appropriate context for their discussion.

PROBLEMS OF THE POLICE

The following discussion of the problems of Australian police is necessarily selective. That these are problems are indisputable, as this chapter had indicated. It is axiomatic that the police enterprise is universally problematic, an axiom attested by Skolnick's (1966) seminal work, and Goldstein's (1977) opposite description of police as an anomaly in democratic society. The task here is to identify which of the problematic aspects of policing provide the most instructive account of the present circumstances of Australian policing.

This section outlines a number of broad areas in which this writer believes the most prominent problems facing Australian police are evident. These areas both take in some aspects of issues identified in earlier sections and introduce several new ones. The areas are these: police work and the community; police powers and resources; police accountability and malpractice; and police personnel and organizational structure.

Within the arena of police work and the community, there are two general issues which require comment: the nature and changes in that nature of police work itself; and the nature and change in that nature of the community within which police conduct their enterprise. Concerns that might be raised in the first issue include changes in the levels and types of criminal activity that require police attention. Concerns in the second sphere include general levels of public support, and more particularly, support from those groups in the community that police find problematic, such as young people and aboriginals.

Australian police, like their counterparts overseas, generally believe that crime is increasing at an alarming rate. They believe that they are less able to prevent crime, and less able to solve that crime which has been committed, as Australia heads towards the twenty-first century. Victoria police point towards increases in all categories in its Major Crime Index between 1985/86 and 1986/87: homicide (11 percent); serious assault (5 percent); robbery (26 percent); rape (9 percent); burglary (14 percent); theft (10 percent); motor vehicle theft (24 percent); and fraud (18 percent) (*Victoria Police Statistical Review of Crime*, 1986/87). They also report decreases in clearance rates. These are absolute figures and do not take into account population parameters. Nationally, crime rates have been calculated on the basis of per 100,000 heads of population, a more reliable statistic. Mukherjee et al. (1987) report on crime rates for those offenses that have an acceptable degree of interstate definitional consistency. They note that between 1973/74 and 1984/85, the homicide rate remained relatively stable at between 1.61 and 1.91; the serious assault rate rose from 20.76 to 58.77; the rape rate rose from 5.62 to 12.12; the robbery rate rose from 23.34 to 42.88; the "break, enter, and steal" rate rose from 880.98 to 1746.67; the motor vehicle theft rate rose from 374.85 to 663.18; and the fraud rate rose from 233.92 to 437.29. The clearance rates over the same period were: murder (stable between 86 percent and 93 percent); serious assault (stable between 73 percent and 78 percent); rape (mildly fluctuating between 61 percent and 74 percent); robbery (stable between 25 percent and 31 percent); break, enter, and steal (steadily decreasing from 20 percent to 12 percent); motor vehicle theft (stable between 12 percent and 16 percent); and fraud (decreasing from 81 percent to 70 percent). In a revealing statistic (Mukherjee et al., 1987), the clearance rate per police officer in Australia improved by 87 percent between 1973/74 and 1984/85 for violent offenses and by 19 percent for property offenses.

Reported crime statistics should, of course, be treated with considerable caution (see Galvin and Polk, 1982). Challinger (1983), for instance, argues a strong case for the existence of a "crime reporting wave" rather than a crime wave in the explanation of Australia's apparently increasing crime rate. Nevertheless, police clearly believe that movements in crime constitute a serious problem for both themselves and the community (see Victoria Police, 1986/87). That belief has had important consequences in the public image that police have created in terms of the problems they see themselves as facing.

In addition to movements in the general crime rate—reflected by index crime statistics—emerging crime patterns within some index categories and sometimes outside the index categories constitute increasing problems for police. Some of these patterns are new, others are the function of increasing public awareness and hence reporting. A short selective list includes organized crime and drug trafficking, "white-collar" and professional crime, and domestic violence and child abuse. Because of our general reliance upon reported crime statistics, it is difficult to be sure of how much the apparent increases in these forms of criminal activity are true increases or the results of heightened public and police sensitivity. In either case, the magnitude of these offenses and the difficulties police have in dealing with them are real enough.

Organized crime and drug trafficking have been subject to considerable public scrutiny in Australia in the last decade or so, particularly in the form of Royal Commissions (for example, the Stewart Royal Commission, 1983, and the Costigan Royal Commission, 1984). While Wardlaw (1988) points out the lack of substantive empirical knowledge about both the extent of organized crime and drug trafficking and the connection between the two in Australia, it is generally agreed that both aspects of criminality constitute serious social and criminal justice problems. This is reflected in part by the establishment of federal and state agencies such as the National Crime Authority and the New South Wales Drug Crimes Commission (Wardlaw, 1988), as well as federal and state initiatives in the educational and preventive areas (for instance, the federal "Drug Offensive" campaign which began in the mid-1980s, and initially targeted narcotic use through massive media advertising). State Police drug squads have been increased in size, and so also penalties (Wardlaw, 1988). The problem for police is two-fold: (1) an apparent lack of effectiveness in their efforts to deal with such criminality; and (2) the corruptive influence upon police of the networks of organized crime and the massive profits to be made from drug trafficking. Wardlaw (1988) argues:

> ...such evidence as is available (and it is of a very poor quality in Australia...) indicates that all these initiatives (that is, new agencies and increased police agency attention to drug law enforcement) are having little, if any impact upon drug markets and drug use. Larger numbers of drug arrests (many at a higher level in the system than in previous times), much larger seizures of illicit drugs, and an apparent willingness of the courts to hand down longer sentences for major drug crimes all seem to have little effect. Heroin use appears reasonably static, cannabis use remains widespread, and cocaine use appears to be increasing. (second parenthesis added)

At the same time, many police and some police commentators have regretted that setting up of federal agencies to tackle these issues. Swanton's (1985) critique of the National Crime Authority has already been noted; he argues that all law enforcement should be left in the hands of the state police whose traditional role it has been to hegemonize law enforcement. Major-General Ronald Grey, the retired commissioner of the Australia Federal Police, also argued that resources and powers which went to the National Crime Authority would have been better allocated to the Australian Federal Police and the state departments (*The Age*, 15 February, 1988). In Australia, we are currently seeing the beginnings of a significant debate concerning the most appropriate means of dealing with drug trafficking and abuse; many theorists and practitioners are now doubting the wisdom of relying upon increased law enforcement capacity given its hitherto poor results (Wardlaw, 1988). Decriminalization in some form for narcotic use received favorable attention (Ward and Dobinson, 1988); a retired Deputy Commissioner of the Victoria Police, Paul Delianis, publicly called for a serious consideration of decriminalization, on the grounds that traditional enforcement strategies did not work (*The Age*, 8 June, 1988). "White-collar" professional and corporate crime has also received increasing attention in Australia. There is good evidence that Australians are not as tolerant of crimes committed by the powerful as was once assumed (see Grabosky, Braithwaite, and Wilson, 1987). Medical fraud by doctors and corporate crimes or breaches of regulations have been brought to prominent public attention (Fisse and Braithwaite,1988; Grabosky and Braithwaite, 1986; Wilson, 1986), as have tax evasion offenses (Costigan, 1984). On a more prosaic level, newly-emerging forms of fraud, such as credit card fraud and computer fraud are increasing in number (Victoria Police, 1986/87). These new forms of fraud represent significant challenges to traditional police practices in dealing with crime, given their high levels of technical sophistication and the consequent need for police to improve their expertise in these areas. In other areas, such as corporate crime and negligence, tax evasion, and medical fraud, police either share the responsibility of law enforcement with other agencies (such as regulatory control boards) or have little or no role to play in investigation and prosecution. Many commentators (for example, Fisse and Braithwaite, 1988) lament the lack of coordination and clear lines of accountability for the enforcement of laws proscribing the crimes and offenses of the powerful. Police are in an obvious dilemma here. If they abrogate any responsibility for the control of such crimes, they can be accused of emphasizing traditional street crimes at the expense of dealing with what, in terms of financial losses to the community, are undoubtedly the more important criminal behaviors (see Grabosky and Braithwaite, 1986). If, on the other hand, they wish to become more fully involved in these areas, they require considerably improved resourcing and training, requirements increasingly unlikely to be met in times of financial stringency; and they need greater levels of cooperation and coordination with other relevant agencies. This latter necessity has always constituted significant difficulty in Australia, given traditional state hegemonies over law enforcement and the different criminal and regulatory codes across the states. At the same time, observers are clearly divided over the issue of the appropriateness of orthodox law enforcement strategies in the realm of the crimes of the powerful (Fisse and Braithwaite, 1988; Grabosky and Braithwaite, 1986). There is little obvious sign that these dilemmas are currently subject to satisfactory resolution.

Domestic violence and child abuse are topical concerns in Australian society. Police particularly are embroiled in debates about the nature and extent of such activity, and the appropriate strategies for dealing with them. The general theme running through critiques of police performance in the domestic violence sphere is one predominantly of a lack of positive police attitude and willingness to solve complex social and family problems. It seems apparent that police have at times abrogated responsibility for the handling of domestic violence, partly as a function of this presumed attitude set and partly because of their belief that they did not have sufficient powers to intervene successfully. Heightened public awareness of the extent and unacceptable nature of domestic violence has forced police to be more responsive in this area. Nevertheless, they remain enmeshed in a fundamental dilemma when it comes to complex social problems which require both law-enforcement and welfare considerations. Police are criticized for taking aggressive law enforcement action in a range of community issues, such as the policing of public order and in their dealings with young offenders; at the same time, their lack of aggressive law enforcement in matters such as domestic violence also render them open to attack.

Child abuse and sexual assault is a complicated phenomenon (see Hewitt, 1986), with jurisdiction over its investigation and prosecution typically split between police, government, and non-government welfare agencies. The Victoria police (1983) have suggested that difficulties in the area are due to : (1) lack of training across disciplines to recognize and adequately deal with maltreatment cases; (2) lack of pragmatic and coordinated approach to welfare problems which renders the role and responsibility of welfare agencies ambiguous and confusing; and (3) the innate conflict perceived by police when social workers are placed in situations of authority and coercion. The last is an especially important consideration to police, who are generally reluctant to see other agencies in the community vested with quasi or full police powers of coercion. A newspaper report (*The Age*, 7 April, 1988) cited the findings of an unreleased Victoria Police report, which was highly critical of the performance of the premier government welfare agency in its handling of child abuse cases. Citing examples of lack of resources, lack of clear lines of accountability, and negligence within the welfare agency, the police report called for the handing over to police the primary responsibility for child abuse cases in the short term. Police argue that as the only well-resourced, disciplined, accountable, and 24-hour-service available in the state, they ought to be given the major responsibility. In the long term, they envisage the creation of an independent coordinating body which would combine the resources of all relevant agencies.

The behavior of young people, especially young males, historically has brought them into conflict with police. The Neesham Inquiry (1985) stated:

> Public survey in Australia and overseas have almost invariably found that younger people tend to have the greatest antipathy towards the police. These findings are supported by our own surveys as well as a great deal of anecdotal and other evidence.

Young people represent a particularly problematic group for police (see Muir, 1977). They are disproportionately involved in official crime rates, reflecting the attention that police believe they ought to be devoting to juvenile offending. In Victoria, young people aged below 17 represent approximately 19 percent of the state's population yet of all people proceeded against for criminal offenses, they represent 42 percent of burglary charges, 34 percent of theft and motor vehicle theft charges, 20 percent of robbery charges, 9 percent of serious assault and fraud charges, 3 percent of homicide charges, and 1 percent of rape charges (*Victoria Police Statistical Review*, 1986/87). While these figures hardly support police allegations about the violent nature of modern youth, they do point to a significant offending problem in property crimes. Murray and Borowski (1986) argue:

> With regard to property offences, the community and law enforcement agencies would appear to be justified in expressing real concern over the high juvenile arrest rates. It should be remembered, however, that many juvenile property of-

> fences are petty in nature, executed in a very "amateurish" manner, and may invoke little property loss or damage.

Aboriginals present ongoing problems for police. They comprise 1.4 percent of the total Australian population; however, they represent 14.5 percent of the prison population. That is, they are ten times overrepresented in the system (Hazlehurst and Dunn, 1988). Aboriginals are disproportionately represented in prison for offenses against the person, traffic and vehicle-related offenses, and offenses against good order (Hazlehurst and Dunn, 1988). These writers notce that alcohol-related violence constitutes the bulk of the serious offenses for which aboriginals are imprisoned. Besides the alarming rate at which aboriginals are imprisoned, they also endure disproportionately high rates of deaths in custody (Grabosky, Scandia, Hazlehurst and Wilson, 1988). The bulk of the deaths have taken place in police holding cells and clearly raise concerns over both the nature of aboriginal offending and their subsequent treatment by the justice system, especially police.

Aboriginals in Australia are a dispossessed people, with high rates of alcohol abuse, unemployment, and homelessness. They are a clear example of a marginalized group within society that gets into trouble with the justice system. Allegations are often made that aboriginals are singular victims of racism, especially generated by police (see Stafford, 1986). But the historical legacy of white Australia's treatment of aboriginals and their current disadvantaged socioeconomic status are complex factors that render any one explanation for their differential treatment in the justice system as simplistic. As Grabosky et al. (1988) argue:

> The issue of Aboriginal deaths in prisons and police holding cells is particularly complex. To suggest that so disturbing a series of events can be explained entirely as a matter of police brutality, official negligence, white racism, cultural disintegration, emotional despondency, accident, or natural causes is to oversimplify it. No single explanation nor solution will suffice.

Gale and Wundersitz (1987) examined juvenile arrest rates in the state's capital city of Adelaide over a twelve-month period from mid-1983. After their very thorough analysis, they concluded:

> It is well documented that Aborigines, both juveniles and adults, experience disproportionately high rates of arrest. This

> has, at times, been attributed to the fact that Aborigines live in remote, spatially separate communities and exhibit marked cultural differences. Yet even when controlling for these factors by studying only Aboriginal and non-Aboriginal youths resident in Adelaide, we still found substantial differences in arrest patterns....(We) found no statistical evidence that, at the point of arrest, police overtly discriminate against Aborigines on racial grounds.

Police apparently predictably considered unemployment status as a factor influencing formal action; because the aboriginal youth were more likely to be unemployed, they were thus more likely to be arrested. While noting that the data did not reveal specific racial discrimination, the researchers argued that they clearly indicated the disadvantaging of aboriginal youth.

Police believe that their capacity to both prevent crime and deal with it following its commission has steadily eroded in recent years. Thus, police understandably argue for improved powers and resources to control this erosion. Second, police administrations and unions have become increasingly more willing and able to argue their case in the public arena, through the mass media, and by way of industrial action or agitation. It is clear that law enforcement has always been part of the political processes of society; but it is only in relatively recent times that police have explicitly entered the political fray as a significant lobby force. Third, resistence to both the fact of police arguing their case in public and to the logic and desirability of those arguments themselves have entailed a vigorous public debate, conducted largely at this stage between police and civil libertarians. Fourth, in Australia the cost of funding public services has come under considerable scrutiny in recent times because of the country's economic recession; it is clear that steady, generous, and automatic growth in public enterprises, including policing, is a thing of the past.

Police, like all public sector enterprises, are facing more detailed review of their efficiency than has occurred in the past. A recent article captures the nature of this change:

> ...Australia's financial crises means that police increasingly will have to justify their budgets and to demonstrate that their resources are being used efficiently. This concept of accountability is one familiar to private business and to all other areas of the public sector and, yet, Australian police historically have been allowed to hide behind a veil of "necessary secrecy"

> with constant claims that bigger budgets were the only solution to increasing crime rates accepted without investigation. (*The Bulletin*, 31 May 1988)

The emergence of this treatment of policing as a public sector enterprise like all others, at least from an accounting perspective, clearly has important implications. It means that police must enter the public arena to defend themselves and their capacities and enlist public support for continued expansion and upgrading of their powers. In order to avoid the consequences of economic recession felt by other public sectors, it has become useful for them to argue the direct social consequences to the community in terms of increased crime of a weakened police service. Police powers, it can be argued, need not have direct cost implications, and can be seen to offset the disadvantages of being unable to grow in personnel and resource terms at the same rate as in the past.

Freckleton and Selby (1988) have argued a trenchant case that in almost all aspects of accountability, police in Australia have been found wanting. Echoing the assertion quoted from the *Bulletin* above, they maintain that police have managed to avoid the "dramatic changes in Australian public administration" that were heralded in during the mid-1970s (Freckleton and Selby, 1988). They point to the lack of formalized inspectorates within police departments and the general lack of management skills at executive levels brought about by rigid promotional structures and insularity in training and development procedures.

Police malpractice (a generic term used here to encompass corruption, brutality, and other criminal and disciplinary offenses) has been the subject of a sufficient number of detailed inquiries into police departments in recent years to enable a broad indication of at least its nature. The Williams Royal Commission of Inquiry into Drugs (1984) provided a list of allegations made to it concerning police across Australia during the course of its hearings:

- Police officers, by recourse to violence or with a threat of violence or other threats, extract confessions (frequently false) or other evidence;
- Police officers were involved, usually in combination with others, in the illegal importation of, production of, or trafficking in, drugs;

- Police officers accused and charged persons in respect of drugs after the drugs had been "planted" by police officers; Drugs, money and other goods seized by police officers were not appropriately accounted for but were diverted by the police officers to their own use and profit;
- Police officers were influenced by criminals, by the payment of money or otherwise, to turn a "blind eye" to criminal activities, or to provide criminals with information, or to influence the course of an investigation or ensure it did not proceed, or to conceal the results of the investigation.
- Police treated those alleged to be involved in drugs with unnecessary and unjustified roughness, often subjecting them to personal abuse and physical ill-treatment;
- Police officers treated the goods and property of those claimed to be involved with drugs with scant respect, frequently wilfully damaging them or putting them into disorder—particularly if a search for drugs proved unsuccessful.

The Committee of Inquiry into the Enforcement of Criminal Law in Queensland (the Lucas Committee, 1977) has said:

> We have come to the conclusion that the fabrication of evidence by police officers—particularly of confessional evidence—does occur. The sad truth is that "verballing," as it has become known, is a device that is not uncommonly employed by certain members of the police force. And, for what it may be worth, we are also satisfied the practice is by no means peculiar to the State of Queensland.

The Stewart Royal Commission into Drug Trafficking (1983) reported that its own findings concurred with those of the Lucas Committee, adding: "It is impossible to ascertain how widespread these occurrences are but this Commission is satisfied that in some areas the practices are common." Elsewhere, the Stewart Commission (1983) reported that it has "encountered many breaches of the criminal law and abuses of power by police and other law enforcement officers." In a newspaper interview, Tony Fitzgerald of the Commission of Inquiry into corruption in the Queensland Police said (*The Age*, 13 July 1983):

> I have personally been surprised at the extent of what has come to our attention...I suppose the initial shock is that in what is basically a tranquil society there are any of these

> problems. But that is probably excessively naive. One accepts that there is likely to be some misconduct where there is a confluence of power and affluence.

Among the many allegations and admissions of misconduct arising from the Fitzgerald Inquiry has been the admission of corruption by a (now former) assistant commissioner of the Queensland police: "That was the end of the single rotten apple theory and it also demonstrated how far corruption went" (*The Age*, 13 July 1988). Fitzgerald called for a permanent anticorruption commission in the state, and the Criminal Justice Commission has since been established. New South Wales has also established its Independent Commission against corruption.

Allegations (and findings) of malpractice have not been confined to Queensland. The Beach Inquiry into allegations of misconduct against members of the Victoria Police (1976), the Moffitt Royal Commission of Inquiry in respect of certain matters relating to allegations of organized crime clubs (New South Wales, 1974), and the Lusher Commission into the New South Wales Police Force (1981) all found examples of police malpractice. It is worth repeating that there are no reliable estimates of the pervasivencess of malpractice among Australian police. It ought not be concluded that all Australian police departments are systematically corrupt and regularly condone or encourage the breach of criminal and disciplinary codes. Nevertheless, the findings of the commissions cited above clearly point to significant problems.

In two reports (1975 and 1978), the Australian Law Reform Commission recommended the establishment of specialized investigation units in all police departments. Brown (1985) describes the typical procedure:

> Investigation of public complaints is monitored by Internal Investigation section which reports directly to a Deputy Commissioner or Assistant Commissioner responsible for discipline. More serious complaints, such as commission of criminal offences or mistreatment of prisoners, usually have to be reported to Internal Investigations for a direction as to the subsequent investigation. Where a sustained inquiry is required, a task force of experienced investigatiors may be established. Complaint registers and indexes are maintained to record the progress of the investigation. Public complaints of a minor nature are usually investigated locally, although

line supervisors are not appointed to investigate allegations against members under their direct supervision.

Whatever the veracity of the respective criticisms that have been levelled against complaints investigation procedures, it is clear that the effective and fair monitoring of the behavior of police personnel in matters of malpractice has proved to be an elusive goal. It is not, therefore, surprising that the strengthening of the capabilities of oversight bodies like ombudsmen and complaints authorities has developed apace in recent years with, at least initially, almost universal endorsement. Freckleton and Selby (1988) describe what has happened:

> Police and Police Associations have been significantly involved in the negotiations leading to the vesting of jurisdiction in Ombudsmen and Police Complaints Authorities to monitor the performance of Internal Investigation units around Australia. Generally they have not opposed in principle the existence of external review mechanisms, but have cavilled when it threatened to interfere with the management or operations of police.

The Stewart Royal Commission (1983) cites with approval the Australian Law Reform Commission's view that:

> The machinery for action must be fair and just to the police and public alike. For the appearance of justice and for the protection of the standing of the police, the procedure cannot be left wholly to the police themselves.

Complaints investigation procedures cannot by themselves satisfactorily solve the problems of police malpractice, of course. Many aspects of serious malpractice, such as corruption, take place among willing parties on a convert basis, and there is little opportunity for them to come to light by way of public complaints. Concerted action across the spectrum of police organization and structure has been called for. The Stewart Royal Commission (1983) made a series of wide-ranging recommendations to control corruption (following its recognition that corruption can at best be controlled and moderated rather than eliminated altogether). Among those recommedations are: the setting of strict guidelines concerning the acceptance of gifts, favors, and concessions; the appointment of chief executive officers from outside a particular department; and the establishment of an Inspectorate of Australian Police Forces, along the same lines as the British Chief Inspector of Constabulary. It was this last recommendation that the Commission considered the most powerful potential mechanism for controlling corruption. While this recommendation has not been implemented to date (nor even contemplated, to the writer's knowledge), it is interesting to note, as described above, that several states have before them either suggestions or draft acts regarding the establishment of permanent anticorruption commissions. Stewart, in fact, rejected such a model after the Commission's examination of the structure, powers, and procedures of the best known extant example of such a unit, the Hong Kong Independent Commission Against Corruption.

Swanton (1983) argues that the best and most desirable form of control in policing is self-control. While he acknowledges the difficulties of engendering the requisite professional attitudes amongst police that would allow effective peer review and control, he sees such engendering as vital. Swanton (1983) says:

> If police, both unions and management, do not operate to seize the initiative in areas of disciplinary and ethical control, governments and special interest groups will continue to advocate and introduce control measures diametrically opposed to professionalisation—the very process capable of providing a long-term solution to the problem of police control and accountability.

The focus of this section is upon some aspects of organizational structure. The broad dilemmas imposed upon Australian policing by the tensions between a centralized, highly ranked, hierarchical disciplined service and the realities of autonomous and complex decision making in the operational sphere have already been noted. The Lusher Inquiry into the administration of the New South Wales Police (1981) details the dilemma as follows:

> Senior police officers are very heavily involved in day-to-day events which could easily be, for the most part, dealt with and finalised at lower organisational levels...policy executives are unable to devote adequate attention to policy formation and planning for the future development of the Force. A further consequence is that the skills and capacities have not been developed in police personnel to the extent that would enable them to satisfactorily handle these key management func-

> tions. The practice of referring trivial matters to senior police is also inefficient in that it requires documents to pass through numerous hands on the way up.... Certain talents of younger officers are underutilised.... A new idea has to pass through so many hierarchical levels that it is unlikely to find acceptance at all levels. Senior police have frequently adopted a defensive attitude towards suggestions for change.

Besides the general problem of lack of delegation and incentive for decentralized decision making, the Lusher Inquiry also commented upon the problems generated by dual levels of accountability in many areas of the department, especially in terms of the command and control of specialized officers. A typical example is the deployment of detectives at district and divisional level, where they are nominally responsible to the general duty (uniformed) duty officers, while at the same time they are under the control, often directly, of their CIB chiefs at headquarters. In their submission to the Neesham Inquiry (1985), the Victoria Police Association pointed to a similar phenomenon:

> Within one Police District there are usually officers from the Operations Department (uniformed general duties officers), Crime Department (detectives), and Traffic Department (traffic patrol specialists). Only those from the Operations Department come under the direct control of the Officer in Charge of the District. Those...in the task forces and from Crime and Traffic virtually can enter a District, remain in it for a considerable time, perform good work or create havoc, and leave. The Officer in Charge of the District never knows about it and there is really no system by which he can find out unless we load up the system with further reporting responsibilites. (parentheses added)

The Lusher Inquiry (1981) recommended for New South Wales: "an organisational structure which provided clear lines of responsibility, removed dual control of specialists, encouraged greater delegation and increased district autonomy." When John Avery became commissioner of the New South Wales police some years later, he presided over a large-scale implementation of the Lusher recommendation (*The Bulletin*, 31 May 1988). A consultant study team which reviewed organizational redevelopment for the Neesham Inquiry (1985) in Victoria also recommended sweeping changes. These included a reduction in the number of operational districts, the integration of uniformed crime and traffic departments at a regional level, and a strengthened inspectorate which would supervise regional performance. The Chief Commissioner of the Victoria Police opposed many of the regionalization recommendations on the grounds that there was poor understanding within the department of the implications for such a move, and that it would involve a massive increase in public service (that is, civilian support) infrastructure to allow satisfactory devolution of administrative decision making and management (Neesham Inquiry, 1985). The Inquiry, amongst other considerations, relied upon the finding from its contracted attitude survey amongst members of the department that central administration of the department was seen to constitute problems of morale. Forty-two percent of respondents stated that departmental administration "significantly" lowered morale (Neesham Inquiry 1985). Comments by officers emphasized the lack of delegation, the remoteness of central administration, and the inefficiency of a rigid paramilitary command structure. The Inquiry essentially accepted the recommendations of the study team and argued that regionalization and integration of the three major operational departments should take place. Many of these recommendations have in fact been implemented in Victoria.

The recommendations of the Neesham Inquiry in Victoria and the Lusher Inquiry in New South Wales reflect the identification of enduring problems in Australian policing regarding the capacity of police departments to respond to the needs of professionalized decision making and accountability at all levels of the organization. From their modern conception, Australian police departments were amongst the most highly centralized in the western world. This development made considerable sense in the early days of Australia's history given the relatively small populations in the colonies and states and the absence of a legacy of other forms, such as the military, of law enforcement, and social control. The problems identified in that high degree of centralization in recent years reflect changes in both the work and social environments in which police operate, and in the nature of police organizations themselves. An important aspect of those changes was touched upon in the last section: the growing demands for police to be held accountable not only for the propriety of their occupational behavior, but also for their organizational behavior in terms of budgetary and resource allocations. Once again, it remains to be seen what effect attempts to decentralize police organizations and devolve decision making to smaller more autonomous units will have upon the development of improved accountability.

While at least some state police departments are considering or implementing decentralization initiatives, Swanton (1985) warns of what he sees as the continuing federal centralization of many state police functions. His view of the "steady expansion of federal interests into what was previously a State's domain" (Swanton, 1985), exemplified by the creation of the National Crime Authority in 1984, has already been noted. He argues that this has come about at least partly because of the "puzzling" reluctance of the various police commissioners to form themselves into a group to coordinate state police initiatives in such areas as organized crime (and, by implication, to thus eliminate the necessity of federal intrusion into these areas) (Swanton, 1985). He goes so far as to argue:

> A point has now been reached at which, due to a confluence of technology and political as well as social trends, the developmental process may be slowed..., or even, in some cases, reversed. That is to say, police organisations may experience functional erosion and de-skilling. The present trend to homogeneity, centralisation of exercising of functions and responsibilities that were previously exclusives (sic) of police preserves, could well contribute to a broad decline in police effectiveness.

However, despite Swanton's pessimism, it is not at all apparent that the problems faced by Australian police departments are largely or even significantly functions of federal intrusions. Such intrusions as exist can be seen as responses to existing problems rather than as causes. At the same time, there is little evidence that the fundamental arrangements in which state and territory police retain hegemony over most aspects of traditional law enforcement and order maintenance functions are under major threat. The movement towards greater accountability of police departments need not be seen as an attempt to alter crucially interdepartmental responsibilities. Rather, they would seem to be concerned primarily with rendering more efficient and accountable each individual department, according to the social and political contexts of each polity. Nevertheless, on another reading, Swanton's concerns can be aligned with those expressed at state level regarding some of the negative consequences of enduring or developing centralized bureaucracies which restrain creative problem solving and the development of professionalized policing.

CONCLUSIONS

The present chapter has been an attempt to capture the important characteristics of Australian police and policing. There are three obvious restraints upon such an attempt. First, a comprehensive account would require many more words than were available to the writer. Second, there is much about Australian policing which is under researched or not yet publicly available. Third, there are sufficient diversities within and between Australian police departments to render improbable an acceptably succinct description of what Australian police are like and what they do. Nevertheless, there are commonalities enough in the history, development, and contemporary organizational structures and practices across Australian policing to make the present chapter's contribution worthwhile, as long as the aforementioned qualifications are recognized. At the same time, when the narrative relates exclusively to one or a small number of Australian police departments, from which Australian-wide policing phenomena should not be inferred, then the discussion needs to be treated as particularistic.

In the writer's view, a number of characteristics of Australian policing can be singled out as important in terms of possible comparison with policing in other countries. The first of these is the historical background to the development of Australian police. Australia's relative youth as a nation, its penal colony origins, and the existence of an indigenous culture effectively destroyed by white settlement have left their mark on policing. The rapid development of centralized policing bureaucracies in the colonies in the nineteenth century was in large measure a response to a sparsely-settled land with perceived criminal and public order problems in the shape of aboriginal resistance to white settlement, a dangerous class constituted by convicts, and the perceived anarchy generated by gold discoveries. The later federalization of the country, with the entrenchment of state rights and state mandates over policing and criminal justice, consolidated the strengthening of largely autonomous but firmly centralized state police departments. At the same time, the creation of police in industrial disputes, invariably in favor of employers, in a country which has traditionally had a high rate of unionization, helped create a particular public and occupational image of police.

The net effect of these historical characteristics cannot, of course, be determined with any precision. But it is possible to argue that two crucial outcomes occurred. The first is the significant structure of Australian policing, with its quasi-military hierarchical command apparatus, which owes more in many regards to the Royal Irish Constabulary of the nineteenth century than it does to Peel's more civilianized urban model of 1829. The second outcome is the occupational image generated by early developments. This includes the low social status of policing as an occupation and of police officers as reputable people. Conflicts with particular groups, (such as aboriginals and gold miners) and with the working class in general did little to improve the negative connotations of this image.

The second important characteristic flows to some extent from the first. Recent attempts to improve the calibre of recruits, the training provided within police departments, and the enhancement of career development, all reflect a recognition that these aspects of the organizational administration of Australian policing have been found wanting. The highly bureaucratized nature of Australian policing, with its implications of a conservative public sector, has meant that police departments have been slow to respond to the manifest inadequacies of both the quality of its personnel and the quality of police management.

The third characteristic also relates to the centralized nature of policing in Australia. Until the creation of a number of federal agencies in recent years, state police handled almost all aspects of law enforcement and order maintenance. Their mandate and operational coverage has been, in consequence, probably broader than that found in other countries. Thus state police departments have independently generated a wide range of specialist divisions and officers with, until recently, little interchange or coordination with other state agencies in those spheres. Demographic and organizational differences between states have meant that the development of policing competence and professionalism in these areas has been uneven.

The last two characteristics are at some odds with the negative implications of the previous ones. First, while it is clear that police have endured poor relations with some sectors of the various communities in which they operate, it is also apparent that in contemporary times they enjoy a generally positive public image and degree of respect from the community. Qualifications to that assessment were made elsewhere in this chapter, and we need to have a better understanding of the functional reality of public support for police. Nevertheless, relations between the police and the community in Australia cannot be characterized in general as impoverished. Second, this chapter has highlighted a number of areas where police departments have attempted (or been pressured into) reforms of various sorts. The present writer would describe the processes whereby police are publicly scrutinized regarding their performances and practices, and whereby police allow and at times encourage themselves to be so scrutinized, as democratically healthy. While it is unwise to offer a judgment on the performance, competence, or worth of Australian police departments, it can be argued that Australian society is in the positive position of being able, increasingly, to make such assessments. This would not have been possible had police departments remained isolated and alienated from the communities they serve.

REFERENCES

Articles, Books, and Monographs

American Bar Association. *The Urban Police Function.* Chicago: American Bar Association, 1973.

Avery, J. *Police: Force or Service?* Sydney: Butterworths, 1981.

Bradley, D. and Pursley, R. "Behaviorally Anchored Rating Scales for Patrol Officer Performance Appraisal: Development and Evaluation." *Journal of Police Science and Administration,* 15 (1987): 36-45.

Brennan, F. *Too Much Order With Too Little Law.* St. Lucia, Queensland: University of Queensland Press, 1983.

Brown, G. "Discipline and Accountability." In B. Swanton, G. Hannigan, and T. Psaila (eds). *Police Source Book 2.* Canberra: Australian Institute of Criminology, 1985.

Brown, G. and McNeill, A. *Report on the Victoria Police Personnel Assessment System.* Melbourne: Victoria Police, 1978.

Chappell, D. and Wilson, P. *The Police and the Public in Australia and New Zealand.* St. Lucia, Queensland: University of Queensland Press, 1969.

__________(eds). *Australian Policing.* Sydney: Butterworths, 1988.

Chisholm, R. and Nettheim, G. *Understanding Law: An Introduction to Australia's Legal System.* Sydney: Butterworths, 1978.

Clark, C. M. H. *A History of Australia, Vol. IV.* Victoria: Melbourne University Press, 1978.

__________. *A Short History of Australia.* South Melbourne, Victoria: Macmillan, 1981.

Clyne, R. "South Australia." In B. Swanton, G. Hannigan, and T. Psaila (eds). *Police Source Book 2.* Canberra: Australian Institute of Criminology, 1985.

Critchley, T. *A History of Police in England and Wales: 900-1966.* London: Constable, 1967.

Das, D. "The Image of American Police in Comparative Literature." *Police Studies* 8 (1985): 74-83.

Doherty, V. "Western Australia." In B. Swanton, G. Hannigan, and T. Psaila (eds). *Police Source Book* 2. Canberra: Australian Institute of Criminology, 1985.

Erwin, D. "Tasmania." In B. Swanton, G. Hannigan, and T. Psaila (eds). *Police Source Book* 2. Canberra: Australian Institute of Criminology, 1985.

Finnane, M. (ed). *Policing in Australia: Historical Perspectives.* Kensington, New South Wales: New South Wales University Press, 1987.

Fisse, B. and Braithwaite, J. "Accountability and the Control of Corporate Crime: Making the Buck Stop." In M. Findlay and R. Hogg (eds). *Understanding Crime and Criminal Justice.* Sydney: Law Book Company, 1988.

Fogarty, C. "Training and Education" In B. Swanton, G. Hannigan, and T. Psaila (eds). *Police Source Book 2.* Canberra: Australian Institute of Criminology, 1985.

Foremen, L. and Allan, K. "Promotion Procedures in State and Territory Police Forces." In B. Swanton, G. Hannigan, and T. Psaila (eds). *Police Source Book* 2. Canberra: Australian Institute of Criminology, 1985.

Freckleton, I. "Police and the Media." In I. Freckleton and H. Selby (eds). *Police in Our Society.* Sydney: Butterworths, 1988.

Freckleton, I. and Selby, H. "Piercing the Blue Veil." In D. Chappell and P. Wilson (eds). *Australian Policing.* Sydney: Butterworths, 1988.

__________. "Police Accountability." In M. Findlay and R. Hogg (eds). *Understanding Crime and Criminal Justice.* Sydney: Law Book Company, 1988.

Froemel, E. "Objective and Subjective Measures of Police Officer Performance." In C. Speilberger (ed). *Police Selection and Evaluation.* New York: Praeger, 1979.

Gale, F. and Wundersitz, J. "Police and Black Minorities: The Case of Aboriginal Youth in South Australia." *Australian and New Zealand Journal of Criminology* 20 (1987): 78-94.

Galvin, J. and Polk, K. "Any Truth You Want: The Use and Abuse of Crime and Criminal Justice Statistics." *Journal of Research in Crime and Delinquency* 19 (1982): 135-164.

Goldstein, H. *Policing a Free Society.* Cambridge, Massachusetts: Ballinger, 1977.

Grabosky, P. and Braithwaite, J. "Corporate Crime and Government Response in Australia." In D. Chappell and P. Wilson (eds). *The Australian Criminal Justice System: The Mid 1980s.* Sydney: Butterworths, 1986.

Grabosky, P., Braithwaite, J., and Wilson, P. "The Myth of Community Tolerance Toward White-collar Crime." *Australian and New Zealand Journal of Criminology* 20 (1987): 33-44.

Grabosky, P., Scandia, A., Hazlehurst, K., and Wilson, P. "Aboriginal Deaths in Custody" *Trends and Issues* 12 (1988): Canberra: Australian Institute of Criminology, 1988.

Haldane, R. *The People's Force: A History of the Victoria Police.* Carlton, Victoria: Melbourne University Press, 1986.

Hannigan, G. "Industrial Relations." In B. Swanton, G. Hannigan, and T. Psaila (eds). *Police Source Book 2.* Canberra: Australian Institute of Criminology, 1985.

__________. "Legal Powers and Prosecution." In B. Swanton, G. Hannigan, and T. Psaila (eds). *Police Source Book 2.* Canberra: Australian Institute of Criminology, 1985.

_________. "Queensland." In B. Swanton, G. Hannigan, and T. Psaila (eds). *Police Source Book 2*. Canberra: Australian Institute of Criminology, 1985.

Hazlehurst, K. and Dunn, A. "Aboriginal Criminal Justice." *Trends and Issues*, 13, Canberra: Australian Institute of Criminology, 1988.

Hendry, B. *Retirement from the Victoria Police*. Melbourne: Criminology Department, University of Melbourne, 1988.

Hewitt, L. *Child Sexual Assault Discussion Paper*. Melbourne: Victorian Government Printer, 1984.

Hogg, R. and Findlay, M. "Police and Community." In Freckleton, I. and H. Selby (eds). *Police in Our Society*. Sydney: Butterworths, 1988.

Hughes, R. *The Fatal Shore*. London: Collins,1987.

Inglis, K. *The Australian Colonists*. Carlton, Victoria: Melbourne University Press, 1974.

James, S. *Police Occupation Interview*, Melbourne: Criminology Department, University of Melbourne, 1972.

_________. "Some Observations on Police Selection Methods in Australia." In B. Swanton, G. Hannigan, and T. Psaila (eds). *Police Source Book 2*. Canberra: Australian Institute of Criminology, 1985.

James, S. and Hendry, B. "The Money or the Job? The Decision to Leave Policing." *Australian and New Zealand Journal of Criminology* 24 (1991): 169-189.

James, S. and Polk, K. "Policing Youth Themes and Directons." In D. Chappell and P. Wilson (eds). *Australian Policing*. Sydney: Butterworths, 1988.

James, S., Campbell, I., and Lovegrove, S. "Personality Differentiation in a Police Selection Interview." *Journal of Applied Psychology* 69 (1984): 129-134.

Jones, S. "Police and Public Perceptions of the Police Role: Moving Towards a Reappraisal of Police Professionalism." In J. Yuille (ed). *Police Selection and Training: The Role of Psychology*. Dordrecht, Netherlands: Martinus Nijhoff, 1986.

Lefkowitz, J. "Industrial-Organisational Psychology and the Police." *American Psychologist* 32 (1977): 346-364.

Lester, D., Lewis, T., and Swanton, B. "Cynicism, Job Satisfaction and Locus of Control in Queensland and New Jersey Police Officers." In B.

Swanton, G. Hannigan, and T. Psaila (eds). *Police Source Book 2.* Canberra: Australian Institute of Criminology, 1985.

Lundman, R. *Police and Policing: An Introduction.* New York: Holt, Rinehart and Winston, 1980.

McIver, J. and Parks, R. "Evaluating Police Performance: Identification of Effective and Ineffective Police Action." In R. Bennett (ed). *Police at Work: Policy Issues and Analysis.* Beverly Hills, California: Sage, 1983.

McKillop, S and Vernon, J. (eds). *The Police and the Community.* Canberra: Australian Institute of Criminology, 1991.

Marx, G. "Alternative Measures of Police Performance." In R. Larson (ed). *Police Accountability.* Lexington, Massachusetts: D. S. Heath, 1987.

Milte, K. and Weber, T. *Police in Australia: Developments, Functions, Procedures.* Sydney: Butterworths, 1977.

Muir, W. K. *Police: Street Corner Politicians.* Chicago: University of Chicago Press, 1977.

Mukherjee, S., Walker, J., Psaila, T., Scandia, A., and Dagger, D. *The Size of the Crime Problem in Australia.* Canberra: Australian Institute of Criminology, 1987.

Murray, J. and Borowski, A. "Perspectives on Juvenile Crime and Justice in Australia." In D. Chappell and P. Wilson (eds). *The Australian Criminal Justice System: The Mid 1980s.* Sydney: Butterworths, 1986.

Northern Territory Police. *Staff Development and Appraisal Scheme Manual.* Darwin: Northern Territory Police Department, N.d.

O'Brien, G. *The Australian Police Forces.* Melbourne: Oxford University Press, 1960.

O'Malley, P. *Law, Capitalism and Democracy: A Sociology of Australian Legal Order.* Sydney: George Allen and Unwin, 1983.

Reiner, R. *Blue-Coated Worker: A Sociological Study of Police Unionism.* Cambridge, England: Cambridge University Press, 1978.

Remfrey, P. "Conditions of Service." In B. Swanton, G. Hannigan, and T. Psaila (eds). *Police Source Book 2.* Canberra: Australian Institute of Criminology, 1985.

Rippon, T. "The Rise of Police Militancy." In K. Serong (ed). *Police Industrial Relations Seminar.* Melbourne: Airlie Police College, 1982.

Ronalds, C., Chapman, M., and Kitchener, K. "Policing Aborigines." In M. Findlay, S. Egger, and J. Sutton (eds). *Issues in Criminal Justice Administration.* Sydney: George Allen and Unwin, 1983.

Rowe, K. "Police Recruitment and Selection: Some Vital Conceptual and Practical Issues." In B. Swanton, G. Hannigan, and T. Psaila (eds). *Police Source Book 2.* Canberra: Australian Institute of Criminology, 1985.

Silver, A. "The Demand for Order in Civil Society: A Review of Some Themes in the History of Urban Crime, Police and Riot." In D. Bordua (ed). *The Police: Six Sociological Essays.* New York: Wiley, 1967.

Skolnick, J. *Justice Without Trial: Law Enforcement in a Democratic Society.* New York: Wiley, 1966.

Smith, D. "Police/Community Involvement, A Planned Approach to Effective Crime Control." In B. Swanton, G. Hannigan, and T. Psaila (eds). *Police Source Book 2.* Canberra: Australian Institute of Criminology, 1985.

Stafford, C. "Aborigines: A Comparative Analysis of Institutionalised Racism and Violence." In D. Chappell and P. Wilson (eds). *The Australian Criminal Justice System: The Mid 1980s.* Sydney: Butterworths, 1986.

Sturma, M. "Policing the Criminal Frontier in Mid-nineteenth Century Australia, Britain and America." In M. Finnane (ed). *Policing in Australia: Historical Perspectives.* Kensington, New South Wales: New South Wales University Press, 1987.

Swanton, B. "Developments Affecting Police." In B. Swanton, G. Hannigan, and T. Psaila (eds). *Police Source Book 2.* Canberra: Australian Institute of Criminology, 1985.

__________. "The Police in Australia: A Critical Review." In D. Chappell and P. Wilson (eds). *The Australian Criminal Justice System.* Sydney: Butterworths, 1977.

__________. *Protecting the Protectors.* Canberra: Australian Institute of Criminology, 1983.

Swanton, B., Hannigan, G., and Biles, D. *Police Source Book.* Canberra: Australian Institute of Criminology, 1983.

Swanton B., Wilson P., Walker, J., and Mukherjee, S. "How the Public See the Police: An Australian Survey." 1 *Trends and Issues* 11, Canberra: Australian Institute of Criminology, 1988.

Van Maanen, J. "Police Socialization: A Longitudinal Examination of Job Attitudes in an Urban Police Department." *Administrative Science Quarterly* 20 (1975): 207-228.

"Victoria Police. A Search for Sanity." *Police Life,* (1983): 8-10.

Victorian Ministry for Police and Emergency Services. *A Comparison of Police Selection and Training in Australia.* Melbourne: Victorian Government Printer, 1985.

Ward, P. and Dobinson, I. "Heroin: A Considered Response?" In M. Findlay and R. Hogg (eds). *Understanding Crime and Criminal Justice.* Sydney: Law Book Company, 1988.

Ward, R. *The Australian Legend.* Melbourne: Oxford University Press, 1970.

Wardlaw, G. "Drug Control and Organised Crime." In M. Findlay and R. Hogg (eds). *Understanding Crime and Criminal Justice.* Sydney: Law Book Company, 1988.

Whitrod, R. "The Accountability of Police—Who Polices the Police?" In K. Milte and T. Weber (eds). *Police in Australia: Developments, Functions, Procedures.* Sydney: Butterworths, 1977.

Wilson, P. "Public Attitudes to the Police." A paper delivered to the *Australian and New Zealand Association for the Advancement of Science Centenary Congress,* May 1988.

__________. "Professional Crime: The Case of Doctors." In D. Chappell and P. Wilson (eds). *The Australian Criminal Justice System: The Mid 1980s.* Sydney: Butterworths, 1986.

Wilson, P. and Western, J. *The Policeman's Position Today and Tomorrow: An Examination of the Victoria Police.* St. Lucia, Queensland: University of Queensland Press, 1972.

Reports and Determinations of State and Federal Commissions, Committees and Boards (available from respective State or Commonwealth Government Printer)

Australian Law Reform Commission. *Complaints Against Police,* 1975.

__________. *Complaints Against Police*—supplementary report, 1978.

Report of the Board of Inquiry into Allegations Against Members of the Victoria Police Force, (Beach), 1976.

Report of the Royal Commission on the September Moratorium Demonstration, (Bright), 1971.

Report of the Royal Commission on the Activities of the Federated Ship Painters and Dockers Union, (Costigan), 1984.

Report of Commission of Inquiry into Possible Illegal Activities and Associated Police Misconduct, (Fitzgerald), 1989.

Report of the Committee of Inquiry Into the Enforcement of Criminal Law in Queensland, (Lucas), 1977.

Report of Inquiry Into New South Wales Police Administration, (Lusher), 1981.

Report of the Royal Commission of Inquiry in Respect of Certain Matters Relating to Allegations of Organised Crime in clubs, (New South Wales) (Moffitt), 1974.

Royal Commission of Inquiry Into Aboriginal Deaths in Custody, (Muirhead), 1988-1990.

Report of the Committee of Inquiry into the Victoria Police Force, (Neesham), 1985.

Report of the Royal Commission of Inquiry into Drug Trafficking, (Stewart), 1983.

Report of the Royal Commission into Drugs, (Williams), 1984.

Victorian Police Service Board *Determination 308*, 1980.

Annual Reports

Australian Bureau of Statistics (1987)

Police Board of New South Wales (1984)

Police Complaints Authority (Victoria) (1986/87)

Victoria Police (1981)

Victoria Police (1986)

Victoria Police (1986/87)

Victoria Police (1989/90)

Victoria Police Statistical Review (1986/87)

Newspapers and Magazines

The Age:

20 January 1984

26 January 1984

2 February 1984

13 February 1988

15 February 1988

24 February 1988

24 April 1988

8 June 1988

22 June 1988

4 July 1988

13 July 1988

The Bulletin:

31 May 1988

POLICE IN FINLAND

by Ahti Laitinen

INTRODUCTION

The following brief description of the sociopolitical environment and the history of Finland is intended to serve as a prelude to the account of the police. As the police are closely linked to the social and cultural milieu of the country, this description is expected to help in understanding the developments in regard to the police in Finland.

Finland is one of five Scandinavian countries, namely Denmark, Iceland, Norway, and Sweden. The social and political systems in these countries are very similar to each other. There is strong cooperation among the Nordic countries. The total area of the country is 338,145 sq. kilometers; it is the one of the largest countries in Europe. The population of Finland is about five million and the population density of the country is low. Administratively, the country is divided into 12 provinces. There are 461 municipalities which have been, since 1977, two different types: urban municipalities and rural municipalities. The majority of inhabitants are mostly formal members of the Lutheran Church, which is an official state church.

Finland is a bilingual country. The official languages are Finnish and Swedish, but the Swedish-speaking people are only 6 percent of the whole population. Although the Swedish-speaking part of the population is a small minority, its economic and political position has traditionally been strong. Two other ethnic minorities, the

Gypsies (approximately 6,000) and the Lapps (approximately 3,000) are in weak positions.

Up until 1809 Finland was a part of Sweden and thereafter till 1917, it remained annexed to the imperial Russia as a Grand Duchy. The imperial Russian connection as a Grand Duchy of the Russian Czar was a result of the 1808-1809 war. It was in 1917 that Finland got her independence. After she became free from the Russian control at the time of the Bolshevik Revolution in 1917, she chose to become a parliamentary democracy with an elected president as the head of the country.

There are more than fifteen political parties in Finland. The leading political parties in governments after the Second World War have been the Center Party (agrarians) and the Social Democratic Party. Sometimes, also, the Communists have participated in coalition governments. The National Coalition Party (conservative) has been a leading opposition party. After 1986 there has been a coalition government of Social Democrats and Conservatives in the country. Presently the Center Party is the main opposition party. Almost all governments during the last 20 years have been committed to consensual politics.

In its relations with other countries Finland had been neutral after the Second World War. It was not a member of any bloc or treaty organization. In 1948 Finland signed a Treaty of Friendship, Cooperation and Mutual Assistance with the then Soviet Union which accepted the neutrality of the country. Finland is a member of European Free Trade Association (EFTA), but it does not belong to the European Community. In 1973 a mutual agreement was made between the European Economic Community (EC) and Finland. At present the issue of European integration and relationships with the EC countries is a challenge to the Finnish politicians. The economic advantages of Finland demand integrated relationships and cooperation with other European countries. Fortunately, the fear that political neutrality of the country may be put in jeopardy by the membership in this organization has become irrelevant today.

MANDATE AND PHILOSOPHY

To give an account of the mandate and philosophy of the police in Finland, it is necessary to look at the history and evolution of the Finnish police. The history of the Finnish police dates back to the Middle Ages when Finland was part of the Kingdom of Sweden. At that time, public order in towns was maintained differently from that in the countryside. In fact, it was not until new legislation was passed in the 1960s that these differences were done away with. The beginning of the real police institutions is closely associated with the industrialization in the 1800s. We can, however, find certain types of police activities a long time before that period.

The towns of Sweden-Finland were at first allowed broad autonomy in keeping public order. According to a town law enacted in the 1350s, the maintenance of public order and safety was the responsibility of town councils, although the King's bailiff was supposed to keep watch over it. In the seventeenth century, the administration began to be concentrated in the Crown. An indication of this development was that the administration of the towns was transferred from the town councils to royally appointed provincial governors. Various classes of civil servants existed for maintaining order and public safety. So called "Servants of the Town" were closest to what we now call police officers. In 1776 an ordinance for improving the deteriorating order and public safety of Stockholm, joint capital of Sweden and Finland, was passed and it created the position of the Master of Police (Jousimaa, 1986).

Compared to other countries, police departments in Finnish towns were established early. The first Chamber of Police under the Czar was established in 1816 in Turku, the capital of Finland until the Russian occupation. While the famous London Metropolitan Police was established in 1829, The Chamber of Police in Helsinki, the contemporary capital of Finland, started functioning in 1826. The duty of these chambers was to keep order, prevent crime, maintain peace, and to act as a court for minor offenses. The Chamber of Police's judicial powers were not abolished until 1897. Since the State appointed the members of the Chambers of Police, there was a considerable governmental authority over the police.

Following the example of Turku and Helsinki, the other large towns in Finland received their own Chamber of Police, and the policemen were given uniforms. In 1861 the expression "Police

Department" was officially used for the first time. At the turn of the century town police were divided into the uniform and the detective or plainclothes branches. During 1903 and 1904, town police finally became part of the state administration. This, however, did not immediately result in any improvement in the handling of police affairs, as noted in a report of the Ministry of Justice in 1906 which referred to the various shortcomings in the police. Politics, it was alleged, had interfered in police operations. Nonetheless, the town police continued to be administered under the system described above in the early years of independence until 1925 (Jousimaa, 1986).

The primary reason for the early establishment of the Finnish Police Chambers was not the increasing population of the cities as it was in many other countries. The Russian authorities wanted to have a strict control over the citizen's movement. When the Russian General-Governor (the top representative of the Czar in Finland) in 1870s and 1880s demanded the increasing number of policemen in Helsinki, the Helsinki city council resisted the proposal very strongly. It resulted in a fight for power between the rich Finnish citizens and Russian state officials because the Helsinki city council regarded the police as the tool of Russian emperors. At the end of 1800s the situation changed. The Russians began to integrate Finland more closely with Russia. The nationalists in Finland considered it reasonable to develop the Finnish police for avoiding Russian integration. On the other hand a revolutionary working class emerged in Finland. A strong police were considered to be important for Finnish bourgeoisie.

Policing in rural areas was originally different from urban areas. Progress regarding the development of policing in the countryside was slower. Old provincial laws make mention of country sheriffs as some sort of order keepers. In the sixteenth century, independent feudal lords became King's bailiffs and it was their duty to oversee the state of law and order. Sheriffs were originally the people's representatives to the king, and prosecution was one of the sheriff's many functions. After the sixteenth century, however, the sheriff was appointed by the King's bailiff, and he was the representative of the state entrusted with administrative duties including maintenance of law and order. Since the sheriff's office required a certain amount of personal expenditure in carrying out of some duties, wealthy peasants were usually selected for the post.

During 1634 and 1635, the administrative system of Sweden-Finland was overhauled. The governors became King's bailiffs and administrative districts were known as "kihlakunta." According to the Ordinance of 1688, the administration of the district was placed under the direct jurisdiction of the King's bailiff and it included many responsibilities including the supervision of law and order and prosecution. By the Royal Decree of 1675, provincial governors were required to appoint sheriffs. They were to be loyal peasants living in the area. The duties of King's bailiff were later transferred to the sheriff (Jousimaa, 1986).

Originally sheriff's duties were proclaimed in 1814 by the General-Governor which remained valid until 1898 when rural police were given their own statutes and regulations. At the end of the last century different alternatives were considered for improving policing in the countryside. It was decreed in 1891 that each sheriff's office would have a sufficient number of constables hired by the state. Constables were appointed by the provincial governor. Since then policing in the countryside has been the responsibility of the state and the role of the communes has been only nominal (Sinisalo, 1971). Town and rural police were brought under the same set of regulations by the Police Act of 1925. Towns, however, still had the responsibility of providing one-third of the cost of the police department. This financial burden was removed in 1977.

There were other police reforms. The police became civil servants under the jurisdiction of the Ministry of Interior. A special police affairs department was created to direct, supervise and coordinate police operations of the country. Under the twelve provincial governors, there were police inspectors in the provinces for police affairs. Criminal investigation improved in 1927 following the creation of additional positions for detectives in the provinces. These positions were transferred to provincial criminal investigation police units started in 1938. In 1926 a Crime Research Center was set up in Helsinki which was also entrusted with the local Interpol responsibilities. In 1955 the Central Criminal Investigation Department was formed in the country's capital, Helsinki, by the combination of the Crime Research Center and the Criminal Investigation Center of the Uusimaa province.

At the end of the 1920s and the early 1930s many occurrences of unrest and civil disturbances took place in Finland. One reason was the political situation of the time and another was the Alcohol

Prohibition Law of the period. At this time a Mobile Command Force was commissioned to deal with the situation. Over the years this Command Force was given additional duties, its personnel were increased and in this way the present Mobile Police was formed. The Second World War interrupted the active development of the police. During the war the historical office of the King's bailiff was abolished and the bailiff's duties were transferred to the sheriff. The statute regulating inspectors of police in the provinces was amended and they were given the power of prosecutor in addition to administrative and law enforcement duties.

Until the end of the Second World War there was a police unit called the State Police charged, in practice, with the task of preventing communist activities in the country. Formally, their main task was to deal with activities against the state. After the temporary peace agreement with the Soviet Union in 1944, the State Police unit was led till 1949 by Communists or left-wing officials. During this period the main duty of the State Police was to reveal the activities against the Soviet Union. They were abolished in the beginning of 1949. A unit of Security Police, with lesser authority than that of the ordinary police and without a political agenda, was established.

The Police Act (No. 84/1966) was put in operation in 1967. It was the first comprehensive law in Finland covering all police activities. It cancelled all separate regulations governing different branches of the police. In 1973 the Act was amended and provisions were made for advisory boards in units. This allowed members of the public limited opportunities to actively cooperate with the police (Jousimaa, 1986). In 1973 the Police Department of the Ministry of the Interior became the Supreme Command of Police in Finland while police bureaus were given the command of police in the provinces. The new legislation did not change the field organization of the police. The Central Criminal Investigation Department was reinforced by putting the remaining provincial criminal police units within it.

As the figures in Table 1 covering a period of twenty-six years between 1960 and 1986 show, the number of sworn and civilian personnel working in police departments all over the country increased slowly all the time. The figures do not include the sworn personnel and civilians working in the Finnish province (laani) of Aland which is an island with an autonomous status in Turku archipelago.

TABLE 1: THE NUMBER OF POLICE OFFICERS AND OTHER PERSONNEL

Year	Police	Civilians	Total	Police/ population ratio
1960	6,161	872	7,033	1.39
1961	6,258	883	7,141	1.40
1962	6,700	1,103	7,803	1.49
1963	6,777	1,117	7,894	1.50
1964	6,928	1,143	8,071	1.52
1965	7,056	1,171	8,227	1.55
1966	7,119	1,134	8,253	1.55
1967	7,286	1,156	8,442	1.58
1968	7,292	1,186	8,478	1.58
1969	7,370	1,191	8,561	1.60
1970	7,330	1,249	8,579	1.60
1971	7,374	1,467	8,841	1.60
1972	7,398	1,555	8,953	1.59
1973	7,649	1,851	9,500	1.64
1974	7,761	2,932	10,693	1.65
1975	7,769	2,984	10,753	1.65
1976	7,776	3,093	10,969	1.67
1977	7,880	3,130	1,1010	1.66
1978	7,891	3,145	1,1036	1.66
1979	7,899	3,163	11,062	1.66
1980	7,941	3,216	11,157	1.66
1981	8,011	3,216	11,377	1.67
1982	8,126	3,386	11,512	1.68
1983	8,211	3,378	11,589	1.69
1984	8,226	3,414	11,640	1.69
1985	8,239	3,424	11,663	1.69
1986	8,252	3,348	11,600	1.69

(*Source: Committee Report,* 1986).

In Figures 1 and 2 the number of police officers and the ratio of police officers per 1,000 inhabitants are shown. It can be seen that the number of police officers has increased from 1960 to 1986 by

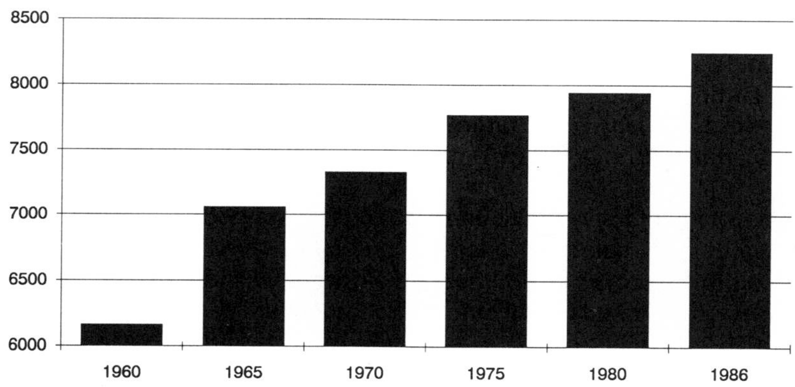

Fig. 1: The Number of Police Officers Over the Years

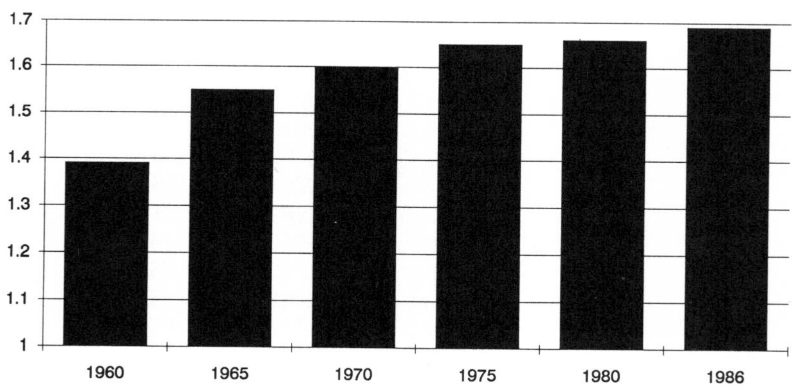

Fig. 2: Police Officers per 1,000 Inhabitants During the Same Period.

about 34 percent. Nevertheless, the growth per 1,000 inhabitants is quite small.

The size of the local police as a whole is large compared with all other groups of the police. This position in 1986 which developed at the end of a period of continuous growth beginning in 1960 is illustrated in Figure 3.

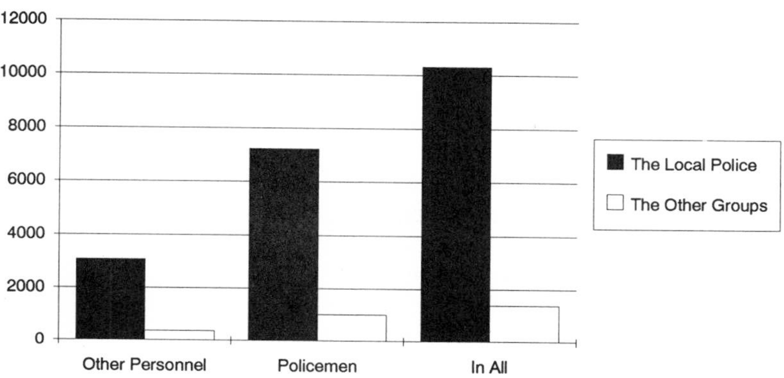

Fig. 3: The Number of Police Personnel in Different Groups.

In Finland the police are part of the state administration. It was the first Nordic country with a purely national police organization at the beginning of this century. In Norway the police were nationalized in 1937, in Denmark 1938, and in Sweden 1965. The most important laws for the police in Finland are the Police Act of 1966 (No. 84/1966) and the Police Decree passed in 1985 (No. 737/1985) which bestow on the Ministry of the Interior the powers and authority of supervising the country's police. Accordingly, the police have traditionally been under the control of this ministry. In the other Nordic countries the police come under the Ministry of Justice.

FUNCTIONS

Based on the relevant laws[1] and regulations, the functions of the police can be described briefly as follows:

I Emergency duties

II Supervising activities:

1. General supervision
2. Maintenance of public order
3. Traffic control
4. Supervision over foreigners
5. Miscellaneous functions

III Investigation work

IV Administrative tasks:

1. Administration of public licenses
2. Rescue work

V Preventive work

1. Preventive information
2. Justice and traffic education for the public
3. Youth work
4. Crime prevention activities
5. Community policing

VI Prosecution and recovery proceedings

VII Protection of the safety of the state

VIII Executive assistance

According to the research findings, different emergency duties of the police have increased during recent years. There are two main purposes for emergency duties. First, the state authorities want to guarantee that citizens are able to contact police at any time in the day and night. Second, emergency duties, among some other things, help to organize the police through patrols and communication centers. The most important parts of general supervision are maintenance of public order and traffic control. These are mainly concentrated in populated, urban areas. A typical task of the Finnish police and, also, a problem, is the control and arrest of drunken persons in order to help maintain public order. Annually, the number of the arrested drunks is more than 2,000,000 which is high compared to the population of Finland consisting of 5,000,000 inhabitants.

Traffic is controlled by the Mobile Police who operate centrally and, also, the local police engaged in general police duties. One part of the traffic control is the regulation of the boat traffic on the lakes and the seas. In 1984 Mobile Police spent about 43 percent of their working hours in traffic control. The corresponding figure for the local police is four to five percent. Controlling speed limits is one primary traffic police responsibility.

All decision making concerning foreigners is made by the Bureau for Aliens at the Department for Police Affairs in the Ministry of the Interior. Their tasks can be described as follows:

- Administration of the different licenses which include:
    (1) residence permits/working permits
    (2) visas
    (3) frontier crossing permits
- Citizenship affairs with such activities as:
    (4) citizenship applications
    (5) announcements of the citizenship
    (6) different certificates concerning citizenships

Deportations, different inquiries, and passport control are also undertaken by the police in this connection.

Miscellaneous supervising functions are numerous. Enumerated below are the areas in which supervision is at least partially a police task. Some of these tasks are:

(1) Trade and business
(2) Entertainment and games
(3) Traffic affairs
(4) Social security and health
(5) Legal administration
(6) Internal administration
(7) Economic and environment administration
(8) Miscellaneous administrative matters

The investigation activities are handled by the Central Criminal Police as well as the local police. Presented in the figures on the next page are the recent crime statistics and the crime trends to indicate police activities in this regard.

Compared to the other Scandinavian countries, Finland has the lowest theft rate. This is explained by the prosperity, urbanization, and population density differences between the nations. In narcotic offenses Finland again ranks the lowest. With regard to assaults, Finland and Sweden rank well above both Norway and Denmark.

One branch of administrative activities is the administration of public licenses. This branch is wide and versatile. However, it is confined to three main areas: driving licenses, registrations of vehicles, and issuing of passports.

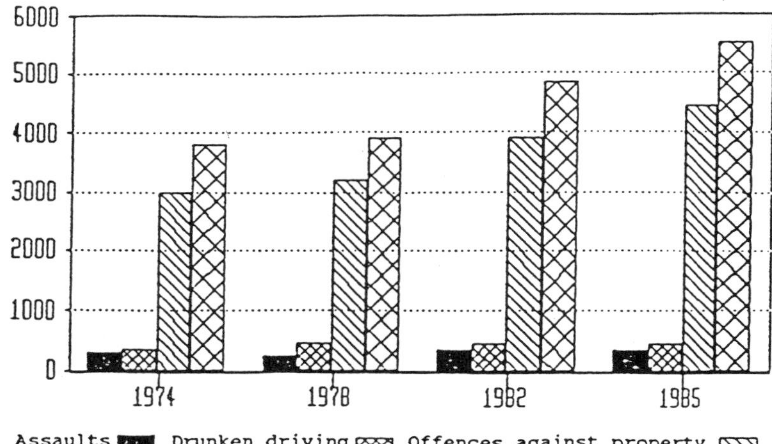

Fig. 4: Rates of Some Crimes in Finland Per 100,000 Inhabitants (*Source:* Rikollisuustilanne, 1979, 1986).

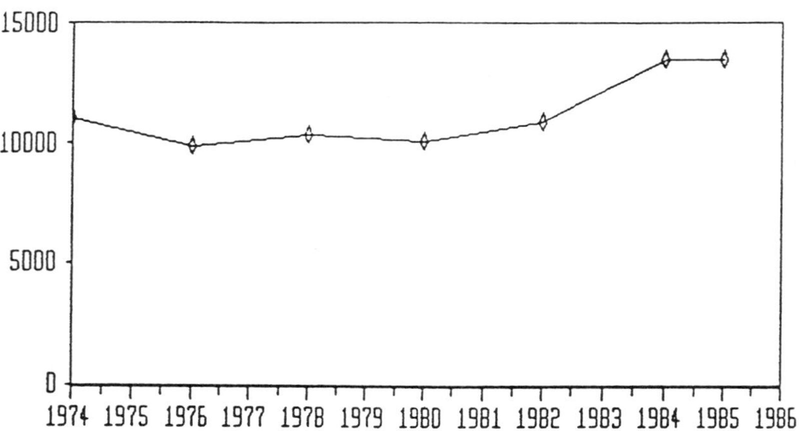

Fig. 5: Rates of All Crimes in Finland Per 100,000 Inhabitants (Source: Rikollisuustilanne, 1979, 1986).

The following list includes the licenses the police are competent to issue:

(1) Guns and shooting facilities
(2) Lotteries, games and collections
(3) Trade and business
(4) Entertainment
(5) Traffic matters such as (a) drivers' licenses; (b) licenses for public carriers; (c) special transportation licenses; (d) registrations of vehicles; (e) passport and identity cards; (f) matters pertaining to foreigners including visas; and (g) miscellaneous.

Another aspect of administrative activities is rescue work. The police are responsible for the planning and execution of different rescue operations together with other state officials.

Preventive work, the preventing of crime and accidents, began in 1930s on a voluntary basis. At the beginning such work was mainly traffic-related. During 1960s preventive work was institutionalized and at the moment it is an essential part of policing. The police arrange and deliver lectures on justice and traffic education for school children. In 1983 such lectures amounted to 22,500 hours for 525,000 children. At the time of writing the number of policemen participating in youth work was 620 and they devoted approximately 44,000 hours to this work annually.

Community policing was not initiated in Finland until 1978. In 1981 official instructions were issued on the matter. At present, there are about 160 community police officers in some 40 different police districts and those engaged in this work approximately two percent of the entire police force in Finland. The principal forms of community policing are block policing and area policing. In block policing, a police officer is assigned to a certain neighborhood, where he becomes its "own" officer. Neighborhoods are usually city areas, suburbs, and municipal blocks. The officer has his own office in the area where at certain times he is available to the public. Area policing involves subdivision of the police districts into smaller areas.The primary responsibility for a particular area is assigned to one officer although other police officers also work in the area. This special officer is expected to develop a close relationship with the residents and understand their problems better.

Generally, area officers operate without a local office, the area may be more artificially delineated, and it may include a larger locality than a block officers' jurisdiction (Mantila, 1987).

Prosecution and recovery proceedings fall within the jurisdiction of the Ministry of Justice. The highest-ranking prosecutor is the Chancellor of Justice and sheriffs are the prosecutors in their respective areas. The security police are responsible for some special tasks in connection with the security of the state. Two main tasks that they perform are counterintelligence and deterrence of terrorism. According to the Police Decree, the police must provide assistance to all officials, with such executive assistance from the police being regulated separately for every branch of administration.

According to a *Committee Report* (1986) the police have engaged as follows in 1985:

Administrative tasks	4.8
Emergency duties (patrols)	27.6
Supervising functions	23.3
Crime prevention	1.2
Investigation	27.2
Miscellaneous matters	15.6

(*Source: Committee Report*, 1986)

All police functions are administered in a sense by the Department of Police Affairs located at the Ministry of the Interior. The Statute for the Ministry was issued in 1926, when the Department for Police Affairs came into being. Since its inception the Department for Police Affairs has undergone many changes. It became the highest policy-making body for the Police only in 1973. The Police Department, and through it the entire police force, is under the control of the government. The department's civil servants report to the cabinet. This means that all far-reaching decisions are made at the ministerial level. The Ministry of the Interior gives the basic guidelines for police operations and is, therefore, continuously kept informed of important police matters. Since its inception in the year 1926, the Department of Police Affairs in the Ministry of the Interior has been the Supreme Command of the police supervising all these tasks allocated to the country's police. In order to administer the various responsibilities, this department functions in five bureaus with the personnel shown against each of these bureaus as follows:

(1) Administrative Bureau	17
(2) Police Bureau	13
(3) Technical Bureau	10
(4) Bureau for Aliens Affairs	41
(5) Automatic Data Processing Bureau	11

The principal tasks of different bureaus are briefly enumerated below:

Administrative Bureau

- Legislation
- Territorial division of police administration
- Economic planning and budgeting
- Personnel administration
- Establishment and control of associations
- Control of business affairs
- Control of lottery and collections
- Information and public relations
- Labor protection

Police Bureau

- Public order and safety
- Leadership and management of policing
- Transfer of criminals
- Granting of police authorities
- Police training and study trips of policemen
- Labor research and rationalizing
- Physical education and sports of policemen
- Police dogs
- Appeals (complaints)

Technical Bureau

- Police storage depots and the Police Dog Institute
- Real estate and apartments
- Equipment, tools, and fixtures

- Confiscation of the objects
- Graves of foreign soldiers

Bureau for Aliens Affairs

- Finnish citizenships
- The supervision of foreigners travelling and resident in Finland
- Passport control and frontier crossing (This has been taken away from the police recently.)

Automatic Data Processing Bureau

- Automatic data processing

Included within the functions of the Department of Police Affairs are the duties performed by such sections as (1) the Police School and the Police College; (2) the Police Dog Institute; (3) the Police Storage Depots; (4) the Central Criminal Police; (5) the Mobile Police; and (6) the Security Police.

The Police School and the Police College are responsible for the training of police personnel in Finland. Police training will be discussed later which will show the various functions performed by these institutions in the field of police training, continuing education, and professional advancement.

The tasks of the Police Dog Institute are acquisition of dogs suitable for police work, and the training of dogs and their handlers. In addition, the Institute is in charge of tactical development of the dogs. There has been a tendency in Finland in recent years to put police dogs into groups in the operationally most important police districts. This has resulted in better emergency capabilities. It has been possible to use the special vehicles required for dog patrolling more effectively and advanced training has been easier to organize.

The work of police dog squads, which is part of the public order and safety, is accomplished in special vans. In disturbance-prone areas patrolling is done on foot. With the help of police dog patrols criminals have often been caught successfully at the scene of the crime or tracked and caught in Finland's forest. (It is easy to become lost in a sparsely populated country with large, heavily forested areas, such as Finland.) The prompt use of police dogs in locating persons lost in forests has saved many lives each year. Dog searches for drugs and bombs during and after the 1970s and 1980s became a new duty. Some police dogs and their handlers have had special training in these duties in addition to the basic training.

The Police Storage Depots are responsible for the arms, cars, information systems, and other equipment. At the time of writing the number of personnel working in the different police depots was about 70.

An important segment of police duties is criminal investigation. Crimes are usually investigated first by the local police and the difficult cases are handled with the cooperation of the Central Criminal Police. According to the Police Act, the duty of the Central Criminal Police is to investigate crimes which, due to the complicatedness of the investigation or other reasons, are not suitable for the local police. The Central Criminal Police provide scientific and technical assistance to local police in investigation.

The Central Criminal Police headquarters are in Helsinki. There is a provincial department for investigation in every province. The Criminal Police Department is divided into five bureaus, namely, the Bureau of General Administration, Bureau of Investigation, Bureau of Fingerprints, Criminal Laboratory, and Information Bureau, which keeps the different kinds of national registers and maintains liaison with the Interpol. In the Tundra area of Lapland an officers' unit composed of two individuals from the Central Criminal Police is in charge of investigation of crimes regarding reindeer. The number of the personnel employed by the Central Criminal Police was 342 persons at the time of writing.

The Mobile Police operate throughout the whole country. They maintain a branch in each province and these branches are divided into command forces (29 such units at the time of writing) which are located in the larger communities. The headquarters, located in Helsinki, also constitute the branch for the province of Uusimaa. Their strength was 199 at the time of writing.

The Police Act states that the Mobile Police must assist other police units, maintain public order and safety, aid in crime prevention and traffic control as well as function as the national police reserve. The Police Act divides the Mobile Police's primary duties into four categories: (1) the control, organization and guidance of land traffic as well as traffic education and research; (2) the prevention of the illegal importation of alcoholic beverages and their unauthorized manufacture, transport, or sales; (3) the supervision of water traffic, hunting, fishing, and nature conservation; and (4) assisting other police units in searches and investigations and in capturing fugitives from justice. In addition, the Mobile Police aid other authorities and perform such additional duties as are specifically assigned to them by the Ministry of the Interior. The special duties of the Mobile Police include the provision of security for the President of the Republic, passport control at some border stations, police operations at Helsinki-Vantaa airport, and providing police escort for state visitors.

As mentioned previously, the present Security Police were established in 1948. Their main duties are investigation of crimes against the State, operations against anti-state activities, prevention of terrorism, surveillance of subversive elements, and other tasks of similar nature. They are divided into bureaus with district offices in various parts of Finland.

The distribution of the police personnel in different sectors of policing is presented in Table 2. It should be noted that the table does not include the personnel working in the autonomous province of Aland where there are 80 sworn and nine civilians at the police department at the time of writing.

TABLE 2: THE NUMBER OF POLICE PERSONNEL IN DIFFERENT SECTORS

	Police	Civilians	Total
Local Police	7,222	3,076	10,298
Central Criminal Police	191	151	342
Security Police	94	54	148
The Mobile Police	722	57	779
Police Academies	24	41	65
Police Storage Depots	70	70	70

(*Source:Committee Report*, 1986).

The duties of the police may also be understood by looking at the organization of the police. The Finnish police are organized in three levels. The Central administration is located in the Ministry of the Interior; the regional police administration is handled at the level of the provincial governments; and within the provinces there are the local police units in the cities, old and new, and rural areas. The organization in its various dimensions is shown in Figure 6.

One special department in each county government is the police department. The duties of these units are similar to those of the Department for Police Affairs in the Ministry of the Interior. They, however, act only on the provincial level. Therefore, any detailed description of the county-level administration of the police will not be presented. At the time of writing Finland had 461 municipalities and 253 police districts. There were urban police departments in 29 municipalities and 432 municipalities were grouped into 224 rural police districts. While 33 police districts operated on an individual

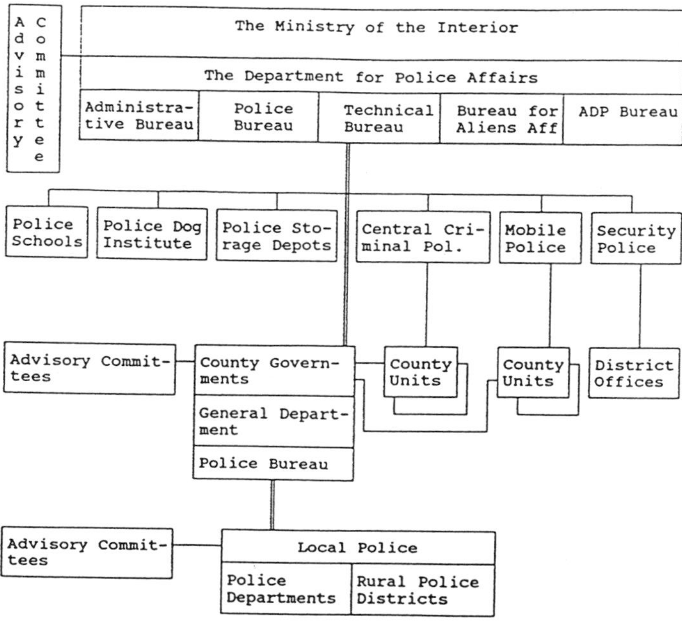

Fig. 6: Police Organization in Finland

basis, 220 of them operated through 66 cooperative centers. These departments share resources and duties with others on a cooperative basis.

Urban police departments are located in the towns established before 1960. In Helsinki, the capital of Finland, the police department which has more than 2,000 personnel is divided into several units. They are administrative, public order and safety, and criminal investigation units. Although in smaller towns the number of personnel is smaller, the organizational structure is basically the same as in Helsinki.

A rural police district of medium size is headed by a Sheriff who is assisted by a commissioned office, a komisario, and about 15 sergeants and constables. The largest rural police districts are divided into divisions such as public order and safety, traffic, criminal investigation, and administration. The last mentioned division handles, among other things, a variety of permits and the collection of debts. The urban police have no debt collection duties.

Most police districts in Finland are small (10 to 12 policemen) with no division of labor. In these districts every police officer attends to all kinds of duties. A separate administrative unit, however, usually exists staffed by two to four female civilian employees. While police duties are performed only by men and women who have gone through police training, clerical jobs are carried out by those employees with general office clerks' training and a special course in police administration.

Analyzing the cost of policing for performing the legally mandated functions, based on annual national budgets of Finland, it is seen that the police share is quite low (see Table 3).

TABLE 3: THE PERCENTAGE SHARE OF POLICING IN ANNUAL BUDGETS

Year	Share of policing
1980	1.52
1981	1.63
1982	1.57
1983	1.55
1984	1.40

Year	Share of Policing
1985	1.39
1986	1.45
1987	1.44
1988	1.55

The cost of policing as reflected in annual budgets has been quite steady during 1980s, and, compared with many other countries, it is really low. Mostly the annual rise in the cost of policing has been lower than the total increase of the budgets. (See Figure 7 below.)

Some explanations can be presented for this situation. One of the main tasks of the police is to prevent and investigate crimes. Compared with most European countries the level of criminality is low in Finland. Further the problems related to drugs and minorities are minimal. There is no problem with terrorism. Finland is a peripheral European country, its population is low (about 5 million inhabitants), but its area is large (the fourth largest in

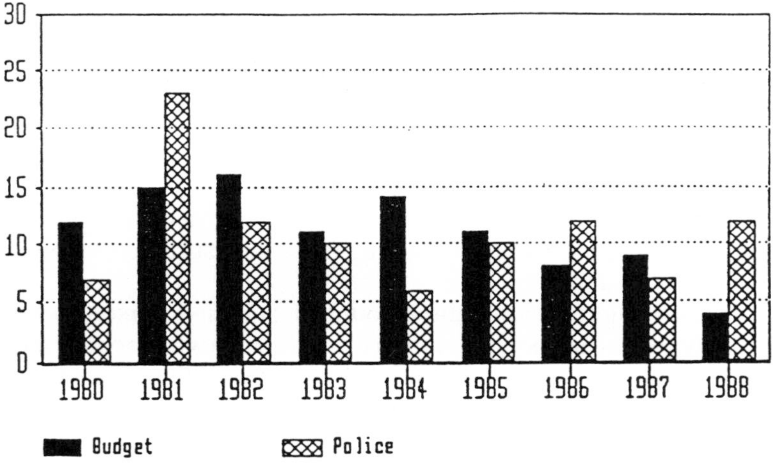

Fig. 7: Comparison of the Rise of Annual Budgets With the Cost of Policing

Europe). Industrialization and urbanization in the country have taken place late. Both started in large scale only after the Second World War. In Finland there are only two small minorities: about 6,000 Gypsies in different parts of the country, and a few thousand Lapps who live in the northernmost part of the country. On the other hand the Finnish policy toward aliens has been very restrictive—too restrictive in many citizens' minds—and that is why the number of foreign refugees is very low. There are only a few hundred immigrants mostly from Vietnam and Chile who have settled in the country.

It is, however, necessary to mention that as the European countries are drawing closer, there are considerable fears in Finland that drug, terrorism and other criminal problems of Europe may spread in this country, too. This is why in the recent years there has been a demand for stronger policing, tighter immigration policy, and better security arrangements.

PERSONNEL PRACTICES

Recruitment: In Finland there is no special bureau for recruitment and the main reason is that there have always been more applicants than those who qualify (about eight to nine percent of the former) for admission to the police school. In Finland the reasons people are drawn to police work are the variety and flexibility of the job; the short, cost-free training; good salaries; career opportunities; and job security (*Committee Report*, 1985).

An overall picture with the school levels of those who apply for entry into the police school including those who succeed is shown by Tables 4 and 5.

As these figures show, the amount of qualified persons who have passed the school graduation examination (who are referred to as "students" in Finland) has been growing all the time. In the late 1980s it is about 80 percent. A more detailed description about formal qualifications is provided ahead.

TABLE 4: APPLICANTS TO THE POLICE CADET COURSES AND THEIR SCHOOLING BACKGROUND BETWEEN 1974 AND 1984 (With Percentages in Parenthesis)

Year	Basic School	Middle School	High School	Total
1974	1,521(47.7)	1,088(34.1)	1,582(18.2)	3,191(100)
1975	1,314(38.7)	1,417(41.7)	1,664(19.6)	3,395(")
1976	1,434(33.9)	1,741(41.2)	1,051(24.9)	4,226(")
1977	599(23.4)	1,077(43.3)	850(33.3)	2,556(")
1978	816(17.7)	2,080(45.1)	1,720(37.2)	4,616(")
1979	767(16.4)	2,012(43.0)	1,898(40.6)	4,677(")
1980	595(15.1)	1,677(42.6)	1,668(42.3)	3,940(")
1981	361(12.7)	1,133(39.7)	1,357(47.6)	2,851(")
1982	443(14.0)	1,325(41.8)	1,404(44.2)	3,172(")
1983	497(13.3)	1,420(38.0)	1,820(48.7)	3,737(")
1984	370(10.9)	1,269(37.3)	1,764(51.8)	3,403(")
Total	8,717(21.9)	16,269(40.9)	14,778(37.2)	39,764(100)

TABLE 5: QUALIFIED PERSONS TO POLICE CADET COURSES AND THEIR SCHOOLING BACKGROUND BETWEEN 1974 AND 1984

Year	Basic School	Middle School	High School	Total
1974	98(28.6)	190(55.6)	54(15.8)	342(100)
1975	143(26.9)	250(47.0)	139(26.1)	532(")
1976	20(5.2)	186(48.6)	177(46.2)	383(")
1977	8(5.1)	54(34.2)	96(60.7)	158(")
1978	15(5.6)	104(38.5)	151(55.9)	270(")
1979	8(2.2)	112(31.1)	240(66.7)	360(")
1980	6(2.9)	50(24.0)	152(73.1)	208(")
1981	5(1.9)	78(29.5)	181(68.6)	264(")
1982	29(3.0)	71(23.8)	219(73.2)	299(")
1983	9(3.0)	101(33.8)	189(63.2)	299(")
1984	2(1.2)	31(18.7)	133(80.1)	166(")
Total	323(9.8)	1,227(37.4)	1,731(52.8)	3,281(100)

(*Source: Committee Report,* 1985).

Although the number of applicants is large, there are some special problems concerning adequate representation from the Helsinki area and the Swedish-speaking population. In the years following 1962 till the time of writing, there were about 4,000 applicants from the Uusimaa province (Helsinki and its neighboring areas) which constituted only about 7.1 percent of all applicants. There have been only 400 qualified persons (5.8 percent of all) from this area, although it contains 25 percent of country's population in the country's police force. Although there is no simple answer to this problem, the awareness of this deficiency is increasing. A recent survey refers to some unique difficulties for officers working in Helsinki area. These are excessive cost of living, scarcity of housing, transitory characteristics of the city population, and comparatively hard working conditions and demanding work (*Committee Report*, 1985). The Helsinki Police Association found similar reasons for this phenomenon through another survey which it conducted. These were lack of noticeable prestige associated with police work in Helsinki area, the monotonous nature of the work, the bad working conditions, loneliness in the big urban setting of Helsinki, and the mechanical attitudes of superior officers (Weckman, 1988). The expensive standard of living in Helsinki seems to be the main economic disincentive for police officers in this area. Working conditions in Helsinki area, particularly in regard to the kind of violent resistance faced by police officers during 1980-1984, has been the same in Helsinki area as elsewhere in the country. Such matters constituted about 36-39 percent of all police cases in Finland during that period. In the year 1984 there were 343 such cases in Helsinki area (*Committee Report*, 1986).

In approximate numbers, there are 300,000 people in Finland (6.2 percent of all inhabitants) whose language is Swedish. Until 1985 there were only two cadet courses (in the years 1980 and 1983) for Swedish-speaking people. There were only 234 applicants for these courses and just 54 qualified (*Committee Report*, 1985). It is not known why the situation is so. Perhaps the Swedish-speaking people, who seem to maintain a strong identity of their own, regard the police as a symbol of Finnish power.

Due to this situation, Swedish-speaking applicants and those from Helsinki area are given special consideration and ensured greater success than other groups in the selection tests. The test scores of the Swedish-speaking applicants are compared only with each other to select the maximum number of qualified candidates from the group. Despite these measures, the lack of representation of the Helsinki area and the Swedish-speaking people continues. To help rectify this situation, special drives for recruitment from the Helsinki area and amongst the Swedish-speaking people have been stressed (*Committee Report*, 1985; *Committee Report*, 1986).

Vacancies for the Police School are published twice a year in the main newspapers. The announcements are rather official looking. There are no advertisements on television. At local level police chiefs make a preliminary assessment of the candidates from their own jurisdictions. Their recommendations are sent to the Police School which makes the initial selection. A check for a possible criminal record and other personal particulars occurs at this stage. However, the final selection to the test is made by the National Selection Board, which is appointed by the Ministry of the Interior. Since 1985 the Board has included representatives from the Helsinki, Tampere and Turku Local Police, the Mobile Police, the Capital County Police, the Police School, the Finnish Police Federation, the Finnish Criminal Investigators' Federation, the Police Corps' Central Union, the Finnish Sheriffs' Association, and one specialist member. Additionally, representatives of the Police School teachers of Finnish language, psychology, and sport are also on the Board. There are two applicants for the selection test for every one who passes and who qualifies for hiring.

In the two-day-long selection test the following items are included: writing abilities, i.e., national language, personal characteristics, intelligence (essentially a measurement of logical reasoning and thinking speed), knowledge of current affairs, and physical fitness and skill. Every recruit will get an extra point if he has at least a noncommissioned officer's rank in the army, or success in sports, well-known confidential posts, or special vocational training. Finally, there is a personal interview. Personal interviews included in the preliminary selection process can cause subjective bias in the selection of candidates, however. Therefore, the Parliamentary Police Committee suggested that it would be better for experts from universities to develop special tests for policemen. It recommended that the weight given to interviews should be reduced and that a special formula to minimize subjective errors be considered as necessary. There has been no study, however, concerning the selection process in terms of its success or failure (*Committee Report*, 1986).

The formal qualifications which are specified in the Police Decree (No. 737/1985), and stated briefly in the job advertisement are as follows:

(1) The minimum age for a police officer is 18 years. There is no upper age limit. However, an applicant over 30 years can be recruited to the department if his personal characteristics, education, and experience provide special reasons for his suitability.
(2) Higher secondary school or at least vocational school level education is required.
(3) Involvement in crime and arrests for drunkenness can disqualify a candidate. Physical requirements including good eyesight, color perception, normal hearing, absence of debilitating disease, and a good physique are stringent. Work experience of at least a year's duration is considered advantageous.
(4) Every officer has to have a record of military service before entering the police.
(5) He must have gone through Reserve Officer's or Noncommissioned Officer's School in the army or have compensatory qualifications.
(6) A candidate can be qualified for the job only if he gets the driver's licence before the training.

The following certificates are also required:

(1) Official certificate which shows the applicant's family history, his religion, etc.;
(2) School and job certificates;
(3) Military pass;
(4) Passport picture;
(5) Doctor's certificate with a special reference to color perception; and
(6) Other certificates according to applicant's preference.

(*Source:* Police Decree No. 737/1985, *Policeman*, 1988).

The Ministry of the Interior is directly responsible for development and coordination of training for all police personnel. The police academies are directed by the Police Department of the Ministry. There is no special Bureau for this purpose. It has been suggested that there should be a Bureau in Police Department only for training (*Committee Report*, 1986).

History and Structure of Training. Police training in Finland began at the Helsinki Police Department in 1918. Up until 1961, police training was conducted at the Police School in the island of Suomenlinna near Helsinki. In the beginning, the curriculum consisted of courses on general education supplemented by training in criminal police work or ordinary law enforcement (Luntiala and Meronen, 1986).

In 1962 police training underwent a significant revision as there began in that year a new system of basic training called "cadet course," at the new Police College in Espoo, near Helsinki. Until 1973 all police training took place in that college when the police training center, known as the Police School, was first located in Helsinki and later moved to Tampere. In the beginning the school provided training only to cadets, but in 1977 it was expanded to include the training of all policemen as well (Luntiala and Meronen, 1986). At the moment there are two police training centers in Finland: Police College in Espoo, which gives higher training and Police School in Tampere where police officers receive their basic training (See Figures 8 and 9).

Police training in Finland underwent important changes in 1988. First, new courses (Figure 9) for police officers began in August 1988. In the new system the increase of hours for police officers and for noncommissioned officers is quite small. The increase was 12 and eight weeks of training respectively. But for commissioned officers the increase was quite marked. It went up from 32 weeks to 64 weeks. They were required to take their examination after a preparation of two years instead of one year as happened previously. Figures 8 and 9 represent the former and revised training system.

As these figures indicate, one stage is essential for moving into the next one.

The Ministry of the Interior has forged plans for college credit for courses taught in the course of police schooling. Now, the basic as well as other courses of police training are so designed that they

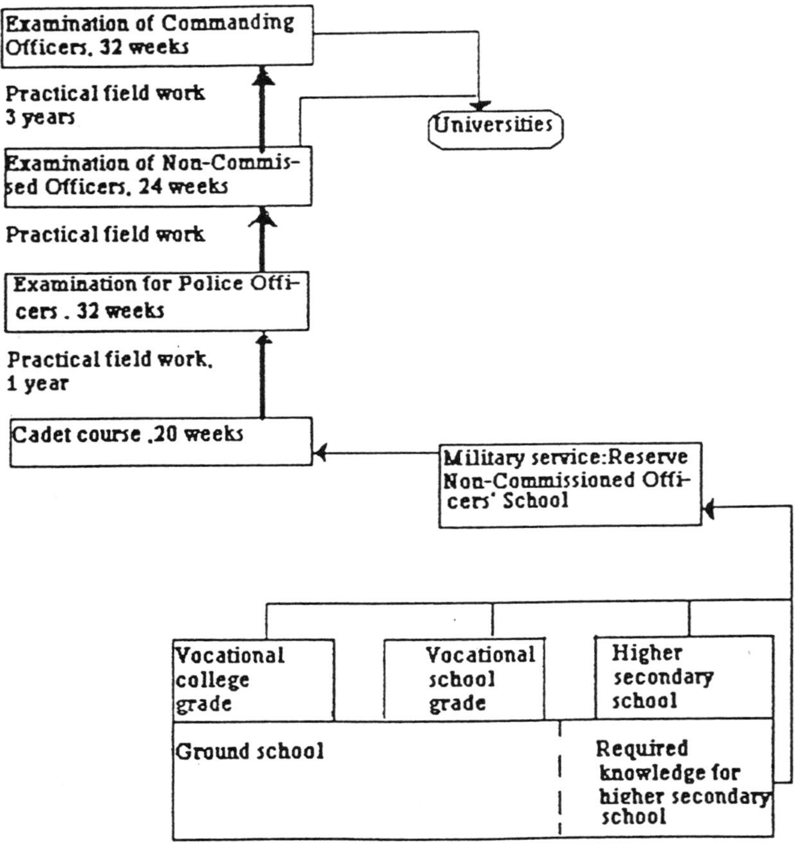

Fig. 8: The Structure of Police Training (Former) (*Source:* Petterson, 1987b: 34).

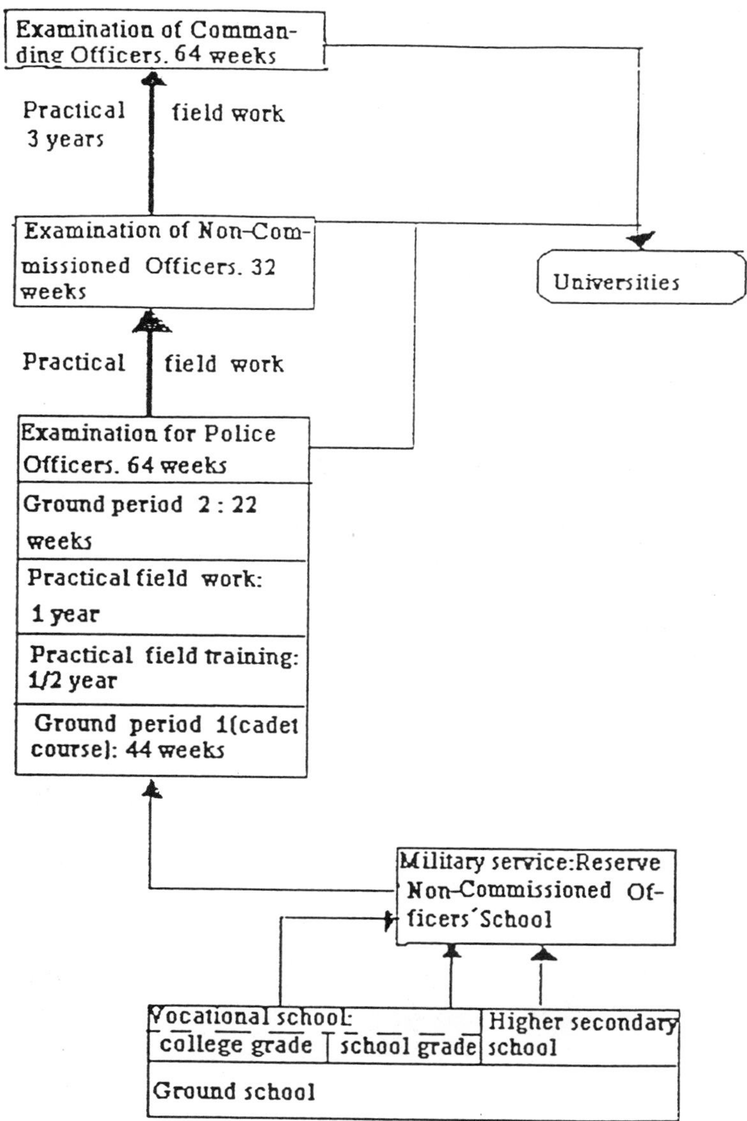

Fig. 9: The Structure of Police Training (Since 1988) (*Source:* Petterson, 1987b: 34).

enable police officers to enter institutions of higher education of various levels. Further, the present plan is to develop police training with an emphasis on:

- Increased vocational skills
- Acquisition of special skills
- Adjustment of training to the needs of society and labor market
- Synchronizing police training with secondary and higher levels of general education (*Committee Report*, 1984).

Training at the Police School in Tampere is free. Food, housing, and health care during training also are provided free of charge. Trainees get ten Finnish marks (about 2.5 U. S. dollars) a day, and they can also apply for a study loan from the government. They are required to serve the police at least one year after the course.

The total program of Finnish Police training is illustrated in Table 6 on pages 154-155.

The percentages shown within parenthesis represent the proportions compared to the total period of training. Trainees work 38 hours a week. Police officers are trained for 66 weeks which constitute 16.5 months. Noncommissioned officers undergo 37 weeks

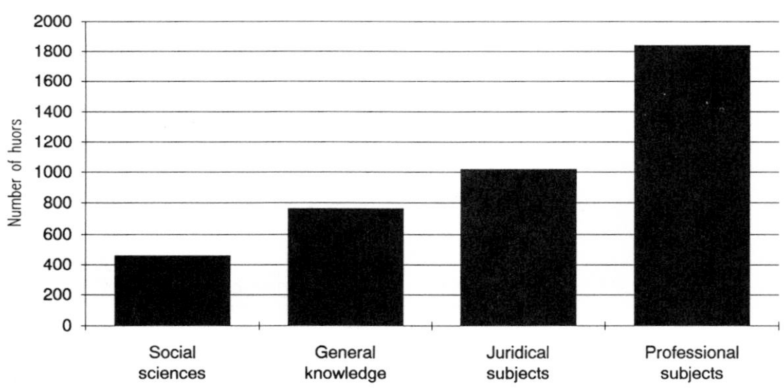

Fig. 10: Different Topics in Police Training

i.e., eight months of training and Commissioned officers are trained for 64 weeks or 16 months (*Committee Report*, 1984).

The comparative importance of different topics in police training is shown in Figure 10 on page 152. It is noted that professional and juridical subjects constitute the main bulk of police training in Finland. Humanistic topics are only marginal.

Women in Training. In regard to the representation of women in police training, it is to be noted that women were allowed to join the police starting in 1973. There were only 53 positions for policewomen until 1975. But four years later there were 180 women in police jobs which constituted 2.2 percent of all police officers. In the cadet courses the representation of women has been minimal; only barely 2 percent and, in this regard, Finland is at the bottom among the Nordic countries. In the beginning of 1987 when the Act for equal rights for men and women was passed, recruitment of women received a new impetus. Until then women also occupied the lowest level positions in the police. The future of women in police is yet uncertain. Recommendations have been made to study the question and to proceed with care (Petterson 1987; *Committee Report*, 1986).

Training - Personnel. In the Police School in Tampere there are 29 full-time teachers; 12 of them are faculty members with police training and the rest are civilians with university education. In 1987 there were also 159 part-time civilian instructors who were responsible for 26 percent of the entire training program (*Annual Report of the Police School*, 1987).

In the Police College in Espoo 16 full-time teachers taught in 1987. Nine of them received police training and the rest had university education. Almost 500 civilian instructors were associated with the college. Besides normal training as discussed above, the Police College is responsible for supplementary and special training on contemporary problems. Instructions by civilian teachers amounted to 28 percent of commissioned officers' training and 85 percent of special training (*Annual Report of the Police College*, 1987).

The new training system is expanding the need for new police academy trainers. While in 1989-1990 there was a requirement for only five persons, it rose to 18 in 1990-1991. In the area of training there have been numerous developments over the years.

Training, Promotion, and Leadership: Criteria for promotion are not clearly defined in Finland. Besides formal qualifications

TABLE 6: FINNISH POLICE TRAINING (Percentages in Brackets)

	A P1 1st yr.	P2 2nd yr.	Total	B	C 3rd yr.	D 4th yr.	5th yr.	Total
SUBJECTS:								
1. GENERAL KNOWLEDGE:								
Math				114				114
Soc.	50		50					50
Fin.	76	44	120		50	60		230
Swed.	57		57		30	70		214
Lang.	57		57	57	30		70	157
	240	44	284	171	110	130	70	765
			(11.3%)		(8.9%)		(8.2%)	
2. VOCATIONAL SUBJECTS:								
(Juridical courses)								
Administrative Law						50	80	130
Traf.	75	40	115		95			210
Civ.	20	10	30		20	20		72
Crim.	65	50	115		95	25	66	301
Proc.	20	45	65		40	40	40	185
Com.	30		30		40	30	20	120
	210	145	355		292	165	206	1,018
			(14.1)		(23.6)		(15.2)	
(Professional courses):								
Pol.	131	76	207		110	80	120	517
Tra.	100	60	160		80	50	50	340
Auto.	15	35	50					50
Driv.	20	20	40					40
Crim.	40	60	100					100
Tech.	45	45	90					90
Self.	105	44	149		40	35	35	259
Sign.	47	20	67					67
Arms.	50	20	70					70
	613	380	993		360	225	265	1,843
			(39.1)		(29.1)		(20.1)	
3. SOCIAL SCIENCES:								
Mgmt.					60	60	65	185
Psy.	95	40	135		20	30		185
Soc.					30	50		80
Ethi.	4	2	6		2		4	12
	99	42	141		112	140	69	462
			(5.6)		(9.1)		(8.6)	
4. SPECIAL COURSES:								
Type.	40		40					40
Faid.	25	10	35		6			41
Data.	60							60

	1st yr.	2nd yr.	Total		3rd yr.	4th yr.	5th yr.	Total
Bkk.								
Psy.					20			20
Med.					20			20
Meth.					20	10		30
Stat.						36		36
						65		65
	125	10	135 (5.4)		66 (5.4)	111 (4.5)		312
5. OTHER SUBJECTS:								
Res.	12	179	21				50	71
Rev.					10	10	100	120
Ftra.	40	30	70		30	30	40	170
	52	39	91 (3.6)		40 (3.2)	40	190 (9.4)	361
6. SELF-TRAINING:								
	352	660	528 (20.9)		256 (20.7)	416 (34.0)	416	1,616
	1,691	836	2,527	171	1,236	1,227	1,216	6,377

Explanations:
Fin: Finnish; Swed:Swedish; Lang: English or German; Traf: Traffic Law for Police; Civ: Law for Civil Servants; Crim: Criminal Law; Proc: Legal Procedure; Com: Civil and Commercial Law; Pol: General Police Topics; Tra: Traffic; Auto: Automobile Knowledge; Driv: Driver's Training; Crim: Criminal Tactics; Tech: Criminal Techniques; Self: Self-Defense and Sports; Sign: Signal Communication; Arms: Arms Education and Shooting; Mgmt: Organization and Management; Psy: Psychology; Soc: Sociology; Ethi: Police Ethics; Type: Typewriting; Faid: First Aid; Data: Data System of the Police; Bkk: Bookkeeping; Psy: Forensic Psychiatry; Med: Forensic Medicine; Meth: Methodology; Stat: Statistics; Res: In Reserve; Rev: Reviews and Seminar Work; Ftra: Field Training.
A: Police officers' course
B: General knowledge requirement for noncommissioned and commissioned without high school diploma
C: Noncommissioned officers' course
D: Commissioned officers' course
P1: Cadets' course
P2: Police officers' course

acquired through training, a person must have skill and ability for successful job performance (Moment 51 of the Police Degree No. 737/1985). It is alleged that political considerations enter into promotions. The Chairman of the Helsinki Criminal Police Association, Heikki Salmi, mentions that even in the local police level such considerations are not absent (Salmi, 1988).

At present, the selection process for noncommissioned officers' courses is under revision. Formerly there were no established criteria for selecting such officers. As a practical matter, only six years of field experience were required. Now candidates are evaluated according to five factors: performance at police school examination, other education, language skills, job experience, and suitability for supervising positions. The evaluation of the two last items is made by police chiefs. Job experience evaluations are based on professional skills, activity, initiative, responsibility, cooperativeness, organizational abilities, and written as well as oral skills. The evaluations are arranged by the heads of the county police establishments who are the provincial police heads in Finland. The final selection is made by the Police College through a selection board.

Getting selected for the noncommissioned officers' courses has been a problem for a long time. In 1987 there were only 2,045 sergeants' vacancies and already 232 persons qualified through these courses were available for those posts. In that year there were 905 applicants and only 78 qualified (Vesterinen, 1987). As indicated above, the selection process was under revision. Now noncommissioned officers go through proper tests like policemen and commissioned officers do. Such tests include items like jurisprudence, personnel administration including supervising and contemporary issues, and subjects like order, crime, and traffic.

For selection to commissioned officers' courses, a candidate can send an application once a year to the Police College. His Chief is a recommending authority and the Police College makes the selection. The most important means for selection to the commissioned officers' course is the test score. It is much like the one taken by the noncommissioned officers, except that the questions are more advanced. However, written tests have been criticized as too narrow to measure qualifications for the positions of commissioned officers. At the time of writing, a working group in the Ministry of the

Interior was reviewing the selection process for these officers too (Weckman, 1988).

No quota is fixed for the number of qualified persons selected for commissioned officers' courses. Under normal circumstances the number of applicants is between 100 and 120, and of them about 25 qualify. Unlike the other courses, there has been a shortage of applicants to commissioned officers' course and this is considered troublesome (*Committee Report*, 1986). It is suspected that the age of retirement for commissioned officers which is 63 compared to the lower age limit of 57 for noncommissioned officers, is an important discouraging reason. Another reason is that commissioned officers are required to pass an examination on jurisprudence. Generally, those who join the police at lower ranks do not possess such qualifications. It has been suggested that there should be an alternative examination to accommodate aspirants coming up through the ranks. However, there has been no change in the examination procedure for commissioned officers as yet (*Committee Report*, 1984).

LEADERSHIP AND SUPERVISORY CALIBRE

As leadership and supervision are discussed here together, it is intended to include within this discussion all supervisory positions of the police in Finland. In accepting the American equivalents of the Finnish supervisory positions, it should be noted that they are based on their similarity to the designations used in numerous American police departments. It may be borne in mind that it is always imprecise to describe one country's police department's supervisory designations in terms of another country's rank structure. Since it is also proposed to deliberate here on the nature of "supervisory caliber," education and training of supervisors is also discussed in this section. We will keep in mind that under the section on personnel practices, there is an account of the promotion system in Finland showing how supervisory positions are filled in. There will also be a section later in this chapter on standards used in evaluating individual performance in which supervisory practices are discussed.

To begin with it may be observed that, unlike some other police departments included in the present volume, the police in Finland have a flat hierarchy. The supervisory positions are *ylikonstaapeli* (sergeants), *komisario* (lieutenant), *ylikomisario* (captain), *apulaispoliisimasteri* and *apulaisnimismies* (deputy police chief and deputy sheriff) and, finally, the *poliisimasteri* and the *nimismies* (police chief and sheriff). These are the field supervisory positions. Apart from them, there are supervisory positions known as *tarkastajas* (inspectors) who are the heads of the provincial police units. Also, there are such inspectors in the Police Department of the Ministry of the Interior headed by the *ylijohtaja* (general director of the police). It is interesting that top-ranking positions in another country included in this book, namely, India, carry the designations of inspectors. The chiefs of police in the Indian states were till recently called inspector generals.

In Finland there are two ways to rise to top leadership positions—police chiefs (*poliisimasteri*), sheriffs (*nimismies*) and inspectors (*tarkastajas)*—in regional or national establishments of the police. Police officers can earn promotions through police training but it is rather rare for an officer to rise to the highest leadership positions through promotion. Generally, they occupy the top positions by achieving higher education at universities. For leadership positions like police chiefs in large cities or the sheriffs in new cities and rural areas, law degrees are required. The rank-and-file personnel cannot attain these positions since they are without such degrees (*Committee Report,* 1986; Petterson, 1987).

In the course of discussion on the promotion system in the previous section it has been explained how the supervisory positions of sergeants (*ylikonstaapeli*), lieutenants and captains (*komisario* and *ylikomisarios*) are acquired. Among the various factors considered useful for promotion, good job performance and success in the promotion examinations are considered most important. For the captain's position, however, there is no special examination. Senior lieutenants may automatically occupy them depending on suitable vacancies. In one sense, these are indeed professional police supervisors who rise up from the ranks. These positions are not open to persons without police experience, and to obtain that experience one must join as constables (*neurempi konstaapeli*) and go through the academy and field training. Police chiefs and sheriffs are not professional police personnel in that sense. They do not need to have police experience, and they are all required to be law graduates. They need not go to professional police schools to achieve vocational education. In that sense they are somewhat like the police presidents (*polizeipräsidenten*) in Germany.

Das (1993) mentions that during the course of his field research he found that "supervisors with the rank of komisario or lieutenant-captain said that Finns generally resent supervision." He adds:

> Therefore, police supervisors are very discreet and circumspect in supervising personnel. The absence of strict supervision seemed satisfying at the Police Training School in Tampere where candidates in the pre-service training compared their compulsory time in the army with the relaxed and pleasant climate at the police school. Police chiefs and sheriffs also claimed that most satisfactory aspect of their jobs was that the police inspector or Laaninpoliisitarkastaja was not in a position to interfere in their day-to-day activities.

According to Das, reflected in the police supervisory style and practice is the influence of Finnish culture, more particularly, the Finnish administrative culture. One observes the relative absence of social barriers, class distinctions, and official protocols. Added to this cultural trait, is the reality that no sense of emergency envelops the police environment. Emergencies associated with drugs, terrrorism, violent crime, and difficult problems of law and order do not threaten the police obliging them to act as a domestic army. He mentions that "a policy based on respect for individual autonomy and freedom seems to be an objective pursued by the government in all civil service." Individual police officers are allowed to function without interference from supervisors. It has been noted that although the Ministry of the Interior in Finland enjoys the power to give police orders, that power is very rarely used.

While legitimacy of the police leadership is generally invulnerable, it has been mentioned (Das, 1993) that the influence of party politics has increased in the police hierarchy in the recent days. Political influence, however, is very subdued in police appointments. It is believed that although there may be some political considerations in the appointments to the highest police positions, the promotion system or appointments to the positions of police chiefs and sheriffs in general are non-political. Sheriffs are considered officers of the law in the sense that traditionally they were also prosecutors. But, as Das (1993) rightly observes, insistence on legal qualifications only as the basis for appointments to the highest police positions coupled with the Finnish historical respect for law has also produced a legalistic leadership style. Accordingly, Finnish police leaders may be found to be not so experimentation-oriented or innovation-minded. Conservative impact of legal discipline on the leadership may be responsible for this situation. This requirement has also practically prevented the rank-and-file officers from aspiring to rise to leadership positions.

STANDARDS USED IN EVALUATING INDIVIDUAL POLICE PERFORMANCE

As mentioned in the previous section, police officers in Finland even at the lowest street level are allowed to function with certain degree of autonomy. In other words, supervision is relaxed. Quantitative measures of performance, such as traffic citations and arrests, are not utilized in assessment of individual performance.

What seems to be the most important criterion is the every day performance of the individual officers including his behavior, attitude, and reputation among peers. Public complaints against police officers are not a problem. Although there is no civilian complaints authority in Finland, complaints are investigated by two independent agencies, namely, the Ombudsman and the Chancellor of Justice.

Most police departments in Finland are small, and the officers function as generalists. Supervisors remain in close touch with them. Street-level officers are also personally known to the highest officers in the departments like sheriffs, police chiefs and other executives. Officers conduct their business always in pairs. It is because of these conditions that the performance evaluations tend to be subjective and personal. It was explained by a former chief of the patrol division in Helsinki (Das, Personal Conversation, 1990) that any misdeed on the part of a police officer comes to his attention through the grapevine. He added that corruption of a police officer could be instinctively felt as a boil in one's own body. The Helsinki executive also said that even in a big city like his, the members of the public were bound to come to know if there were misdeeds on the part of the police and accordingly, these would be brought to the attention of the proper authorities. These remarks are illustrative of the informal and subjective nature of performance evaluation in Finland.

As explained in the relevant sections above, the hierarchical ranks in the police organizations are rather limited in Finland. The only street-level supervisor's position is that of the sergeant and promotions are strictly on the basis of the examinations as well as the successful completion of training. The officers like lieutenants and captains are also selected on the basis of promotion examinations and, they have to undergo lengthy training in the Police College. Police chiefs and sheriffs are brought in from outside on the basis of their suitability and legal qualifications. They enter these positions without any further chance of promotion except that they may work at the Department of Police Affairs as inspectors, general director of the police, or the provincial inspectors of police. These positions are a few only and mostly the occupants are selected on the basis of their general reputation, suitability, and willingness to move to the new positions. General reputation seems indeed to be an important factor at all levels of the organization in the matter of performance evaluation. This is because, as indicated above, most departments are small, the police work is of general nature, the country does not have tough crime or law-and-order problems, and Finnish society is homogenous, welfare oriented, and affluent.

PROFESSIONALIZATION

The following is an account of the Finnish Police professionalism. In this account the quality of police profesionalism has been assessed taking into consideration some usual indicators of professionalization, namely, access to higher education, licensing, code of ethics, and membership in professional associations.

In regard to access to higher education, it should be noted that before 1962 police training was not geared toward making it a stepping-stone to higher education. The access to university education was not facilitated by professional police training courses. However, such courses have been now integrated with the general education system based primarily upon universities. True, even now these courses prepare a police officer for the special tasks that he or she performs. Judged against the second indicator, namely, licensing, it appears that the police officers were not granted the status of regular civil servants till some years back. Prior to the Civil Servant Act (No. 755/1986) and, the Decree (No. 723/1987), there was another Act (No. 202/1926) regulating the relations between different civil servants and the state. According to this Act, certificates of appointment issued to police officers were different from other civil servants since the police were regarded as servants under special control and hierarchical order. Their rights and privileges as civil servants were somewhat unique. Currently, there is no difference in the certificates issued to civil servants except that the new laws specify two appointment alternatives, namely, permanent and temporary. Police officers are generally classified as permanent civil servants. As civil servants of the state, the code of ethics governing police officers is the new Civil Servant Act (No. 755/1986) and Decree (No. 723/1987) which came into force in 1988. The Police Act (No. 84/1966) and the Police Decree (No. 737/1985) also provide important guidelines for police conduct. General rules for civil servants are also found in the Act for Administrative Procedures (No. 598/1982) and in the Constitution of Finland.

The new Civil Servant Act has brought civil servant laws closer to normal labor laws, intending to make administration more effective and flexible. Now employment relations are more simple, less rigid, and not so bureaucratically controlled. The Civil Servant Act defines the employment relation as a service relation to the state in the line of public law. Article 21 of the Act states some general principles and states, for example, that civil servants have no right to take any advantage, which can weaken the public trust.

The Police Decree (No. 737/85) enunciates the broad principles concerning police duties and these principles are more demanding than those found in the Civil Servant Act. This has been justified because of the role of the police in society, and the hierarchial, paramilitary nature of police administration. So the police officers have a service relation to the state, but they work in police organization under authority relations. A police officer at all times must act as "police," if the situation so requires. This means that he/she must not let his/her ethical image be tarnished by undesirable acts in private life as provided for specifically in the articles 47 and 49 in the Police Decree, 1985). Moreover, a police officer can be discharged from service more easily than other civil servants. He or she can be dismissed from his/her position "if there is a reason to that" (Police Decree, 1985: article 47). Further, unlike his counterparts in other government jobs police officers have no right to complain about such dismissals. Regarding the final condition, namely, the membership in professional associations, it may be observed that a rank-and-file police officer is not a member of professional associations. The police have their trade unions. Although these bodies conduct small training programs they are not professional associations. This situation is quite different in regard to command personnel, who acquire academic degrees. Those who are lawyers by education belong to appropriate associations of their discipline.

In brief it can be argued that the police have come a long way in the matters of education and training. For the older generation of police officers, training was much less comprehensive and educational methods inferior. Many changes have taken place now giving the police a better professional image as well as status.

WAGES, STATUS, SUBCULTURE, AND MORALE

Police salaries have increased at a remarkable pace over the past several decades. At the beginning of this century their salaries were quite low. In 1924 a new law concerning the salaries of the civil servants took effect. Table 7 illustrates the differences in income of civil servants in 1914 and 1924 as computed in Finnish marks (at the present rate of exchange one American dollar is equivalent to approximately four Finnish marks).

The new salary regulation of 1924 created 30 different wage categories in civil service employment. The highest annual salary was 100,000 Finnish marks and the lowest, 10,000 marks. Junior constables were generally at the bottom of the pay scale. Compared with the school principal's salary, that of the police chief outside Helsinki changed rather drastically in 1924. Table 8 presents comparative wages of police officers and other professional groups some sixty-plus years later.

TABLE 7: THE ANNUAL WAGES OF SOME CIVIL SERVANTS IN THE YEARS 1914 AND 1924 (In Finnish Marks)

	1914	1924
School principal	7,000	57,000
Police chief (Helsinki area)	6,000	36,000
Senior constable (Helsinki)	1,960	19,500
Train Conductor	1,390	18,000
Junior constable in city	1,360	14,400

(*Source:* Ruotsalainen, 1973)

TABLE 8: WAGES OF POLICE OFFICERS AND OTHER PROFESSIONALS IN PUBLIC SECTOR (Total Monthly Emoluments in American Dollars)

Architect	2,768
Planning engineer	2,594
Librarian	1,656
Cleaner	1,368
Sheriff	2,996
Lieutenant (police)	2,637
Constable	2,008

(*Source: Statistical Report,* 29, 1987).

One can see that the police salary is not so bad compared to other public-sector professionals.

In Finland two standard socioeconomic classifications exist in regard to various occupations. The one is a nine level (number one for the highest rank and number nine for the lowest) and the other is a three level (I for the highest and III for the lowest) classification. In the first classification a police constable is in level 5, a lieutenant in level 4 , and a police chief or a sheriff in level 3. In the second classification the corresponding levels are II, II, and I (Rauhala: 1966, appendix 1). Thus, these old classifications put a police officer in the middle, and a police chief in the high socioeconomic category.

In Finland research concerning police status, subculture, and morale is rather fragmentary. Administratively the Finnish police are united since they constitute only one national police force. But there is a geographical difference in police work between metropolitan areas, particularly, Helsinki and the rest of the country. Emoluments and social status vary between supervisory personnel and the rank-and-file personnel. There, also, seems to be a gap between the police officers of the older generation and the officers who have joined the police in the recent years. This distance is noticed basically in attitude and mode of operation.

Historically the image of police has not been attractive as they were regarded as the tool of the Russian emperor. This fact was acknowledged by the police too (Ruotsalainen: 1973). The police have also been complaining that the public perception of police work as a lowly occupation has caused the police to suffer inadequate salary (Aherma: 1986).

The key variables that affect the police image are shown in Figure 11.

In Figure 11 in which all variables affecting police prestige are interwoven together, it is easy to stress the connection between variables 1, 2, and 3. The connection from 1, 2, and 3 to variables 4 and 5 is much more difficult to analyze. If we suppose that there is a common ideology or a subculture shared by the police in Finland—which can be part of the dominant ideology, then it is easy

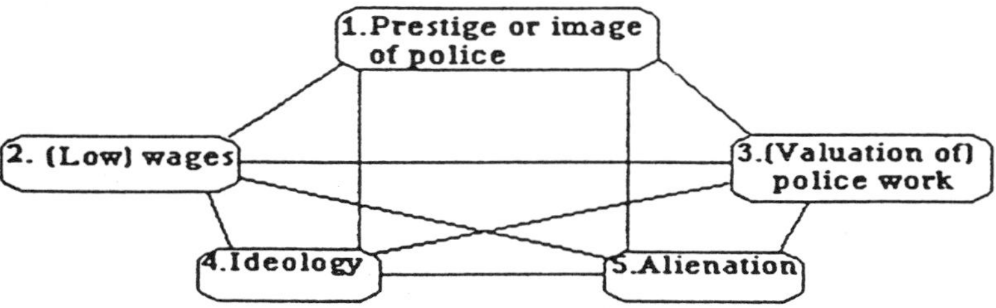

Fig. 11: The Interconnection Between Presige Variables.

to believe that the police are alienated from the common people. According to Martti Grönfors (1979), the police organization has a tendency to solidify police attitudes and encourage conservative ideology. Although he had little empirical evidence that police officers tended to cling together even socially, they did appear to have "felt at odds with society and with society's support for their work." There is evidence demonstrating that the political attitudes of the police had shifted to the right. This can be seen from Table 9 below in which the percentages of police support to various political parties have been shown between 1981 and 1987.

TABLE 9: THE POLITICAL SUPPORT BY THE FINNISH POLICE FEDERATION, 1981 AND 1987

Party	1981	1987
Moderate Party	31.7	36.0
Center or Liberal Party	14.9	13.5
Other Right-wing Parties	5.4	5.0
Social Democrats	5.4	3.4
Folk Democrats and Communists	1.4	0.3
Non-Allied	24.3	30.7
Greens		1.0
Refused to say	17.6	10.9

Source: Virta (1987).

Grönfors (1979) maintains that younger police officers display harder attitudes toward minorities like Gypsies than their older colleagues. The better educated officers seem to be "hard-liners." As a matter of fact, the popular TV-serial *Reinikainen* shows an older constable who has better humor and knowledge, more able to accept the common public side than his younger counterpart who is mostly a stupid bureaucrat.

Morale of the Finnish police officers can be described as fairly high. As mentioned above, the job is highly attractive as can be seen from the fact that a large number of people apply for police jobs. The turnover rate is rather low. A near total absence of complaint on the part of the police is also remarkable. In his survey of Finnish police (Das, 1990; 1993) Das assesses police perceptions and attitude in respect of their work, environment, deviance and pride as well as any possaible changes that they desired. He found that police officers in Finland were highly satisfied with what they did. They also had good feelings about their organization, superiors, and the job itself. By and large, they had a benign feeling regarding the society at large, the media, and other government agencies. Police officers thought that their colleagues demonstrated some of the best qualities found in respectable and honorable members of the Finnish society. Generally, the officers indicated that they were satisfied with the present state of the police and did not favor many changes. Their attitude, as revealed in the Das survey, indicated that since they consider that nothing was broken, there was no real need to fix anything. Such views and opinions are indicators of high morale of the police in Finland.

UNIONS AND ASSOCIATIONS

In Finland the history of police trade unions is a lengthy one. As mentioned elsewhere, early on their wages were meagre and the prestige low. These reasons helped unionization of the rank-and-file police officers. However, unionization based on hierarchial work structure has resulted in many unions among the police. Many unions also reflect the conflicting interests and views among police officers.

The Finnish police have four main associations, established as follows:

1921: The Finnish Sheriffs' Association

There are about 260 sheriffs who are the heads of rural police districts and belong to this association. It may also be pointed out here that its members all have law degrees, several have training to work as judges, and they also have had prosecutorial experiences.

1923: The Finnish Police Federation

It has over 70 local associations and had in 1982 about 7,100 members who are uniform police personnel.

1930: The Finnish Criminal Investigators' Federation
In 1982 this Federation had about 1,500 members. Police investigators and the uniform police officers function fairly separately. This investigating branch of the police has its own sergeants, lieutenants, and captains, etc., who take the honorific, *Rikos* (criminal), before their designations.

1943: The Police Corps' Central Union
In 1982 it had about 2,400 members and, this union has a broad mixture of police personnel (Aherma: 1986).

The members of the Finnish Police Federation, as mentioned above, are mostly uniform constables, and the Finnish Patrolling Police Association is a member of it. The Police Corps' Central Union includes the Finnish Police Chiefs' Association, the Police Officers' Association, the Association of the Officers of the Central Criminal Investigation Department, the Staff Association of the Security Police, and the Staff Association of the Police Academy (Aherma: 1986).

These Associations are also members of Central Trade Unions. The Sheriffs' Association and the Police Lawyers' Professional Association which were established in 1976 are members of AKAVA (The Central Organization of Professional Associations in Finland) and all the rest, except Criminal Investigators' Federation, are members of TVK (The Confederation of Salaried Employee Organizations) in Finland. The Criminal Investigators' Federation has tried all kinds of arrangements concerning the question of the Central Union. For a long time they were members of the Finnish Police Federation. In 1975 they demanded two special salary increments which they did not get. Consequently in 1976 they decided to separate from the Finnish Police Federation (Aherma, 1986). Following the separation they started on their own with their union which was a member of TVK. Now, the Criminal Investigators' Federation has decided to separate from TVK and join another Central Trade Union. These quarrels date back to 1976 when there was a civil servant strike. Criminal Investigators' Federation did not join the strike. Many of its members decided not even to pay the solidarity strike-money although their own union directed them to do so. This event weakened the relations between the TVK and the Criminal Investigators' Federation.

For many years the Finnish Police Federation belonged to the VTY (Joint Organization for Civil Servants and Workers) which was member of the SAK (The Confederation of Finnish Trade Unions). The SAK is the central organization for Finnish labor unions whose members are industry workers and it has a pronounced leftist image. This is not the image of the TVK which is an organization for office workers, as stated above. According to a decision supported by more than 90 percent of the members, the Finnish Police Federation changed their affiliation to this organization in 1984. This change possibly reflects new identity of the police in labor market as well as in society. It can also be interpreted as an indicator of the police identity with the political right, or, at least, with centrist politics.

Trade union membership is high among police officers. About 95 percent of Rikos Police officers (detectives) in Helsinki belong to the Criminal Investigators' Association (Salmi, 1988). It is difficult to assess the effects of unionization in the social situation of police officers. Annually the Central Unions enter into bargaining with the management. Smaller police unions are given a chance to voice their opinions, although how effective they are in doing so is somewhat questionable. Clear expressions of discontent with the social situation and with the Central Unions, namely strikes, are rare.

There were some police strikes in 1917, but these were small and local. In 1970 Civil Servants' Work Relation Act (No. 664/1970) formally gave civil servants the right to strike. In February 1976 for the first time in Finland, there was a major police strike under the auspices of the Finnish Police Federation. However, only the patrol officers, uniform constables, went on strike. It lasted 17 days. The results achieved by the strikers were not spectacular. They derived a benefit of 24 U.S. dollars as an increase in pay (Aherma, 1986). Contrary to what the strikers had hoped there was no collapse of law and order in society. The winter was severe. Command officials and the detectives stayed on the job during the strike. In fact, the strikers admitted that the lesson they learned from this experience was that if there was a need for such a strong action as strike the police front should be united (Orasmala, 1983). The National Research Institute of Legal Policy conducted an extensive research concerning the effects of the strike and its conclusion was that there was no big collapse for the society (Takala, 1979).

PUBLIC RELATIONS, PUBLIC CONFIDENCE, TRUST, AND RESTRAINTS ON THE POLICE

In this section the public image of the police will be examined taking into account the different surveys conducted in Finland. Elsewhere in this chapter we have made a reference to the number of civilian complaints against the police to the Chancellor of Justice and to the Judicial Delegate. We have also mentioned the number of cases filed against the police. These statistics, however, do not really give a true concept of the public image of the police in Finland. A typical feature of the Finnish culture is a tendency to complain about civil servants. Police officers are civil servants, and as such, there will always be many complaints against the police every year. In Finland the duties and rights of the police are regulated in detail by law and, because of this, too, it is considerably easy to file complaints against the police.

Following the Civil War during the 1920s and the 1930s, it was usual for leftists to criticize the police as the violent tool of the wielders of state power. Such criticism did not endear the police to the people. Although the situation nowadays is different, maybe, such concepts linger in some minds even today.

Traditionally there have been numerous anecdotes which tend to depict the police as foolish or silly. For example, a popular joke has it that police officers walk in twos because only one member of the team can read (he can not write), and the other has to write. However, the police always walk in twos even in remote villages because an eyewitness account of two police officers is more credible in courts and, of course, the officers feel physically more protected when they are allowed to work in twos. There are many other such jokes.

In recent years Finnish police officers seem to have been affected by U.S. television shows. Some papers say that they apparently behave more aggressively. They are apt to display their revolvers more frequently. They also display more urban manners and attitudes (Uusitalo, 1980). Maybe, such changes will provide the stuff for more jokes in the future.

The findings (Kamppi and Aro, 1987) of a survey concerning the opinions and attitudes of the Finnish public toward the police shows that the status of the police is ambivalent. While citizens consider the police necessary and important, particularly for the maintenance of the public order and safety, as well as for rendering help when one is in trouble, they regard the police also as a restricting and punitive institution. Generally speaking, people's attitudes toward the police are colored by emotions. Ordinary people's contacts with the police are not anyday occurrences. Most people consider the police reliable and objective. According to Kamppi and Aro, the most important duties of the police are traffic control, general supervision, maintenance of public order and safety, and investigation of crimes.

People tend to look upon policing as a vocation. They consider that police officers possess sportsmanship, athletic skills, aggressiveness, and masculinity. However, they do not regard such characteristics as necessarily the best possible combination for police officers. Popular opinion holds that the police should be human, patient, and considerate.

According to Kamppi and Aro, the police officers are impersonal, distant, and difficult to contact. They are viewed as lonely riders in their cars. They appear to concentrate on meticulous control and imposition of fines instead of general supervision and providing information. Finally, the public also considers police organizations to be authoritarian, bureaucratic, and control-orientated.

In a study Ylikangas (1984) found that the people regard the younger police officers as arrogant towards the public. According to Ylikangas, this attitude causes tension between police and citizens. Another survey (Luntiala, 1988) was conducted regarding the attitudes of car drivers towards traffic control by the police. That study found that 50 percent of the respondents were satisfied with the behavior of the police. Only seven percent were totally dissatisfied.

It has been said that the relationship between the Finnish press and the police is not satisfactory. Journalists complain that the police frequently conceal information about crime investigations and other police matters. Hence they tend to develop a more negative opinion of the people than the general public.

Minority groups, especially Gypsies, held more critical views towards the police. In Finland the Gypsies are the largest ethnic minority numbering about 6,000. One important reason for this bad relationship is that the Gypsies do not share the police concept of social order. According to Mäkinen (1985), this seems to be at the heart of distrust and conflicts between Gypsies and police.

According to Grönfors' research findings (1979), the police view the Gypsies as opposed to everything they regard as important. The Gypsies complain that the police are unable to understand their society and culture. Further, the police are found to equate Gypsy culture with criminal culture. In their dealings with this section of the Finnish society, the police are apt to act upon their views regarding the Gypsy way of life. The Gypsies, therefore, perceive the police as a section of the Finnish community whom they should avoid at all costs. Contact with the police means an inevitable break with the Gypsy community. They scrupulously limit their contacts with the police. The Gypsy attitude towards the police is most unfavorable while the police look for criminals in the Gypsy community. The latter expect to be treated by the police discriminatorily, disrespectfully, and violently.

Generally speaking, however, it can be said that today the police generally enjoy public trust and confidence in Finland although certain police methods, certain aspects of their behavior, and the bureaucratic organization of the police are sometimes criticized. Police officers do seem to create difficulties for themselves. According to Aromaa (1986), they are quite worried about their safety in certain conditions. They suffer tensions. They are afraid of violent situations. Sometimes they do not clearly know what to do and how to behave. In many instances they are also afraid of the consequences of their decisions. They seem to be afraid of public threats of complaints to their superiors or the courts.

Sometimes press and other mass media have been critical of the police. Their criticisms have concentrated in few areas, namely, investigation methods, styles of operations, and information services. Since these are also the problems for the police in Finland we shall discuss them in the next section concerning the problems of the Finnish police. In connection with this controversy it is good to bear in mind that it is police practice to divulge information about ongoing investigations to the extent permitted by law and ethics.

According to the Publicity of a Public Document Act (No. 83/1951), documents concerning crimes and their investigation can be made public only after trial. This is why the police must exercise great care when informing the public and mass media about crimes and suspects. They must carefully determine whether it is necessary to publish the names of suspected criminals because it involves individual privacy.

In certain cases the police are directed to use radio or television broadcasts for informing citizens about important matters. According to the order given by the Ministry of the Interior, the police must send messages by radio or television in the following cases:

- To warn people against dangerous person/persons (murderers, terrorists, pyromaniacs, etc.) who the police are looking for.
- To circulate news about lost or missing persons suspected of being in danger due to their age, illness, or similar circumstances.
- To reach person/persons who have been sold or given by accident dangerous substances (medications, poisons, explosives, arms, etc.) when it is impossible to contact them by other means.
- To caution a person/persons against an accident, economic loss, crime, physical danger, etc.
- To inform about roadblocks caused by natural disasters.

In an effort, however, to disseminate more information about police matters in areas where it is possible without legal or ethical restrictions, the police over the last few years have produced educational programs concerning traffic conduct, crime prevention, and certain other topics. They have also made use of short educational advertisements. As mentioned elsewhere, the 1973 amendment to the Police Act created an advisory committee system within the police administration. These committees which consist primarily of laypersons are found at every level of police administration including the police districts. The committees do not have decision-making powers. However, they are able to improve relations between the police and the general public through recommendations based on public opinion.

In Finland, as indicated earlier, there are two authorities which are responsible for legal and ethical conduct of public servants, namely, the Ombudsman and the Chancellor of Justice. They can inquire into public complaints against the police. However, so far there has never been any grievous charge against the police. Even the number of such charges are not large.

Restraints on the police in Finland were very limited indeed till recently. The police could detain a suspect for a long period in their own jails for investigation. Such powers of detention were curtailed only recently following the Finnish move to be a member of the European Community. It was necessary to bring the Finnish legal provisions to the European standards.

As indicated elsewhere, the Finnish courts are not hard on the police. As a matter of fact, the courts tend to rely on the police. The press is vigilant but officers are generally happy with the press coverage of their activities. There is only a little complaint against the evening newspapers about being sensational. In order to cater to the taste of sensationalism, they are accused of sacrificing the truth in favor of spicy details. Informal restraints prevail in the sense that officers are quite concerned about one another. They are also proud of a lack of misdeeds among their colleagues (Das, 1993).

PROBLEMS OF THE POLICE

We can divide the problems of the police in Finland into the internal and external ones. Included in the first category are the problems of the resources of the police. These problems are partly linked to today's rapid social changes, as well as the late urbanization and industrialization of Finnish society.

Finnish politicians and government leaders realize that in contemporary society the demand for police services is increasing. Urbanization is generating a greater awareness for security and safety. Corporate crimes, computer crimes, and so on are calling for greater resources in crime investigation. Connected with these developments is more urgent requirement for police training (*Committee Report*, 1986).

Now leaders are making appeals for better relations between the police and citizens which call for improved methods of public relations. They want to see the police develop as a helping institution avoiding the military image. These goals, too, demand new ideas in the area of police training.

An internal problem of the police today is non-availability of police officers in certain parts of the country. The Helsinki district, the most populated and industrialized area in the country, is chronically short of police officers. In Espoo, some 15 miles north of Helsinki, for every 1,000 inhabitants there are 0.97 police officers while on the average there are 1.49 police officers for every 1,000 inhabitants in Finland as a whole. The lack of the personnel has caused backlog of work. It has worsened as well as delayed police response to public demand for police services. However, the shortage of police officers in Helsinki is not only an economic matter. Young police officers prefer to work in the countryside or small cities because these places are more convenient and the cost of living is cheaper. These districts are also considered safer than Helsinki. So the turnover of the police personnel in Helsinki area is very high. Complaints are also heard regarding the lack of police resources, such as computers, telecommunication devices, cars, and other technological resources (*Committee Report*, 1986).

The demands for reform of the police organization are heard constantly. Organizationally the police are hierarchical and centralized. Sometimes troubles have arisen because of the hierarchical culture of the police. Bureaucratic regulations have hampered rapid action. These features with law-oriented philosophy of police administration have decreased effectiveness at the lower levels of the department. Perhaps because of the tight control from the top, illegalities and crimes at the rank-and-file level are quite unusual. During the last several years only few briberies, for instance, were found in Finnish police ranks.

Police reforms have, however, a political dimension. During recent years leading political parties, the Social Democratic Party, the Center Party and Conservatives since 1986, have been vying to install their people at the top positions in the department. Thus, these police appointments at the national as well as state levels have been politically influenced. In the process, however, administrative reforms have slowed down.

The police have also been complaining about some constraints on their organization. There is, for example, a blanket ban on all wiretapping. According to the proposal of the Parliamentary Police Committee in 1986, the police must have a right to listen to telephone calls as well as access to other means of communication in certain cases such as drug trafficking, organized crime, terrorism, and other serious offenses. But these rights are still politically debated. Advocates of the rights to privacy are strongly opposed to this move (Aallas, 1986; Nortamo, 1986).

Certain groups of Finnish citizens called attention to the fact that the police have established certain semi-secret units inside their organization. The Bear Unit, consisting of 60 police officers with eight supervisors, for example, is kept in reserve to tackle terrorists, skyjackers, and hijackers. There are other similar groups organized for a quick response in unusual or emergency cases. These elements have special training, weapons, and modes of operations. It is claimed that there are additional units of such nature inside the police about which there is very little public knowledge (Aallas, 1988). Some interpret this kind of development as a harmful trend toward developing "security state" in which the citizenry can be kept under strict control (Hirsch, 1980).

CONCLUSIONS

The police in Finland, which are historically closedly linked to the Swedish police, did not develop exactly like their Swedish cousins. Finland was the first Nordic country with a purely national police model. Nor do the Finnish police resemble the police in Scandinavia in some other important respects. In Finland, for example, the police have no connection with the Ministry of Justice which controls the police in other countries neighboring Finland. The influence of Russia seems to have been responsible for strong structural linkage with the center of government. In many European countries, including Germany, that central controlling institution happens to be the Ministry of Interior and the police are under the direct control of that ministry. In that sense, Finland falls into this European tradition. The Finnish police share a major tradition of the European policing in having two distinct styles and structures for rural and urban police. In Finland the rural policing is responsibility of sheriffs, but unlike U. S. police they are neither elected by the people nor appointed by provincial courts or governments. In all rural areas the sheriffs are the representatives of the national government. Unlike the Italian Carabinieri or the French Gendarmerie, the Finnish police do not have armed police for policing the countryside. Their emergency police are the Mobile Police who are engaged in traffic control.

In order to give police operational muscle and control over crime-control activities the police in Finland have been entrusted with very strong legal powers in carrying out their business. This was particularly noticeable in the police powers of arrest and detention which have been drastically reduced only recently so as to bring Finnish laws into conformity with the needs and requirements of human rights. This new step dismayed the police, but now they seem to have accepted the new situation.

Notwithstanding their unusually strong legal powers and authority the police in Finland have never had a reputation of being trigger-happy or autocratic. They have a positive image and complaints against the police are not anyway distracting. The police have also been largely noncontroversial and nonadversarial in the sense that the problems of crime, drugs, terrorism, and public disturbances have not rocked Finland. Blessed with an acceptable image, peaceful condition, and high standard of affluence, the Finnish police also receive prolonged and careful training at all levels. In this regard, German police training has had a marked influence upon Finnish police training; indeed, in length, thoroughness, and the quality of instructors, Finnish training programs are like their counterparts in Germany.

Finnish police leaders, both in the countryside and in urban areas are law graduates like their counterparts in other Scandinavian countries. In rural areas they also performed the tasks of prosecutors. It may be noted here that many sheriffs in remote areas also have been *varatuomari*, the people who have had training to fill in judges' positions. In spite of the fact all police personnel must have completed compulsory military training with a limited work experience as a supervisor during their army attachment, the culture of militarism is not pronounced in the police organization in Finland. As a matter of fact, the hierarchy in the police is rather short. Supervisors seem to be sensitive to the Finnish intolerance of close supervision.

The unique factors mentioned above have made police work in Finland very attractive and charming. Indeed, police problems are not serious now. Mostly these are problems relative to the scarcity of human resources, and that is partly a historical legacy. Towns have had numerically stronger force and, in the recently developed urban areas, the force has been thinly distributed. That anomaly continues even today. As mentioned previously, the police have had a fairly easy time as they have not been challenged by terrorism, crimes, drugs, and other evils that plague many an affluent society. Finland has also kept its borders closed to foreigners. But with the fall of communism, greater European integration, and surging waves of drugs, organized crime and related problems, the police will have to gear themselves to face these and other new challenges.

---

[1]During the first years of the 1990s, a Committee on Police Legislation started to plan a new Police Law. At the beginning of 1994 the Committee made its proposals to the Finnish Government. In April 1994 the Government Bill for a new Police Law was given to Parliament. Most probably some changes will be made during the legislative process. The Government has reported that the law will come into force at the earliest in the second half of 1995. This new legislation will modernize the definition of the rights and duties of the police.

REFERENCES

Aallas, Esa. Terroristit tulevat ellei poliisin valtuuksia lisätä (Terrorists are coming if there is no increase in the power of the police). *Ydin* 20 (5) (1986): 4-8.

__________.Valtion salaiset vartijat (The secret guards of the state). *Ydin* 22 (2) (1988): 4-7.

Aherma, Roy. Suomen Järjestyspoliisien Liitto r.y. 20 toiminnan vuotta, 1966-1986 (The Finnish Patrolling Police Association. 20 Years of Action, 1966-1986). *Poliisimies* 57 (4) (1986): 21-24).

__________.Poliisin ammatillinen järjestäytyminen *Poliisi Suomessa* (Police in Finland). Helsinki, 1986.

__________.Professional Associations of the Finnish police, The Police of Finland, 1986.

Annual Report of the Police College, 1987.

Annual Report of the Police School, 1987.

Aromaa, Kauko: Mitä poliisi pelkää? (What is a policeman afraid of?). *Poliisimies* 57 (10) (1986): 29-31.

Committee Report 1984:4. Poliisin ammatillisen koulutuksen sopeuttaminen keskiasteen koulunuudistukseen (The Adjustment of the Police Training to the Middle Level School Reform). *Sisaasiainministerion poliisiosaston julkaisuja* 4 (1984).

__________1984:10.Poliisipäällikoiden virkatutkintotyoryhman mietintö (The Report of the Committee for the Examination of the police chief officers). *Sisäasiainministeriön poliisiosaston julkaisuja* 10, 1984.

__________1985:5.Poliisikokelaiden rekrytointitoiminnan tehostamista selvittäneen työryhman mietintö (*The Report of the Committee for the Advancement of Police Recruitment*). *Sisaasiainministerion poliisiosaston julkaisuja* 5, 1985.

__________1986:16.Parlamentäärisen poliisikomitean mietintö (*The Report of the Parliamentary Police Committee*), 1986.

Das, Dilip K. *Policing in Six Countries Around the World: Organizational Perspectives.* Chicago: OICI, University of Illinois, 1993.

__________. Personal Conversation with Ahti Laitinen, 1990.

Eerola, Satu. Poliisimiehen tyoturvallisuudesta (About the labor protection of a policeman). *Poliisimies* 55(12) (1984): 25-34.

Grönfors, Martti. "Ethnic Minorities and Deviance: The Relationship Between Finnish Gypsies and Police." *Scandinavian Studies in Criminology* 7 (1979): 147-156.

Hirsch, Joachim. *Der Sicherheitssaat (The Security State)*. Frankfurt am Main, 1980.

Jousimaa, Kyösti. "The History of the Finnish Police." *The Police of Finland.* Helsinki:Finnish Chapter, International Police Association, 1986.

Kamppi, Terttu and Antti Aro. *Poliisimielikuvat (The images about the police).* Helsinki: Consumer Compass/Kuluttajatieto Oy, 1987.

Luntiala, Pertti. Poliisi yleison palvelijana (The police as the public servant). *Poliisimies* 59 (5) (1988): 24-25.

Luntiala, Pertti and Esa Mearonen. "Police Personnel Training." In Reino Orasmala et al. (eds). *The Police of Finland.* Helsinki: Finnish Chapter, International Police Association, 1986.

Mäkinen, Tuija. Diskrimininering i Finlands zigenares erfarenheter (Discrimination in Finnish Gypsies experiences). *Nordisk tidsskrift for kriminalvedeskab* 72 (1) (1985): 49-57.

Mantila, Anu. Lähipoliisi—Kortteli ja aluepoliisit kertovat työstään (Community policing—the opinions of neighborhood and district policemen of their work). *Publication 83,* Helsinki: National Research Institute of Legal Policy, 1987.

Nortamo, Simo-Pekka. Puhelinkuuntelua (Listening secrectly on telephones). *Helsingin Sanomat,* November 23, 1986.

Orasmala, Reino (ed.). *Poliisikunnan keskusliitto ry. 1943-1983. Historiikki (The History of the Police Corps' Central Union), 1943-1983.* 1983.

__________. *The Police of Finland*. Helsinki: Finnish Chapter, International Police Association, 1986.

Petterson, Valtter. Nainen poliisina (Woman as a policeman). *Poliisimies* 58 (5) (1987): 24-25.

__________.Poliisikoulutus uudistus (The Reformation of the Police Training). *Poliisimies* 58 (2) (1987): 33-35.

Policeman 58 (7-8) 1987: The Announcement of the Police Cadet Course, p. 41.

__________ 59 (1) 1988: The Announcement of the Police Cadet Course, p. 45.

Rauhala, Urho. *Suomalaisen yhteiskunnan sosiaalinen kerrostuneisuus (The Social Stratification of the Finnish Society)*. VAPK Kampin VALTIMO, 1966.

Rikollisuustilanne 1979, 1986 (Criminality 1979, 1986). Helsinki: National Research Institute of Legal Policy, 1979 and 1987.

Ruotsalainen, Veikko. *Suomen Poliisien Liitto R.Y. 1923-1973 (The Finnish Police Federation 1923-1973)*. Helsinki: Police Federation, 1973.

Salmi, Heikki. Kolumni (A Column). *Rikospoliisi* 59 (1) (1988): 35.

Sinisalo, Kari. Poliisin toimivallan määräytyminen (The determination of the competence of the police). Unpublished paper, 1971.

Statistical Report, 29. Helsinki: Central Statistical Office of Finland, 1987.

Takala, Hannu (ed.). Poliisilakko (The Police Strike). *Publication 30*. Helsinki: The National Institute of Legal Policy Research, 1979.

Uusitalo, Paavo: Poliisin aseenkantotavan vaikutuksista (The effects of the policemen's way of carrying guns). *Oikeus* 9 (3) (1980): 164-171.

Vesterinen, Seppo. Poliisiopiston valintalautakunnan kokous (The Meeting Report of the Selection Board of the Police College). *Poliisimies* 58 (6) (1987): 16.

Virta, Sirpa. Poliisijarjestötutkimus (The Study of the Police Associations). *Poliisimies* 58 (12) (1987): 51-53.

Weckman, Markku. Poliisin jatkokoulutuksen valinnasta ja menettelyn kehittämisestä ym (About the selection and development of the post graduate-training of the police etc.). *Polisimies* 59 (2) (1988): 12-13.

Ylikangas, Mikko. Poliisi ja poliisin arvostelu (Police and the criticism against the police). *Poliisimies* 55 (9) (1984): 9-13.

POLICE IN INDIA

by S. M. Diaz

INTRODUCTION

India is a peninsular land mass surrounded by the Himalayan Mountains in the north and 4,000 miles of coastline with the Bay of Bengal, the Indian Ocean, and the Arabian Sea in the other three directions. It has long borders with Pakistan in the west, Nepal and Bhutan in the north, and Bangladesh and Burma in the east. Its 25 autonomous states as well as Union Territories which are directly administered by the Center, cover an area of two million square miles and hold a population of 850 million. About 24 percent of Indians live in urban areas.

A democratically elected government which is parliamentary in character operates from the country's capital of New Delhi, and the states within the country also have similar governments. Political power is divided between the governments at the center and the states, and in that sense the set-up can be called federal. It has a strong central tendency. Some of the states, particularly at the periphery, have been governed by parties different from, and sometimes in opposition to, the Congress Party which originally led the national movement for independence and controlled for a long time the governments at the center and most of the heartland states. This has led to an emerging phenomenon of regionalism of varying degrees all round, primarily arising from political rivalries intensified by perceived disparities in economic development between different regions and states. In recent times a National Front

Government was in power in New Delhi, and in the heartland states, while the Congress Party was forced to make do with some of the distant states like Maharastra, Andhra, and Karnataka. This minority government did not last long and today a Congress Party government is in the saddle.

The original tribal inhabitants of the country probably lived in the tablelands of Central and South India. Some of these tribes still predominate in the states like Madhya Pradesh, Bihar, and Rajasthan. In other parts of the country they live in some remote hill and forest areas but in rather smaller numbers. The Dravidians were the first organized and civilized people to inhabit India. The urbanized civilization of Mohanjadaro and Harappa is believed to be Dravidian, and is placed around 2,500 to 3,000 years before Christ. The pastoral Aryan people came through the northwestern passes a little later and fanned out in different directions in the north of India, primarily. They either overwhelmed the Dravidians or merged with them, or drove them down south. In the northeast, people of Mongolian origin made their inroads. The people of India, as they are today, are therefore a mixture of all these races, to a greater or less degree.

On the spiritual front, first Animism, then Proto-Hinduism, and finally Vedic Hinduism, could be considered the early religions of India. But in the sixth century B.C., Mahaveera and Buddha sponsored Jainism and Buddhism, which were in essence reform movements against the ritualism and priestcraft of the then prevalent Hinduism. In due course, however, resurgent Hinduism, with a philosophic base and orientation, absorbed the good features of all these reformist movements and reestablished itself as India's dominant religion and principal way of life. Christianity came to India in A.D. 52 with Apostle St. Thomas, and Islam in A.D. 712, when the Arabs reached Sind in India's west. Thus the people of India belong to many racial origins, religious persuasions, and distinct regions that speak different languages and dialects. But still one does not have to labor hard to discern an underlying sociocultural unity, which is a synthesis of contributions from all these sources. Unfortunately, however, there has been a fundamentalist slant recently among the adherents of the principal religion leading to communal confrontations on many issues in spite of the basic secularism enshrined in the Constitution.

Vasco da Gama is credited with having opened the sea route to India for the first time in A.D. 1498. This is true only so far as western Europe is concerned. On the contrary, after the discovery of the monsoon in A.D. 47, people from the Middle East as well as Greece and Rome, did come and establish trade relations with India in spices and fine-spun cotton fabric. Apart from literary evidence on both sides, the digs of Arikamedu near Pondicherry and the finds of Roman gold coins at other places on their route, from west to east across the south of India, vouch for this. Much later, after 1498 in succession, the Portuguese, the Danish, the Dutch, the French, and the British, established trading posts in different parts of India. The British East India Company, originally established in Surat in A.D. 1600, gradually spread out conquering many Indian states and annexing territory or obtaining tribute from rulers, thus becoming for the first time in history a commercial institution taking on territorial and governmental responsibilities. This continued till 1858 when after the bitter but not so organized struggle for freedom in 1857 by a bulk of the army men and some rulers, the British Government took over direct control of its Indian Empire. It is a fact of modern Indian history that Britain ruled over India for nearly 200 years. There was peace in the land, by and large, Pax Britannica. Other benefits were marginal, such as establishment of a few industries and some plantations as well as rail transportation and communicational progress. But then, no nation ever ruled another nation primarily in the interest of the subject nation. However, the British did bequeath to India a liberal English education, as a result of which the educated Indian community imbibed the western concepts of nationhood, democracy, and the rule of law, all of which not only served India during its struggle for freedom, but also later after her independence from the British colonial rule in 1947. Fortunately, India has managed to retain in the midst of many stresses and strains the essence of these values and ideals in the decades after independence too, which accounts for the measure of the prestige that the country commands in international circles.

According to Pandit Jawaharlal Nehru, a veteran freedom fighter and the first Prime Minister of India, independence was the means of redeeming of a pledge to the common man in India for social and economic independence and the dignity of the individual. In the years following independence, India has acknowledgedly done fairly well in many respects. The country has had the advantage of a stable government, which many newly independent countries in Asia, Africa, or South America have not had. India has a criminal justice system, which, with all its problems of delay, delivers legal justice to the humblest citizen of the land. India does not face the recurrent famines, like the Bengal famine of the old days, because the country has improved its food production from 47 million tons in 1947 to 173 million tons at the time of writing. The country has a comfortable provision of buffer stock of grain to meet emergencies, such as failure of monsoons. The world at large and the World Bank in particular have appreciated this progress. The First and Second Five Year Plans gave a meaningful boost to agricultural infrastructure and heavy industry, which was followed up in the early 1960s by the Green Revolution. Later plans, however, were to some extent thrown out of gear by defense problems and related needs.

The planning process itself was started by Pandit Nehru, as a response to widespread call of the people to banish the prevailing evils of ignorance, disease, and poverty and the need for the rapid development of a nation with totally limited resources. In the directions of improving national levels of education and health, something has been achieved, with the latter considerably better. The literacy rate has increased from about 10 percent to about 40 percent. In fact, it is 70 percent in Kerala. But the national average is not good enough considering the constitutional provision for free, compulsory primary education. Higher education as well as professional education and training for skills progressed farther, so that India today stands quite high in the world as regards educated, professional, and skilled human resources. As regards health, with preventive medicine and improved medical care epidemic incidence and mortality rates have declined substantially. That is the reason why expectancy of life in India has also increased from 27 years in 1947 to 55 at the time of writing. Despite considerable efforts, it is only on the front of eliminating poverty that the country has not fared well on account of various reasons. The first and most important of the problems is just that there are too many people in the country. In 1947 India's population was only 340 million. The 1981 census figure was 683.8 million, and the rate of growth over 2.4 percent. The estimated population today is 850 million with only a slight reduction in the growth rate to 2.1 percent. Steps are being taken within democratic limitations to control the growth rate further. Another important issue that arises in this context is quality of life. The primary indicator that determines this is education, particularly women's education, as it has been vindicated in Kerala state. For many reasons India is still lagging behind in "threshold" education, particularly among females. Some programs recently introduced for promoting full registration and minimizing dropouts, as well as encouraging adult literacy, are expected to improve matters within a reasonable timeframe.

In this context, a problem of considerable relevance is the gradual erosion of societal norms and the increasing lawlessness that pervades Indian society today. Durkheim (1932) spoke of the anomie or normlessness that was the prevalent feature of Western Europe after the First World War. Merton (1957) delineated the nonconformist adaptive patterns of criminal innovations and rebellion that young people individually and in groups tended to adopt in the United States after the Second World War in pursuit of the socially ordered objectives of reaching positions of prestige, power, and money. The contemporary situation in India is not very different from what Merton envisaged in the postwar U.S.A. In fact, the dominant concern of most people in India today appears to be to make money somehow with as little effort as possible, and in the process questionable practices like white-collar crime and even violence are not taboo. This is perhaps a tendency generally perceived in all countries of the world, but the Indian situation is seen to be in marked contrast to its own historical and cultural traditions. Apart from this, the processes of accelerated democratization and distorted individualization, as well as misinterpreted secularism, in free India exist side by side with not so well planned industrialization, haphazard urbanization, and uncontrolled spread of slums in industrial centers. All this has led to overwhelming permissiveness.

As a result, it is noticed that there has been a definite fall in standards of public life, with widely prevalent laxity, deviance, and corruption. There is also today a volume of recorded crime, which is far in excess of what could be considered reasonable or as normal due to any corresponding increase in population. Crime figures increased approximately by 56 percent from during the last decade as against population which increased only 25 percent during the same period. Even among common people, such as students, townsfolk, and villagers, there has come about a feeling of discontent and frustration and a predisposition to group deviance and mass violence provoked by a disparity between promise and performance. What is worse is the dichotomy between profession and practice and a prevalent perception of extreme deprivation, due to political, economic, or other reasons. Regionalistic terrorism is an extreme exhibition of this malaise. Terrorism in the Punjab as well as Jammu and Kashmir has continued far longer than the country's social health can withstand. Communal disharmony has become endemic and is bursting out into sporadic violence with alarming frequency in many places. Perhaps India and Indians have lost the moorings they derived from the moral ideals of the Gandhian era by going all out for material benefits. In such a context, it is heartening to see some right-thinking elders joining together in a Movement for National Resurgence. These developments and trends naturally have had their impact on policing in the country.

MANDATE AND PHILOSOPHY

Policing of some kind was always part of the statecraft in India. In the kingdoms, big and small, that existed in the country from time immemorial the king invariably assumed the responsibility of preserving peace and order within his realm. He also sought to prevent criminal activities by antisocial elements and to deal with wrongdoers when they did come to notice for criminal misconduct. In smaller territories, the king personally attended to the policing responsibilities, occasionally by going out in disguise to see things for himself, but generally by sending out his agents for collecting intelligence and using units of his military formation, such as it was, to restore order where necessary. In the larger kingdoms or empires, like the Mauryan Empire, which commenced in 321 B.C., a part of this responsibility of the ruler was delegated to the City Superintendent and others in the form of preventive and enforcement duties as outlined in the *Artha Sashthra,* a compendium of statecraft written by the Prime Minister Kautilya for the first Mauryan Emperor, Chandragupta Maurya. The reference to policing and the relevant laws occurs inter alia in Kautilya's book, which is in the nature of a guidebook of pragmatic principles for rulers to follow in handling political and economic matters. A similar book appeared centuries later in the West and that was Machiavelli's *The Prince.* In the kingdoms and empires that emerged later in India, policing in its essence existed in some form or the other. In the Tamil country, however, a far superior value-based treatise of guidance to rulers called *Thirukural* has been widely in use for nearly 2,000 years. Policing by the king as well as intelligence services are included in this work.

In the long interval between the Mauryan and the Moghul Empire which came into existence in 1526, policing of a well-organized and commendable variety evolved principally designed to ensure effective intelligence as well as fine watch and ward. This evolution could be gleaned, by inference, from the writings of Chinese travelers Fahien and Hieuen Tsang, who visited India during the Golden age of the Guptas in the late fourth, fifth, and sixth centuries A.D. and later during the rule of Harshavardhana in the seventh century. In the south the reign of the great Raja Chola around the turn of the tenth century, A.D., witnessed an acme of administration in all aspects including policing as could be inferred from the epigraphs and literary evidence of the period. About the police administration during the Moghul period, we have more precise information with description of the role of the Kotwals and the Daroghas as well as the procedures of policing. When the British came, they were naturally subject to the laws of the land and the procedures of policing in the respective areas where they operated. The only exception occurred when some outright grants of large territory were made by the local rulers to the British. Even in such cases it was rare that policing responsibilities went with the territorial grant. Normally the local ruler's police attended to this work. All this would show that some sort of policing did exist in all parts of the country, all the time.

Sometime after the British East India Company firmly established itself in 1600 and later started to rule India as an agent of the Crown with a Governor-General, the British Army Commander, General Napier, was sent to conquer and annex Sind, which he did in early 1840s. In 1843, in order to tone up the civil administration, Napier organized a police system in the annexed territories on the model of the Royal Irish Constabulary of Northern Ireland (Ulster), which was seen to work better than other systems like the Moghul Kotwal or Darogha system or the time-honored watch and ward pattern tried out elsewhere in the country. The British system introduced a few decades earlier in the Metropolis of London also was not considered suitable. Consequently, the Sind model was adopted, first in Bombay in 1853 and later in Madras in 1859. The Police Commission of 1860 placed its seal of approval on the system and the Indian Police Act of 1861 followed. This Act, which is 125 years old, still provides the current mandate for the functioning of the Indian Police. The three basic features of the enactment are:

(1) Policing is a state responsibility, and so structurally the regular police are a state-level administrative apparatus.
(2) Police are organized in a hierarchical form on the model of the Royal Irish Constabulary under an Inspector General of Police who is answerable to the State Government.
(3) The internal administration of the police organization of the state is responsibility of the Inspector General of Police himself.

The mandate of the police is envisaged as prevention of crime and maintenance of order, and in the process the police are expected to carry out orders issued by all lawful authority. This is spelled out in section 23 and the related provisions of the Police Act of 1861. In the district, the most important center of administration in India, they are expected to function under the direction and control of the District Magistrate in maintaining law and order in the jurisdiction. The same mandate was allowed to continue even after India attained independence in 1947. No serious attempt was made at that critical time by the Indian national leaders to remould the Indian police as a more effective instrument of service to the people in proper accord with the changed situation and in response to the needs of the free citizens of India.

Policing philosophy in India has been colored by the fact that the Indian police are a ruler-appointed police; they are structurally different from the people-oriented police, as is the case in regard to the police of Britain (Mullik, 1972). Unlike the British police evolving as a local institution in the shape of watch and ward and providing the foundation of Britain's Home Secretary, Sir Robert Peel's 1829 Metropolitan Police, the police in India have always served the ruler more conspicuously. They were always drawn from the men who served the chieftain or the local king. The Sind model of policing spread everywhere in India during the British rule as a state-level organization serving the government of the state more directly as a ruler-appointed force.

When India awoke to freedom on the midnight of August 14/15, 1947, the founding fathers of the nation including the great Sardar Vallahbhai Patel, the first Home-minister of India, did not take the steps to introduce a new enactment for the police service, spelling out police objectives for a free India that would be in tune with the changed context and circumstances of the country. Nor was a new mandate and philosophy of policing through statutory innovations adopted. On the contrary the new rulers of India went on adding new laws, as well as all and sundry functions to the already heavy burden of the police. As a result, the police continued as the law enforcement and order maintenance arm of the rulers. Writing nearly four decades after independence, a dispassionate British observer commented that the police in new India had only changed their masters from the British rulers to the Indian ruling-elite groups (Arnold, 1986). This is not to say that no attempts were made at all to reorient the approach and functioning of the police after independence. There certainly was a serious effort made. Pandit Jawaharlal Nehru gave a stirring call to the leaders of the police to reorient their thinking and redirect the activities of their organizations toward effective service of the people. Sardar Patel established a well-designed National Police Academy which trained the Indian Police Service officers, the superior members of the police in India, under the new dispensation. Nevertheless, there was no radical departure in thinking as regards the laws or their enforcement. All attempts made by police leaders were either on individual initiative or half-hearted activities in the group. There was no change in the system itself. There was no change in the basic law governing the police organization and its functioning.

The first realization of this hiatus came in the late 1970s and appropriate action was taken with the appointment of a National Police Commission under the chairmanship of Dharma Vira, a former top-level bureaucrat of the central government and the Governor of Karnataka as well as West Bengal. The Commission went about its job very systematically and gave quite a few good recommendations, all of them very valid, reference to which will be made at the appropriate places later in this chapter. But for now what is relevant is that the Commission's recommendation for a new Police Act, for which the Commission members even developed a well-considered draft incorporating many of their important recommendations, is still under consideration even today. The hiatus in adopting the proposed new Police Act may be due to the procedures outlined therein for police accountability which are so radically different from what the rulers of the country are used to that the powers that be need a lot of time to rethink and adjust themselves. It is hoped that the pressure of public opinion and a broad democratic consensus in favor of the carefully-drafted and relevantly-oriented new philosophy and mandate for the Indian police will assert themselves and lead to the adoption of a new Police Act.

FUNCTIONS

In brief, the function of the police in every society is considered to be the protection of society. This may be amplified to mean the protection of life and property and the constitutionally guaranteed and cherished rights of the people against a backdrop of well-maintained public peace and order. This is so in India too. The Constitution (1950) incorporates in full the human rights envisaged in the U.N. Declaration of 1948. The functions of the police have been listed by the National Police Commission of India (1979) as follows:

(1) To promote the nation's integrity and preserve public order.
(2) To investigate crimes as well as to apprehend offenders and participate in the connected legal proceedings.
(3) To identify problems and situations that are likely to result in commission of crime.
(4) To reduce opportunities for commission of crime through preventive patrols and other appropriate police measures.
(5) To aid and cooperate with other concerned agencies in implementing measures for prevention of crime.
(6) To aid individuals who are in danger of physical harm.
(7) To create and maintain a feeling of security in the community.
(8) To facilitate orderly movement of people and vehicles on the roads.

(9) To counsel and resolve conflicts and promote amity.
(10) To provide other appropriate services and extend relief to people in distress situations.
(11) To collect intelligence on public peace and crime, especially affecting national integrity, security, and economy.
(12) To perform such other duties as may be enjoined on them by law for the time being in force.

The above functions naturally cover a wide spectrum of police duties, extending from the maintenance of the nation's integrity and security as well as public peace and order, to the prevention, investigation, and prosecution of offenses of various kinds, including white collar crime and offenses against codified public morality. By and large, these functions have been based on the police duties, as outlined in Sec. 23 of the old Indian Police Act of 1861 as well as the nine principles laid down in England during the London Metropolitan Police Reforms in 1829, but relevantly updated in the context of the social changes and developments of today as well as the needs of the present and the future environments. These functions fall under the three broad heads of police duties classified as social control, social defense, and social welfare services. Of these naturally, the social control function is the most important and covers public peace and order maintenance, enforcement of law including social legislation, right from the stage of prevention, reporting, and detection through investigation, to prosecution and disposal in court. Social defense and social welfare too are vital components of police work, particularly in a changing and developing welfare-oriented democratic society like India.

Crime today has become the major concern of the people in India as it has become so everywhere in the rest of the world. A comparative study of the crime figures over a decade in our country too has shown an increase in crime, by more than double of what would be warranted only by the yardstick of increase in population. Apart from the quantitative increase, the current trend is pronouncedly more toward violence. Noticeable is a general tendency toward permissiveness and lawlessness. There prevails a mood of tolerance for questionable methods provided there is heavy money to be had at the end of it all. Indians would be better off with less crime. The Indian criminal justice system inherited from the British, and based on rule of law was all right during the

British days. In spite of the delays and other defects it could ensure justice for the humblest citizen of the land if he or she had the stamina to pursue their case. That system designed to meet the requirements of the people and the country of over a century ago, is not fully relevant to the aspirations of the people of independent India today. It is now bursting at the seams under the weight of its own work load. Complaints are heard that the system is on the verge of collapse. It certainly is faced with a tremendous crisis. The relevant problems primarily relating to the law's delays have been referred by the Government of India to the Law Commission, a constitutional and statutory body, continuously in session to review and update the country's laws, and to suggest ways and means for improvement. It would, however, have been more appropriate if the Government of India had appointed an integrated criminal justice commission to study the whole system of criminal justice delivery, taking into consideration all the subsystems together, and to make its recommendations for effective and coordinated functioning. Nevertheless, the existing system is basically sound, and essentially it is respected and complimented by right-thinking people nationally and internationally. There certainly are shortcomings, though, which must be speedily rectified in order to make the system meaningfully to meet the country's current needs.

It must also be mentioned here that certain ideas for decentralization and speedy disposal are now being widely canvassed. Some of them have been adopted and tried out successfully, like the Nyaya-Panchayat system at the grassroots level, and the Lok Adalat. These are ad hoc courts for delivery of speedy justice in pending cases of a relatively simpler nature with the consent of the parties concerned. These have been adopted in selected centers all over the country. The latest suggestion, well received all over the land, is the one of a national court of appeals, between the high Courts of the states and the Supreme Court of India. The present Prime Minister has also endorsed it. But what is really required is an integrated streamlining of the whole system, with an accent on prevention of crime with due consideration for the rights of victims, side by side with promoting of ways and means of also controlling the filing rate, while trying out various methods of improving the clearance rate of cases. Reducing the filing rate, for example, may involve matters such as decriminalization, diversified and compounding disposals, as well as the simplification of procedures. In such a context, the police as the principal agency of the system, in mass contact with the public, will have to reorient their approach and functioning to ensure effective public cooperation all around.

The police in India had a reputation for competent handling of crime even during the British days even though they were undermanned, overworked, ill-paid, and badly equipped. Bayley (1969) clearly acknowledges this fact and notes the following achievements of the Indian police:

(1) Conducting of numerous massive general elections to the satisfaction, by and large, of all concerned.
(2) Maintainenance of public peace and order in spite of the mounting stresses and strains.
(3) Handling of the problem of crime fairly satisfactorily ensuring legal justice to those who seek it.

During the last two decades, however, conditions in India have steadily deteriorated. The environment for police work has been definitely getting worse. The police also have had to carry on with ill-suited legal instruments. They suffer fron extreme inadequacy of modern equipment and the level of professionalization is low.

PERSONNEL PRACTICES

The personnel practices, obtaining in the police organization of India, are substantially different from the practices adopted in England, the United States, and many other countries. As regards recruitment of police in India, there are at least three different entry levels, as against only a single level of entry in England and the United States. The three levels in India are as a police constable at the lowest level, a sub-inspector at the middle level, and as an Assistant or Deputy Superintendent for the supervisory levels in the higher reaches. The system also provides for some upward mobility; it is possible for deserving persons from the lower cadres to be promoted to a percentage of the higher-level jobs. This three-level entry is justified in this country by the far-flung massive structure, vast numbers, low educational level, and the poor quality of life of the majority of the population, to which the police have to cater, as well as the type of work that is expected to be performed at the different levels by the police personnel deployed in remote rural areas. The police constable in the main is expected to attend to the job of order maintenance and to carry on the patrolling of the distant and sometimes sensitive beats. For this purpose, in the olden days, even individuals who had barely completed about ten years in school were hired. Most of them had to retire as constables, however. Promotions to higher levels were not possible because they were poorly educated. Nor was their service potential good enough for promotion in most cases. As a result, the minimum qualifications for recruitment at the constable level have been raised to a higher level in recent years.

The sub-inspector, hired at the middle level, is often described as the backbone of the police service, which in a large measure is true. He functions under law as the station-house officer, maintains peace and order, registers and investigates crime, and supervises the constabulary in regard to all their duties. He again acts as the cutting edge of the organization in the implementation of policies decided at the state level. Through his functions he represents the state administration, particularly in remote areas. Higher-level entry of well qualified and competent persons, suitable for ultimately manning senior positions in the service, is facilitated through competitive examinations and interviews conducted by the public service commissions at the national and state levels. This procedure is similar to the pattern of ushering in managerially qualified and trained personnel at the higher levels of business and industry, and has been continued from the days of the British, who had their special recruitment for the higher services in England first and later in India too. For the present, the three different levels of entry perhaps need to continue; maybe later the levels of entry to the police can be reduced to two.

The recruitment and selection for the constabulary is done at the district level by the superintendent of police with the assistance of his senior officers after suitable advertisement in the local media. The educational qualification for the position of a constable is a high school diploma generally called a matriculation certification in India. Minimum physical requirements are a height of 5 ft. 6 in., an appropriate girth, and a reasonable performance in a sextet of track-and-field events. Short-listed candidates are put through a brief written test, an interview, and finally, a medical examination before appointment.

After appointment constables are sent for training in the police training schools. The period of training varies from state to state; it is from six to nine months. Recruit training consists of outdoor and indoor work, equally balanced, with perhaps an extra emphasis on physical rigor, parade ground work such as foot drill, arms drill as well as weapon-training. In the classroom trainees are taught the rudiments of police work, basic laws, and public relations. After training in the school, they are given practical on-the-job training in police stations. The period of practical training could be better utilized to mold the personality of the young constables under proper guidance and supervision before they are posted to regular work in police stations. At present the best is not done, both because of the pressure of law-and-order work everywhere and the absence of due care and attention for providing a purposeful practical training before sending recruits out on diverse duties.

The recruitment to the vital position of sub-inspector of police is made from among young men, and also women are hired in recent years. They are required to possess a university degree in any discipline. Successful candidates must be also physically well built and medically fit. The candidates are put through a written examination in general education and awareness, and the final selection is made through personal interviews of the qualified candidates.

Selected persons are trained in the police training college of the state, and their one-year training is structured reasonably well on the lines suggested by the Gore Committee on Police Training (1972). They are trained to perform the role of station-house officers who exercise considerable authority under Indian criminal laws. Criminal laws, both substantive and procedural, take pride of place in their course content. In addition, they are trained in all aspects of enforcement of law including criminal investigation. They are given an appreciation of criminological concepts. Sub-inspector trainees are also trained regarding the procedures and practices for maintenance of public peace and order. The updated syllabus, after the Report of the Gore Committee, also has a reasonable content of management principles and techniques as well as ideas and approaches for good public relations and securing public cooperation. Trainees also receive a reasonable amount of physical training, parade ground work, weapon-training, and target practice. After completion of this training, they are also expected to do a period of practical on-the-job training for six months. Very often this program gets abridged due to the needs of emergency law-and-order work. Such duties become necessary all the time and naturally these youngsters are more readily pressed into emergency duties. Under such circumstances they have to pick up their lessons as they go along, and learn what they can by trial-and-error.

The senior-level personnel of the Indian Police Service (IPS) who are allotted to all the states by the central government are selected by the Union Public Service Commission on the basis of the results of a fairly stiff competitive procedure. It consists of a two-tier examination, a preliminary screening test and a main examination, followed by a personality test in a half-hour interview. The states also select a few senior personnel by a similar procedure through their own public service commissions. These persons get absorbed in due course in the Indian Police Service itself on the basis of their record of performance.

The officers selected and appointed to the IPS are trained in the National Police Academy (NPA). Initially they attend a brief Foundational Course of about four months in three selected centers. The Foundational Course is designed to give an insight to the country's economy, its problems, and the role of the public service in the society to all superior civil service personnel.

The one-year professional course at the NPA at Hyderabad is now split into eight months and four months. The full course of professional training is completed during the first eight months. The course content lays emphasis on criminal law and its enforcement, criminology, police science, starting with the history, organization, and administration of the police, and going on more importantly to maintenance of public peace and order as well as investigation of crime. Concepts and practices of management, with special reference to personnel management and police community relations occupy a prominent place in the syllabus. Wherever possible, theoretical postulations are supported by observations of real-life situations and simulated exercises as well as case-law discussions. Apart from these, a couple of sessions in the morning and evening are devoted to physical training and unarmed combat exercises, parade ground work and weapon training with target practice using small arms. Equestrian exercises and rock climbing are also special features of the outdoor training program.

After this intensive training, the probationary officers are sent to the states to which they are assigned. There they undergo a period of practical training in the field which involves learning the problems and challenges in different aspects of police work. During this period special care is also taken to enable the probationary officers under training to learn the local language as well as the local and special laws of the state. They may be required to spend a couple of months in the state police training college to learn the local laws and the language. Thereafter, the trainee officers are posted to independent charge of a subdivision, having earlier been exposed to the responsibilities of those who command police stations and circles. Subdivisions are administrative units into which districts in states are divided. Circles are parts of subdivisions. A circle consists of a number of police stations.

After they have acquired a thorough knowledge of conditions, problems, and methods of actual police work, officers of the Indian Police Service are brought back to the National Police Academy for another short spell of four months, to complete their institutional training. The primary purpose of this second phase of training is to reconcile the concepts learned and internalized in the Academy with the practices found in the states to the extent possible. During this period they are also exposed to democratically differing views of leading personalities from different walks of life on sensitive issues so that they may acquire an effectively balanced approach to problems.

Only upon completing the full period of their training are the probationary officers posted to the first effective charge of a subdivision in a district. Apart from the Assistant Superintendents of Police of the Indian Police Service, as already indicated, states hire a few probationary Deputy Superintendents of Police through a local process of selection, with the assistance of state Public Service Commissions. These officer-recruits are trained in state police training colleges and also put through practical training, after which they are given a job in a police department. They continue to work in junior positions, like the IPS officers, till state governments and the Union Public Service Commission agree that they are suitable to be absorbed in the IPS, which happens at the level of the Superintendent of Police. While an IPS officer takes charge as Superintendent of Police in about five years, a Deputy Superintendent of Police hired by a state may take about ten years to reach that position.

Before going into the matter of promotions, obviously it is necessary to examine the rank structure of the organization in some detail. In the police organizations of most states, between the police constable and the sub-inspector, there are at least two ranks, Head Constable and Assistant Sub-Inspector. In some states there is also a rank of Grade I Constable between Constable and Head Constable. In the next stage, between sub-inspector and Deputy or Assistant Superintendent, there is another rank, namely Inspector of Police. But some states have been experimenting with a rank of Deputy Inspector of Police. From the rank of Deputy/Asst. Superintendent of Police, the promotions take place to the ranks of Superintendent of Police, Deputy Inspector General of Police, and Inspector General of Police. In recent times, the higher rank of Director General of Police has been introduced in most states, and a number of positions of Inspector Generals of Police have been created so as to remedy the perceived lack of promotional avenues in the police service as compared to other civil services.

It is an acknowledged principle of promotion in Indian public administration that in the normal course of events, any entrant into public service at a certain level has a right to expect at least two promotions. The first one is on a consideration of seniority, subject to the rejection of the unfit. The second promotion is also based on seniority and is given to those who have already secured the first promotion, but moderated to some extent by merit. Any promotion beyond that will be solely on merit. As regards the promotion prospects of constables, as stated already, this principle only operates in the breach. Many persons hired as constables retire as constables. There are two reasons for this. The first, as mentioned earlier, is that many who join the police as constables do not possess the educational qualifications required for promotions. And the second is that the proportion of promotional avenues open to constables is very meager, with the result, even among those who were qualified, only a few get promoted. That is one of the reasons why most police commissions appointed by states and the recent National Police Commission have recommended a high school diploma as the minimum qualification for police constables, and that provision be made for an increased proportion of promotion opportunities for them.

At the sub-inspector's level, opportunities for promotion are better. A reasonably good sub-inspector of police normally reaches the level of Deputy Superintendent of Police. Some of them become Superintendents of Police too. This happens more often than it did before because of an increased vista of promotional positions created in recent times. Similarly, where formerly it was the normal expectation of an IPS Officer to reach at least the position of a Deputy Inspector General of Police and only sometimes succeed in becoming an Inspector General of Police, the present ambition of such an officer is to become at least an Inspector General of Police if he cannot attain the rank of Director General of Police. This is because many senior-level posts have been liberally created in states in recent times.

What is more important is the question of whether in the context of the three levels of police recruitment deserving persons recruited at one level do have free access to cross the barrier and go to the next slab and even beyond. Many persons who enter as police constables with fairly good educational qualification and reasonable background have become sub-inspectors and some of them have earned promotions as Inspectors of Police too. There have also been a very few cases of constables promoted as Deputy Superintendents of Police. This sort of thing should happen more often now, and more of them should become Deputy Superintendents of Police. If at the sub-inspector's level, direct recruitment is restricted to 60 percent, and the remaining 40 percent is kept open for promotion from the lower ranks, as suggested by the Administrative Reforms Commission, there will be greater opportunities for deserving persons among well qualified constables. More and more of such constables have been hired in recent times. Incidentally, this will also provide motivation for better quality of work of all ranks at all levels.

In the same way, if a 40 percent reservation is ensured for deserving persons to be promoted from the sub-inspector/inspector level to the rank of Deputy Superintendents of Police, and if a direct recruitment to Deputy Superintendents of Police in the states is avoided, as suggested by the National Police Commission (1978-81), there will be a greater number of suitable persons crossing the barrier between the middle to the senior level. One can then freely visualize the chances of a competent sub-inspector getting into the IPS, and also an occasional case of an outstanding police constable gaining entrance into this superior police service. In the state of Tamilnadu people talk with admiration of one constable who was promoted to Superintendent of Police and made a mark in the olden days, and of a sub-inspector who was promoted as Deputy Inspector General of Police. The latter did outstandingly well as the Deputy Inspector General of the Criminal Investigation Department of the state. With better standards of recruitment and training, more promotional avenues should open up. And with a 40 percent reservation for promotion from the lower ranks to the higher, it should be possible to report many more cases like those in Tamilnadu in the future.

LEADERSHIP/SUPERVISORY CALIBRE

Leadership at the various levels of the police goes to qualified and acceptable persons who have been selected to the pre-top leadership level and placed there already on the basis of certain norms laid down by appropriate commissions. The concept that a leader is one who is capable of influencing his team to strive willingly for the group objective does not always suit the persons on whom the leadership mantle falls in the police organizations of India. But the persons chosen from among the acceptable seniors too normally do not adhere to this concept of leadership.

One may look first at the number one position of the state police organization, the Director General of Police, for which the most meritorious officer should be selected from among all the competent and available senior-level persons. But in actual fact a chief political executive of a state chooses, even superseding many seniors, that particular officer in whom he has confidence. Often this means a person who is most acceptable to the party in power, and not the best person with the ability to perform well and to carry the whole team with him. However, there is at least one point in favor of such a leader. He is in a position to get things done for the organization during his tenure, particularly as regards finance, by obtaining the requisite sanctions more easily from the political executive of the government. That is perhaps good for the police. But a police leader is judged by the public on the basis of the results he has achieved in pursuit of the organization's primary objective, which is protection of society. He is expected to gear the organization up to meet developing situations, not only during the period he is in charge, but in the days to come as well. It is equally important that his leadership contributes effectively to the building-up of a cohesive team. Individuals in the team need to be appropriately motivated. The team must have a high morale. Such achievements and the consequent public support for police programs and policies are the hallmarks of a good police leader. It is gratifying to note that the top police leaders of recent times in India at least seemed to have known what was expected of them. They made sincere efforts towards that end, and also achieved a measure of success in various states in different types of environments. Problems have, however, been acute in some states in regard to the issue of team cohesion due to split loyalties and undesirable political contacts at various levels.

The next level of leadership that is to be considered is the aggregate of senior leaders in the making. They consist of Inspector Generals of Police and Deputy Inspector Generals. They are generally in charge of territorial police divisions in states, or separate functional divisions in state police organizations like crime, intelligence, traffic, or armed police. Their job is to supervise the work of the Superintendents of Police in charge of districts in states and to guide, coordinate, and monitor the work of officers in headquarters or in regional centers in carrying out their functional assignments. In such capacities they assist the top leaders of police organizations. Their personal motivation is to prepare themselves to reach in due course the topmost positions of Director Generals or other equivalent assignments. And this seems to work well enough, except in the case of some police officers who prefer to play politics instead of concentrating on their job.

Police organizations located in various states in India operate by virtue of the Indian Police Act of 1861 which provides for three vital positions of leadership. First, there is the chief executive of the organization, or the Director General of Police at the top. Second, there is the Superintendent of Police in charge of the district at the middle level. The third level is the station-house officer at the cutting-edge level, sometimes referred to as the service-delivery level. He is of the rank of a sub-inspector or an Inspector of Police. The Superintendent of Police is the leader of the police in the district and is in charge of all aspects of police work there. Though the police is a disciplined hierarchical organization, this functionary at the helm of the district police has substantial freedom of action. Within the framework of the law and the budget, he enjoys a measure of flexibility in handling his functions. While occupying this position police officers of senior level get a chance to build up their careers. They can earn a reputation for even-handed maintenance of peace and order as well as for effective crime work. It is at this level again that they have an opportunity to develop a habit of cultivating a good relationship with the public and delivering other services that will stand them in good stead right through their career as they go up the ladder. The annual administration report of a district is a record of their work for the year, and gives a fairly clear account of the performances of the district police under a particular Superintendent of Police's leadership.

In the major cities, law and order, criminal work, as well as police administration is vested with a Commissioner of Police who usually holds the rank of a Deputy Inspector General of Police. In the case of major metropolitan cities the police chief is of the rank of Inspector General of Police. These functionaries combine in themselves some part of the authority of the Executive District Magistrate or Collector of the District and the head of the police organization of the area. Many Superintendents of Police work under them, dealing with different functional charges. But the law and order and crime functions in metropolitan area are so heavy that these functional charges are also further separated into territorial divisions. The Commissioner of Police system in the major cities avoids the old anomaly of the Superintendent of Police having to work under the direction and control of the District Magistrate/Collector as stipulated under the Indian Police Act of 1861. That arrangement, requiring the Superintendent of Police to work under the general direction of the District Magistrate, is universally resented by all police Superintendents as an uncalled-for interference by a civilian administrator in the professional affairs of the police.

The police leadership of the lowest level is that of the officer-in-charge of the police station. He is normally a sub-inspector, and sometimes an Inspector of Police. This is the individual whom the law of the land recognizes as the person competent to implement the law and in whom the authority envisaged by the law is vested.

As a matter of fact, even senior officers of the police draw their authority only as his lawful superiors who may help, guide, and supervise him as well as monitor his work. The station house officer is also the person who is expected to maintain law and order in his jurisdiction as well as prevent crime. When crime does occur, he must register cases and investigate them with a view to placing the matter for adjudication before a court of law.

Unlike the pattern obtaining in the U.S.A., where the District Attorney decides whether the evidence gathered in the case is good enough for the matter to go before a court, in India the Investigating Officer is the final authority regarding the disposal of a case. He may obtain legal opinion from a competent prosecuting counsel and his superior officers may advise him on valid grounds in this regard, but under the law the disposal of the case depends on what the police investigating officer ultimately decides. In *Dinesh Mishra v. the State of Bihar* (1968), the Supreme Court of India laid down that even a Court of Law could not give the officer-in-charge of a police station a direction one way or another. In theory no executive, political or administrative, has the authority of directing the course of investigation or the method of disposal of a case. But in actual practice political interference does happen to a recognizable extent as confirmed by several recent studies including the one done for the National Police Commission. The National Police Commission did (1978-81) suggest a way out of this state of affairs with public safety committees at the state and central levels. But no action has been taken yet on the Commission's report. Political authorities who have benefited over the decades by having full control over the police are not likely to agree to surrender such control without a fight.

Leadership of the station house officer, which is at the grass-roots level, has immense potential in India for determining public attitudes towards the police and for shaping the image of the organization. People are good judges and they cannot be deceived all the time by pseudo-leaders or insincere administrators. A good police leader of a station can make a significant impact in his jurisdiction, particularly in rural areas. Able station house officers are the persons who may be trained and developed so that they can go up higher in the departmental hierarchy as leaders of the middle level. The same applies also to middle-level police leaders. Those among them who achieve success as community leaders deserve to go higher up and occupy senior positions in due course. Unfortunately, only a few junior police leaders with such calibre reach the top. This writer knew one such police officer who was regarded by the citizens of his jurisdiction as one of God's own good men devoted to the service of the people. He rose up the leadership ladder in the organization, received a few police medals, and contributed in a large measure to improving the quality of life of the people whom he policed.

Leadership qualities and supervisory calibre are important at all levels of the police organization in India as can be noted from the account given above. It is also right to say that essentially leadership qualities need to be fairly evenly distributed at all levels of police leadership and supervision.

STANDARDS USED IN EVALUATING INDIVIDUAL POLICE PERFORMANCE

Evaluation of individual police performance is not an easy task even under normally favorable circumstances. The police in India function under extremely trying conditions. They have been facing very difficult situations during the last two decades. Under these circumstances evaluation of individual police performance is an almost intractable problem. While successful detection or prosecution of cases may perhaps be easily recognized, crime prevention efforts could not be satisfactorily assessed at all. Further, in India so far, no quantitative or qualitative standards have evolved or been validated by empirically-tested scientific research for measuring general police performance. Nevertheless, some rough-and-ready yardsticks have been adopted by consensus among competent senior police officers over the years. The findings so arrived at have not been unsatisfactory, as confirmed over the years by application in the field.

These rough-and-ready methods consist of three approaches, which may be jointly adopted and administered in a coordinated manner. These approaches are:

(1) A direct on-the-spot field check, monitoring of performance and related inspection reports.

(2) A check of statistics, such as the rate of detection, which have been gathered and meaningfully evaluated.
3) An over-all assessment of the goodwill that an officer has created over the years and left behind in the jurisdiction upon his routine transfer out of the area.

The first method of evaluation provides an opportunity for the competent authority to evaluate the performance of the individual police officer on the job in carrying out the tasks assigned to him for execution as a matter of day-to-day routine. Checking of patrols, monitoring of field work, and inspection of police stations would all come under this category. The second approach enables a more comprehensive assessment of the individual police officer's performance over a period, normally a year. It can present a true picture of his work performance during the period provided that the statistical information for this assessment is collected without any bias. The evaluation must be done fairly, taking attendant circumstances of the environment into account. The third technique has unerringly been found in practice to project the prevalent state of affairs more realistically. But the evaluating authority should utilize all the three methods in a coordinated fashion and then come to an independent conclusion. Sometimes contradictory findings flowing from a particular method may have to be reconciled, clarified, and moderated with findings resulting from the other methods. It is because of a failure to ensure objective evaluation that one hears tirades against the conventional annual performance evaluation records, called Annual Confidential Reports. One state government, namely, the Government of Tamilnadu, has abolished the system of keeping confidential annual reports in the personal files of officers as evidence of performance.

Very often one also hears complaints that because of an inclination on the part of evaluating senior officers to rely blindly on interested hearsay or distorted statistics many subordinates take to the easy way out by burning case files and selective registrations of criminal complaints in order to improve their clearance statistics and show effectiveness of their crime control activities. Subordinates resent the religious zeal with which some evaluating officers adhere to the statistics for evaluating performance. Citizens at large are not satisfied with it. Blind adherence to statistics on detection of crime defeats the purpose of meaningful evaluation of an investigator's work. The percentages of detection cannot be accepted without taking into consideration diversity of regions and other unique factors. In the State of Tamilnadu 40 percent detection of crime may be considered good in some localities. But in some others even 55 or 60 percent detection may not be evaluated as good enough. Certain prevalent environmental factors affect the rate of detection over which investigators can exercise little control. At the same time statistics cannot be dispensed with; such a practice may surely set a premium on inefficiency. The long and short of the matter is that statistics has a role to play in meaningful evaluation of performance and proper planning for the future. However, the data should be collected painstakingly and in an honest fashion. Evaluation should be done taking all circumstances into consideration in a balanced way, and not haphazardly. In other words statistics alone should never be the basis of individual performance evaluation in view of the complex nature of the work the police perform.

The third method, which may be described as "goodwill measure," is qualitative. It is an assessment based on public opinion regarding an officer who has worked in a particular community for a number of years. It is, no doubt, a democratic method. Nevertheless, it is obvious that there are many difficulties in encouraging people to come forward to ventilate their views on the performance of an officer. Many people may simply not be well-informed about police performance. It is not a reliable indicator by itself. However, as hinted above, "goodwill measures" can be effectively used in conjunction with the other methods for accurate performance evaluation.

Side by side, police organizations of states may commission coordinated research by groups consisting of experienced academic researchers and competent police officers to arrive at a proper system of evaluation of the performance of individual police officers, at the three different levels of the service. Once these instruments are properly designed and scientifically tested, perhaps we might be able to achieve a better standard of evaluating police performance.

PROFESSIONALIZATION

As regards improving the police image, experts who have studied the subject have categorically stated that two major steps are vital for this to come about:

(1) Professional upgrading of the police services
(2) Promotion of popular respect toward and cooperation with the police

The purpose of this section is to review the state of professionalization in the Indian police.

Professionalization naturally involves thorough initial training of the prospective members of the police service in the objective and technical foundations of that service. It calls for an acquisition of a specialized body of knowledge and related skills. Accreditation in respect of these members has to be granted by a competent evaluating agency only after systematic tests and careful assessment of the standards they have attained. These standards are measured against certain minimum levels that they are expected to reach. This is done quite well in India at the level of the Indian Police Service officers by the Union Public Service Commission in New Delhi, and the National Police Academy in Hyderabad. Senior officers, selected and trained to man the superior cadres of police organizations all over India, in the Indian Police Service, are sufficiently qualified and suitably trained. They must be regarded as professionals. What is required further is a system of professional self-regulation based on certain accepted service-oriented and ethical norms. The Indian Police Service should have prescribed this in detail for itself. What exists now is a built-in pattern of monitoring and correction when things occasionally do go wrong. The National Police Commission (1978-1982) has made some useful and valid recommendations including the introduction of public safety committees at the national and state levels. These committees are expected to form the base for suitable special agencies for dealing with accreditation problems as well as effective monitoring and correction of professional standards.

In this way, the tone and standards of professional functioning of the police at the higher levels, and their purposeful supervision of the lower-level operations, may be effectively ensured. This will require only some marginal adjustments to bring the Indian Police Service and its system of operation to acceptable professional standards. The sooner this is done, the better. But professionalizing the Indian Police Service alone without effectively professionalizing the service-delivery or cutting-edge level in the middle does not serve much of a purpose.

As regards the middle level of sub-inspectors of police, the selection procedure, the training and accreditation as well as self-regulation, monitoring, and correction process will require substantial alterations. There will be need for further planning and streamlining before professional standards can be established and inculcated. But this can certainly be done in due course because the basic material selected at this level too is suitable for such upgrading. As regards the training, the course content itself has to be considerably improved, widened as well as made more in-depth. It needs to be updated too from time to time in keeping with changing society. The Gore Committee on Police Training (1972) made some good recommendations in this regard and many states have implemented them reasonably well, but the process must be steadily ongoing.The accreditation procedure may also have to be further tightened up and vested with some competent agency attached to the state-level Public Safety Commission and the police department. The same agency could also look after the laying of standard guidelines for self-regulation, as well as for the institution of control and monitoring systems, leading to effective correction when things go wrong occasionally. All this involves considerable planning for changes in organizational design, structure, and functional as well as procedural implementation.

But in respect of police constables, it must be admitted that neither the personnel selected, nor the body of knowledge imparted to them as of now in India, satisfy even remotely the requirements of professional standards. This body of men normally perform only routine law-and-order duties, and are expected only to carry out in a disciplined manner orders and instructions issued to them. Under no circumstances, therefore, could it be envisaged that professionalization would be ushered in among them if this state of affairs continues. But on the other hand, it will also be appropriate to plan ahead for a time, when the regular police service itself in India will have only two levels of entry and will, therefore, require full professionalization as far as membership of the service is concerned.

At the same time in a poor country like India entry at such a low level as that of an Indian police constable cannot be avoided. But such entry may be restricted only to the armed police units to be trained, suitably armed, and kept ready as riot squads to deal with emergent law-and-order situations. Such squads will be capable of deployment at a moment's notice to operate under the direction and control of the senior-most regular police officer of an affected area. Thus police stations need not have a huge constabulary, officially detailed for patrol, process-service and other duties but frequently routinely mobilized to deal with grave problems of law and order which occur with amazing ease in India because of a variety of reasons. Police stations will then have only a small contingent of assistant sub-inspectors to help the sub-inspector or Inspector of Police in all aspects of police work. Work in the police stations will normally be functionally separated as law and order, crime, and traffic. It is already so in city police stations of some states. Custodial jobs like guards in jails and hospitals as well as escorts of prisoners can be legitimately given to the state prisons department. In recent years police commissions at the national and also at the states levels have been steadily converging toward such a point of view.

As a result, police stations will be headed only by a station-house officer of the rank of Inspector/Sub-Inspector of Police, assisted by functional sub-inspectors in charge of the divisions of "law and order." Assistant Sub-Inspectors will be made available to them. Riot Squads will be kept ready in police stations as and when necessary. Crime units will also have only assistant sub-inspectors to support Sub-Inspectors/Inspector in charge of police stations. Traffic branch also will consist of assistant sub-inspectors and where necessary, traffic wardens. Assistant sub-inspectors of Police may be directly recruited from among graduates. Proper training must be given to them in a prescribed body of knowledge and that should be an appropriate base for their professionalization. A provision for adequate clerical and communication assistants with reasonable chances for upward mobility should also be made.

At the same time, suitably qualified and carefully selected personnel would be continuously mobilized as assistant sub-inspectors after a period of practical experience and special training in armed police units. Forty percent of the trainees will be inducted into police service after a period of special training lasting four-to-six months. They also will be required to obtain practical experience at police stations.

Very often the rank of the Sub-Inspector of Police is referred to as the backbone of the police organization. This is indeed the level and position which should receive priority attention in the matter of professionalization. In most states at least 60 percent of sub-inspectors' posts are filled by direct recruitment. In some states direct recruitment is also done for the preparatory level of Assistant sub-Inspectors of Police who become sub-inspectors in about three-years time, and so the beginning of professionalization is possible at that level also. About 40 percent of these posts are also filled by promotions. Induction of professionalization into this mixed bag is not going to be an easy job. With a planned effort, it should be possible to achieve it.

As at present the basics of professionalism exist only in the higher reaches of the police service. But it should be easy enough to make the Indian Police Service really professional within a short period of time as indicated above. At present, however, only a sort of semiprofessional pattern exists which helps to some extent in the work of the police. But there is a need for more systematic and rapid process of professionalization in the higher levels. This alone will not be enough. In due course the middle level of the police hierarchy, consisting of the Inspector, the Sub-Inspector, and Assistant Sub-Inspector of Police, should be made more professional. They will then be capable of profesional service to the people at the cutting-edge level, and in a manner that will reciprocally lead to public satisfaction. This is also the way to ensure public acceptance of police performance and for a concomitant emergence of spontaneous public cooperation. Consequently, the police image will also improve substantially.

WAGES, STATUS, SUBCULTURE, AND MORALE

When we consider the matter of police wages in the Indian situation, we naturally must examine it in relation to the three levels of recruitment and the career prospects and opportunities at each level. Taking first the level of the constable, there was a time at the turn of the century during the British days when the police constable's monthly wages were only rupees eight as against rupees three thousand for the top officers of the Indian Police, the predecessor of the Indian Police Service. They were mostly British personnel. With the advent of independence in 1947, the constables' pay was increased to a reasonable level while the top officers' pay remained the same and was even marginally reduced. Since then the constable's pay has been progressively increasing; they are doing better than other higher ranks. Following the recommendations of the last pay Commission, the Tamilnadu Government has upgraded the minimum pay to all Government services at rupees 750 per month (at the time of writing, twenty rupees are equal to one American dollar). In other states too the position should be similar. The police constable naturally would fit into a level slightly higher than the minimum.

According to the recommendations of the recent Tamilnadu Pay Commission, the present arrangement placed the police constables in the pay scale of rupees 825-15-900-20-Rs.1,200 for Grade II and rupees 950-20-1,150-75-1,1500 for Grade I police personnel. The recent Tamilnadu Police Commission has recommended the abolition of Grade I constables. It was suggested that only those with education up to the school leaving examination should be recruited to the lowest level in the police. The pay scale suggested would merge Grade I and Grade II. The Head Constable's pay scale would be rupees 1,200-30-1,500-40-2,040. It should be noted that the present pay scales are one hundred times greater than the corresponding scale in 1902. In addition police constables are entitled to free housing, uniforms, and free education up to the high school level as well as free delivery of health and medical facilities. Over and above these official facilities, recreational amenities and scholarships for higher academic and professional courses of study are provided by departmental Welfare Services which are fairly well organized in all police services of the country.

Suitable candidates from the rank of constable quite often were promoted to the category of sub-inspector on the basis of selection and training. The Administrative Reforms Commission had suggested a 40 percent reservation of these posts for such promotion. As noted previously, the middle level of recruitment takes place at the cutting-edge or service-delivery level of the sub-inspector of police. The salary scale of the sub-inspector of police now is rupees

1,600-50-2,300-60-2,660. This position acknowledgedly is the most important in the police hierarchy administratively and operationally. The first promotion from this post is to Inspector of Police. At this level the pay scale is rupees 2,000-60-2,300-75-2,200-75-2,800-100-4,000. Free housing and uniforms are provided to the rank of Inspector of Police too. In addition, families of these officers also benefit from government's free health delivery and medical care facilities as well as education services. For the deserving candidates the promotion from this category is to the rank of Deputy Superintendent of Police whose scale of pay is rupees 2,200-75-2,800-100-3,800-150-5,000. This position is a supervisory one. It is equivalent in rank and responsibility to the Assistant Superintendent of Police which is the juniormost position in the senior level of officers. These officers, as discussed above, belong to the Indian Police Service looked after by the Union Public Service Commission at the national level.

The Indian Police Service has its initial recruitment at the Assistant Superintendent's level on an All-India basis. It takes place once a year through the Union Public Service Commission which conducts written examinations and interviews for this purpose. The pay-scale of the Assistant Superintendent of Police, the juniormost member of the Indian Police Service, is approximately the same as for the state rank of Deputy Superintendent of Police ranging from rupees 2,250 to 4,000. But nobody stays in the position of Assistant Superintendent of Police longer than four to five years except if held back on disciplinary grounds. Within that period all Indian Police Service officers, recruited as Assistant Superintendent of Police, become Superintendent of Police. In all eventualities they get promoted as joint Superintendent of Police in the senior scale of the Indian Police Service. The Superintendent of Police's scale of pay is 3,000 to 4,500 with a selection grade going up to 5,500. The rank of Superintendent of Police is the position in which officers of the Indian Police Service spend a good part of their careers. It is in this position that they deepen their job experience as well as build up their professional expertise and reputation. After about 14-to-16 years of service, they become Deputy Inspectors General of Police on a scale which ranges from rupees 5,000 to 6,150. The next promotion is to the rank of Inspector General of Police for which the pay ranges from rupees 5,600 to 6,700. The top position of Director General of Police varies in respect of its pay scales among smaller states and bigger states as well as the police organizations under the national government. In the smaller states the pay of the Director General of Police is rupees 6,500 to 7,300. In bigger states the pay goes up to rupees 7,600. For some of the Central Police Organizations, it is flat rupees 8,000.

The status of the police in India, particularly at lower levels, is not as good as it should be. This is obviously related to the poor image of the police arising from a historical perception of them since the colonial period as a poorly educated and oppressive agency of a foreign power, namely, the British Raj. Unfortunately after independence no basic changes took place in the legal and administrative framework of police functioning in general or of criminal investigation procedures in particular. On the other hand, the influence of political power and money power increased. A dispassionate British observer was of the view that the Indian police appeared only to have changed their masters (Arnold, 1986). Nothing much was done till very recently to improve police emoluments which is also a concomitant determinant of status and image of the police. Accordingly, the status of the police continued to be poor. This was what visiting Police Superintendent Pollard from U.K. found in the Punjab, Gujarat, Bombay, Goa, Andhra Pradesh, and Tamilnadu. He observed that the Indian police lacked status, were poorly paid, and had an unfortunate public image as oppressive, untrustworthy, and corrupt (Pollard 1978). After visiting the National Police Academy where he was able to perceive the quality and status of the young officers of the Indian Police Service, he added that his earlier comments were true largely of the middle and lower levels of police officers. He felt that the recruitment of poorly educated persons as constables was not helping the police improve their status.

As already discussed, in a vast country like India with a population of about 850 million, a low rate of literacy, and a low per-capita income, a three-tier recruitment system which presently operates in the country is inevitable. It ensures a fair distribution of employment opportunities in the public sector of the economy. Perhaps, the lowly paid personnel are able to establish better rapport with the poor and uneducated rural population. When the country attains a full literacy and achieves a greater level of income, perhaps it will be possible to adopt a two-tier system of recruitment. The solution, for the present, is to select for the constabulary level only high school educated persons. The need is to train and orient them for a clean and efficient delivery of police service, particularly to the poorer segments of the population. Police personnel should also be effectively motivated to realize that they are a service, not a force, responsible for safety and security of the community entrusted to their care (Nath, 1987).

The next issue is subculture of the Indian police. Culture is defined as the complex of traditions and value systems as well as historical and educational background developed over the years which is cherished and promoted systematically by a well-knit society. Socialization is the process by which the members of a society become familiar with its culture. But, because of culture conflicts or cultural lags, there may emerge a group which pieces together some exclusive and not desirable ideas based on certain grievances and feelings of alienation. The resultant attitudes drive the group toward a separate identity, a deviant culture that is at variance with the main culture of the society. This is a subculture. The police in India appear to have a subculture. It is based on a perception that the people are always critical of them, whether they do well or badly. They complain that their successes are never acclaimed while their failures are always trumpeted in the media in a big way. They are resentful that the public attitude to the police is generally negative and hostile. As a result, the members of the police feel that they must cling together and stand by each other through thick and thin. Under such circumstances even where there are legitimate public complaints against the police, these are not taken seriously at appropriate levels of the police force. Thus, suitable action is seldom taken against police personnel on account of public complaints. People feel that there is no use complaining against the police to their own superiors. They complain that the police at all levels form a solid phalanx and only support each other. They lose confidence in the police and develop negative attitudes toward the system as a whole. Naturally the police image suffers grievously. The National Police Commission of India (1978-81) recommended systematic enquiries by different executive or judicial bodies into different kinds of allegations against the police.

Morale is the feeling of healthy group cohesion that the members of a well-knit and successively well-performing group develop about themselves. Such a group is characterized by a sense of belonging. They display pride in their own organization and its achievements. They take responsiblity for failures and share credit for successes. None of them is prepared to leave their organization for a position elsewhere even for some substantial benefits. They are even prepared to make sacrifices for the sake of the team. The police in India cannot be said to have such morale. Political influence seemed to have destroyed their organizational pride, belongingness, and team spirit. Police officers at different levels have developed the habit of seeking political interventions in matters like recruitment, posting, promotion, and even for retention in a particular position. Professional superiors have no longer effective control over their rank-and-file. This is a development that has stood in the way of professionalization, effective performance, and organizational health. Good morale is conspicuous by its absence. On the one hand, unscrupulous politicalization has resulted in depriving individual officers of motivation and robbing them of enthusiasm. On the other, this sad state of affairs is further aggravated by cynical public attitude toward the highly politicalized, frustrated, and partisan police.

UNIONS AND ASSOCIATIONS

In recent times the Indian police at different levels and in all the states have been permitted to form professional associations, but not unions. Such associations exist in many places and are meant to advance the professional interests and expertise of their members while protecting and safeguarding the rights and legitimate interests of the police personnel. But professional associations are different from unions in the sense that the members of such an association, unlike those of the union, have no right to stage strikes as a way of enforcing their right of collective bargaining. In actual fact, however, there have been cases in which some professional associations of the lower ranks in certain states of India have misunderstood their position as members of an association and not a union, and have resorted to strikes. In such cases legal recognition has had to be withdrawn until the authorized role was accepted.

The police admittedly are placed in a difficult situation in this regard. Obviously they are an essential service, have little or no right of collective bargaining, and cannot go on strike. At the same time they do have many grievances and little or no public support.

Under the circumstances, they need an effective machinery for timely redress of their legitimate grievances which at the moment is not effectively available to them. They tend to "unionize" their associations at least at the lower levels, and do not really appreciate the basic differences between associations and unions. A situation like this warrants a permanent and effective grievance-redressal machinery for the police, built directly into the administrative system. Such a body has been recommended by the National Police Commission of India (1978-81). The distorted unionization of police associations in the past in some states like Uttar Pradesh and Bihar has led to police strikes. In some other states, too, similar situations almost led the police to the brink of strikes. Such eventualities were averted by prompt action under the Essential Services Maintenance Act. The deployment of personnel from the police organizations working under the control of the Government of India like the Central Reserve Police Force in the states have enabled the state administration to weather such situations without too many problems. Organizations like the Central Reserve Police Force have enabled the state Administration to get over such situations without too much problems or difficulties.

The normal functions of police associations in India are envisaged as follows:

(1) To objectively analyze the general problems of the police personnel such as wages, service conditions, and welfare measures, and to make appropriate representations to the concerned authorities in a timely manner in order to seek constructive improvement and remedial measures when there are genuine grievances.
(2) To review and organize professional development measures, within the parameters of the service conditions, for better delivery of police services to the people at large.

It is noted that service associations tend to concentrate more than perhaps is necessary on the first objective. They seldom attend to the second one. They may only occasionally organize some lectures by higher level associations. In one special situation, associations play a very useful role for the benefit of the members. This happens when a Pay Commission or a Police Commission holds meetings. Associations present carefully prepared representations to these bodies which are of immense use to them in coming to appropriate conclusions and making plans for the progress and advancement of the police.

There are three levels of associations normally in the police of most states of India corresponding to the three levels of police appointments. There is the association of Constables covering also Head Constables and other higher-grade Constables. The second association is that of the middle-level personnel, namely, sub-inspectors, inspectors, and the related next higher ranks. The third and last is the Indian Police Association. There have been instances of unionization and strikes, as well as threatened strikes by the first two types of associations in some states on some occasions. But the Indian Police Service Association has not had problems of that type. A complaint against this association is that it has not been active enough as regards the expected role of such a high-level service association. One of the major recommendations of the National Police Commission (1978-1981) is an active role for this association in solving the problems of the police.

Very often problems arise because high-ranking police officers do not develop a meaningful rapport with the junior members. If supervising officers take sincere steps to ensure that all personnel receive their entitlements of emoluments and allowances, and look into individual grievances personally and compassionately with a view to obtaining redress, very little room will be there for grievances to assume serious dimensions. In a uniform service where subordinates believe that their entitlements, postings, and promotions are justly earned without subjective and extraneous influences no major problem normally arises. Where there are legitimate grievances, it should be possible to seek redress effectively. Further, if higher-level officers associate freely with their juniors in service without reservation everywhere, including the sports field and cultural activities, and if they are ready to help junior colleagues in their personal problems relating to the housing and health of the family and schooling of children, the response from the lower-ranking personnel is likely to be positive. Such a response helps avoid all possible friction. Wherever a police organization encourages proper procedures, redress of grievances, proper rapport between the rank-and-file and the officers in higher positions, and appropriate welfare facilities, the "unionization" of police into professional associations will not normally occur. Moreover, strikes are unlikely to take place.

POLICE PUBLIC RELATIONS, PUBLIC CONFIDENCE, TRUST, AND RESTRAINTS ON THE POLICE

Police public relations in India seems to be extremely unsatisfactory. It is not difficult to fathom the reasons for this situation. The police in India came into existence as a ruler-appointed agency of the colonial Government. The role of the police then, as the British saw it, was to maintain peace and order, a "Pax Britannica," in the occupied land and to handle problems of crime as they arose. The question of police performance in accordance with the aspirations and expectations of the people of India was naturally not part of their terms of reference.

And what is worse is that, even after independence steps were not taken by the national leaders to reform the objectives, functions, and activities of the police and bring them in tune with the needs of the people of free India. Thus, an opportunity to bring the police nearer the people was lost. Today public cooperation with the police is not abundant. The public attitude continues to be negative toward them. The police image is poor. True, public relations itself is a relatively new idea in the field of management. But the police of India, except in individual exceptions, have not understood and practiced it at all.

Perhaps public relations for the police can be viewed as open relationship between the police and the public. It involves fact-finding regarding the needs and expectations of the public by the police, effective performance of police functions against the background of these expectations, and a partnership between the police and the people. The police need to explain their needs, work, and achievements to the people. Such communications lead to a mutual appreciation between the police and the public. Police community relations is a slightly more inclusive concept than police public relations. Besides public relations of the police, it covers community services organized by the police and community participation in such services. Both are ways of establishing better police public relations. Radelet (1986) popularized this enlarged concept of police public relations. He included in it "the reciprocal attitudes of the police and the public," and "general public relations, community services and community participation." Apparently the St. Louis Police Department (Missouri, U.S.A.) was the first to give meaning and shape to this definition in 1957 through its community-based work. While acknowledging that it may be so, this author recalls with some pleasure that three years prior to St. Louis work, in 1954, he, as a police officer in India experimented with a police village adoption scheme in Coimbatore district of Tamilnadu state. The village adoption scheme involved community service, community participation, and public relations. But this was an individual effort which was not taken up anywhere else in India and consequently, the Coimbatore experiment did not hit the headlines.

Britain has always led in the matter of good relationship between the police and the public. The credit for appreciating this need and establishing it on a sound footing goes to the first Commissioners of the Metropolitan Police of London, Rowan and Mayne. They made it clear that police authority was dependent on public approval and befriending the public was the first job of the police. A pioneering British scholar in the academic field of the police and community, Michael Banton (1964), described the British police officer as a special professional, an Ombudsman at the street-corner. He is expected to administer society's moral standards with good judgment, based on the public point of view and with public cooperation and support.

Historical evidence seems to indicate that the British police developed good police-public relations slowly, steadily, and systematically right from the beginning. As a result, they became a model for police organizations of the world in regard to relations with the public (Reith, 1952). Some Indian police leaders have tried to improve relations with the public, drawing lessons from the practices of the first Commissioners of the Metropolitan Police. Their ideas had to be modified to adapt them to the Indian conditions. In some cases such efforts produced good results. However, the concept of police-public relations did not receive its due place in the Indian scheme of things.

Public relations of the police in India was evaluated through a survey done by the Banaras Hindu University in 1972. It confirmed the fact that the image of the police was decidedly poor. According to a 1978 study by the Indian Institute of Public Opinion which was commissioned by the National Police Commission, 82 percent of the respondents opined that police personnel at lower levels did not discharge their duties in a straightforward manner. They were found rude. Threatening behavior as well as corrupt practices were widely prevalent. Unfortunately, the police image seemed to have remained as unsatisfactory as it was six years back.

Public confidence arises primarily out of clean and efficient police work. The delivery of police service that the community needs must also be effective. Effectiveness as a management concept is different from efficiency. It involves an additional dimension of police service being "in-time" and "in-place." It must also be acceptable to those who are its beneficiaries. The question of acceptability is determined on the basis of whether police performance is in accord with the people's expectations. Such expectations are connected with their overall aspirations as free citizens of a free country. If popular expectations are sensibly perceived by the police and their performance is geared toward meeting them, there will normally be no problem in regard to public acceptance of the police. When there is such acceptance public confidence in the police is automatic and public cooperation ensues.

The Indian Police have not been getting much needed public cooperation to any desired level in the performance of their functions. In the absence of such cooperation, police performance has not been of a very high standard. It has not been acceptable to the people because it is not in accordance with their expectations. Acceptability is a dimension that results normally from good police performance which in turn is contingent upon police perception of the expectations of the people. When there is public cooperation resulting from good police performance, it also leads naturally to even better police performance. As a result, public attitude to the police improves and records a positive rating of a fairly high level. This leads automatically to a good police image. There is a lot more to be done in India in this direction. The establishment of good police community relations would be the effective first step to ensure good public cooperation in due course.

Unfortunately the police in India are not in a position to command much public confidence. There is a complete lack of mutual trust between the police and the public. It is due to the unfortunate public image of the police as oppressive, untrustworthy, and corrupt. Such an image has emerged because of a hang-over of the colonial era. As elsewhere, misbehavior of individual policemen tends to be generalized to all police personnel. It is widely believed that only political influence or money power could move the police to act. Such an impression has served to dampen the enthusiasm of the limited number of right thinking officers who have been making efforts consistently to establish a better rapport with the people.

The absence of popular trust is further accentuated by the fact that the law of the land reposes very little trust in the police. According to the Indian Evidence Act, an admission made to the police by a person accused of an offense is not admissible as evidence in court. Only a part of it may be admissible if a material object is recovered following such admissions by suspects. According to various Criminal Justice professionals from all over the country, this restraint on the police does not serve any useful purpose. Unfortunately, it has tempted some members of the police to padding of evidence. They do so in order to produce such evidence as will be acceptable to the court for conviction of an offender. This habit of fabricating evidence can have wider consequences. Under the circumstances the correct solution to the problem is an amendment of the Indian Evidence Act making the statement made by the accused to police investigators admissible as evidence. In any case, the court is entitled to have before it the totality of evidence. The test should be based on the reliability of evidence. It should be disconnected from the tendency to restrain the police.

If this major restraint against the police, namely, lack of trust by the law and the people is removed, the police for their part would also respond with better standards of behavior. Trust begets trust. It is a question here only of admissibility and not acceptability of evidence. Before accepting such evidence, the court can make sure that it was not obtained by coercion and that it was properly corroborated in material facts by other evidence including scientific physical evidence wherever possible. The adoption of such a procedure would be perfectly in order. It is not in keeping with dignity and standards of the court itself to shut out a vital part of the totality of evidence.

The Gore Committee on Police Training (1973) called for reorientation of police training with emphasis on integrity, impartiality, and a sympathy for the weaker sections of society. According to the study commissioned by the National Police Commission (1978-1981), political influence in urban areas affected all echelons of the police; the higher officers were not spared. This seems to be the prevailing pattern all over the country.

In recent years the Delhi Police have been doing their very best to blaze a new trail. In the first place, they have tried to inculcate a sense of individual motivation and pride in their organization and in the quality of service they render to people. And then, they have also adopted programs of crime prevention, public cooperation, and many innovative projects for public service. In all these areas, an Independent Research Organization called the MODE had done studies on behalf of the Delhi Police at different stages and come to the conclusion that there has been progressive improvement in all fields. In the most recent study done in early 1990, over 90 percent of the Delhi Police Personnel, a much higher percentage than before, have expressed a feeling of motivated pride in themselves and in their organization, and also with the service rendered by them to the public. There are also increased indications that the crime prevention and accident prevention efforts are systematically bearing fruit. The innovative measures practiced by the police are also appreciated more and more by the public. And the police themselves have acted with commendable patience and restraint individually while dealing with provocative situations. The research also has confirmed that the police effort at systematically converting every interaction between the police and the public into a goodwill-producing occasion has resulted in a steady improvement of the police image. If these efforts continue systematically and produce increasingly better results, other cities of India will naturally emulate this role model and there will be substantial improvement in the total situation relating to the behavior and performance of the individual police officer all over India.

In recent years more and more academic institutions and opinion survey groups have been associated with police commissions, and even with police performance in certain states and cities such as the city of Delhi. The National Police Commission (1978-1981) pressed into service many research organizations to study individual and collective police performance in many different areas which included a number of specific subjects. Earlier in 1972 an organization attached to the Department of Politics of the Banaras Hindu University and involved in the study of state governments made a survey of public opinion about police work. They examined 9,000 respondents in and around the city of Banaras. Their findings indicated that the people expected the police to maintain peace and order effectively. They wanted the police to protect life and property meticulously. But because their expectations were met either partially or were not entirely fulfilled the image of the police was considered far from satisfactory.

PROBLEMS OF THE POLICE

Among the problems facing the police in India in recent times, a major one is that of having to deal with incessant confrontations arising out of protests and demonstrations. Indians with one grievance or the other take to the streets in open demonstrations fairly routinely. Such demonstrations may be against the government in general, or against one particular government establishment, or against one particular group by another. Whatever be the genesis of such grievances and the shape the demonstration takes, very often it deteriorates into a confrontation with the police. According to Bayley (1969), an ordinary grievance which in the U.S.A. or the U.K. would only warrant a letter to the editor, would be taken to the streets in India, with its attendant problems. Antisocial elements only wait for chances afforded to them by protests and rallies to take sneaking advantage by creating trouble and profiting by it. And so, frequent street demonstrations and confrontations—with the need to handle them effectively with use of force where necessary—are constant problems for the police.

It is a credit of the police in India that, by and large, they have handled such problems of confrontation reasonably well. Bayley (1969) compliments the Indian police on generally ensuring peace and order during the post-Independence decades. He particularly commended the police of India for the smooth conduct of numerous massive general elections to the satisfaction, by and large, of all parties concerned. Law and order problems in the recent times are getting increasingly difficult. They are characterized by a general permissiveness that has affected all sections of the community.

The police are finding it more and more of a serious problem to deal with increasing number of confrontations of varied types in the different parts of the country. An added dimension to these developments is the tendency on the part of the people to resort to violence at the slightest provocation.

In order to handle the problems of popular unrest and mass disturbances, the governments both in New Delhi and the states realized that an increase in police strength was called for. What has occurred is a constant and ad hoc increase in the armed police strength to deal with law and order situations everywhere. Behind this development there is a belief that a demonstration of force by government was inevitable for smothering challenges to the established order. As a result, there has been an inadequate increase in the strength of the regular police who handle patrols and other normal work. Constant agitation has also necessitated the diversion of the elements of regular work force to special tasks of controlling disorders. Criminal investigation and crime prevention activities have been a casualty of this abnormal situation. Perhaps it is better for the authorities not to rush for haphazard creation of more and more armed police battalions to contain disturbances. Instead, they should develop a strategy of highly mobile and widely dispersed but compact units of specially trained personnel to handle problems of disorder. This strategy may prevent the ad hoc growth of armed police and make some valuable resources available to maintain a timely growth of personnel for regular police work.

A second related problem is that in most police establishments, the primary police function of prevention of crime and prompt investigation of reported crime does not receive appropriate attention because of the law and order preoccupation of the police everywhere and the diversion of even the staff earmarked for routine preventive patrols and criminal investigation to emergent law and order duties. Traditionally, a priority for the police is preventive patrols. This strength is normally not expected to be diverted to what has now become a routine: watch and ward as well as security for fairs and festivals, VIP visits, and containing disturbances. As a result, units deployed for investigation of crime cannot be left alone to do their job. Effective peace and order calls for the prevention of crime as well as the prompt and successful handling of incidents of crime. Unfortunately, such is the pressure of disturbance-related work that work relating to criminal investigation and routine order maintenance is not appreciated and diversion takes place all the time.

The third problem of importance is that the police lack technological support in regard to transportation, communication, and scientific aids. Compared to similar cities of the West, the number of wireless mobiles available to Indian city police are inadequate. They are unable to ensure effective coverage of the needs of the area. They have failed to achieve the international standard in regard to response time on emergency calls. Some years back efforts were made to modernize the city police departments with better scientific aids, communication facilities, and vehicles. But this touched only the fringe of the problem. In the past two years a substantial improvement has been seen in the capital city of Delhi in regard to wireless mobile coverage and response time. Other cities like Bombay, Calcutta, Madras, Ahmedabad, Hyderabad, and Bangalore have not yet improved much in this direction. A communications network has been developed in bits and pieces throughout the country. This network is reasonably good in Tamilnadu. But efforts at developing a computerized network, which started a decade ago, have not yet resulted in the requisite coverage or been standardized. Further, even where the network exists, the persons who provide the inputs at the grassroots level have not been properly trained for the purpose and as a consequence the input concerning criminal information can not be utilized generally. The police do not have the means to gain instant access on traffic and crime matters to the National Crime Records Bureau in Delhi or State Crime Records Centers.

For modernizing the Forensic Science Laboratories at state level some updating of the sections of physics, chemistry, biology, ballistics, and questioned documents took place. In some states, like Tamilnadu, both regional laboratories and mobile laboratories have been developed. While this is all for the good, modernization has not taken place everywhere and the facilities have not achieved the standard of developed countries. Forensic Science Laboratories with improved facilities and trained personnel have done well in certain areas. But problems such as better identification of physical evidence at the scene of crime, getting the right expert promptly to come and handle such evidence, and sending the material properly to the laboratory for examination exist. There is also the problem stemming from the failure to suitably integrate results of laboratory examination analyses into the totality of evidence in particular cases. For this aspect of the work, uniform police and detectives must also be trained and oriented properly.

One special problem that the police in India have to face is the ambivalent attitude that different sections of the people exhibit toward legal propriety of police work. In regard to the third-degree methods, for example, the villagers of Bhagalpur in Bihar who suffered atrocities at the hands of the local dacoit groups, demanded that when arrested these criminals should suffer physically at the hands of the police. The so-called "Bhagalpur blindings" took place as a result of this demand and the local police got into trouble as a consequence. However, it is not only at the level of villagers that this problem exists. Even educated and influential complainants want the police to use third-degree methods against suspects in order to improve detection. But the press, the law, and the courts frown upon such tendencies, the defaulters face the music, and the police earn a bad name. The solution to the problem lies in strict avoidance of third-degree methods. Scientific methods of investigation, including psychological approaches to interrogation, are more important. The police must educate all the people regarding the legal limits of what they can do in the investigation of crime. The Delhi Police in recent years have done commendable work in this regard (Rustamji, 1991).

The next important problem faced by the police in India, which has been touched upon in various earlier sections of the chapter, is the absence of public cooperation. Cooperation from the people in India is not forthcoming because they perceive that the performance of the police is not in keeping with their expectations. As a result, they do not regard it as acceptable. Where the police take pains to learn what the people really want and endeavor to satisfy the popular needs, people's acceptance will improve. Their cooperation naturally will follow their acceptance. Such a development will result in better police performance, a concomitant popular recognition of police work, and a good police image obviously will emerge. In order to create the appropriate conditions for cooperation from the members of the public, the police should painstakingly professionalize themselves. They should energetically organize programs for promoting police community relations. Both these processes have not yet properly taken place (Diaz, 1991).

Because of the three different levels of recruitment, the relatively lower qualifications for constables and the poor quality of police training at this level, professional standards cannot be expected at lowest level of the police in India. But it is possible for the middle and higher levels of the police service to attain these professional standards in due course. Perhaps with a little additional effort, the senior levels can professionalize themselves almost immediately. A special feature of professionalization naturally is a service-orientation. That orientation needs considerable emphasis in respect of the police service of India. In India a large percentage of the people are illiterate. They live below the poverty-line, and substantial sections of the population are also underprivileged both socially and economically. Police discretion, wherever it is exercised, should generally be in favor of the disadvantaged without causing injustice or prejudice in the process to any other person or group. This is a problem that arises more in India than in other countries because of the large segments of the people who lead an existence of enormous deprivation.

CONCLUSIONS

India is the world's most populous democracy with a very long history of poverty, political dissension, religious upheaval, and social discontent. Although there have been police as part of the administration in India throughout its history, the present system of policing was established by the British through the Indian Police Act of 1861. The Indian police were modeled after the Irish Constabulary as opposed to Sir Robert Peel's Metropolitan Police of 1829. The Irish Constabulary were ruler's police, an organ of the state administrative apparatus, and it was designed to act as the strong arm of the government of the day. After independence of India from the British colonial rule in 1947, not much happened in regard to giving the police a new philosophy and a more modern mandate. Their narrow role inherited from the days of the colonial regime remained virtually the same.

Many of the insurmountable problems of the Indian police today can perhaps be traced to the anachronistic role which has produced a mindset not in keeping with the modern developments in India. But that is perhaps not the whole story. Independence could not wipe away the centuries of economic disparities, religious hostilities, and diverse forms of social injustice. However, independence gave people new hopes, greater freedom of expression, and a higher degree of individual autonomy in pursuit of their objectives. In a poor country where millions live in poverty, the rate of literacy is deplorably low and the exploitation of women, children, and the poor is rampant. India's political independence has instead led to the development of complex social problems. The police in India have to tackle these problems with a very low level of professional, technological, and popular support.

The problems of the police in India appear to be gigantic. Popular coperation and goodwill is almost nonexistent. The bulk of the police force, the constables, are inadequately educated, badly trained, insufficiently paid, and largely deployed as menial workers. Traditional police work such as preventive patrol, crime prevention, and criminal investigation has been completely neglected because of unrest and disturbances that the police must constantly tackle. Almost all extra resources have been expended in recent years in building military-like prowess of the police to save the country from chaos. But this is contrary to what the police role should be: a humble functionary working the beat as a helper, a friend, and a counsel.

The hope seems to lie in making the police work with the people. To achieve this, what the police must do is to professionalize themselves. In the Indian context, the level of professionalization must not be measured in terms of technological sophistication like computer capability, speedy transportation, development of a costly network of communication, and so on. What is important in the Indian situation is the service-orientation of the police. Perhaps in a country like India, where the larger segments of the people have been historically facing the problems of hunger, disease, exploitation, and other social evils, the police must also regard themselves as the police of the poor. Policing a nonaffluent society perhaps needs, most of all, a people-orientation. The Indian police must learn to work with the poor and the deprived, and in carrying out such work, an attitude of people-orientation is likely to be the most important asset.

REFERENCES

Arnold, David. *Police Power and Colonial Rule, Madras (1859- 1947).* Madras, India: Oxford University Press, 1986.

Banton, Michael. *Policemen in the Community.* London: Tavistock, 1964.

Bayley, David H. *Police and Political Development in India.* Princeton, New Jersey: Princeton University Press, 1969.

Diaz, S. M. "Sensitization of the Indian Police for Effective Role Performance." *Denouement,* January-February, 1991.

Durkheim, Emile. *Sociology and Psychology Translation.* New York: Free Press, 1953.

Gore Committee on Police Training. *Report.* New Delhi: Government of India, 1972.

Merton, Robert K. *Social Theory and Social Structure.* New York: Free Press, 1957.

Mullik, B. N. *A Philosophy for the Police in India.* New Delhi: Asia Publishing House, 1972.

Nath, Trilok. *Indian Police: A Case for a New Image.* New Delhi: Asia Publishing House, 1987.

National Police Commission. *Report 1-8.* New Delhi: Government of India, 1978-1981.

Pollard, David. "Community Relations Officer of U.K." *Police Review* February, 1978.

Radelet, Louis A. *The Police and the Community.* Mission Hills, California: Glencoe Publishing Inc., 1986.

Reith, Charles. *The Blind Eye of History.* London: Faber and Faber 1952.

Rustamji, K. F. "Wrong Tests of Policing." *Denouement,* January-February, 1991.

The Supreme Court of India. *Dinesh Mishra v. the State of Bihar,* New Delhi, 1968.

POLICE IN JAPAN

by Haruo Ueno

INTRODUCTION

The police reflect the society, they are a product of its institutional traditions and its offspring. It is necessary to understand Japanese society and culture in order to understand the Japanese police. Hence, we start with a brief introduction of Japan. A brief and perfunctory introduction is of very limited use in appreciating the highly organic relationship between the police and culture. It is hoped that this introduction will encourage interested readers to delve deeper into Japanese history, society, politics, tradition and values, and other elements that have given the Japanese a unique characteristic and identity.

Japan is an island country consisting of four large and many small islands with a total area of about 377,700 square kilometers (187,200 square miles). Japan is regionally divided into 47 prefectures which are subdivided into cities, towns, and villages. Towns and villages are administratively grouped into counties. The total population in 1986 was 120,720,542 according to annual census by the Ministry of Home Affairs. The islands are covered with steep mountains and volcanoes, and less than one-fifth of the land area is habitable. In this sense, Japan is the most densely populated country in the world. It is a very homogeneous country with a single ethnic group and a single language. Almost all Japanese are Buddhists.

Japan is an old country with more than 2,000 years' history. Because of its remote location in far east Asia, it remained unknown to Europeans until 1542 when a Portuguese ship reached one of the southern islands of Japan. The appearance of the Europeans contributed to reunification of Japan as they brought with them new military technology. After several decades of contact with Europeans, Japan under the Shogunate closed her ports to outside commerce. This self-imposed isolation continued for more than 200 years until an American, Commodore Matthew C. Perry, with four naval warships, arrived in Tokyo Bay in 1853. Japan accepted the American proposal to open up her ports. The Shogunate returned sovereignty to the emperor and after the restoration of the emperor, his government began to adopt many European standards. A constitution was adopted. A diet, or legislature, was set up. An American public school system and French army and police systems were introduced.

An island country isolated from the outside for a long time, Japan continues to be almost totally homogeneous. More than 99 percent of the people are ethnic Japanese who are mostly Buddhists. The majority of the non-Japanese are Koreans and Chinese who speak Japanese. Almost all of them, too, are Buddhists. The vast majority of the people belong to the middle class with very small upper and lower classes. According to the national opinion survey of 1985 conducted by the prime minister's office, 88.5 percent of Japanese stated that they were middle class. While 0.5 and 8.1 percent identified themselves as upper and lower class respectively, those claiming no class identity were 2.8 percent.

Education has become popular and illiteracy is almost nonexistent. Basically, there is no difference in social customs, way of living, or world view among the people. Buddhists disfavor disputes, violence, and bloodshed. Traditionally, crime has been very low, and law enforcement agencies are not overworked.

Japan has historically been overpopulated. Expulsion was equivalent to a death penalty. It was difficult for anyone to find livelihood once he or she lost his or her niche. If members broke a community regulation, they were ostracized. Thus, the community played a more important role in keeping peace and order than the government. Even after the introduction of European laws and culture, community customs and values have largely remained unchanged. "Don't become a nuisance to others" was the most important rule in the community. Respect for community leaders was highly prized. As the basic unit of the community was the family, respect for ancestors and heads of families was encouraged, and patriarchal authority was given a great deal of importance.

As Japan has been a densely populated country with a very narrow landmass and the situation has remained unchanged, the people wisely realize that they cannot exist unless they make mutual concessions to live together. In Europe those who were discontented with their own society were able to emigrate to the new world. But in Japan it has been actually impossible for citizens to leave the society, even if they were dissatisfied or opposed to it. In order to maintain a harmonious society, important matters are decided by consensus in Japan. They do not decide by majority. The majority are expected to take the minority's feelings into consideration and do their best to appease the discontent of their opponents. If the majority continue to run the organization only by majority rules, majority leaders will lose their confidence not only from minority members, but also from majority supporters.

According to Reischauer (1977), in Japan the general desire for consensus decisions and the popular dissatisfaction with narrow majority decisions on important matters give the political minority an even stronger position. If the Liberal Democratic Party (the group dominating politics at the time of this writing) were to use its narrow Diet majority to run through great numbers of bills against determined opposition, as it theoretically could, it would be seen by the public as acting undemocratically and would run the risk of organized demonstrations to the point of civil disorder and possible repudiation by the public at the next election. This situation makes it imperative for the party in power to limit the number of controversial bills presented in the Diet as much as possible. Less controversial matters are carefully tailored to avoid any serious controversy and important controversial issues are made as palatable to the opposition as possible and are strictly limited in number. For these reasons, Japanese communities do not want to make minority groups bitter. The majority amends its decisions to make matters acceptable to, or at least endurable for, the minority.

Basically, the community was formed along geographical lines, but after industry developed and people moved from the country to urban areas, the unity of local communities weakened. But new types of community activities were organized, usually functionally in working places like factories and offices. Political parties, religious organizations, educational institutions and even hobby groups became new units for networking with a strong sense of solidarity. Such units—or communities—are usually small, and if they are large, small subgroups are organized so that each member knows all the others and his/her role in his/her community. He or she can feel pride and honor through a sense of belonging to that unit. For example, the Japanese feel pride and honor in belonging to various organizations; an individual, for instance, may feel pride and honor in being a member of a Rotary Club or a Lions' Club. Recently, however, communities have become larger and larger in the urban areas where many people are frustrated and hopeless. At the same time, when young people leave villages, elderly people are often left without anyone to take care of them. When such a gap occurs in a community, very often the police in that community may fill in the gap.

Japanese industry also made rapid progress. Factories and railroads were built and foreign trade grew. Japan became a modern industrial nation. The population increased rapidly along with her trade and industry. But the Depression undermined Japan, which didn't have enough natural resources to support her large population. Japan tried to gain influence in Asia by military means in World War II. But by August of 1945, Japan was thoroughly defeated and she surrendered unconditionally. The American occupation forces advanced to Japan. All of Japan's great cities except Kyoto were destroyed. Industry was at a virtual standstill. Agricultural production had fallen off drastically. Urban housing vanished in flames. Food ran short and all consumer goods disappeared. City dwellers suffered a collapse of morale and increase of crimes. But American democracy was introduced as disarmament and demilitarization was pushed on by the occupation forces and welcomed by the Japanese people. Miraculously, Japanese economy revived from the ruins. Today, Japan enjoys a prosperous economy. But even now, the land is too narrow to maintain the large population and housing conditions are very bad. This is one of the most serious social problems in Japan.

MANDATE AND PHILOSOPHY

The mandate and philosophy of the police in Japan can be appreciated by tracing the major stages of the evolution of this important and unique institution. It will be noted that in their origin the police in Japan had a certain aura of nobility, grandeur, and magnificence. They were connected with the traditional authority and respect Japanese reserve for the symbols of the state.

One must also remember that, according to Japanese wisdom, social order should be preserved by communities and families, not by force or governmental control. So law enforcers should perform their tasks by guiding, supervising, advising, and assisting the people in fulfilling their role in maintaining social control. Traditionally, criminals were at first interrogated by community members who encouraged them to surrender to the authorities. When a criminal surrendered, he was accompanied by some members of his family and the community. Even if the offense took place in their presence, law enforcement officers encouraged the people to take an important role in all criminal matters. Sentiments expressed through such sayings as *akami-no-ohihi* ("mercy of the government") and *toku-no-shihai* ("rule by virtue") were symbolic of the normative nature of Japanese law enforcement. When officers responsible for law and order patrolled, offenders surrendered to them accompanied by their families and saying, "Onawa Chodai" which meant "please bind me with your rope." Since the Shogunate considered that the law should not be compulsively enforced, but be voluntarily followed, surrenders by offenders were encouraged. Although informants were sometimes exploited to surprise burglars' dens or a gang of pickpockets, such practices were not encouraged because the Shogunate believed that the law should be enforced without stratagem.

It was in the second decade of the ninth century that the first formal uniform police, *Kebiishi,* which literally means Criminal Investigation Agency, was founded in Japan. Their mandate was to patrol the streets and guard the gates in Kyoto, the then capital of Japan, in order to maintain public order and apprehend criminals. Sometimes a squad of *Kebiishi* was dispatched to the countryside to raid bandits' dens and to apprehend them. The directors of *Kebiishi* were appointed from the nobility. The members of patrol squads were recruited from the sons of powerful families in the countryside. They were honorably discharged after three or more years of service. They received the official title of swordsmen from the emperor. Young and ambitious countrymen gladly went to the imperial capital, Kyoto, to serve the guards for many years without pay. When they returned home with the honorable title of *Kebiishi*, their political power was guaranteed and they became influential in their regions. They and their clans became Samurai who constituted the ruling class in the feudal age. After the *Kebiishi* was abolished, these official titles were used as first or second names. Even today not a few Japanese retain these titles in their names.

During the control of the *Kebiishi*, there was capital punishment. Abolished by the emperor for religious reasons, this policy continued for three-and-a-half centuries, A.D. 818 to A.D. 1165, and the period is known as the Peace Era. Buddhism was strong and order was maintained well. But in the late twelfth century, local rebellions and disturbances occurred in various districts. Accordingly, the authority and power of the central government declined. A number of local Samurai leaders in the provinces banded together for mutual protection. Local peace and order was maintained by the Samurai in towns. But in villages vigilance systems were established against robbers' attacks. Villages were fenced around. Night watch and ward were kept at village gates. All adult male villagers were mobilized, and social ostracism was applied to breakers of village rules. After a few centuries of confusion, decentralization, and rivalry among warlords, a more efficient and tightly organized feudal system developed.

In A.D. 1602, the Shogun government was established and the capital was moved from Kyoto to Edo (Tokyo). To maintain public order in Edo, town magistrates (*machi-bugyosho*) were introduced. Magistrates with 50 *yoriki* (inspectors) and 240 *doshin* (sergeants) worked a monthly shift. If one magistrate and his staffs were on duty, the others were off duty during that month, while in the following month the other magistrate and his people performed the shift duty. The main job of town magistrates was public safety and order in Edo, and judicial administration including supervision of the courts, jail, and parole. Additionally, they managed a free hospital for the needy, an industrial training institute for the poor, and the release of prisoners. The magistrates' office was divided into several departments: patrol and street enforcement (local community); secret activity (criminal investigation and inspection of the vigilante system); judicial inquiry; parole and pardon; prisons; criminal records; and management of poor houses. Most *yoriki* and *doshin* were assigned to the patrol and street enforcement departments which gave them a lot of contact with local inhabitants.

Although such an official police system existed, peace and order was substantially maintained by the inhabitants. Edo had a little less than a million population and the metropolitan area was divided into about a thousand blocks (semi-incorporated towns) in the beginning of the eighteenth century. The blocks handled firefighting, sanitation, registration of birth and death, law and order, frankpledge, treatment of misdemeanants in protective or educational custody, mutual aid, and arbitration of neighbors' disputes. The block officials were not salaried but rather appointed from elderly and leading persons.

Each block had an office with a watch host at the crossing of important streets which were called *jishinban*, a voluntary watch, where block people assembled and fire-fighting articles were stocked. These houses were sometimes shared as joint offices by two or three small blocks. All adult male inhabitants in the blocks had responsibility to keep night watch, to guard the gates, and to fight a fire. In order to find people for these tasks, houses of *kidoban*, gatekeepers, were built where full-time or part-time employees worked as substitutes. The tradition of *jishinban* and *kidoban* still exist in the koban system today.

Beside these block systems, there were neighborhood organizations which were called the *boningumi* (five-family associations). These were neighborhood organizations like tithing in old England. Five-family associations consisting of neighbors (usually five families) were collectively liable to the government for any crime or disorder caused by members. They had a joint responsibility to make offenders surrender to the magistrate and to restore peace. The five-family and frankpledge system was introduced from China in A.D. 652. The tradition continues to the present day as *chonaikai* (neighborhood associations).

In 1868, the Shogun's government was abolished and the emperor's reign was restored. This new government sought after European technology and methods. A national police system was introduced similar to the one found in France and Prussia in 1874. By 1886 about 1,000 police stations were founded in cities and counties and more than 15,000 police boxes were established as bases of police operations in towns and villages throughout Japan. A single police officer was posted in each box, but in densely populated areas there was more than one officer. According to the regulation of 1896, one police officer was stationed for every 300-to-800 inhabitants in densely populated city areas, and for every 1000 to 2000 inhabitants in other areas. This system has continued to the present day. A single officer's post is known as the *chuzaisho,* residential police box, and a multiple officers' post, the *koban,* a nonresidential police box. They can be found in every town and village.

As a result of the Restoration, the Samurai lost their positions and social rank. Some re-entered the new government as police officers and schoolmasters, bringing with them the characteristics of the well-educated, ethical, self-sacrificing, and responsible servants of the society. These characteristics were cultivated by Confucianism. Samurai ideals learned through Confucianism became the official ideology and the subculture of the Japanese police.

Confucius, the Chinese scholar and aristocrat, who lived from 551 B.C. to 479 B.C., taught standards of personal conduct and government. The most important of his teachings was respect for ancestors, family, and government. According to his teachings, family relations were to be very highly regarded and every person was to work for his or her family. Everything he or she earned belonged to the family. A person obeys his or her father as he or she knows his/her father always thinks of the family's happiness; "Contribute all you can, take only what you must." Learning and education was held in the highest reverence. "Learning, undigested by thought is labor lost; thought, unassisted by learning, is perilous." Everyone was expected to behave in a just manner and with consideration. Shaming in public was considered one of the worst evils. So, people didn't criticize anyone before others for fear those criticized would lose face. People desisted from crimes in order to maintain their dignity, that is, to save face. Confucianism was introduced into Japan during the sixth century, and the Shogunate adopted it as the government's ideology.

The political leaders under the Meiji government, which carried out the modernization plan by introducing European culture and technology into Japan, regarded the police as an instrument for creating a new nation. Police officers were expected to play the role not only of law enforcers, but also of teachers to instruct the people in the new moral and political vision. Traditionally, the social status of police officers has always been very high in Japan. The police in Japan receive the same respect as community leaders, educators, mediators, or consultants. So, police officers, schoolmasters, and village headmen were called the "Big Three" of the village, and respected by the people as persons of established virtue. As the people felt respect and confidence in their police officers, they developed a high reputation, and it became easy for the citizens to have a deep regard for the police and submit to their leadership.

During the Restoration period, European jurisprudence, especially French and German laws, were introduced in Japan. But as stated in an old Japanese saying, namely, "three articles of law," Japanese criminal law is simple like the Sermon on the Mount. The first emperor of the Han dynasty of China (206 B.C.-A.D.220) was a benevolent despot who used his power to serve the people by following Confucianism. He proclaimed that only killing, wounding, and stealing should be punished. Since then, these wrongdoings have been called "three articles of the criminal laws" (*Hoh-San Shoh*), which implies that the laws should be simple. In the Edo era, a parent who killed a child was not guilty of murder if it were done to punish the child, to uphold family honor, for educational purposes, or to maintain family happiness. On the other hand, if a child killed a parent, capital punishment or life imprisonment was mandatory. This law was in operation until 1973 when the Supreme Court found it unconstitutional. Such a tradition helped maintain community order.

As indicated above, the modern Japanese police system was introduced from Europe as a means of modernization. Meiji leaders were deeply conscious of the necessity of learning everything from Europe, although it was almost impossible to infuse the borrowed institutions with Japanese spirit. Public order in local communities, however, was well maintained and an external police system was unnecessary to borrow. Nevertheless, a national police system, from the central organization to the police station, was introduced. But the traditional peacekeeping mechanism continued to function with the added supervision of the police station. The responsibilities of the police station were to inspect, supervise, advise, and assist community peacekeeping machinery. As is usual with a developing country, people were poor and uneducated. Policemen worked as guardians of the community and as deputies of the emperor.

The mandate and philosophy of the police in Japan is to keep the peace and to protect the weak from criminal victimization. To do this, they use the powers invested in them as law enforcement officers as well as their moral powers as ideal citizens. As guardians of the peace and protectors of the weak, a police officer must be impartial, and act without prejudice, favor, fear or malice, and should conduct his private and public life so that the public will regard him as an example of stability, sincerity, and morality. He is always expected to act for the good of the public, not merely as an enforcer of the law, but as a helpful and reasonable public servant. In order to do his daily tasks effectively and efficiently, he is expected to use discretion which is regarded as the art of suiting actions to particular circumstances. He exercises discretion when he decides which offenses to report, which he should warn the offender for, and which he should allow to pass without intervention. His discretion is a product of wisdom and skill. Although a policeman's mandate is specified by law, he enjoys wide discretion in performing it. Courts are seen to uphold the principle that a police officer may accept any alternative so long as it does not violate the law.

Preventing crime is viewed as an important task of patrol officers. Each koban officer is assigned a small district in which he must maintain the peace and protect the people. He is responsible for maintaining an environment which does not generate crime. Patrol officers, therefore, visit every residence and small business in their assigned districts twice a year to ask them questions regarding their personal particulars, jobs, and so on. They spend 15 or 20 minutes at each residence talking about domestic and local matters, including problems of the neighborhood, suspicious neighbors, crimes, any need for counseling, complaints against the police and other municipal officers, questions about criminal law, advice for preventing burglary and traffic accidents, and other topics concerning general welfare.

As the industrial revolution went on, well-educated and talented young persons began to get jobs in the business world. Police administrators experienced a shortage of well-educated aspirants. After the 1920s, farmers' sons began to enter into the police force instead of Samurais' sons. In spite of this change, the tradition of the Samurai and Confucianism continued to be the backbone of the police.

But, unfortunately for both the police and the people, the Japanese police were influenced by fascism and militarism in the 1930s and 1940s. And the police became agents of the extremists, and their coercive and haughty attitudes created a gap between them and the people (Ames, 1981). The centralized police had a range of responsibility that went far beyond the ordinary police duties. The Special Higher Police was established to regulate conduct during World War II. They censored and regulated publications, motion pictures, political meetings, and associations.

After World War II ended, the democratization of Japan was promoted by the Occupation Army. Fascism, militarism, and imperialism, movements that led to World War II, were thoroughly ousted and abolished. Those officers who were involved in these movements were purged from the government. In 1947, the police law was enacted in line with the occupation policies of the Allied Forces. A democratic and municipal police system was introduced with the following major points of reform:

1. Responsibilities of the police were limited to maintenance of the peace, criminal investigation, and protection of citizen's life and property. They were no longer responsible for fire-fighting, public health, and other administration duties.
2. To democratize the police, the National and the Prefectural Public Safety Commission system was introduced in Japan.
3. Cities, towns, and villages with a population of more than 5,000 were to maintain their own police. That resulted in the establishment of more than 1,500 independent municipal police forces. Towns and villages of less than 5,000 inhabitants, too small for the financial burden of an autonomous police force, were policed by the National Rural Police. With their headquarters in Tokyo, they were organized prefecturally for policing the assigned districts and for ensuring minimum standards of training, communication, identification, crime detection, and crime records for all municipal police forces.

As a result, the police in Japan became more democratized than ever before. However, it soon became apparent that the decentralization was not well suited to the country's situation and it seriously reduced the efficiency of the Japanese police forces (Bayley, 1991). This, in turn, tended to impose a heavy financial burden on small municipalities. To correct these defects, a new police law was put into effect on July 1, 1954. This law brought a new police system into being, one that combined the concepts of democracy and centralization. The system embodied the concept of a democracy suited to the Japanese tradition. The National Rural Police and municipal police forces were abolished and they were integrated into one unified service, namely, the Prefectural Police throughout the country.

According to Japanese police philosophy, a good police force embodies an arrangement for efficient protection of citizens through democratic methods. More than one hundred years ago, Japan borrowed a police system from Europe as a means of modernization. However, only organizational aspects were initiated. Basic police work, which is maintenance of peace and order, continued to be performed in accordance with the traditional method combining the Japanese spirit with the European knowledge and enriching the eastern experience with western technology.

FUNCTIONS

The functions that the police perform can be understood better by looking at the present divisions, hierarchy, and structure of the police in Japan. As one looks at the organization chart, one can appreciate the extent and kind of functions the police perform.

The police today are organized into prefectural divisions. While police are autonomous in their routine operations within the prefectures, general supervision over the force rests with the National Police Agency (NPA). Designed to guide and coordinate the administration of the prefectural police forces, the NPA operates under the control of the National Public Safety Commission (NPSC) consisting of six members. A cabinet member is appointed to preside over the Commission. Although it comes under the jurisdiction of the prime minister, he is not authorized to command or give orders to it. Nevertheless, members are appointed by him although they are to be approved by both houses of the Diet. Their term of office is five years. In order to ensure political neutrality, the Commission is not allowed to have two members from the same political party. The National Police Agency actually plays the role of headquarters or central command for the Japanese police. It directs and supervises all prefectural police operations from the national standpoint. It is responsible for police education and training, communications, criminal identification, forensic activities, criminal statistics and technology.

The Director General of the NPA is appointed by the NPSC with the consent of the prime minister. Under the overall direction of the NPSC, the Director General exercises control over all administrative matters including appointment of personnel and supervision of their duties. The Commission sets basic policies and monitors their implementation through the Director General. Its control does not include direct supervision of daily police operations. The National Police Agency has a Secretariat and six internal bureaus covering administration, criminal investigation, safety, traffic, security, and communications (Figure 2). Included among them are the National Police Academy, the National Police Research Institute and the Imperial Guards Headquarters. It also included the Regional Police Bureaus, each of which is responsible for such functions as training, inspection and interprefectural matters (Figure 1).

In Japan police matters are within the jurisdiction of prefectures. The country is divided into 47 prefectures including the one covering Tokyo Metropolitan area. Prefectural police are responsible for all police matters in their jurisdiction. As noted at the national level, a Prefectural Public Safety Commission (PPSC) heads the prefectural police. Such commissions, which are set up for supervising prefectural police, work under the direction of the governor of the prefecture. It is composed of three or five members appointed by the governor with the consent of the prefecture legislative assembly.

Within the overall direction of the PPSC, chiefs of the concerned Prefectural Police Headquarters (PPH) are responsible for all police matters in their jurisdictions. These chiefs are appointed by the NPSC with the consent of the respective PPSCs. Usually, chiefs and other high officials of the PPH are among the senior officials of the NPA. All other officers are appointed by the prefecture. A prefec-

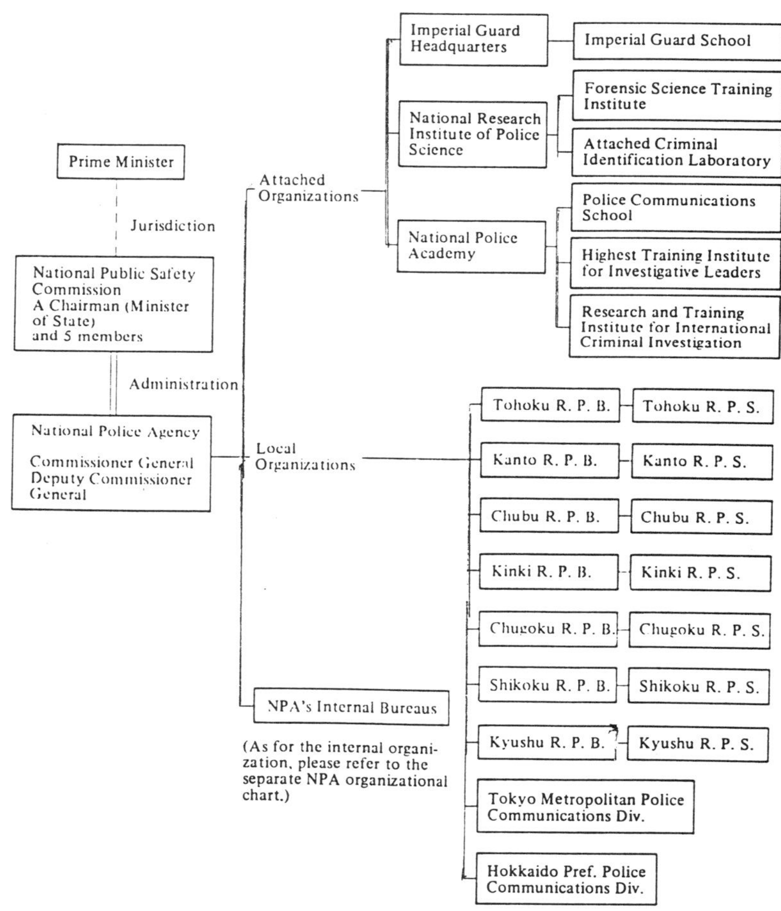

Fig. 1: Police Organization (National Level), as of August, 1989.

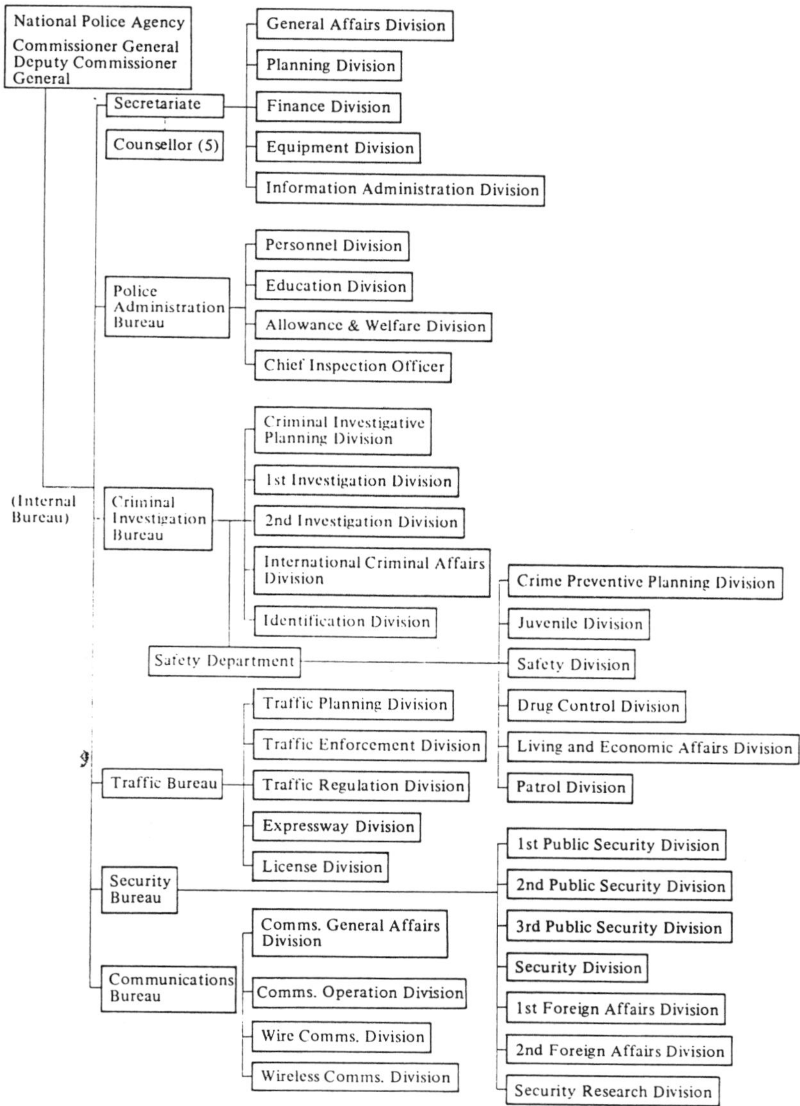

Fig. 2: Organizational Chart of the National Police Agency, as of August, 1989.

tural police headquarters consists of several divisions equivalent to the bureaus of the NPA. Each prefecture is divided into several sections. The Meiji government decided to establish police stations in each of them. These stations are the front-line operational units. Their responsibility is to handle all police matters within the precinct. Naturally, the performance of police stations is closely related to the daily life of the citizens.

Tokyo Metropolitan Prefecture is one of the 47 prefectures. The police here are organized differently from other prefectural police forces. The Metropolitan Police Department (MPD) falls under the administration of the Tokyo Metropolitan Assembly. The Superintendent General of Police, who heads the Metropolitan Police Department, is appointed by the NPSC and approved by the Prime Minister. The MPD is directly supervised by the NPA but not through the regional police bureau.

The country has experimented with the national police system. But the central responsibility for maintaining peace and order has remained with the *koban* and *chuzaisho*. In important districts, the government built police boxes at the national expense. But usually police boxes, sometimes even police stations, were set up with local resources. Even salaries were sometimes borne locally. Such police officers were called "petitioned officers" and such boxes "petitioned police boxes" as they were established through local people's petitions. Petitioned officers had the same powers and responsibilities as ordinary officers. Even today, some police stations and boxes, though fewer and fewer, are products of local appropriations.

At the time of writing there were 1,248 police stations, 6,392 nonresidential police boxes (*koban* or *hashutsusho*), and 8,901 residential police boxes (*chuzaisho*) throughout the country. Usually 50 to 300 police officers are posted in a police station and there are ten or twenty police boxes in each police station. *Kobans* are set up in densely populated areas, busy streets, amusement centers, or in front of railway stations or famous temples in urban areas. And, *chuzaishos* are set up in rural areas. At *kobans* more than two officers serve by shifts. At *chuzaishos* a single police officer serves and lives in its residential quarters with his family.

In large cities, there are several police stations. In 1992, there were 72 police stations in the old city area of Tokyo, 28 in Osaka, and 14 in Kyoto. There is more than one police station in 63 cities.

The number of personnel working for the Japanese police was 258,000 at the time of writing, out of whom 9,600 are assigned to national and regional level organizations including sworn police officers, Imperial Guards, telecommunications and computer specialists, and civilian employees. Among 250,000 employees who work for the prefectural police forces, there are 230,000 sworn police officers, 4,000 traffic wardens, and 26,000 civilian employees. The numerical strength of the prefectural police force is authorized by cabinet order every year on the basis of population, crime rate, traffic, and other such factors. There are about 4,300 female police officers throughout the country. There is one police officer for every 556 persons.

For performing variety of functions including supervision over police functionaries, there are nine ranks in the Japanese police. The total authorized strength of each rank throughout the country as of October 1, 1991, is as follows:

Superintendent General	1
Superintendent Supervisor(s)	50
Chief Superintendent(s)	120
Senior Superintendent(s)	560
Superintendent(s)	5,100
Inspector(s)	10,900
Assistant Inspector(s)	31,800
Sergeant(s)	74,300
Constable(s)(Patrolman, Detective)	97,600

Articles 1 and 2 of the *Police Law* define the responsibilities and duties of the police as protection of life, property, the constitutional rights of individuals, and the maintenance of public safety and order, including prevention, suppression, and investigation of crimes, apprehension of suspects, and traffic control. This is a modification from what the police were required to perform ealier. This change was introduced by the amendment of 1947 as the duty of the prewar Japanese police had extended from maintenance of public peace, investigation of crimes, and protection of life and property to sanitation inspection and labor protection, firefighting, and issuing permits for building construction. After the Second World War, specialized and technical responsibilities of administrative nature were transferred to special ministries and agencies.

According to the prewar Code of Criminal Procedure, the police were under the direction and supervision of public prosecutors. But the new Code of 1947 and 1953 conferred upon them independent authority for investigating all offenses including collection of evidence and apprehension of suspects. Thus, the police are empowered to investigate not only criminal offenses, but also all kinds of violations punishable under any national law or local regulation. For further action, cases are forwarded by the police to a public prosecutor who also has the investigative right and responsibility. Actually, however, they confine their activities to supplementary investigation and prosecution of the cases received from the police. Recently, however, prosecutors have been concerned with white collar crime, especially corruption by high officials and corporate crimes. In 1975, the Tokyo Public Prosecutor's Office arrested former Prime Minister Kakuei Tanaka on charges of receiving bribes from the Lockheed Corporation. The Lockheed Scandal increased the reputation of prosecutors greatly.

There are special judicial police officers for certain offenses prescribed by special laws. Maritime safety officers handle crime on the sea and in the harbor. Postal inspectors handle postal crime. Narcotics enforcement officers are responsible for offenses related to narcotics and stimulant drugs. The National Tax Agency brings accusations of tax evasions to the public prosecutor's office. Forest service officials and immigration inspectors enforce these special laws. Although there are more than ten special law enforcement agencies usually described as special judicial police, there are instances of overlapping jurisdiction between them and prefectural police who also have the responsibilities for investigating violations of special laws. Actually, most judicial duties are handled by the prefectural police.

In addition to judicial duties, the police perform various tasks which are defined as administrative responsibilities. Under the Road Traffic Law, the police regulate vehicular and pedestrian traffic and prevent and investigate traffic violations. They also issue, suspend, and cancel drivers' licenses. They set up traffic lights, control signs, and issue permits for the use of roads for special purposes. Under the Morality Business Control Act, the police issue business licenses to bars, cabarets, massage parlors, strip show theaters, adult shops, love hotels, gambling parlors, and other entertainment establishments and control their business activities. Moreover, the police administer the Security Business Law, the Pawn Brokers Law, the Used Goods Dealers Laws, the Gun and Sword Control Act, and the Crime Victims Benefit Law.

In order to perform these mandated tasks, prefectural police headquarters and criminal stations usually have six divisions: criminal investigation, crime prevention and citizen's safety, criminal patrol, traffic, security, and administration. The criminal investigation division handles investigation of all crime including white collar crime and organized crime. The crime prevention and citizen's safety division handles special investigations concerning drugs and stimulants, guns and swords, juvenile delinquency, moral offenses, as well as matters affecting environment and consumer protection. This division also undertakes crime prevention activities and counseling for juveniles, aged persons, and families. It issues licenses to moral and security businesses, including permits for possession of guns, swords, or dangerous substances. The traffic division is responsible for the enforcement of traffic laws, prevention of traffic accidents, safety education, issue of driver's licenses, and permissions for road use. The security division looks after relief arrangements during natural disasters, riot control, and protection of dignitaries. It also conducts operations concerning counterterrorism, intelligence, and counterintelligence for national security. The administration division takes care of administrative matters including police schools, police detention facilities, and criminal victims compensation schemes.

Police responsibilities performed under the Code of Criminal Procedure such as arrest, search, and investigation are termed as judicial responsibilities. Other responsibilities are classified as administrative responsibilities. Under the prewar criminal procedure law police officers had to perform judicial responsibilities under the direction of public prosecutors. These officers who performed judicial tasks were called the judicial police. The concept of the judicial police is akin to the police judiciare in France and the Kriminalpolizei in Germany.

PERSONNEL PRACTICES

It is realized in Japan a police force's most important resource is the people who work for the organization. Just as business organizations need good facilities to increase their productivity, the police need good officers. In the area of recruitment, Japanese police are somewhat unique in the sense that there is an emphasis on moral strength of the recruits. In Japan police officers are valued, not because they issue traffic citations and arrest criminals, but because they must act as community leaders. Since the primary responsibility for peace and order falls upon the family and the community in Japan, an officer's principal mission is to guide and assist citizens in these efforts. No doubt, the police have the final responsibility for maintaining peace and order. However, ideally a police officer should not have to impose the law upon the citizens. Police officers must be credible leaders whose virtues attract people to follow their example. This idea dates back to Confucius' saying, *Sonomi Tadashikereba Reisezushite Okonawaru*, loosely translated, meaning: "when a ruler's deeds are upright, the result is good government without the need for force or coercion."

Police officers are expected to be honest, diligent, courteous, warmhearted, well-educated, emotionally stable, courageous, and dignified. These qualifications are regarded as essential for being respected as persons of upright character. This is in accordance with the motto, "Rule by Virtue," and it is based on a deep-rooted Japanese tradition of following the example of upright leaders. Accordingly, a model police officer, is also an upright and respected citizen. In order to develop and refine these virtues, police recruits must undergo extensive training to strengthen their moral character and, therefore, the most important criterion for the selection of recruits is the potential for development of moral character.

Recruits must be between 18 and 26 years of age, at least five and one-half feet in height, and 100 lbs. in weight. They must have a high school diploma. Applicants must pass physical and medical examinations, intelligence tests (intellectual capacity and knowledge), and vocational aptitude tests (psychological evaluation). These tests are done through written and oral examinations. In addition, applicants must undergo background investigations which are the most useful for selection boards in assessing an applicant's personality, capacity, and potential. Police officers must possess a law-abiding spirit, a sense of duty, an ability to get along with people, and a capacity for sympathy for the weak. Applicants are required to possess these attributes as well. Selection boards place considerable weight on future potential.

About 7,400 applicants pass the entrance examination every year. One out of every eight or nine applicants is found suitable to enter the police. Forty-five percent of successful applicants are university graduates. There are no requirement in regard to residency. It is difficult for the Tokyo Metropolitan Police Department and other urban prefectural police forces to recruit the full quota of their officers from their own jurisdiction. In Tokyo 20 percent of police officers come from Tokyo and in Osaka, 42.4 percent from Osaka. But in the Akita prefecture, which is located in the northern part of Japan, 97.1 percent of police officers come from its own prefecture as per records available with the National Police Agency. In the rural prefectures, most recruits grew up in the prefectures in which they serve. Generally speaking, most recruits come from rural middle class and lower middle class families.

Education and training is a distinctive feature of the Japanese police. All police researchers from overseas admire the Japanese police training system which is long, extensive, and systematic. Police officers continuously receive formal training at police schools. Besides such courses, on-the-job training is customarily given at the police station. Those on day shift often spend part of the work period in some training.

During the Meiji regime education was regarded as the most important means for modernization of the country. In order to catch up with the modern and industrial countries of the world, a police training school was created as early as 1880 where police recruits had to undertake training for three months. In 1885 the National Police Training Institute was established in order to impart special training for a year to promising sergeants and inspectors selected for promotion by prefectural governors. By 1930 all prefectures had generally extended recruit training to six months. Since 1959 pre-service training for a year has been made compulsory for all recruits. And now training is likely to be for an extended period of two years.

Since education and training are regarded as the responsibility of the national government, all expenses were defrayed from the national treasury. According to the Article 5 of the Police Act, the NPSC and the NPA "shall take charge of maintenance and management of police education facilities and other affairs relating to police education and training." According to the Article 37, all educational expenses are met by the national government.

According to the Article 2 of the Police Act, the police protect lives and property, prevent and process crime, control traffic, and maintain public safety and order. For this purpose, a police officer is given more powers than other public officials. In order to exercise these wide powers without violating individual rights, proper decision making, human values, and right intellectual skills are required. Consequently, the purpose of police education is to develop in police officers the following principles:

(1) No law enforcement agency can protect liberty and democracy unless it is enthusiastically supported by the public. Police officers are public servants who have the unique position of enforcing the law in a way that can also generate people's respect for democratic values.
(2) To realize fully the duties and responsibilities and, at the same time, to develop necessary moral character as a police officer, it is also important for the officer to possess such virtues as respect for discipline, perseverance, self-sacrificing spirit, and a sense of responsibility.
(3) A police officer must be a person of high principles with good education and a pleasant nature. The police are in frequent contact with people. They must act on their own judgment and good sense. They must exercise strict self-control since they are in a position to rectify anything wrong and unlawful. Their public and private life must be such that the public should look upon them as an example of stability, fidelity, morality, and fine personality. A police officer's personality should be characterized by such traits as loyalty, magnanimity, determination, alertness, intelligence, selflessness, and honesty. He or she must add to his or her effectiveness by diligent study and sincere attention to self-improvement.
(4) A police officer must possess the knowledge and ability to meet the requirements of a true profession. An officer's daily duties often require him or her to make decisions concerning the application of criminal law, and the officer must make such decisions without a delay. The officer does not have the time to consult his or her law books. He or she must be able to treat injuries and apply first aid.

(5) A police officer must be mentally and physically stronger than people in general because of the sensitive nature of his/her duties. The officer must suppress crime, arrest criminals, and save human lives. Thus, the practice of judo is useful not only physically but mentally also. To be a good citizen is regarded as the most important goal for a good police officer. The best officer is the best citizen. If the key to police morality is public respect, the reverse is also true. The key to public respect is police morality and the proper performance of duty. Since Japanese police officers fully understand the high expectations of the public regarding morality and the strong criticism police misconduct is bound to incur, they train themselves and help one another to ensure that their duties are properly performed and that they are not involved in scandals. [These principles are provided for in the Article 4 of the *NPSC Regulation for Police and Training*.]

Japanese police education is divided into two categories: school education and general culture. The former is subdivided into recruit education, education for promotion, and in-service and special training. General culture includes on-the-job training.

All successful applicants must receive long and extensive education and training before they are posted in the field. Newly recruited police officers with high school education are admitted to prefectural police schools for a year, and for six months if they are university graduates. Policewomen receive shorter training. Until July 1986, policewomen were differently treated from policemen. For example, the labor standards act forbids policewomen from being on duty after ten o'clock at night and working on dangerous assignments. Small in number, most policewomen leave their position after marriage. Administrators were, therefore, reluctant to give them extensive training. Since policewomen have begun to work for longer periods of time, and are now engaged in various fields, training for policewomen is being reviewed.

Professional education and training is given to police officers in the schools they are admitted to. They study primarily law and police practice, including sociology and psychology, and are required to master judo and kendo, the traditional Japanese martial arts which build strong bodies and minds, and are useful for self-defense and the apprehension of criminals. They also study history, literature, and art. All the newly recruited officers are accommodated in the dormitories at the police school. They are also taught to enjoy sports, arts, movies, music, and the traditional tea ceremony and flower arrangement.

As mentioned above, the purpose of the education is to develop professional ability of the police officer. To be of sound body and mind is regarded as the most important quality. To be a good citizen is to be an efficient police officer. An officer should have a bit of the knowledge of a lawyer, doctor, and engineer. He or she must possess the tough-mindedness of an athlete, the insight of a scientist, and the compassion and understanding of a priest.

Duration of police education and curricula are uniform throughout Japan. This education requirement is also a very serious hurdle to successful entry into the police profession in Japan. About ten percent of the recruits of the prefectural police schools fail to complete the requirements. The word "education" is usually used rather than "training" because this training is formal, systematic, and theoretical. However, practical "training" in the strict sense of the word, is also required for police recruits. Accordingly, school education has been integrated with training on the street.

All recruits must stay in the dormitories and follow a rigorous routine. This is fixed as follows:

6:00 A.M.	arise
6:15 A.M.	morning call
6:50 A.M.	breakfast
8:30 A.M. - 12:00 P.M.	classwork
12:00 P.M. - 1:00 P.M.	lunch and break
1:00 P.M. - 4:00 P.M.	classwork
4:00 P.M. - 5:00 P.M.	club activities
5:00 P.M. - 7:00 P.M.	bath and dinner
7:00 P.M. - 9:30 P.M.	study on their own
9:30 P.M.	night call
10:00 P.M.	lights out

Recruits are expected to learn the police spirit and ideals by leading a regular school life for a year. New recruits with high school diplomas receive a year's course consisting of the following:

General Culture	256 hours
Civics	25 "
Ethics	25 "
Health Care	24 "
Japanese Language	40 "
Current Topics	30 "
Natural Sciences	16 "
Law	248 "
Criminal Law	80 "
Criminal Procedure	80 "
Civil Law	28 "
Police Activities	692 "
Patrol Duties	384 "
Criminal Investigation	86 "
Communication	110 "
Role Playing Exercise	112 "
Physical Training	548 "
Etiquette and Drill	112 "
Firearms	72 "
First Aid	40 "
Judo and Kendo	136 "
Athletics	50 "
Driving	34 "
Miscellaneous Training	324 "

Included within miscellaneous training are orientation, examination, visits to cultural centers, sightseeing, and athletic competition.

After completing a year of police school, recruits are sent into the field for about a year. While they are assigned to the police station, tutors are carefully selected, and individual training is given to them. They return to the school for a four-month refresher course to reflect on their experience and to receive additional training. This completes their official recruit training and education. At the time of writing, recruit training was under review for further expansion up to two years. Recently, 44 prefectural police forces have opted for one-year-and-ten months' comprehensive training for high school graduates, and one-year-and-three months for university graduates. Training for high school graduates will consist of initial basic training for twelve months, field training for four months, and refresher training for six months.

Constables qualified to be promoted as sergeants are sent to regional police schools to attend an elementary leaders course which lasts nine weeks. This course consists of two parts: a five-week segment for training as leaders or supervisors at the junior level, and a four-week technical training stage. Students can choose one of the four specialized courses, namely, criminal investigation, crime prevention, traffic control, and public security (riot control and intelligence). Generally speaking, students are posted to the division in which they are trained.

Sergeants promoted as assistant inspectors are trained for fifteen weeks in the middle-level leaders course at regional police schools. It consists of two parts. Nine weeks are devoted to training as supervisors and six weeks to technical training.

After the successful completion of inspectors' examination, officers are sent to the National Police Academy where they study for six months. Police inspectors or above are commanding officers. They are qualified to make a request for an arrest warrant. They are generally placed in such posts as assistant chief of division at prefectural headquarters or deputy chief of a police station. Consequently, highly sophisticated education is given to these officers in order to train them professionally as executives fit in character, intelligence, and attitude for service.

Close attention is given to a program of continuous training and research in order to meet the needs of the times and to keep abreast of the demands of social change. For this purpose, one to three weeks of in-service training is given to all police officers, usually assistant inspectors or below. These courses are intended to re-educate low ranking police officers at least every four or five years. There are more than one hundred in-service training programs such as highway safety, criminal identification, organized crime, juvenile delinquency and so on. In-service training is conducted in various fields of police activity such as: motorcycle driving; traffic engineering; highway safety; traffic law enforcement; investigation of hit-and-run crimes; criminal identification; death investigation; scientific investigation; forensics; fingerprint techniques; white collar crime; corruption; organized crime; counterespionage; intelligence production and analysis; antihijacking; riot control; bomb threats and search techniques; drug law enforcement; juvenile delinquency; first aid; crime prevention; pollution; law enforcement data processing; criminal statistics; management and organization; police discipline; patrol operation and supervision; personnel administration; languages (Korean, Chinese, Russian, and English); judo and kendo; and athletic leadership.

Included in in-service training are also courses such as criminal investigation (for detectives), crime prevention, juvenile delinquency, public security, and traffic control. Suitable courses are given to police officers who desire to be transferred from the patrol section to another branch.

Generally, a graduate of refresher courses is posted to the police station as a patrol officer for a few years. Later, after due consideration of the officer's vocational aptitude and ability, he or she is transferred to another section and an introductory course is imparted to him or her. The content of training varies with the courses. For example, a young patrol officer who desires to become a detective is admitted to the special training course for detective candidates if he or she passes the detective aptitude test. This course usually runs for eight or ten weeks. They are given additional instruction by experienced detective officers at prefectural police headquarters. During that time, they go to the prosecutor's office, criminal court, and jails for lectures. After they pass the examination for detective candidates, they return to their respective police stations and receive on-the-job training at the hands of experienced detectives. These trainers are carefully selected and trained for imparting appropriate instruction.

Once it is decided to transfer a patrol officer to detective work, the officer has to undergo an initiation which the police call "rough work." This starts from shoplifting and bicycle thefts. The officer is called a "probationer" or an "apprentice." The relationship between the tutoring detective and a new police officer is somewhat parental or brotherly/sisterly which helps the newcomer in learning much about the spiritual side of being a police officer. The officer learns pride and dedication through this relationship. For example, a police officer must take "three years of tea-serving" to learn self-discipline and concentration. At one time, all apprentices started their jobs from cleaning workshops, washing tea cups, arranging tools, and so on. Among them, tea-serving was regarded as the most important job for apprentices. Usually this apprenticeship continued for at least three years. After this term of apprenticeship was finished, and the apprentices were entitled to investigate crimes on their own, they had to continue to study in order to develop their ability and knowledge of criminal investigation.

In-service training courses are held at prefectural, regional, and national police schools. At the prefectural police schools, in-service training for low-ranking officers runs for two to four weeks. At regional police schools special training in Korean language, counterintelligence, and explosives disposal is given for three weeks to one year. At the National Police Academy, there are six-month-long courses for Judo and athletic leaders and also those lasting for three to seven weeks for death investigation, crime against business, and so on, which are given to assistant inspectors or above. Special courses on bookkeeping and accounting, statistics, foreign languages, computer operation, and psychological analysis are sometimes given in external facilities. Prefectural police forces pay for these courses.

In Japan law enforcement is viewed as a difficult and challenging job. It is recognized that professionalism as well as genuine regard for human rights must be inculcated in all personnel working for the police. Sensitivity to the constitutional rights of the individual, and his/her innate worth and dignity is essential and indispensable. Law enforcement and judicial officers have observed similar changes all over the world. Of course, Japan is not an exception to that development. The Miranda rules and other leading cases were introduced in Japan within a few days after these decisions were handed down by the United States Supreme Court. The police have to be more sensitive than ever about the constitutional rights of individuals. They must be more professional in law enforcement practices. In order to meet the changing demands of society, the police must continue to change.

This is why the Training Institute for Leading Investigators was established in 1967. Advanced training for criminal investigation is given to superintendents and inspectors who are below 45 years of age with more than five years experience as inspectors. Senior detective managers of prefectural police come from the graduates of this institute. They receive instruction in management and administration of criminal investigation for six months.

To sum up, there are three kinds of police educational facilities in Japan: prefectural police schools, regional police schools, and the National Police Academy. While the main function of prefectural police schools is to provide education for recruits, regional police schools provide advanced education and the National Police Academy offers training for superior police officers.

Instructors are selected from inside and outside the police force. Recruit instructors in prefectural police schools are usually selected from among officers of the rank of assistant inspectors. They are required to be well experienced, considerate, and incisive. It is believed that they provide the first impressions of policing to the recruits and hence, they must be good models. The NPA prepares textbooks and teaching materials for both students and instructors. Instructors can read these books before they start teaching. Certain instructors on promotion and special training courses are selected from outside the police. They may include individuals who teach languages or cultural topics. While such instructors have adequate knowledge, they may lack the sense of mission as law enforcement officers. Police officers as instructors are preferred more often. However, in order to avoid self-complacency and criticism from the public at large, it is necessary to recruit outside instructors from time to time.

Superintendents and senior superintendents are appointed as professors of the National Police Academy. Ten of these professors have experience as chiefs of the PPH and twenty of them are qualified executive elites. All high-ranking officers of the NPA deliver lectures several times a year. To maintain close relations between the police and the society, many civilians are invited as special lecturers from universities, the mass media, community leaders, and the artistic, sports, and business communities. About a fifth of all lectures at the inspector course are given by senior NPA officers, and the rest by guest instructors. At the prefectural and regional schools, experts such as professors of civil law, psychology, geography, anthropology, and public accounting are appointed as part-time instructors. Community leaders, representatives from the mass media, artists, and business leaders also are invited as guest instructors.

A story of an Inspector is narrated in Appendix A to illustrate how one can advance in a police career.

As indicated elsewhere, there are nine ranks in the Japanese police. Sergeants and assistant inspectors are classified as front-line supervisors; inspectors and superintendents as middle-level managers; and senior superintendents and above as top-level managers. The number of officers in each rank is fixed by cabinet order.

Promotion, essentially based on merit, is open on an equal basis to all regular police officers hired by the prefectures. Merit is judged primarily through competitive examinations that are given every year by prefectural police headquarters. These examinations are divided into three parts: the first part consists of multiple-choice questions about police work, law, and general knowledge including current topics. The second part is an essay test on various aspects of technical knowledge such as law, management, investigation, crime prevention, traffic, and security. During the final part the candidate has to pass a series of interviews with senior officers at the headquarters and a number of physical-fitness tests covering arrest techniques, field operations as the commander of a small unit, and so on. All qualified officers are urged to take the promotion examinations because they are thereby encouraged to study new laws and regulations and all aspects of police work. In some prefectures, the first part of the promotion examinations is called an achievement test and all police officers are required to take it. The achievement test is given every year by the chiefs of prefectural police forces to determine police officers' knowledge of police work.

In Japan officers are told to become specialists in their own field, which means acquiring skills of a generalist with comprehensive understanding of police responsibilities. Their experience, the record of routine performance, and personal qualities, as rated by their supervisor, are also considered at the time of promotion. Constables have to serve for three years (four years in Metropolitan Police Department in Tokyo) before they can apply for sergeants' examination. University graduates may take it after a year's experience. High school graduates have to serve for three more years as sergeants before they apply for the promotion examination for assistant inspectors.

Until recently the examination was the only criteria for selecting supervisors. But in 1968 the title of Senior Constable was created for suitable officers who had many years of experience minus the requirement that they have to pass the sergeants' examination. Since 1972, veteran police officers have been awarded the rank of sergeant as a reward for years of police service. Every year the ratio of these sergeants has been increasing. Moreover, the functions of sergeants have been changing. Previously, sergeants were regarded as supervisors who went around police boxes to oversee patrol officers to ensure they were working properly. Today their function is to instruct young officers by showing them how to handle their assignments and to coordinate their activities. Assistant inspectors perform the task of front-line supervisors, though they were regarded as middle-level managers until 1972.

After a successful completion of promotion examinations for sergeants and assistant inspectors, the officers are required to enter regional police schools where they have to attend one of the supervisors' courses. There is a nine-week junior level supervisors' course for sergeants. The course for assistant inspectors runs for 15 weeks to prepare them as middle-level supervisors. They are promoted during or after the completion of these courses.

Selection of candidates for promotion to the rank of inspector is made through a similar procedure consisting of examination and evaluation. But more weight is placed on their capability as middle-level and top-level managers than their experience and previous accomplishments. Those who pass the examination enter the National Police Academy for six months. Annually, approximately a thousand assistant inspectors are sent to the Academy from the prefectures in Japan. They are trained not only as inspectors but also as future managers of prefectural police. Persons above the age of fifty are usually exempted from the requirement because they have little chance of becoming top-level managers.

The subjects studied at the Academy include law, police practice, and general culture. The purpose here is to learn how to manage the police organization. Another objective is to develop solidarity among police executives throughout the country through the process of living under the same roof and eating at the same mess. All officers are required to stay in the dormitory even if they live near the Academy. Most instructors of the Academy are superintendents, senior superintendents, and chief superintendents who are experts in their respective fields. All senior members of the National Police Academy talk to the trainees concerning their own tasks. University professors, business executives, political critics, musicians, medical doctors, litterateurs, artists, and others are invited to raise students' skills, knowledge, cultural awareness, and develop artistic capabilities.

Inspectors play an important role in police work. Usually in their 30s and 40s, the prime of life, they are section chiefs or deputy chiefs of police stations or assistant section chiefs at the prefectural headquarters. They stay in this rank for seven or eight years before they are promoted to superintendents.

Promotion to superintendent depends on selection by prefectural police chiefs. In some prefectures, chiefs are advised by selection committees. Selections are based on the applicant's capabilities, leadership, and the needs of police agencies. Superintendent is the rank held generally by chiefs of police stations, chiefs of sections, and divisions at the headquarters, deputy chiefs of big police stations, and, also important sections at headquarters. In small prefectures, deputy and assistant chiefs are superintendents. Senior superintendents are generally deputy and assistant chiefs at prefectural headquarters and chiefs of very large police stations where the strength of officers is about 300. Chief superintendent is the rank held by chiefs of prefectural police and deputy chiefs of very large prefectural forces. Superintendent Supervisors are chiefs of big and important prefectural police headquarters as well as deputy chiefs of Tokyo and Osaka police offices. Senior superintendents and above are officially appointed by the NPSC on the advice of the PPSC. Persons recommended by chiefs of prefectural police are promoted without exception.

In Japan, both in governmental organizations and private companies, promotion is usually based on experience and school background. So, the promotion system in the police service is attractive for young persons, especially for ambitious high school graduates who cannot go to university for economic reasons. This is one of the main reasons they apply for police jobs. Theoretically, one can reach the top positions. University graduates and those without such education can rise as high as their talent can take them. At the time of writing four superintendent supervisors and 39 chief superintendents were promoted from the rank of constables.

Described above is the normal promotion procedure. But the National Police Agency has adopted a unique recruitment system known as the Executive Candidate Examination which was introduced in the nineteenth century to attract highly educated persons to the police. Entrance into the police through this system is made at the level of assistant inspector. Like all other ministries and agencies in Japan, the NPA has taken up this special measure to attract ambitious and talented people with high educational standards. Applicants must pass an advanced civil service examination conducted by the National Personnel Authority in which one out of every forty applicants is successful. Most successful applicants are graduates of the Law Faculty of Tokyo and Kyoto Universities which were established by the Meiji government to produce high-class bureaucrats.

This is similar to hiring practice in regard to elite bureaucrat corps in France. Every year 15 to 20 persons are recruited through this examination. Known as executive elites, they are given special training. After three years' apprenticeship at a prefectural police office, they return to the NPA where these future leaders are promoted to the position of superintendents. They are commonly assigned to prefectural or overseas posts and occasionally transferred to other ministries. They are rotated every one-and-a-half or two years. Thus, they are trained as administrators of varied responsibilities. The former prime minister, Nakasone, started his career as an executive elite of the police force and resigned to run for election when he was Superintendent of the MPD. Senior administrators, including chiefs of prefectural police, are usually these specially trained executive elites. Now, about 500 elite executives work in the NPA and prefectural police establishments. This elite system has been criticized at times since the participants do not have a lot of field experience as low-level police officers. But, they can concentrate their time on things essential for the nation as a whole (Bayley, 1991; Ames, 1981).

LEADERSHIP AND SUPERVISORY CALIBRE

The most important quality for good leaders in Japanese society is understanding and sympathy, which is expressed through the phrase *enman na jinkakau* or "well-integrated personality." A strong and aggressive personality is considered unsuitable for leadership. The qualifications of a leader in Japanese society are his or her ability to understand and attract the support of citizens. Ability to work efficiently in a group is more highly valued than intellectual skills. A person who can arrive at a satisfactory solution or conclusion to a problem for everyone concerned is regarded as possessing good leadership qualities.

According to Japanese norms and beliefs, if superiors attract their subordinates emotionally, subordinates are likely to sacrifice their personal interest for the sake of their superiors or organizations. Also, it is believed that when subordinates feel personal commitment to their superiors, they work more ardently for them. The words, "I would walk through sea and fire if you wanted me" are often used by subordinates who feel personal commitment to their superiors, and wish to devote themselves solely to them. If superiors fail to hold their subordinates emotionally, they will lose leadership. Japanese workers consider human relations as more important than rational direction. Leaders are expected to accommodate subordinates' opinions and wishes as much as possible.

The seniority system rooted in the Confucian tradition is still influential in Japan. Under this system, the highest offices are usually held by the senior persons. Seniority is usually based on the length of service. But young persons know that their turn will come and that they will occupy these high posts in the future. These conditions of leadership are common to any Japanese community, including the police.

In Japan a crime is simply viewed as a breach of a law which is a social promise made by community members. The vast majority of the community members are able to keep such promises. Nevertheless, a very few cannot do so. Since social promises constitute the laws, those who break them are considered criminals. However, criminals are a minority. Police officers, who have been regarded as community leaders both before and after modernization, are required to act as representatives of the majority and to show understanding and sympathy to criminals as the minority. In this sense, a well-integrated personality is necessary for all police officers, especially officers in supervisory positions.

Many foreign researchers (Bayley, 1991; Ames, 1981) on the Japanese police have observed that there is very little police misconduct in Japan. One of the biggest concerns of senior police officers in Japan is misbehavior by their subordinates. It would not be an overstatement to say that the problem of police morale can be solved only by ensuring that no misconduct takes place. This is true because even a petty shoplifting by a police officer would certainly trigger strong public criticism. The mass media would lambaste the police for having employed such a thief and tend to impress the public that all police officers were untrustworthy. Additionally, the senior officers of the shoplifter, as his or her supervisors, might be viewed as being responsible for the misconduct and might themselves be punished in one way or another. All officers therefore worry about police misconduct because they fear it would undermine the public's respect for the police as a whole and lead to public refusal to cooperate with the police.

Not only in the community of the police, but also in other hierarchical institutions of Japan, senior officers are required to supervise their subordinates to see to it not only that their jobs are performed properly, but also that their private lives are free from misbehavior. Supervisory offices cannot remain immune from punishment once their subordinates are involved in police scandals. If the misconduct is gross, punishment will reach as high as the top-ranking officers. From an American point of view, this typically Japanese moral code may be far beyond imagination. Nevertheless, it is taken for granted in Japanese society and considered to be the proper accountability of any organization to society. So, virtuous personality is regarded as the most important qualifications of police officers, especially officers in supervising positions. Bayley (1991) observed that the Japanese police are extremely stern with infractions Americans would consider petty, and there is very little police misconduct in Japan.

STANDARDS USED IN EVALUATING INDIVIDUAL POLICE PERFORMANCE

As in other countries, Japanese citizens' expectations and demands vis-à-vis the police are great and always growing. So, it is not easy for police officers to complete their duties perfectly and satisfy all citizens' demands. On the other hand, officers can be severely disciplined when they fail to carry out their assignments. Police administrators consistently maintain the principle of "work and you will be rewarded." In the police stations, chiefs take every opportunity to award honors to those police officers showing diligence, kindness, efficiency, courage, and integrity. Ideal conduct is demonstrated by apprehension of a criminal in the act, obtaining useful information about a fugitive terrorist, the highest number of traffic citations, recovery of a drowning child, proposals for the promotion of efficiency, kindness shown to aged persons or visitors, organizing and assisting boys' baseball teams, advice and support to elderly persons' sports clubs, and so forth.

Traditionally, Japanese police officers have been expected to show an example of good citizenship to the people. They were called teachers of moral and civic education. So, when an honor is bestowed, it is done more so based on how the officer handled the case and how the involved citizen reacted and appraised the officer, rather than on what he or she actually did. Kindness is more highly appraised than strength or perfection of law enforcement. Kindness and sympathy to the weak and poor are the most important elements when people evaluate police officers' deeds.

In Japan, team spirit, a sense of belonging and group activity is more highly emphasized than individual activity. What a member has contributed to his or her organization is the most important factor in his or her evaluation. A prefectural police chief usually gives an award to a unit such as a station, a section, a project team, a task force or a group organized when a homicide is solved or when officers perform well when a big accident happens. Sometimes more than a hundred investigators are mobilized to organize a task force for a homicide case. Individual heroism is discouraged. To do the job as a part of the team is highly encouraged. When an organization receives an honor, a party (usually buffet) is held, and all members participate to celebrate the achievement. But it is unusual for individual members to be awarded honors.

Officers who serve for many years are honored with service medals at 20, 25, and 30 years. These medals are awarded on police anniversary day each year. On this occasion chiefs of the prefectural police hold commendation ceremonies and invite governors and other dignitaries as guests. When veteran officers receive 30-year service medals, their wives accompany them. They are invited to go on two- or three-day trips. When 30-year service medals are awarded, police chiefs also give medals to the police officers who have maintained good conduct for a long time. Meritorious officers and their wives are invited to the Imperial Palace garden in Tokyo where the emperor honors them with a few words expressing his thanks for their service. In this way the emperor shows his appreciation for their efforts, which makes the officers feel greatly honored. They often say that the emperor's kind words more than make up for their long years of dedicated service.

PROFESSIONALIZATION

The Japanese police have never discussed professionalism in an American sense of the word. In other words, professionalism has not been advocated to wean the police away from malpractices like brutality, corruption, politicalization, discrimination, perjury, and other forms of misconduct. In Japan there is also not much reference to the bad apple theory. As members of a highly traditional group, a police officer is expected to maintain strict discipline. Rules controlling police behavior are stricter than American standards.

When a police officer is in uniform, he or she cannot smoke or eat outside the police station. A police officer is expected to be unfailingly courteous to the public, remaining cool even if verbally abused, yet unbending in carrying out his or her responsibilities. When Japanese senior police officials are asked to identify the most troublesome problems of police behavior, they now mention off-duty traffic accidents, drunkenness, and indiscretions with the opposite sex. There are virtually no disciplinary problems on duty.

Once a Japanese person enters a company or organization, he or she will continue to work there until retirement. Japanese seldom change jobs. Even if they wish to change, it is not easy for them to find good jobs, especially if they are in the prime of life. Moreover, they will lose the privileges of longevity. So, their sense of belonging and loyalty to the organization is very high. In Japan, all jobs have their own morals and ethics. Japanese people feel professional pride in their work. They are conscious of the social functions and responsibilities of their jobs. A person's salary is mainly based on the length of service rather than position or merit. And labor unions are not organized functionally, but rather by enterprise.

Under these circumstances, once a police officer always a police officer! And even an off-duty officer is expected to act like a police officer. A job is regarded not as a position but as a mark of social status in Japan. Moreover, individuals are identified as members of groups, and the group is affected by the reputation of its deviants. So the group is much more concerned and responsible for individual members' behavior. This may make it easier to understand why Japanese police administrators give new recruits long and complete education. All members of the police community try their best to maintain and raise up the social status of the police.

Even if a crime was committed by an ex-police officer, newspapers give a great deal of coverage to such news to criticize the police. Fortunately, Japanese police officers have a great deal of professional pride and confidence in their own work and they enjoy the respect of citizens.

In 1984 the National Police Agency established a new code of ethics. Known as the "Principles of Police Life," it consists of the following five principles:

1. We, police officers, shall serve the nation and the community with professional pride and a sense of mission.
2. We, police officers, shall respect human rights and perform our duties with courtesy and impartiality.
3. We, police officers, shall strictly maintain discipline and develop a sense of mutual solidarity.
4. We, police officers, shall build up a sense of character and develop our own facilities intellectually, physically and morally.
5. We, police officers, shall be honest and keep our public and private lives sound and unsullied.

Traditionally, police officers have been deemed model citizens who support the view that law should not be enforced by compulsion, but rather willingly observed. This way of thinking is the Japanese tradition of law and order. It is repeatedly emphasized that a good police officer ought to be a good citizen. A good citizen is to be sincere, honest, humane, kind, gentle, warmhearted, calm, cool, mild, sound, steady, courteous, polite, faithful, diligent, punctual, self-restrained, impartial, unselfish, self-sacrificing, devoted, well-integrated, frugal, modest, merciful, compassionate, responsible, reliable, sympathetic, moderate, cooperative, and harmonious. These are all the conditions necessary for being good citizens and good police officers. Police officers should satisfy these conditions and continue constant efforts to develop complete support and cooperation of the public. And, if the police accept the public trust with pride and gratitude, it is believed that they will be able to carry out their responsibilities more effectively. This is the Japanese way of professionalization of the police. Vogel (1979) says that the Japanese police have a demanding task.

Police supervisors in Japan are considered responsible for the behavior of their subordinates even to the extent that they may receive criticism and punishment for the mistakes committed by their subordinates whether or not they are specifically responsible for the errors. As in other spheres of Japanese life, the small group has a high sense of solidarity which generates internal discipline over its own members. This helps prevent police corruption.

In the United States, it is assumed that a police officer might act without adequate regard for the rights of the suspect, and judges, therefore, constrain police action. In Japan, however, the police are expected to have inner discipline so that the courts rarely challenge police decisions and the police do not feel on the defensive. In spite of such favorable attitudes, the police in Japan, as noted above, have not relaxed in their efforts to uphold the dignity and importance of the service they are engaged in.

POLICE WAGES, STATUS, SUBCULTURE, AND MORALE

Japanese police officers enjoy good wages and high social status. Salaries are decided based on recommendations from National and Prefectural Personnel Authorities. Every year these authorities make a nationwide study of the salaries and working conditions of industrial workers in the private sector. They then submit reports for the salaries and working conditions of governmental employees to the cabinet. The government has to follow these recommendations to avoid strikes. Salaries of governmental employees are fixed at levels commensurate with those of average industrial workers. The basic salary of police officers is almost the same as that of elementary and high school teachers, and are 8 to 10 percent higher than that of general governmental employees. Police officers also receive various kinds of allowances and benefits.

Overall, then, Japanese police officers enjoy better salaries and benefits compared with other governmental employees and industrial workers. People feel that police officers deserve high wages because their duties are dangerous, unpleasant, and unhealthy. They have to be very knowledgeable and need a great deal of experience. These elements are regarded as important for making decisions about salary standards. As with other governmental agencies and private enterprises, emphasis is placed on experience rather than position and rank. For example, a sergeant with 30 years' experience receives 7.8 million yen a year (65,000 U.S. dollars). He/she receives the same amount of salary as an inspector with 23 years' experience and a superintendent with 22 years' experience. This means that a sergeant receives a higher salary than a superintendent with 10 years' experience. A superintendent with 30 years' experience receives 9.6 million yen a year (74,000 U.S. dollars) which is 23 percent higher than that of a sergeant with the same experience. A rookie patrol officer who just finished recruit training receives 3.34 million yen a year (25,700 U.S. dollars).

In addition to generally favorable compensation and benefits, Japanese police morale is boosted by a sense of self-sacrifice which still forms the basis of solidarity among police officers. Police officers do not feel like blue-collar workers. They enjoy the high respect and reliance from the people.

In Japan, the systems of seniority and permanent employment are in effect in almost all industries, and young employees know their salaries will rise with seniority. They are thus willing to accept low wages during their first few years. This is one of the reasons why Japanese people usually do not want to change their jobs until they retire. It should be pointed out that wages are not necessarily a valid indication of a person's social status in Japan. Scrubwomen, dishwashers at educational institutions, and school guards are all unskilled laborers but actually they receive higher amount of wages than teachers. However, they are considered auxiliary staffs of school and their social status is lower than that of teachers. The high salary of police employees does not necessarily reflect their social status, but people know the police work hard performing their duties in a self-sacrificing manner. They are willing to accept their duties because they know people generally understand and appreciate their efforts.

There is hardly any study on the subculture of the police. American observers like Bayley (1991) and Ames (1981) refer to solidarity, pride, and team spirit of the Japanese police. As Ames (1981) says:

> Solidarity and loyalty among police officers is essential to the strength and effective operation of the police system as it interacts with the community. Loyalty and solidarity are crucial to the police and primary tools in their mission of protecting society from various enemies.

There is no criticism regarding the negative impact of police subculture. The lack of subculture, as has been indicated above, is perhaps due to the fact the police enjoy a high social status with historical links to the Samurai and the emperor. Further, they are given thorough and purposeful training. Police organizations offer congenial working conditions and the police enjoy good salaries, but as has been discussed in the section on police public relations, the police today do not enjoy the same respect and affection they were used to. As a result, certain degree of alienation has set in certain sections of the police paving the way for police subculture. Salary, status, as well as the lack of subculture, have positively contributed to police morale, which is high.

Even in the feudal Japanese society that flourished during the Edo period, the ruling class did not enjoy a very luxurious lifestyle. Confucianism, which was an orthodox philosophy among the samurai, admonished that the samurai should glory in honorable poverty. The ruling samurai class was, therefore, content with a poor but honest life. *Senyu Koraku,* which connotes that people's happiness must be ensured before individual pleasure, still exists in the police community. Hard work, patience, self-discipline, and sensitivity to others are regarded as the most important virtues a police officer can possess. Phrases such as "luxury is the enemy," and "the Samurai (police officers) shouldn't have money on their lips" are often emphasized. Police officers are encouraged to be thrifty and to save for an emergency. More references to police morale are found in the sections dealing with police professionalization and problems of the police.

UNIONS AND ASSOCIATIONS

There are no police labor unions in Japan. Under the public servant law, police employees, like defense personnel and firefighters, are prohibited from organizing and joining a labor union and other organizations to represent them in dealing or negotiating with the government. The government decides the salaries and other working conditions for the police based on the advice of the National Personnel Authority, which is an independent organization that researches working conditions of employees of private companies all over the country. But within the police community there are some friendly organizations such as the Mutual Aid Association and fraternal associations. The Mutual Aid Association is nationally organized and handles medical insurance benefits and pensions, provides housing loans at low interest rates, and runs police hotels in the big cities as well as resort houses in the mountains and on the seacoast that can be used by police employees and their families. Fraternal associations, which are prefecturally organized, handle police hospitals, dormitories, apartments, life and medical insurance funds for employees and their families, police banks, survivor's benefits and pensions, scholarships for police children, travel agencies, and cooperatives.

Almost all matters that would be of concern to police unions in other countries are handled by these two types of associations which are managed and supervised by representatives of all ranks of police officers and civilian employees. But these associations cannot perform the representative functions of the labor union concerning salaries, working hours, and working conditions. The Communist Party of Japan at times has agitated for organizing labor unions within the police, but there has been no real support from the police for these proposals. In police circles this party is regarded as too political and partisan. There is also fear that any close affiliation with the Communist Party might make the police feel entrapped.

True, police employees do not resort to unions to defend their self-esteem. But this does not mean that Japanese police administrators have it easy because unions do not exist. They are required to pay ceaseless consideration and do their best to improve employees' working conditions despite the absence of police unions.

POLICE PUBLIC RELATIONS, PUBLIC CONFIDENCE, TRUST, AND RESTRAINTS ON THE POLICE

Ames (1981) says that the Japanese police think of themselves as "the world's best." Perhaps this pride is well-founded. After all, Japan has "the lowest crime rate in the industrialized world." This American observer also notes that the crime trend in Japan indeed shows a "downward curve." Major Japanese cities are safe at all times. Japan's unique achievement is attributed to "general cooperation by the community in fighting crime" apart from the fact the police are organized efficiently. The police organization is successful in "an almost remaking of individuals." This involves "usually a lifetime commitment to the police profession" on the part of those who join the police. They are moulded into police organization through "extensive training and other formal and informal mechanism."

It is an indication of public confidence and trust that the Japanese police officers enjoy a fairly high social status. The social status of the police profession attracts young recruits of high quality. This ensures good relations between communities and the police. Public trust and confidence are dependent upon the character and behavior of individual police officers rather than the fairness and efficiency of the police organization. Since crime is not so serious and public order is well maintained, dissatisfaction and complaints against the police are not very serious. This does not necessarily mean all people are friendly and cooperative with the police. People respond positively to the small acts of kindness performed by police officers. But they may also be afraid of the police and obey their orders and directives out of fear. Mothers discipline naughty children by threatening to call a police officer to take them away.

Nevertheless, women still come to the police boxes (*kobans*) to ask for help to control their alcoholic husbands and to become arbitrators in family disputes. They do so because police officers are regarded as people of virtue. Such counseling is one of the most important service functions of Japanese police officers. People with problems come to these boxes to talk to their local police officer.

The police have done their best to win the respect of the society and police officers enjoy the esteem of the people, not as law enforcers, but as moral leaders in Japanese society. Police misconduct in Japan is minimal compared to other countries. In 1991, only 11 out of 258,000 personnel were discharged for misbehavior. Another 44 were given departmental punishments such as temporary suspension, reduction in pay, or formal reprimands.

But this respect and confidence seem to be declining lately. Until just recently, public order in Japan was maintained well. The country remained basically peaceful. But lately, the crime situation has begun to change. The circumstances facing the police are growing worse. Now people enjoy an abundant life and high education. More than 40 percent of the people receive higher education and about 90 percent of them feel they are middle class. However, in this process of development, the social status of the police officer has been declining. The educated middle class have wider knowledge and judgment. They are more critical of social phenomena including the government. The police have become a major target of their criticism.

Whenever a police officer's misbehavior is uncovered by the mass media, confidence in the police falls. Traditionally, the Japanese police have been proud of diligence, good discipline, and integrity in both personal and official life, a fact that earned them a good reputation. But unfortunately, there have been several recent examples of police misconduct which have caused a decline in the confidence and trust the people have in the police. There were incidents involving police like the murder of a woman in a love triangle, acceptance of money from an organized crime source in exchange for secret information, and a bank robbery to pay off a housing loan. So the reputation of the police has been on the decline.

Since crime did not become a serious social problem after World War II, citizens have not felt they needed to depend upon the police. So they are quick to criticize the police. Some of them believe that they do not need the police. As a result, the police feel that they are not needed, and the increase of criticism from the people has caused the morale to fall. Fewer and fewer police officers are still extremely diligent and honest. And if anyone of them should commit misconduct, it will be sensationally reported by the mass media and the reputation of the police will be seriously damaged.

The biggest concern for senior officers concerning misbehavior by their subordinate officers are off duty traffic accidents, drunkenness, and indiscretion with women. These are all regarded as intolerable acts on the part of the persons who should defend and develop morals. Morality is considered as the most important and basic factor in preserving the law. Police officers who indulge in these acts are viewed as guilty of betraying people's trust and as such they are considered suitable subjects for reprimands. People expect police officers to be persons of integrity. And, if they fail to meet these expectations, the people consider that they have the right to be angry. However, the same people who get angry with the police when they behave poorly or immorally, seemed to be rather tolerant of the rudeness and rough manner shown by police officers to criminals.

In Japan it is believed by the police that being a police officer is not a job; it is a way of life. Matters such as police dedication, detective spirit, or patrol officer's virtues are commonly discussed among police officers and ordinary citizens.

All those who work in the criminal justice system have to do their best to get to the truth of a matter, not just to win a verdict of guilty or not guilty. The Japanese do not speak well of lawyers who pursue technicalities to get their clients off. They are too proud to accept decisions on the basis of technical legal points or skillful legal arguments. They are concerned whether a suspect has done something fundamentally wrong and whether he or she is likely to engage in such misbehavior in the future. Attorneys at law have not been highly respected. They are called *Sanbyaku Daigen* (pettifoggers), which means persons who bend the truth for petty money.

A police officer's conduct is presumed as proper and lawful unless it is clearly illegal. Citizens must obey police directives. If they fail to do so, they will be punished on charges of obstruction of police duty. The burden of proof is imposed on the suspect. Generally speaking, people are friendly and cooperative with the police. A police officer can perform his or her duty with great confidence. The Japanese police practice restraint in the use of their power. Self-restraint and patience are always emphasized. "Don't be too eager for success. Stand to your post," are police mottos.

There is a good example of police restraint in practice. In February 1972 an incident occurred at a famous summer resort in the snow-covered mountains some 130 km northwest of Tokyo. Heavily armed terrorists of the Japanese Red Army (JRA) took shelter in an expensive villa and held the villa keeper's wife as hostage. Prior to this, they had perpetrated a series of terrorist attacks by using Molotov cocktails and home-made bombs placed in police boxes, which had wounded several patrol officers and had killed the wife of a high-ranking police officer when a letter bomb was sent through the mail. After a long chase, five of the group took over the villa. The police tried everything conceivable over the period of ten days to get the terrorists to surrender. More than 1,200 police officers, ten armored cars, and four water cannon trucks were mobilized. The siege operation was broadcast live and the entire nation watched it on television. The primary concerns of the police were the safe rescue of the hostage and the capture of all the terrorists alive. The police made several attempts to rush to the entrance, but were forced back by gunfire. Several officers were wounded. Temperatures were below zero. After the ten-day operation, the police finally resorted to the tactic of battering down the walls and roof of the villa with a hastily armored wrecking crane, while spraying water cannons. The operation started early in the morning and was viewed on television by the nation. The police went into the villa, and began searching it room by room. After an hour-and-a-half, a police officer was killed, shot by one of the radicals. Only then was an order issued allowing the police to use firearms. The fighting continued throughout the day. Finally, at six in the evening the radicals surrendered. Two commanding officers were shot dead while they led their men in a final assault on the villa, and fifteen other police officers were wounded in the melee. But none of the terrorists were injured and the woman hostage was found alive and unharmed. After this incident, public concern, public trust, and confidence about police activities were highly elevated. Pension and disability benefits systems were also substantially enlarged.

Japanese police continue to practice restraint in the use of powers. They are generally responsive to public demands. Senior police officers are sensitive to public desires and criticism as these are articulated in the media. Police officers, like all Japanese, are very much concerned about losing face. They are apprehensive about being criticized in public. Generally speaking, Japanese don't criticize the government openly, and even when they do so, they do not state their complaints directly. So, the demands of the people are often called the "voiceless voice" in Japan. The upper echelons of the police establishment, as well as other governmental executives, endeavor to seek out and deal with people's complaints before they come to the surface. This is because most people meekly obey the government without complaining even if they are not satisfied. If the police did not make the effort to find out what troubles people, complaints might never come to the surface.

Nevertheless, there are police officers who find themselves alienated from society. They feel that police are not properly appreciated by the people. This stems largely from the fact that people who live in urban areas and who have had the benefit of higher education are becoming indifferent toward the police. They are not concerned about their neighbors either and have almost no idea about what is going on in their local communities. This trend could change the privileged position enjoyed by the police in Japan today.

PROBLEMS OF THE POLICE

As stated in the opening paragraph of this chapter, the police exist and develop within a society, and as that society changes and develops, the police must inevitably change and develop as well. And if the police do not make efforts to improve themselves to meet the new developments, they will fall short of society's expectations.

Among the changes taking place in Japanese society mention may be made of urbanization; motorization; mobility of the population; expansion of social and economic activities; rapid progress of science and technology; expansion of education; economic prosperity; emancipation from poverty; collapse of traditional institutions; authority and public morals; disappearance of taboos; and change of value standards. These phenomena are experienced in other advanced countries, too. They form the underlying causes of problems faced by police establishments all over the world. In the process of these social changes, traditional authority, especially that exercised by professional soldiers, scholars, priests and politicians, has declined. Old taboos have been challenged.

A strong economy combined with democratic process has produced a substantial increase in governmental activity and substantial decrease in governmental authority. People are demanding and receiving increased benefits from the government and yet have less confidence in their government. Higher education has spread, making the general populace better educated and more critical. The police have become the target of their criticism. Generally speaking, public confidence and trust in governmental institutions, activities, and community leaders is still strong. People still obey those who are superior to themselves in age, rank, position, status, experience, and expertise.

Patrol officers are called *Omawarisan,* which means "Mr. Walkabout." They still enjoy an exalted image. They are regarded as models of efficiency and integrity. In order to maintain complete public confidence, the government has always endeavored to improve the quality of police officers. Nevertheless, the number of people who have less confidence in the authority of the government has increased (thus lowering the moral value of law-abiding behavior in Japanese society). This has shaken the morale of the police force.

We have been witnessing changes in a variety of social areas, especially with regard to the authority of institutions: the law, the government, the boss in the workplace, and the elder in the community. It seems that some measures of apathy and noninvolvement or implicit obedience to authority on the part of citizens are needed to maintain the efficiency of a democratic system. This obedience has led to moderation and self-restraint on the part of the government. But today, automatic obedience and respect for established authority is lessening year by year. With this process, disrespect for the authority of the police is spreading, especially on the part of youth, white-collar workers, and suburban residents.

Before World War II, police officers were regarded as the emperor's servants and were expected to behave honorably as the emperor's deputies in the local community. All citizens were considered to be the emperor's dear children. The emperor himself set an example of a modest and frugal life. He was sincere, self-restrained, and devoted to citizens' welfare. On the other hand, people were honest and diligent, but ignorant, innocent, poor, and weak. So it was the emperor's duty and responsibility that he, as a father, treat and protect the people carefully as if they were his children. As a result, the police quite naturally treated citizens as their master's children. It was their duty to treat people carefully and politely and to protect them from crime and danger. Since even criminals were also considered to be the emperor's children, the police were required to protect all their human rights. Police officers were called the "Royal Guardians" of their communities. This way of thinking still exists today. The social status of police officers used to be high, and they and their families found great pride and honor in their profession. They were respected and trusted by citizens. This principle and honor made police officers persons of efficiency and integrity.

After World War II, American democracy was introduced and police officers became public servants. This meant that police officers had to work for the people as servants. Until then the police had believed that they protected people as the emperor's servants. But now Japan was a democratic country, and the police could not work for only one person. So, it was understood that police officers should work hard for public welfare, not for the emperor. The expression, "public servant," has been used since World War II. This phrase, however, is not popular among government employees. This is because Japanese people are very rank conscious and inclined to compare themselves with others to determine their social status. Since servants are under obligation to work for the benefit of their masters and to obey their commands, government employees rank below the ordinary people. This is why the morale among the low-ranking police officers was totally shaken and depressed following the last World War.

Now, the National Police Agency and the prefectural police forces are trying their best to maintain, improve, and develop police officers' morals and morale. As discussed previously, in 1984 the National Police Agency established the new Code of Ethics for police life. The ultimate purpose of the police is not to bring suspected criminals to justice, but rather to protect the weak against the strong. Victims are weak and offenders are strong. Law violators are weak and law enforcers are strong because violators do not have the strength to keep the rules. There are various reasons why the weak are so weak. Each weak person has his or her own causes and reasons for being weak. So the police have to try their best to understand and sympathize with the weaknesses of each person. The police have been constantly taught that the law should not be enforced mechanically. Wide discretion is allowed to each police officer. Patrolling on foot or bicycle is encouraged to maintain contacts with ordinary citizens. Car patrols are supposed to be used only for emergencies. It should be emphasized that if the new Code of Ethics is followed sincerely by police officers, they will be able to obtain complete support and warm-hearted cooperation of the public. This will help them in carrying out their responsibilities more effectively.

CONCLUSIONS

When I was posted as the Police Attaché at the Japanese Embassy in Washington D.C., I was often asked whether Japanese or American police were superior. I made it a rule to answer that Japanese police were best for Japan and the American police for the United States. The police are the product of a nation's history and the needs of a society. In every society laws are necessary for people to live peacefully with one another. In order to maintain these laws, the police are required in every society. So the police must develop along with society and keep up with the changes. The quality of the society determines the quality of the police. They are not expected to stand on their own as an entity separate and distinct from the society where they exist.

What is it that the police must protect? To what should they give priority? Public order, human rights, freedom? Japanese regard the right to live in peace and comfort as their most important constitutional right. This right might also be described as freedom from crime. Fortunately, Japan is peaceful, crime is low, and the police are effective.

I can mention another example. When a Japanese mother scolds her mischievous son, she says, "You have made a nuisance for others and have not made up for it. Get out. You can go any place you wish. Your deed is unworthy of our family. Don't come back!" An American mother, on the other hand, would lock up her son in a small room and forbid him to go out. This illustrates a point of cultural difference between Japan and the United States. Their police are also, therefore, likely to differ in essential characteristics.

Just as the Japanese proverb says, "Children are the mirror of their parents," it can be said that the police are the mirror of a nation and its people. The Japanese police are diligent and disciplined. So, if the police are to be good and reliable, there must be efforts made to establish a good country where honesty pays and crime does not.

REFERENCES

Ames, Walter L. *Police and Community in Japan*. Berkeley, California: University of California Press, 1981.

Bayley, David H. *Forces of Order: Police Behavior in Japan and the United States*. Berkeley, California: University of California Press, 1991.

Clifford, William. *Crime Control in Japan*. Lexington, Massachusetts: Lexington Books, 1976.

Cramer, James. *The World's Police*. London: Cassell, 1964.

National Police Agency. *The Police of Japan 1985*. Tokyo: Government Printing Press, 1985.

Parker, Craig L. *The Japanese Police System Today*. Tokyo: Kodansha International, 1984.

Police Association. *The Police of Japan 1985*. Tokyo: Government Printing Press, 1985.

Reischauer, Edwin O. *The Japanese*. Cambridge, Massachusetts: Harvard University Press, 1977.

Rinalducci, Ralph J. *The Japanese Police Establishment*. Tokyo: Obun International, 1972.

Vogel, Ezra F. *The Japanese as Number One: Lessons for America*. Cambridge, Massachusetts: Harvard University Press, 1979.

APPENDIX A: CAREER OF INSPECTOR HIRAYAMA

INSPECTOR YUKIO HIRAYAMA

I would like to give a good example for the reader to get an insightful understanding of the Japanese police personnel practices.

Mr. Yukio Hirayama is a 36-year-old police inspector who works for me. He is the third son of a middle-class farmer in northern Japan. His father operated a small shop selling seeds and plants to local farmers. According to the Japanese tradition, the oldest son of the family was to inherit the store. Therefore, Yukio was to find employment elsewhere.

Inspector Hirayama recalls that as a child he watched a television program called the "Seven Detectives" and was attracted by the television detectives. An active child, he took up the Japanese martial art of sword fighting, and kendo which, he feels, helped him develop a strong and persistent mind needed to survive the rigors of the police life. Although he says that he hated school, he was able to maintain a good scholastic record through high school which enabled him to get recommendations from his teachers to take the entrance examination for the Metropolitan Police Department in Tokyo. At the tender age of eighteen, he entered the police school of the MPD. It was not easy for him to make the move from a quiet farm to the world's largest city. Aside from being away from home for the first time, he recalls that the year at the school was not easy with its strict regimentation and a heavy load of studies. The only day he could be off from the school was Sunday and even on that day he had to be back at school fairly early. He says that his training in the martial arts at an early age helped him to make it through the year at the MPD school.

After graduation from the school in Tokyo and completing a two-month-long refresher course, Patrolman Hirayama was assigned to a police station in the center of Tokyo. While working at the police station on his assignment, he was constantly thinking about ways to catch thieves and about taking the qualifying examination for detectives. He found time to attend university classes, graduate from university, and marry his high school sweetheart. The most memorable event of his career as a patrolman was the praise that he received from the proprietress of a bar where he went on a call to settle a drunken dispute. He was praised by the owner for his gentle but firm handling of the situation. She gave him the nickname, Kintaro, a famous character in children's storybooks epitomizing strength, humor, and gentleness.

He took the sergeants' examinations when he was eligible for the same and passed it with high scores. It was a proud achievement since he was one of the two in his entire class of 220 colleagues who had succeeded in passing the examination. He then entered the twelve-week-long junior supervisors' course and a seven-week-long investigators' course. After the successful completion of these courses, he was assigned to a residential police station to work as a detective. His experience as a detective gave him greater insights into the police work and enriched his mind as he learned to deal with anger, frustration, and sorrow of victims. He developed a deeper sense of pride in his work as police officer.

A year after being assigned to the detective section, he received special permission to take the examination for assistant inspector because of his college education. A high school graduate usually has a three-year waiting period before he can qualify to take the assistant inspectors' examination. Before any of his classmates was able to pass this examination, he succeeded in getting through on the first attempt. He was thus able to enter the Regional Police School for a nine-week middle-level supervisors' program of training, a two-week patrol supervisors' course and a five-week detective specialist course one after another without a break. On the successful completion of these courses, Yukio Hirayama was promoted as an assistant inspector and was assigned to a downtown police station. He worked as the chief of a larceny unit for about a year when he moved as ordered to the Metropolitan Police Department headquarters.

The work load was extremely heavy and challenging at the MPD headquarters which gave him very little time to prepare for the Inspectors' examination. He then experienced a failure for the first time when he did not pass his inspectors' examination. Fortunately, he had an understanding supervisor who gave him encouragement and support. Hirayama overcame his frustration, passed the examination in the following year, and became an inspector. Within 14 years he had achieved a lot indeed. He then entered the six-month-long inspectors' course at the National Police Academy where he was awarded the top achievement medal as honors graduate by the Director General of the National Police Academy.

At the time of writing Inspector Hirayama is currently assigned to the staff of the Environment and Consumer Protection Division of the National Police Agency. Prior to his assignment, he served as a deputy chief of detectives at a police station. Upon the completion of three years on the current assignment, he is most likely to be posted to a division in the MPD headquarters as an assistant director. After seven years as an inspector he will qualify for the rank of a superintendent, and attend the training institute for six-month-long executive investigators' or a three-week-long administrators' course.

Inspector Hirayama is an up-and-coming officer and the future looks promising for him and his department.

POLICE IN NEW ZEALAND

by Graeme Dunstall

INTRODUCTION

New Zealand is the smallest of the countries whose policing is considered in this volume. Situated in the southwest Pacific, it consists of two large islands and a number of smaller ones whose combined area is larger than that of the United Kingdom but smaller than that of Finland or Japan. The population of some four million is little more than a fifth of that of Australia, and is not as diverse in national origins nor growing as rapidly. Three-quarters of the New Zealand population is in the North Island, with nearly all the remainder in the South Island. With 83.7 percent of its population in urban areas, New Zealand is slightly less urbanized than Australia, but more so than Finland, Japan, or the United States (*Britannica Book of the Year,* 1988). There are five main urban areas with over 100,000 population; three in the North Island: Auckland (829,000 estimated in 1987); Wellington (324,400); Hamilton (102,600); and two in the South Island: Christchurch (299,400) and Dunedin (106,600) (*New Zealand Official Yearbook,* 1988-89). Altogether these main centers contain 50 percent of the country's people. The North Island, and especially Auckland, is gaining from the northerly drift of the population by attracting the bulk of the overseas migrants, and by having a higher rate of natural increase.

Though New Zealand's rate of natural increase has been (and is still) relatively high in comparison with some European countries, it has fallen steeply since the 1960s to 0.8 percent in the late 1980s.

Coinciding with the aging of the New Zealand population has been a decline since 1978 in the overall number and rate of children and young people coming to official notice for juvenile delinquency (Lovell and Stewart, 1983; Norris, et al., 1986). Since the 1960s large swings in the balance of migration have had pronounced effects on the population growth rate and been indicative of New Zealand's changing economic fortunes: a boom brought a net gain from migration of over 100,000 in the years 1972-75; a deepening depression contributed to a net loss by migration (mainly to Australia) between 1976 and 1982; and volatility in migration continued to be manifest during a time of economic reconstruction from the mid-1980s (*New Zealand Official Yearbook*, 1988-89).

Since its economic heyday of the 1950s and early 1960s, New Zealand's position in the league of wealthy developed countries has slipped to a point that its GNP per capita at the time of writing (according to one measure) was US$ 7,290 by comparison with Australia US$ 10,860, Finland US$ 10,900, Japan US$ 11,310, and the United States US$ 16,360 (*Britannica Book of the Year*, 1988). The impact of migration flows (and indeed the economic climate) on the patterns of order and lawlessness is difficult to judge: the overall rate of reported offending rose sharply in the late 1960s and did not slacken significantly before the mid-1980s. The growth in property crime broadly coincided with the growth in unemployment; but direct connections between individual offences and economic fluctuations are not clear-cut. In the early 1970s, however, a popular perception that Pacific Island immigrants had contributed to the growth of disorder in Auckland shaped policing policies in that city.

New Zealand's population is predominantly (82 percent) European in origin, though less so than that of Australia. Maori people, the indigenous Polynesian inhabitants, comprise 9 percent (a proportion that has doubled since the 1920s). Pacific Island Polynesians comprise 2.4 percent and those of mixed ethnic origins some 4.4 percent Both Australia and New Zealand were colonies of British settlement. But by contrast with its neighbor across the Tasman Sea, New Zealand's immigrants between 1945 and the early 1970s continued to be overwhelmingly British, indeed English in origin. Thus within the European population there is a greater degree of cultural homogeneity than is to be found in Australian cities. Even so, the urbanization of Maori and Pacific

Island populations since 1945 have added a unique dimension to New Zealand urban life, especially in Auckland and Wellington where they are now concentrated. In their socioeconomic position however, Maoris and Pacific Islanders broadly parallel that of blacks in Britain and the United States: they are (for example) disproportionately blue-collar workers, less likely to possess a house based on mortgage ownership, much more likely to be unemployed, and to come to official notice of the police (Dunstall, 1981; Social Monitoring Group, 1989).

Despite strong forces for integration into a dominant European culture, a distinctive Maori cultural identity has remained. In fact, by the late 1960s a strong current of Maori cultural resurgence became apparent in the cities. During the 1970s and early 1980s there was an increasingly forceful expression of Maori grievances, especially (in the context of this chapter) concerning the existence of discrimination and what has been termed "institutional racism" in the Pakeha (European) dominated system of justice. Since the early 1970s the concept of a bicultural society has gradually won recognition in official policy and popular parlance (Dunstall, 1981; Greenland, 1984). Government departments and public agencies have been forced to reexamine their policies. In reality however, most public institutions in the late 1980s are still fundamentally monocultural—and a strong sense of grievance remains amongst the Maori. It is in this context then that the origins and development of the New Zealand Police can be examined briefly.

As in other countries of recent European settlement, the police in New Zealand is a fragment of an imported culture refashioned in a changing environment. English precedents shaped the system of criminal justice after Britain acquired sovereignty over New Zealand in 1840. Indeed English criminal law was adopted virtually unmodified for thirty years (Campbell, 1967). From the outset, however, various modes of British policing, acclimatized by prior experience in the Australian colonies, were adapted by the colonial state according to the evolving needs, attitudes, and resources of the British settlers. Most significant in the early decades were the strategies necessary to obtain Maori compliance with British rule (Hill, 1986).

At first, small forces of blue uniformed constables (imitating the London Metropolitan police) were located in the main European settlements and supervised by Police Magistrates. From 1846 they were superseded by paramilitary Armed Police Forces modelled on the Irish Constabulary and controlled directly by the Governor of the colony. At the same time Resident Magistrates were appointed to apply more effectively English concepts of law and order on a biracial frontier. These changes reflected a new Governor's prior experience in Ireland and Australia and his "perceptions of the best way to suppress and civilise a tribal society." It also reflected a "stricter conception of pakeha (European) order and regularity than that hitherto expected by the state from a pioneering society" (Hill, 1986).

Settler control of policing came with self-government. By the 1852 Constitution Act, settlers were given wide powers over internal affairs—powers exercised through both a General Government and six Provincial Councils based on the main European settlements. Between 1853 and 1876 (when the Provincial Councils were abolished) the main responsibility for policing was devolved to provincial governments. The Armed Police were then reshaped into a variety of forces ranging in the mid-1850s from non-militarized "civil" modes in the South Island to more paramilitary ones in the North Island, where the Maori population was concentrated. More coercive modes of policing developed in the South Island from the early 1860s, as gold rushes led provincial governments to look to the Australian state of Victoria for a new system—a distinctive fusion of Irish and London models (Hill, 1986).

In the North Island by the 1860s, the provincial police were little more than small municipal forces with a few men (often part-time farmer-constables) scattered through the outlying areas of European settlement. In the country areas, where Maori predominated, the state sought to work through Maori agents who applied a mix of customary and European norms. During the early 1860s, methods of indirect policing gave way to outright repression when tribes of the King Movement (in the central North Island) asserted a desire for self-determination in the face of growing settler pressure for land. Imperial troops and Colonial Defence Forces enforced settler domination of the Maori by war, and "pacified" the unsettled racial frontier in its immediate aftermath. With the withdrawal of Imperial troops and the disbanding of the Colonial Defence Forces, the General Government established an Armed Constabulary in 1867—a mobile, militarized police force that could act as a fighting corps if need be (Hill, 1986; Hill, 1985).

During the next twenty years, the ending of overt Maori resistance, the growth of a more stable and integrated European society, and the abolition of provincial governments shaped the evolving modes of policing. In 1877 control of policing was centralized when the Armed Constabulary incorporated the provincial forces. In 1886 the policing and military functions of the state were separated. The new civil police force was not visibly armed, symbolizing the gradual shift from the Irish Constabulary mode. By the turn of the century, the London Metropolitan Police had become the exemplar in ethos, training, and organization. Such an identification came to be marked by the constable's uniform with its distinctive helmet in place of a military-style shako.

From the 1880s, the context of policing shifted from that of a biracial frontier to that of a rapidly urbanizing, modernizing, European society. By the 1920s, 60 percent of the European population lived in an urban world. Maori remained largely in rural isolation until after the Second World War. Then their migration to towns and cities brought them ever more disproportionately into the monocultural system of criminal justice. Change in the dominant European culture paralleled that of Britain, North America, and Australia. Technology, fashions, and ideas were quickly transmitted. Social behavior was increasingly subject to similar patterns of governmental restraint until the 1920s, and of greater freedom from the 1960s. The long term pattern of violence recorded by police statistics broadly parallels that of Britain since the 1880s: with a significant decline until the 1920s, and a sharp upswing from the 1960s. Indeed, the research on international crime trends since 1945 shows the close coincidence in those of the English-speaking countries, and especially those of Australia and New Zealand (Gurr, 1977). As with forces elsewhere, the New Zealand Police has grown significantly in numbers and per capita since the late 1960s: from 2,723 in March 1967 to 5,114 in March 1988; increasing the ratio of police per 1,000 population from 0.99 to 1.52 (or more conventionally expressed from 1:1001 to 1:655 population per police officer). In the same period, the ratio of crimes reported per police member increased 70 percent. Nonetheless the seemingly apparent linkage between the growth in both police strength and reported criminality is not a direct or obvious one (Bayley, 1985).

Despite broad parallels in context, local variants have developed from the consciously adopted model of British policing. By contrast with procedures in Scotland, Canada, the United States, and (to a lesser extent) England, but in common with Australian forces, the New Zealand Police control all stages of the prosecution process in the conduct of summary cases in District Courts (Stace, 1986). By the 1930s the police had shed most of its responsibility for traffic control. This function was resumed on July 1, 1992 with the merger of the Traffic Safety Service of the Ministry of Transport with the New Zealand Police. Nor since 1956 has it been concerned with systematic political surveillance. Above all in the English-speaking world, New Zealand stands virtually alone in having one national force. This reflected the development of a state that was much more highly centralized than in Britain or North America. To theorists of the British tradition of policing, such a centrally controlled force could potentially be a tool of government and lack independence in exercising its powers. Nonetheless, by the 1920s the notion of police independence had come to be established in New Zealand as strongly as it was held in Britain.

MANDATE AND PHILOSOPHY

In essence, the distinctive mandate of the New Zealand Police, as with its counterparts elsewhere, is the authority to use reasonable force to effect an arrest for illegal behavior or to suppress disorder (*Crimes Act,* 1961; Bayley, 1985). Though it has been used with increasing pessimism from the 1960s, the phrase, "maintaining law and order" has long summed up government, police, and popular conceptions of the police role in New Zealand. Under the 1913 *Police Force Act,* sergeants and constables were appointed for "the preservation of peace and order, the prevention of crime, and the apprehension of offenders against the peace." In reality, however, police responsibilities have been much broader than this. And indeed the current statutory authority for the establishment of the New Zealand Police, the 1958 Police Act, is silent on the mandate of the police as an organization. In practice the definition of police responsibilities has been shaped by the law to be enforced, by requests for service from governments and members of the public, and ultimately by the police leadership itself.

In 1982, a "functional review" of the New Zealand Police recommended that the legislation governing its activities be reviewed so as to define clearly its "role, functions, and responsibilities" (Hickson et al., 1982). To date, this has not occurred. Police leadership, on whom the initiative for organizational change rests, see a more precise legislative mandate as neither necessary nor desirable. In part, this reflects police reluctance either to broaden (to match the reality of requests for service) or to narrow (and explicitly recognize the impossibility of accomplishing) the traditional definition of their responsibilities. Vagueness of statutory mandate is an advantage: greater precision might promise too much or be unduly constraining. Moreover, an attempt to provide a clearer legislative mandate might trench upon the jealously guarded independence of the police from ministerial direction in law enforcement and order maintenance. Thus, as part of a new strategic management plan in 1984, Commissioner Thompson issued to his senior officers a mission statement which reiterated the longstanding mandate—protecting life and property, preventing crime, maintaining the peace, and detecting offenders by:

- assisting and working together with the community and other agencies; and
- maintaining a police organization capable of providing a high quality of service (Thompson, 1984; *Annual Report*, 1988).

This mandate implicitly eschews a greater social work role proposed for the New Zealand Police by one of its influential members in the early 1970s (Glynn, 1973; 1975). Indeed the publicized definition of the police role for nearly a decade up until 1984 included the provision of "guidance and assistance" in "helping young people to achieve social maturity," and in "cases of tragedy, or family and/or other personal crisis" (*New Zealand Official Yearbook*, 1984). Nonetheless, the traditional conception of the police role allows considerable scope for redefinition of police responsibilities according to changing circumstances: for example, permitting from the 1960s a leading role for the police in search and rescue activities, the development of a social work ethos in "Youth Aid," or an increasing emphasis on community responsibility for aspects of crime prevention and protection of property. And during the 1980s it allowed a greater commitment than hitherto by police leadership to "a full partnership with the community—community policing" (*Annual Report*, 1988). Policing goals, organization structure, and management policies were reviewed during the late 1980s in the light of that new emphasis.

Methods might change, but the basic philosophy of policing has not. Recruits continue to be taught that Rowan and Mayne's "Nine Principles of Police" are "still applicable to today's police" (Royal New Zealand Police College, 1987; Reith, 1952). The philosophy inculcated at the Royal New Zealand Police College and exhorted by successive Commissioners is not codified but nonetheless resembles that published by the Victoria Police in its current "Organizational Philosophy" or by the London Metropolitan Police in *The Principles of Policing and Guidance for Professional Behaviour* (1985). Loyalty, zeal, and efficiency are emphasized, but not at the expense of public approval and cooperation. Recruits study, and have to apply to a variety of situations encountered by the New Zealand Police, the standards of behavior required by the United Nations Code of Conduct for Law Enforcement Officials (Royal New Zealand Police College, 1987). In 1985, Commissioner Thompson reiterated some of the long-established elements of the "New Zealand Police Value System" to which he wished its members to aspire. In particular, police objectives have to be achieved by "fair and legal means," with appropriate discretion and the "minimum degree of force." A "superior quality of service" is to be provided to "all citizens regardless of race, colour or belief." In dress, appearance, and conduct, "pride" in the "profession" is to be displayed (Thompson, 1985; O'Donovan, 1920). The extent to which the police leadership's philosophy has been realized in practice will be examined in later sections.

The police definition of its mandate assumes a consensus on what constitutes crime and disorder: the bald words "protection," "crime," and "peace" convey concepts that are widely perceived to be absolute and clear-cut. Certainly public opinion surveys reveal widespread support for police policies and practice. Increasingly from the 1970s however, critics (to be noted below) pointed to a monocultural system of justice in a bicultural society, and discerned an inequality before the law that was inconsistent with the notion of the rule of law governing the police. Moreover, the extent of civil strife associated with the South African Springbok Rugby Tour of New Zealand in 1981 revealed more clearly than hitherto that notions of lawful behavior and order were in fact abstract, relative, and varying; perceived in different ways by individuals according to their circumstances. To its severest critics then, the New Zealand Police could be seen as ultimately an instrument of government policy and of pakeha (European) values: an inevitable defender of the status quo. In fact, as with other forces in the British tradition, there is no overt political mandate for the New Zealand Police. Clear evidence of ministerial direction of policing is hard to find. More apparent, however, is the inherently monocultural nature of present New Zealand policing, symptomatic of the criminal justice system as a whole.

FUNCTIONS

The 1992 mission statement of the New Zealand Police is, of course, an imperfect guide as to what the organization actually does, or how its behavior is perceived. Summed up in the truism, "maintaining law and order," the mandate at once suggests too little and too much.

Police work in New Zealand, as elsewhere, has always involved more than merely law enforcement and order maintenance. As a centralized organization the New Zealand Police has been seen as a convenient instrument for a variety of administrative tasks, especially in the rural areas. From the 1920s successive Commissioners complained that the police continued to be, as one put it in 1919, "the handy men of the whole of the Government services": then, according to location, registering births, marriages, deaths, aliens, electors and pensions; collecting agricultural and pastoral statistics; inspecting factories, fisheries, weights and measures, hotels and licensed clubs; licensing firearms; and acting as kauri gum and crown lands rangers, customs officers, Receivers of Gold Revenue and Mining Registrars, agents for the Public Trustee, clerks of Courts and Hotel Licensing Committees, bailiffs, probation officers, gaolers (jailers), and court orderlies (*Annual Report*, 1919). Gradually the police shed much of its routine work for other government agencies, especially from the late 1960s. And the Department has shown considerable reluctance to take on new administrative tasks. In the 1980s nonetheless, police still provided services for other parts of the criminal justice system: as bailiffs, part-time probation officers, court registrars and orderlies, and, when prison overcrowding reached crisis proportions in 1987-88, as police gaolers.

Though within the New Zealand bureaucracy the role of the police has ostensibly narrowed, burgeoning public requests for service since the 1950s have prevented a narrow focus merely on criminal law enforcement. In particular the New Zealand Police have committed increasing resources to search and rescue operations, of which there were 964 in the year 1987-1988 (*Annual Report*, 1988). Moreover, in 1987-88, the police responded to 115,605 "incidents" (not necessarily involving law enforcement, such as sudden deaths and vehicle collisions) and 245,976 requests for "services" (such as queries regarding lost property or missing persons, advising relatives, recovering vehicles, and registering firearms). These two categories of activity averaged 23 and 48 events respectively per sworn police member at the time of writing by contrast with an average of 86 offences reported per sworn police member (Annual Report, 1988). In reality the police concern with public safety is construed broadly to include not just criminal acts, but also "those which are natural, accidental or unintentional" (Glynn, 1975; *New Zealand Official Yearbook*, 1984).

Yet the concept of maintaining "law and order" also suggests too much: that without the so-called "thin blue line" society would dissolve into disorder and lawlessness; that increased police resources would do much to solve apparently mounting problems of crime and order. Experience in New Zealand and similar societies during the 1970s and 1980s suggests otherwise. By the early 1970s there was a growing awareness amongst New Zealand police administrators that many in the community had unrealistic expectations of their organization—seeing it as the only or principal solution to problems of order. The emphasis on community policing from the mid-1980s reflects the growing acceptance that the criminal justice system, and within it the police, have only a small, albeit significant part to play in maintaining order and securing law-abiding behavior.

What then do the New Zealand Police actually do? Following Bayley's analytical distinctions we can examine in turn what the police are assigned to do and the situations they become involved in handling (Bayley, 1985).

For budgetary purposes, the New Zealand Police is organized into five programs which represent its main areas of functional activity. On 31 March 1988 there were 5,114 sworn police and 864 civilians who in the preceding year had been allocated to the program in the following proportions (calculated from *Digest of Statistics*, 1988; *Annual Report*, 1988):

	Staff percent	Expenditure(net) percent
I. Corporate Services:	8.7	21.3
II. Community Safety and Security:	72.7	59.8
III. Investigative Services:	13.2	12.0
IV. Drug Enforcement and Intelligence Services:	2.5	3.8
V. Public Affairs:	2.9	3.1

Though these five areas of functional activity have since been refined into thirteen areas of police outputs, the above table provides a starting point for analysis of the assignment of personnel during the 1980s. Corporate Services comprise the administrative and other services used by the police as a whole: planning, engineering, finance, internal affairs, legal, management audit, office examiner, personnel, supply, and training. Altogether, in 1987-88, these services accounted for more than a third of the total budget for operating costs (excluding salaries), and for 71 percent of the allocation for capital expenditure. The exact proportions of civilian and sworn personnel allocated to each program are not available. However, civilians are clearly concentrated in Corporate Services; and they are growing in number in this, as in the other four broad areas of functional activity, as civilianization of non-frontline tasks proceeds. In March 1987 there were 174 sworn personnel at Police National Headquarters: this number represented a 10 percent reduction in three years. This trend has continued as administrative services have been decentralized to the six main police regions comprising 28 districts in 1992.

Services encompassed by the Community Safety and Security program are performed by those who have a visible presence in the community, namely, motorized and beat patrol who comprise the bulk of the staff in this broad area of activity, as well as 120 community constables and the more specialized units deployed on mobile patrol, such as enquiry officers, the police dog sections and team policing and crime control personnel. Personnel needed for search and rescue operations, as well as the staff who perform armed offenders squad duties on a part-time basis, are drawn largely, but not exclusively from the uniformed police. In recent years each of the districts has had an armed offenders squad to attend to a variety of incidents. Selected members of these squads also serve in the Anti-Terrorist Squad which was introduced lately. At the time of writing a further 3,442 staff were deployed (averaging 118 per event) in a variety of special operations: including the visits of the Belgian Royal Family and other VIPs, security for the transit and exhibition of the Te Maori cultural treasures, shadow patrols for mobile gangs, and policing the General Election as well as major sporting and entertainment events (*Annual Report*, 1988).

In New Zealand mobile patrols and their immediate support staff consume the largest proportion of the police resources: recently two-thirds of the total budget for salaries, and 46 percent of that for operating costs annually. The chief element in the patrol force is the double-crewed Incident car (introduced in the late 1960s) which has to maintain a preventive patrol in an allocated zone when not responding to calls for service. At least six staff per day and $NZ 500,000 a year (in 1985/86 figures) are required to keep a single Incident car on the road 24 hours a day, seven days a week (Lines, 1988). Essentially the role of the I car is to quickly assess incidents, make only preliminary investigations, and file reports for further action if necessary. Two-thirds of the incidents attended in 1988 required further attention (*Annual Report*, 1988). In addition then, single-crewed Enquiry cars are allocated to a specific sector to follow up, if necessary, the preliminary reports on incidents from the I car, where they are not investigated by the Criminal Investigation Branch. Also on patrol are Crime cars, crewed with two detectives, for rapid response to reports of crime. During the 1980s, a smaller number of single-crewed Q cars have been deployed during daytime shifts as incident attending cars to record minor complaints where the offender has left the scene, and carry out more extensive scene and area inquiries than permitted I cars (Lines, 1988).

Despite a considerable degree of specialized assignment in types of patrol activity, there is in practice a considerable overlap of work both within and between the main areas of functional activity. This can be seen in traffic regulation where, in New Zealand, there has been till 1992 a separate agency, namely, the Ministry of Transport with a mandate to patrol and enforce the traffic laws. Nonetheless, Incident car officers routinely attended vehicle collisions, frequently took keys off intoxicated drivers, and cooperated with traffic officers in law enforcement and they were responsible for reporting more than 30,000 traffic offenses (7 percent of total offenses) annually. Again, community constables have a role which fits as easily into the brief for the Public Affairs program as it does for Community Safety. The invisible Crime Control Units are formed in the largest cities from both detectives and Uniformed Branch staff to target street crime. Above all, the artificiality of specialized assignment is apparent in the overlap between patrol and investigative units, seen in the often coinciding roles of I, Q, and E cars. Apart from self-initiated activity while on mobile patrol (such as hotel visits, taking keys off drivers, turnovers of people on the street), most Incident car work is essentially reactive: making the preliminary inquiries, then either making immediate arrests, if necessary, filing the matters as unsolvable, or passing them on for further investigation. Thus the patrol force plays a crucial role in the investigative process (Holyoake and Long, 1988).

The Investigative Services program comprises essentially work done by the Criminal Investigations Branch (CIB) and its associated services (excluding drug enforcement and intelligence): document examination, fingerprints, information, modus operandi, photography, and witness protection. In fact, the proportion of staff formally allocated to this program (which includes civilians) understates the proportion of police deployed on investigative work. CIB members comprised 15.1 percent of sworn staff in March 1988; if Uniformed Branch attachments to the CIB are included the proportion rises to 20.1 percent; and if Uniform Enquiry staff are also included the proportion reaches 27.5 percent (*Digest of Statistics*, 1988; Holyoake and Long, 1988). When the multifaceted role of Incident cars is also taken into account, much New Zealand Police work could be considered to be primarily investigative and only indirectly preventive.

Organizationally there were in 1988 a variety of investigative structures amongst the police districts—and the pattern has been changing with decentralization and the move to new structures of community policing since 1989. In five districts in 1988, the Uniformed Inquiry offices were integrated with the CIB; in the remainder they stood alone. Most districts organized their CIB into specialist squads based at the central station, most commonly: fraud, breaks, cars, drugs, and general duties policing. In the outlying police divisions of Auckland and Wellington cities there were merely general duties squads, or (as in Christchurch city) individual detectives based at outstations. For major investigations (especially homicides) relatively large numbers of detectives are redeployed in specially created teams. In most district headquarters there was a criminal intelligence section focusing mainly on serious criminal offending and managing undercover operations and surveillance activities (Holyoake and Long, 1988). Since 1956, when its Special Branch was disbanded and the New Zealand Security Intelligence Service created, the New Zealand Police has not ostensibly been concerned with political surveillance. However, the formation at police national headquarters in 1969 of the National Bureau of Criminal Intelligence (and within it later the National Bomb Data Center and a Terrorist Intelligence Unit) is indicative of a broadly defined focus on intelligence. Concern with public order, especially with the possibility of terrorism and disorderly demonstrations (such as with the Springbok Rugby Tour of 1981, for example), has led to police surveillance that has not been confined to the more usual run of criminal offending.

The Drug Enforcement and Intelligence program is the focus of much of the police intelligence gathering activity. In the districts 72 detectives were deployed in drug squads in March 1988. Probably a similar number of police were involved in surveillance squads, undercover operations and the analysis of criminal intelligence (*Digest of Statistics*, 1988; *Annual Report*, 1988). Liaison officers are also maintained in Bangkok, Australia, Singapore, and at the National Drug Intelligence Bureau (formed at police headquarters in 1972 with representatives from the Health and Customs Departments). This program represents a significant redeployment of the police resources since 1965 when the (then) vice squads in the four main centers received their first instructions and training in drug enforcement.

The Public Affairs program also represents a developing specialization within the New Zealand Police since the late 1960s. It aims "to promote public awareness of law and order and the role of the police in the community" through a variety of activities and specialized staff involved in community liaison, crime prevention, youth aid, and a law-related education program (*Annual Report*, 1988). In their Youth Aid activities, the police come closest to a social work role.

In reality, what police are assigned to do is a poor guide as to how personnel spend their time: the situations they become involved in and the actions taken to deal with them. Research on New Zealand police activity has largely focused on mobile patrols and been undertaken by the police themselves using control room data and end-of-shift reports. During the 1970s it became conventional wisdom that New Zealand patterns of patrol activity paralleled those reported from the United States: mobile patrols were essentially reactive; dealing with a wide range of incidents reported by the public, only 20 percent to 30 percent of which concerned criminal matters (Glynn, 1975; Lines, 1988). However, the sources of information about patrol activity, and how it is analyzed, shape perceptions. Self-initiated activity is not always reported to the control room; and clear distinctions between law enforcement and community service activity are not necessarily apparent in all situations. Police attendance at domestic disputes and noisy parties, for example, has conventionally been labelled a community service (Glynn, 1975) yet it undoubtedly contains a significant element of law enforcement (Ford, 1986). Indeed in August 1987 the New Zealand Police introduced a new policy in dealing with domestic disputes which meant that aggressors would be arrested without a complaint from the victim if there was evidence of an offense, or the victim was in danger (*Star*, Christchurch, 22 June 1988). Complaints of domestic violence, threats, and intimidation which had hitherto been recorded as "domestic disputes" in the incident statistics were henceforth coded as offenses, where applicable. Significantly, in the 1987-88 year, the 16,445 domestic disputes reported as incidents were 11.8 percent less than in the previous year. The reported offense of threats and intimidation, numbering 5,002, had increased 15.4 percent. Minor assaults numbered 12,804 registering a 10.9 percent increase, and serious assaults numbered 5,349 which was a 30.4 percent increase (*Annual Report*, 1988).

In 1980-81, a job analysis survey of New Zealand police constables with six to thirty months service sought to take account of the fact that many of the incidents and tasks they handled contained elements of both community service and law enforcement. On each working day of a five-week roster the constables were asked to record on a questionnaire all incidents, tasks, duties, and offenses they dealt with. These were analyzed according to three categories, with the lesser element of each activity being weighted at half that of the predominant aspect in its contribution to the total score: law enforcement activities were thus found to total 54.4 percent of all work, community service 36 percent, and logistics/departmental/personal activities 20.9 percent. About three-quarters of all activities that were categorized as predominantly community service (such as attending domestic disputes or noisy parties) were seen to include a law enforcement aspect. Just under half of all predominantly law enforcement activities were seen to have an element of community service. Overall, the new constables were apparently engaged in far more law enforcement activities than community services, and roughly a third of their recorded tasks could be viewed as self-initiated. This finding may be flawed by the self-reporting method and the mode of analysis used (Robinson, 1982). Even so, it suggests that the pattern of mobile patrol activity in New Zealand may be less reactive and more law-enforcement oriented than commonly perceived. Certainly, as Bayley has observed regarding the problems of classification and sources of information, "it is too early...to be dogmatic about the character of police work, even in the United States" (Bayley, 1985).

In New Zealand, as has been found overseas, research suggests that mobile patrols are often not as busy as may be thought. In 1988, a Wellington observational study found that, for an I car, calls for service roughly averaged three on early and night shifts, and five on late (afternoon/early evening) shifts. Generally the proportion of time spent in response to calls for service was well below 20 percent of total shift time. Nearly half of all patrol time was spent on correspondence, meals, travel, attending to departmental inquiries, and personal jobs. On average about a third of shift time was found to be uncommitted and spent on mobile patrol which included self-initiated duties, especially turnovers. The Wellington study found that I car crews made arrests, on average, once every four to five days. Just under half the arrests during the study period came from self-initiated activity, particularly as a result of turnovers (Lines, 1988; Robinson, 1982).

In conclusion, the broad outcomes of much police activity can be summarized statistically thus:

A. Main Categories of Offenses Recorded by the New Zealand Police for the Year Ending March 1988:

	Number Reported	Percent Cleared	Number of Prosecutions
Violence	25,485	80.3	13,530
Sexual	3,469	65.0	1,661
Drugs and Anti-Social*	50,427	92.6	28,887
Dishonesty	278,865	24.9	58,671
Property Damage	26,801	33.6	5,215
Property Abuses	16,881	74.8	4,705
Administrative	5,273	74.1	2,228
Traffic	30,841	92.4	19,411
TOTAL	438,042	44.0	134,308

(* 17,704 drug offenses recorded; other types of offense included in this category are: liquor, gaming, disorder, vagrancy, family offenses).

B. Main Categories of Incidents, Services, and Other Activity Recorded by the New Zealand Police for the Year Ending 31 March 1988.

Incidents attended:

	Number dealt with:	Percentage variation on previous year
Alarm sounding	16,790	-58.7
Car/Person acting suspiciously	42,831	+3.1
Domestic dispute	16,445	-11.8
Drunk taken into custody	4,467	-11.9
Sudden death	5,605	+0.5
Vehicle collison	4,102	-6.7
Other incident reports	25,365	+3.4
TOTAL INCIDENTS ATTENDED	115,605	-17.7
Services provided:		
Advise relatives	4,766	+30.2
Firearm query /registration	19,205	+3.3
Liquor licensing	13,972	+11.6
Lost/found property	81,065	+0.4
Missing person	10,238	-3.3
Public relations	5,244	+12.2
Recover vehicle	7,284	-11.9
Summons	24,671	-11.2
Warrant	49,498	-15.8
Licence applications	6,883	+3.9
Other requests for services	23,150	+25.8
TOTAL SERVICES PROVIDED	245,976	-1.8

TOTAL PREVENTATIVE ACTIVITY*	14,686	+32.6
TOTAL OF ALL ACTIVITY	376,267	-6.4

(* Preventative includes crime prevention advice, keys taken, turnover check, watching/observations, and Youth Aid school talks)
Source: Annual Report, 1988.

PERSONNEL PRACTICES: RECRUITMENT, SELECTION, TRAINING, AND PROMOTION

"The continued effectiveness of the police depends largely on the quality of personnel recruited," declared Commissioner Burnside in 1977. This long held view was reinforced rather than supplanted by an increased emphasis on the importance of training from the 1950s. As the police recruiting organizer put it in 1970: "we may make good people better but we certainly do not intend to take on the job of making second rate people good." Much then has depended upon the rigor of selection procedures and the attributes looked for in the ideal recruit. Both have varied somewhat through time according to the balance of supply and demand for recruits and changing social circumstances. But overall in recent years, less than one in five applicants was eventually accepted. Publicity that only a minority meet the exacting standards of the New Zealand police serves to enhance its reputation.

Above all, since the turn of the century at least, the police administration has sought to ensure that it recruited men (and since 1941, women) of unblemished character and untainted relationships. A suggestion of anything less would lower the public standing of the police, and hence its effectiveness. In theory there is no room for extremists, a concept which is supposed to include both ends of the political spectrum and, more recently, those with racist or sexist views. Opinion on prejudices and morals is based on interviews and reputation. Applicants with convictions for crimes of dishonesty, serious assault, or sexual offense are automatically debarred, but not necessarily so for minor breaches of the liquor licensing or traffic legislation. The standing of spouses and near relatives is also investigated to prevent the possibility of smears or blackmail. More than this, close attention to character accords with the bad apple theory of police misbehavior. Malpractice by staff is generally seen within the police as stemming from a deficiency of personal character rather than of training or organization.

Rivaling integrity as the basic attribute for recruits are physical standards which are more susceptible of measurement. Requirements have been altered over the years, but traditional expectations remain. As a matter of fact, they have been reinforced by more violent patterns of public order in the last two decades. Bulk is important, and especially height. The minimum requirement for males was lowered in the 1950s and during the 1980s it was 173 cm and 165 cm for females. In October 1990 the recruit pre-entry standards were again revised, raising the maximum age from 31 years to 40 years at the time of entry primarily to encourage former policewomen who had left to have children to return. The minimum height requirement was lowered to 170 cm for men and 159 for women. Since 1980, greater emphasis has been placed on general fitness. Applicants have now to pass a required fitness level test as well as a thorough medical examination. In part this reflects the changing background of applicants, especially males. However, presently the average male recruit was closer to the ideal of 183 cm, while females averaged 172 cm. Since 1980, greater emphasis has been placed on general fitness. Before the 1960s, they came largely from manual occupations and especially off the land. And so most brought a legacy of strength and an ability to look after oneself in the then occasional rough-and-tumble of policing. From the 1960s recruits came increasingly from more sedentary white-collar, non-manual and service occupations. By the 1980s about half of all new constables came from middle-class urban homes (Robinson, 1982; *South Auckland Police Development Plan,* 1984). Hence, their fitness and skills have needed to be more rigorously tested and developed in training. In the last decade, furthermore, there has been a greater appreciation of stress as a factor in policework and of the need for a high level of fitness to remain in the front line.

Allied to character and physical standards are qualities relating to one's personality, deportment, and worldly experience. The traditional belief has endured into the 1980s that competence in policing comes not so much from training as from personality and experience. Recruiting sergeants, with a checklist before them, look for appropriate qualities: immaculate grooming; articulateness in speech; mental alertness; learning ability (innovative, intelligent); loyalty (dependability, response to discipline, team spirit); frankness; enthusiasm; ambition; motivation; even temperament; stability (as revealed in employment patterns); ability to make one's own decisions; common sense (natural caution, ability to adjust, worldliness); maturity; and confidence. Appraisal is intuitive rather than by psychological testing. Age is important, not just for physical development but also in terms of experience. New constables can be sworn in at the age of 19 years. However most new recruits are typically in their early twenties, and in recent years roughly a quarter have been between 25 and 31 years of age. Prior work experience and skills, such as a trade, can counterbalance a lack of formal educational qualifications.

Even so, the overall educational standards required of recruits have risen. This partly reflects a desire to keep pace with the increasing level of educational attainment in the community at large. More importantly, it reflects the mounting demands of formal police training. In practice the minimum educational requirements have risen since the 1950s, from the final, i.e., sixth standard or grade, at primary school to three years of secondary education. At present, the educational qualifications of recruits are relatively high in terms of the broad span of attainments achieved by pupils leaving secondary school. As many as 62 had passed one or more subjects in the University Entrance Examination, and another five had university diplomas or part of a degree. Since the 1970s a growing number of graduates have been recruited, comprising up to a quarter of some intakes. Skepticism, however, endures that high educational attainments alone are appropriate for entry into the police if not accompanied by worldliness. Instead, they may serve to further mark the police off from most people they deal with. A latent hostility to elitism can be found in an organization where career advancement has been largely in terms of seniority combined with the motivation and ability to pass promotional exams. Whatever their educational qualifications, all applicants have to pass a pre-entry test (introduced in 1956 and subsequently refined) that examines memory, literacy, powers of observation, and listening skills. It is seen as an "excellent predictor of performance at the College" (Gordon, 1984), where the real test of character, fitness, intellect, and commitment begins.

In the buoyant labor market of the 1950s, when most youths left school at least two, and generally three years earlier than the minimum age for recruitment, the police were at a "severe disadvantage in competing for the services of able and ambitious young men" (Report of Committee, 1955). And so growing difficulties in recruitment led to the advent of cadet training in 1957, with the intention that cadets would become the "main source of recruitment" (*Annual Report*, 1957). Their proportion of total recruitment did rise from 11 percent in 1957 to a high point of a third in 1969—but this reflected difficulties in securing older recruits rather than a dramatic growth in numbers of cadets. By 1970 one in five personnel with equivalent service were ex-cadets. Costs of training and lack of facilities at the Training School had limited the cadet intake to a maximum of 80 a year. So too did a policy, formalized in 1973, which attempted to maintain a ratio of one cadet to three recruits in the annual intake. This coincided with current British thinking and reflected concern that the service should not be dominated by ex-cadets. Supervisors and older police officers commonly perceived a lack of worldliness in cadets. They also feared elitism despite assurances that promotion would come to all personnel whose qualities and performance justified it, irrespective of differences in basic training. In fact, experience by 1970 suggested that a greater proportion of cadets would be promoted, and more quickly, than recruits. In part, promotion prospects were influenced by a rate of wastage that was lower for cadets than for recruits. More significantly, cadets had higher levels of educational attainment than did recruits though the gap steadily diminished from that in 1957, when 44 percent of cadets had a School Certificate in comparison with 5 percent of recruits (*Report on Recruiting and Training*, 1971; Gordon, 1984). By the mid-1970s the closing gap in the educational background of cadets and recruits, easier recruitment, and moves to reshape basic training raised the question of whether the cadet system should be ended. And it was, eventually, in 1983.

A year before cadet training ended, the first females were admitted to it (four in an intake of 40) which perhaps epitomizes the tardiness of moves towards full equality for women. In the New Zealand police, formal equality in status, training, promotion, and work responsibility has existed between the sexes since at least 1973, but it has not yet been conceded in recruitment. In practice an informal quota has been maintained, permitted by the section 16 of the New Zealand Human Rights Commission Act 1977 which allows greater numbers of men to be recruited for "the purposes of dealing with situations involving violence or the threat of violence." While successive governments have set the total strength of the service, they have allowed police administrators to determine the number of female officers. Since 1973 this has been done by periodically reassessing the need for policewomen, and also by making up any shortfall in meeting targets for male recruits. The proportion of female officers rose in the four years following 1974 from 3 percent to 4 percent of the service, a ratio that was broadly maintained until 1984 when it began to climb—reaching 6.7 percent in 1990. In 1990, the Deputy Commissioner claimed that the "only bar to a full complement of women within the service is the lack of people willing to apply" (*Press*, Christchurch, August 10, 1988).

However, a much higher rate of resignations by female constables has meant that, in the period 1980-85 for example, women have comprised nearly a fifth of the recruits. Though the images of recruiting publicity have focused on policing as a male occupation, there has been no shortage of women wanting to join. Of the 839 applications dealt with in 1983, over a quarter were from women for whom the winnowing process of selecting out the unsuitable was more severe: only 11.1 percent of the female applicants were accepted, by contrast to 18.4 percent of males. Higher proportions of women than men were declined on educational or medical (physical) grounds, or withdrew their applications. Married women are rarely accepted. Proportionately fewer females than males, however, were selected out on the grounds of general unsuitability. Women eventually accepted for training were, on average, younger with higher secondary school attainments and virtually met the minimum requirements for men in terms of height. According to one observer, they rarely failed their examinations at the Police College (Gordon, 1984). Potentially, enough well qualified female applicants have been available to form a far higher proportion of recruits.

Why then has a relatively small quota remained, albeit one that is now increasing? Despite the Commissioner's directive first enunciated in 1966 (and reaffirmed in 1973) that sex, other things being equal, will cease altogether to be a factor in detailing men and women to police duties, recruiting policy suggests that the irrelevance of gender in the performance of policing was not fully accepted before 1990. In line with government policy an Equal Employment Management Plan was adopted by the New Zealand police during 1990. Indeed recruiting policy since 1973 has apparently been shaped both by a traditional conception of order maintenance as fundamental to policing, and by enduring assumptions regarding the skills and limitations of female officers. Certainly, by the early 1980s, women had come to be found in virtually all spheres of front line policing, meeting violence and sustaining injury. Paralleling their proportion in the service as a whole, there were three women, for example, amongst the 54 members of the two main riot squads that accompanied the Springbok rugby team on its 1981 tour (Meurant, 1982). And, evidence is not lacking of female officers' capacity to deal with situations involving violence or the threat of violence. Even so, policewomen work within a strongly masculine occupational culture where the use of coercion has continued to be seen as preeminently a male function (Macfie, 1985; Sid, 1987; Barber, 1986). Thus the need for policewomen is still implicitly assessed by male police administrators in terms of their traditional role as auxiliaries to male police, especially in dealing with women and children. In contrast to the recruitment of ethnic minorities since the early 1970s, no argument has been sustained that women should be represented in the New Zealand police in proportion to their presence in the wider society.

New Zealand's first Maori policewomen were appointed in 1955 reflecting a changing attitude in the police administration to recruitment of the indigenous race. Pakeha settlers in the mid nineteenth century generally refused to accept the authority of a Maori constable (Hill, 1985). Such ethnocentrism died hard in the first half of the twentieth century. Indeed, for a century following a short-lived phase of mixed-race forces in between 1846 and 1853, Maori were enlisted only to police settlements of their own people. Between 1882 and 1945, a diminishing number of part-time native constables were appointed in remote areas. A survey of senior police officers in 1950 revealed that they were almost unanimously opposed to a suggestion that Maoris should be recruited to police members of their own race. Implicitly most officers accepted the prevailing philosophy of integration or full equality of the races, albeit in terms of assimilation to pakeha norms. In policing, no distinction should be made in terms of race: the significance of cultural differences was not recognized. Some officers thought that Maoris could be recruited for general police work; others saw them as unsuitable. In fact, at least one man of Maori ancestry, but with a pakeha surname betokening assimilation into the dominant culture, had been recruited into the police before 1945 rising to become Assistant Commissioner in 1958. The rapid urbanization of Maori from 1945 was eventually a catalyst for change as growing numbers applied to join the police. By 1970 there were 122 police of Maori ancestry, some 2.5 percent of the total service. But the growth of Maori recruits did not keep pace with the now burgeoning indigenous population: in the late 1960s, Maoris comprised 3.5 percent of all recruits, or less than half the proportion of the 19-to-24-year-old Maori males in New Zealand's population. Far fewer Pacific Island Polynesians were recruited into the service. The number of these recruits did not correspond to the large influx of Pacific Island Polynesians who migrated to the main cities in North Island during the 1960s, nor was it commensurate with their increasing interest in joining the police. That there were only six police of Pacific Island ancestry by 1970 reflected, in part, the rigorous assessment of the depth of assimilation into the dominant culture of such applicants.

Concern about the underrepresentation of Maoris and Pacific Islanders led to a directive from the Commissioner in September 1973 that particular efforts be made to attract suitable applicants. But there was to be no lowering of standards to accept young Polynesians who have had limited educational opportunities. Even so the Department decided in 1975 not to require any formal educational qualification for entrance into the police. A new police pre-entry test was introduced in 1977. And to take account of possible cultural factors, the test results of Maori and Pacific Island Polynesian applicants who performed marginally below the minimum standard were evaluated by the Dean of General Studies at police headquarters. With greater publicity and flexibility, the proportion of Maori and Pacific Island Polynesian recruits increased markedly: from an average of 8.9 percent in the 1976-77 intakes to 15.6 percent of those in 1982-83; or 12 percent overall for the period 1976-87. Depending on the statistical measures used, the New

Zealand police could claim by the mid-1980s to have a significant representation of the Polynesian ethnic minorities within its ranks. However, they were still not found in proportion to their numbers in multiracial communities, such as those in South Auckland (*South Auckland Police Development Plan,* 1984).

The presence of Maori police officers in the cities and at incidents of Maori protest since the late 1970s has had a cosmetic importance: a simple image of pakeha police coercing the indigenous race can no longer be drawn. Conversely, anger has been expressed at Maori police for being used as pawns in confronting Maori protestors (McTagget, 1985). More brown faces do not necessarily make policing more sensitive to the cultural differences and aspirations of Maori and Pacific Islander communities. The police remain part of a monocultural system of criminal justice. Maori and Pacific Island Polynesian recruits are socialized to see themselves as agents of the law (a product of the dominant culture) rather than of Maori, Samoan, Tongan, or Niuean lore. And the chairman of the New Zealand Maori Council has observed that Maori police may not be any more effective than pakeha in dealing with Maori offenders. Even when sent back to their local tribal community, they might not have any standing in Maori terms. In the cities Maori police employ the same techniques as their pakeha colleagues. What was needed for more effective policing (and leaders of the Pacific Islander communities echoed the comment) was close formal co-operation with the leaders and institutions of the ethnic minorities. Similarly an Advisory Committee on Legal Services advocated in 1986 the establishment of a Maori Advisory Committee on Policing "to advise the Police Commissioner on policy, act as a channel for Maori concerns, and foster positive initiatives within the police toward bi-culturalism" (*Report of Police Personnel Policy Committee,* 1983; *Te Whainga i Te Tika,* 1986). By 1988 a senior police officer had been appointed to review the police cultural perspective in consultation with Maori and other community groups. By 1991, again in line with Government policy for all Government agencies, the New Zealand police was seeking to increase the numbers of Maori in all positions in the organization in order to develop the cultural awareness of its staff and establish a closer liaison than hitherto Maori tribal organizations.

Since the New Zealand police remains very much a pakeha male-dominated institution, can it be argued that a distinctive police personality is produced by recruit selection? The evidence, such as it is, suggests not. Recruits and cadets surveyed by two research exercises in the early 1970s were seen as not likely to have authoritarian personalities; and first year cadets without field experience had conservatism scores that differed little from Teacher's College students. However, the conservatism scores of cadets who had acquired field experience (i.e., spent longer in training) were reported as increasing significantly (Gallagher, 1971; Hesketh, 1974). More recently Singer and her colleagues have surveyed the attitudes of recruits, police officers, and university students. Recruits were found to be neither more repressive nor more permissive than students in their attitudes towards offenders (McCormick, et al., 1985). On the other hand recruits and officers (a sample of Police College instructors, noncommissioned officers, and senior constables) were found to have significantly lower Type A scores than other university students. Even so the recruit scores were not significantly different from normal population incidence of Type A behavior (Huang, et al., 1983; Hewson and Singer, 1985). There is evidence that attitudes of recruits and more experienced officers do differ regarding their supervisors, the nature of the police organization, and the way the job is carried out. Experienced officers, as might be expected, have been found to be more cynical than recruits in terms of Niederhoffer's scale of police cynicism (Singer et al., 1984a). Conflicting evidence exists regarding the degree to which recruits and officers differ in their attitudes toward ethnic minorities and especially in their negative stereotyping of Maoris. Nonetheless, recent research suggests that there is a general tendency amongst police personnel, and especially amongst the uniformed patrol staff, to have "negative perceptions of Maoris" (*South Auckland Police Development Plan*, 1984); (Singer and Singer, 1984a; Dance, 1987). However, it is not clear that recruits differ from the wider pakeha population in their racial attitudes. Altogether these surveys suggest, as has been observed from British research, that "police recruits do not self-select according to a coherent set of already existing attitudes" (Fielding, 1986). Instead the formation of a police personality, to the extent that such exists, comes through the effects of training and work experience.

Developments in the training of New Zealand police epitomize the timing and nature of innovation within the Department. Before 1956 the scope, content, and methods of police training changed little from 1898, when a Training Depot was first established at Wellington. Only recruits received formal training—and then only as resources permitted. The Depot was closed during wartime and the Depression of the early 1930s. A sergeant or senior sergeant conducted, without assistance or guidance, the residential courses lasting three (and later two) months for about 30 recruits. They received a basic vocational training: learning the law largely by rote, police powers and duties, departmental regulations and instructions, report writing, and court procedure. Lectures were interspersed with physical training, parade ground drill, and instruction on first aid. After this short concentrated course, the new constables were left to develop their knowledge and skills on the job. So too were the detectives, noncommissioned officers, and officers.

As one of the most important steps in the reorganization of the police force, a committee (comprising an educationist, the director of army training, and a police inspector) was appointed in 1955 to inquire into police training. Its findings were influenced by the second report of the British Police Postwar Committee (1949), and consultation with the recently retired Commissioner of the London Metropolitan police. Following the British model, the committee recommended a probation period of two years training for new constables—with an initial thirteen-week course, followed by general police duties under supervision combined with a correspondence course in law and police practice, and then a final four-week course culminating in an examination before permanent appointment. Such courses began in February 1956 with the opening of a revamped Training School at Trentham military camp near Wellington. In its proposal for cadet training, the committee went beyond the limitations of existing British schemes: 17-to-18-year-olds would have a nineteen-month residential course with periods of station duty and a strong emphasis on general education (*Annual Report*, 1956; *Report of Committee*, 1955).

The committee looked to reshape police training through organizational change. Most, but not all, of its recommendations were followed. In 1955, its chairman (recently retired from the Education Department) was appointed director of training at police headquarters. He issued training directives upon which course syllabi were based, and organized in-service training. A former director of army training took charge of the Training School. As prospective instructors, 18 police sergeants were sent to take a course in what were then seen as very modern and effective methods of teaching at the Army School. Recruit courses, much larger than hitherto, were divided into groups of about 30 (called sections) under individual police instructors. The director of training urged that as much variety as possible be introduced into teaching methods with the aim of full student participation. Thus each section was further divided into syndicates of five or six for discussions, quizzes, and revision. To improve the trainee's literacy and general knowledge, civilian Education Officers with teaching experience were appointed and a police library established. Physical training was now also taught by specialists and the first appointee was an army warrant officer (Mason and Gordon, 1982).

The function of the new Police School was not just to provide basic training for recruits, but also induction and refresher courses for specialists, noncommissioned officers, and commissioned officers. Nor was the scope of training merely encompassed in new syllabi; an ethos and discipline had also to be imbibed. The School's first directive emphasized that a distinct police atmosphere and police spirit was to be engendered and fostered. Thereby the foundation for the future discipline, efficiency, fitness, and morale of the New Zealand police force as a whole would be laid by the School. From 1956 training lay at the core of a developing concept of professionalism in the New Zealand police.

Altogether the innovations of the mid-1950s represented a major advance in police training. Even so the impetus for change was constrained by limitations of vision and resources. In 1960 both the director of training and the Commandant (officer in charge) of the Training School were replaced by police officers whose only qualification as educators was experience as police instructors. On the recommendation of his predecessor, the new director was sent to study police training methods in Britain and Australia. He noted that New Zealand's courses were very short, but he thought the training of recruits and detectives compared favorably. Longer advanced courses and better in-service training were needed, but major improvements were inhibited by the lack of experienced staff and existing demands on the dilapidated army huts that constituted the Training School (*Annual Reports*, 1961; 1962).

Until the mid-1970s then, the nature of police training was largely unaltered. The focus of basic and advanced training within the police remained narrowly vocational rather than more broadly conceived. And teaching methods remained conservative despite the advent of courses for instructors at the Training School. Lectures and rote learning were the norm. Nor was there (by comparison with Britain) systematic on-the-job training of probationary constables. Supervisors (the sectional sergeants) were often too inexperienced or too busy. The correspondence course for the new constables also came to be seen as inadequate. In 1964 it was replaced (along with the final course at the Training School for probationary constables) with an in-service training program of lectures—not just for junior constables, but also for those with up to ten years service. Within a decade this program was seen as unsatisfactory: teaching venues and methods were often poor; timetabling was a problem for shiftworkers; high rates of absenteeism reflected the trainees' apathy; and above all, the system failed to deal with the differing abilities and requirements of the constables (Farrow, 1975). In 1975 the program was abandoned—along with the final examination for probationary constables.

As part of a major review of police organization and methods, training was critically appraised in 1971 by a team of police officers led by Inspector Glynn (Glynn, 1973). A new phase of innovation followed coinciding with, rather than following, similar British developments in police training. Now the cutting edge for reappraisal came not from British models. Instead it came from the officers' appreciation of local changes in policing and its social context since the 1950s, and of wider developments in educational theory and practice.

To a degree the police capacity for reassessment in 1970s was the result of the changing attitudes to training—especially for officers. The first ever training course for officers was held in 1956. From 1964 there was an annual four-week course at the Training School which aimed to give recently appointed commissioned officers a broadened outlook of life and a better understanding of organization and administration. But the need for overseas training was also recognized. From 1961 a growing number of senior officers attended four-month courses at the Australian Commonwealth Police College at Manly (Sydney); first as students, and later as instructors. Some were also sent for six-month courses to the Victoria Police College at Airlie. A few won fellowships to study policing in the United States and Europe. In 1966 and 1971, two senior officers destined to be Commissioner were sent for a year to the Imperial Defence College in Britain.

But perhaps of most significance were the changing attitudes towards a university education. Paralleling trends in North America and Australia, a growing number of police officers thought that a tertiary qualification would be useful, especially for those in executive positions (Chappell and Wilson, 1969). And so, from 1968, the Department provided for part-time (and occasionally full-time) study at a university. The numbers were small (44 part-time and 2 full-time out of 3,214 police in March 1971). Indeed, unless they took extramural courses from Massey University (Palmerston North), they generally needed to be resident in one of the six cities having a university. To improve the quality of promotional examinations for commissioned rank, two University correspondence courses for police officers began at the request of the Department: in criminal law from Auckland (in 1968), and in criminology from Victoria University of Wellington (in 1971). Before 1981, however, there were no other courses specifically tailored to meet their vocational needs. Most worked toward either a law or bachelor of arts degree. A few took diplomas in criminology or in business and industrial administration (if at Auckland); or in public administration (if at Wellington). For some officers, such as J. F. Glynn, such experience provided ideas and attitudes that helped shape the developments in police training during the 1970s (Glynn, 1975).

As a sign of changes to come, the Police School (with its rather junior academic connotation) was renamed College in 1972 on the initiative of its new commandant. In the same year, induction courses for sergeants, which had begun in 1957, were lengthened from ten days to a month. And for the first time senior sergeants received formal training. Their syllabus focused on skills in personnel management, decision making, and operations. Police community relations in a multicultural society were also studied—a focus that was to develop in both basic and advanced courses during the 1970s. Herein could be seen the impact of the 1971 review of training which recommended an increased emphasis on the social, behavioral, and constitutional subjects (*Report on Recruiting and Training*, 1971; *Annual Reports*, 1973 and 1974).

One of the most important fruits of the review of training came in May 1973. A training development unit (under a new director of training) was established at national headquarters with a staff of three officers who were soon joined by a Dean of General Studies—a civilian graduate with experience in adult education. Led by Chief Inspector Glynn, the unit saw as its first task the need to identify the current police role, the qualities required of police personnel, and the broad objectives of police training. Lacking resources and time for extensive research, the unit's findings were inevitably shaped by personal assumptions and perceptions. Its redefinition of the police role was adopted by the department until 1984. In essence, the redefinition sought, for training purposes, to capture the multifaceted nature of policing in a rapidly changing society. And so training had to provide more than merely a knowledge of law and technical skills of practical policing. An understanding of contemporary society and the vagaries of human behavior had to be developed. Training had also to develop the skills of specialists, supervisors, and managers as they proliferated within the ranks of the police. Above all, the unit believed that the overriding and long-term objective of police training/education should be to achieve public recognition of the police as a profession; for prestige leads to public cooperation (Glynn, 1973).

Following the recommendations of the 1971 review the course of basic training for recruits was extended by a week and redesigned in 1974. The proportion of time spent on police law and practice fell from 47 percent to 39 percent; time on drill was reduced (to 5.4 percent of the periods), as was that on firearms training (3.5 percent). Conversely, the periods devoted to tests and examinations were doubled to 44 (7.4 percent), as were those set aside for reserves and revision (6.7 percent) and first aid (3 percent). Time spent on physical training and sports remained roughly the same (13.4 percent), as was that on typing instruction in the evenings (3.7 percent). Periods for general education (now labelled Liberal Studies) increased by nearly a third to 66 (11 percent). Their content was substantially refashioned to promote community-oriented police who are skilled communicators and who understood their role in social and humanitarian terms. Accordingly communication, human behavior in the New Zealand social setting and race/community relations were the main subjects. Though the content of the education course was innovative, it was not yet clearly linked to the teaching of police law and practice. And so there was some resistance from recruits who failed to see the relevance of liberal studies to police work (Gordon, 1984).

Meanwhile, in October 1974, the Training Development Unit proposed more fundamental changes for basic training. "It is not so much that the present basic training system is significantly unsatisfactory," said the Unit's "Review,"..."but rather that the pressing demands on the police service in the future...compel us to discover, plan, implement and experiment with more effective...systems." Recognizing that "considerable disagreement exists" on how training could be "most effectively evaluated," the Unit took a "multi-pronged" approach. Views of new constables and their supervisors were sought regarding the adequacy of basic training. Though "generalized and subjective" their observations could not be ignored. Australian, North American, British, and European systems were studied, but the Unit resisted "the temptation of being unnecessarily influenced by overseas training practices." Current New Zealand police practices were also measured against "characteristics of effective training" gleaned from a literature review. The Unit concluded that existing cadet and recruit courses should be replaced with a 24-week training period with three phases: introductory studies, field orientation studies at stations to which trainees would eventually be posted, and consolidation studies back at the College. Such a combination of theory and practice was seen as best conforming to the principles of effective training. Instead of a few large intakes of recruits each year, there should be a "trickle" system of smaller groups which would allow closer attention to individual needs (Glynn and Watkins, 1974; Watkins and Paterson, 1975).

Administrators, however, focused on practical difficulties rather than the prospect of more effective training. The trickle three-phase system of 24-week courses did not begin until a new Police College was opened at Porirua (Wellington) in 1981. Henceforth the 19 weeks at the College would be broken at midpoint by station duty of four weeks and a week's leave. Recruits spend the same proportion of time as before on police law and practice. However the development of a problem-solving model for handling situations has brought greater sophistication to the teaching of police practice. Furthermore a thematic modular approach was adopted from 1980, more closely integrating some police subjects with general studies topics. With a new emphasis on communication skills and the practical application of theory, police behavioral science was made more relevant. From 1981 there has also been a greater emphasis on self-defense in physical training, and more time spent (at least an hour a day) on learning to use the police computer system. Hours spent on arms training have also been increased to 28 in an overcrowded timetable (Gordon, 1984).

Cadet courses, reduced from 19 to 12 months in 1976, continued until January 1983 when they were suspended as a cost-saving measure. In comparison with recruits, cadets spent more time on liberal studies, learned bush craft, had eight weeks station duty (where recruits did two 8-hour periods before 1981), and were given two weeks' driving instruction (which the recruits did not receive before 1981).

Attempts by the Training Development Unit to improve the effectiveness of instruction and testing in recruit and cadet courses had met with some resistance in the 1970s. Longstanding methods continued, especially in the instruction of police law and practice. In part, pressures for change were blunted by the separation of the officer in charge of the Police College from the director of training (of equal rank) who formulated policy at police headquarters. Between the two there was, according to one observer, a fluctuating relationship with "titanic clashes, interspersed with periods of lethargy" (Gordon, 1984). The 1971 review of training had recommended that the director of training be located at the College and in overall control. Eventually, in pursuit of improved efficiency in the use of resources, the functions of the director were amalgamated with those of the Commandant at the College in September 1985. By then the civilian position of Dean of General Studies had been disestablished and the resources for the continuing evaluation of training had diminished considerably.

Innovative ideas emanating from the Training Development Unit in the mid-1970s were more quickly realized in in-service training over which the director of training had more direct authority. Following the ideas of the psychologist Frederick Keller, the Dean of General Studies advocated personalized training methods. Such methods were first applied (in 1974) to the in-service training of constables on trial for Criminal Investigation Branch (Hartley, 1978). Then in 1976 in-service lectures for probationary constables were replaced by a program of 21 study units to be completed in as many months. Each study unit has a number of self-administer-ing tests. A progress test (administered by the district in-service training instructor) has to be passed before moving to the next unit. Three failures of a test on single unit would call into question a probationary constable's fitness to remain in the service. In fact the new system is not found too arduous: College courses weed out those not likely to pass. While they very effectively enhance the knowledge of new constables, the study units are not supplemented by systematic on-the-job training to further develop and evaluate skills. This deficiency, recognized in the 1960s, continued into the 1980s (Paterson, 1977; *Report of Committee to Review the New Zealand Police*, 1978; Robinson, 1982; *South Auckland Police Development Plan*, 1984).

Late in 1976 the Training Development Unit pressed for the adoption of a national training plan to give all personnel the opportunity to receive training and education appropriate for the career-long needs. Such a plan was not formally adopted, but its objectives underlay subsequent developments. In 1981 a comprehensive district training program was implemented. All personnel up to the rank of Inspector were to participate in at least eight refresher training days a year. From the late 1970s (and particularly with improved facilities from 1981), the range of specialist and advanced courses expanded greatly at the Police College. And senior officers were sent to management courses beyond it: to the New Zealand Administrative Staff College, and (from 1972) to Bramshill College (England). Already, by 1978, 85 out of a sample of 103 commissioned officers had attended one or more specialist courses—26 had attended five or more courses. The ideal of training as an ongoing process had become entrenched (Jamieson, 1978).

To give further impetus to the professionalization of the New Zealand Police, negotiations began in 1976 with Massey University to establish a diploma in police studies which would be available extramurally. The Department was conscious that, compared with the rest of the public service, it had the smallest proportion of graduates: 41 personnel had degrees or diplomas or 0.9 percent of the police in 1976. There was also a sense of falling behind developments in Australia where police in some states could now obtain a vocationally oriented tertiary qualification—albeit not from a university (Paterson, 1976; Jamieson, 1978). Eventually, in 1981 the first students enrolled for a diploma of 14 papers composed largely of existing social science and humanities courses offered by Massey University, together with three papers in police studies taught by a newly appointed director. Numbers taking the diploma did not increase as rapidly as anticipated, partly because (before 1987) its courses could not be credited towards promotion examinations, and also because it was not necessarily seen as the most job-relevant qualification. Degrees in law, arts, and public administration continued to dominate the preferences of students. By 1984 there were 106 graduates in the police, comprising some 13 percent of the commissioned officers and 2.08 percent of the service as a whole: roughly comparable to proportions in the armed forces and nursing, but still far behind those in social work and the public service generally (Working Party, 1985).

Since 1956, and particularly since the mid-1970s there has been greater sophistication in methods and a greater range in the content of police training. Nonetheless, basic patterns and objectives have endured. Though the department came to recognize the importance of tertiary (or college) education for its personnel, it has continued to "educate the hired" rather than "to hire the educated" (Sherman, 1978). To police administrators advanced education might be the prerogative of the universities, but the inculcation of police skills is properly the domain of the Police College (Paterson, 1977). And so the tradition of centralized training within the Department remains. So too does a military flavor in the nomenclature and style of many College institutions: Commandant (College Principal), Wing (each intake of trainees); course directives, standing orders, the duty instructor system, and the pattern of drill and graduation parades. This epitomizes a second, hidden curriculum for basic training which is as important as the formal one of police law and practice. It serves to inculcate police ethics, attitudes, values, and relationships. Discipline, role models, and informal systems of control established within each section (such as jugging—fines towards the price of a jug of beer) socialize the recruit into a distinctive occupational culture (Mason and Gordon, 1982; Gordon, 1984).

Since the early 1980s administrators have claimed much for their training programs, seeing them as basic to police effectiveness and professionalism and ranking highly by world standards. The expertise required by front-line staff, for example, is seen as provided to a large extent by high quality police education and training

(*Annual Reports*, 1980, 1981, and 1984). Yet the effectiveness of formal training in the New Zealand Police is difficult to measure. A survey of new constables and their supervisors in 1980-81 (on the eve of changes in basic training noted above) revealed no major complaints about the general quality of basic training. Supervisors generally saw new constables as well motivated and competent in doing run-of-the-mill police work. Nonetheless a common and consistent thread amongst the critical remarks was the gap between theory and practice (Robinson, 1982). For many new constables confronted with the realities of police work, practical experience counted for more than knowledge and skills learned vicariously. Their main difficulty was in dealing with people—many rookies lacked common sense, tact, and maturity according to their supervisors. In coping, most inexperienced constables turned to others more senior (often their partners in the patrol car) rather than supervisors responsible for on-the-job training. And thereby, work practices might well diverge from departmental norms. Despite the innovations in formal training, most new constables still had to develop practical police skills by trial and error and emulating others. Policing in New Zealand, as elsewhere, remained more a sophisticated craft than an applied science (Bayley and Bittner, 1984; Fielding, 1984).

Even so, developments in formal training have been crucial in shaping the character of the New Zealand police. For one thing the processes of training weed out the timid and the uncommitted. College life instills a sense of *esprit de corps*, pride, team work. And the centralized nature of specialist and advanced training maintains the strong sense of cohesiveness. More than this, training has become increasingly self-critical and systematic in dealing with people and incidents. Thereby an image of professional competence has been maintained in the face of the growing complexities of police work. Circumstances and personality may well shape individual practices, but expectations of appropriate conduct have been effectively instilled. Belief in the rules, voluntary compliance, is as important as control procedures in explaining (for example) the apparent absence of corruption in the New Zealand Police. Above all, the training of senior officers in management skills has enabled the police to maintain their relative autonomy from political interference and to ensure that career police officers rather than outsiders lead the organization.

Though major changes are planned, promotion in the New Zealand police has been to rank rather than to position. And as with all police organizations in the tradition of the London Metropolitan police, promotion to highest ranks is given only to those who have served as constables and passed through the lower ranks. "Every constable...potentially carries the Commissioner's baton," has been the dictum since 1912. Between commissioner and constable there were (in 1987) nine ranks comprising 25.6 percent of the personnel. Rank, and length of service within it, has largely determined remuneration rather than job size or individual performance on the job. And so getting on has generally been seen in terms of movement to higher ranks, rather than personal development in a particular job or movement to more demanding jobs at the same rank (Jones, 1986). Inherent in promotion policy, as in recruitment, is a concept of the generalist rather than of specialized career paths (though in practice these exist). Operational officers, qualified for promotion, are expected to become instructors, supervisors, or desk-bound administrators and possibly return to the front line, as the case may be. Clearly, opportunities for promotion have fluctuated in recent decades in line with the rate of growth of police numbers, the proliferation of ranks, the appearance of ever younger officers in higher ranks, and with the lowering of the retiring age to 60 in 1958 and to 55 in 1985. However, promotion practices and the hierarchical structure (with its narrow pyramid towards the top) have meant that most officers remain in the lower ranks throughout their career.

According to police regulations promotion is on the basis of qualifying examinations, merit, educational qualifications, physical fitness, and readiness to serve in any part of the country. All other things being equal, preference is to be given to seniority. A Promotion Board and a Promotion Appeal Board consider those suitable for promotion up to the rank of chief inspector. In the years 1975-78 (for which figures are available) there were 718 promotions involving rights of appeal; 15 appeals were lodged, ten withdrawn, and two were allowed. For the five senior ranks between chief inspector and commissioner, there is no right of appeal: the commissioner, often after consulting informally with others, recommends to the Minister of Police who are to be promoted. Such informality and the lack of appeal rights produced disquiet amongst commissioned officers during the 1970s. In police circles it is often mentioned that for the ambitious officer there was no certainty of promotion beyond the rank of Chief Inspector.

Until 1964 at least, merit was in practice narrowly and arbitrarily determined by a police-administered examination system. In essence, the system has changed little since its introduction before the first World War. For sergeants, senior sergeants, and inspectors four papers have been required to qualify for promotion to each rank: Evidence, Statutes, Police Administration, and Practical Police Duties. For inspectors, Evidence and Statutes were replaced in 1968 and 1971 by university-administered criminal law and criminology papers. In 1977 a pre-promotional literary examination was removed for those who had (secondary) School Certificate. Since 1987 aspirants for promotion have been able to credit various university qualifications in place of some of the papers. Those taking the police exams face syllabi of increasing complexity: Police Administration, for example, covered 78 topics in 1982 compared with 43 in 1966. Over the years only a small minority of candidates have passed this paper on the first attempt. Cynics have seen in the relatively small and fluctuating numbers of completed examination passes the influence of police administrators, seeking to manipulate the system to meet their needs. More plausibly, the number of candidates and their success reflects changing perceptions of the opportunities and benefits of getting on, and the quality of preparation. Indeed a criticism made with some force in 1979 still held true: "for many candidates, the examination system is something of a lottery; they are given no planned pre-examination study assistance and they then participate in a system which breaches most of the well-recognized modern principles of examination design and testing....It is obvious enough that many candidates qualify who should in fact not do so." (Promotion System, 1979; *The Bulletin*, September, 1986; *Newsletter*, July 1985, January and February 1987; Duncan, 1987). For officers and noncommissioned officers, training courses have followed rather than preceded selection and promotion.

A system of personal reports on efficiency and suitability was introduced in 1964 for all ranks up to Inspector. However, the system carried little weight in the promotion process. Indeed the small number of appeals against promotion suggest that police administrators acted cautiously—seeing the assessment of relative merit as difficult and likely not to stand up in an appeal. Until the early 1980s at least, virtually all promotions below the rank of chief superintendent were apparently based on seniority (Promotion System, 1979; Hickson, et al., 1982). Following a change in the philosophy of rating, a new system was introduced in 1981. Besides assessing potential for promotion, personal reports are now seen as means of individual development: the ratee's aspirations are made known, strengths and weaknesses identified, and counselling given. Of those qualified for promotion in February 1986, 2.4 percent had A ratings, 66.1 percent B, 31 percent C, and 0.4 percent D. However, the validity of the ratings continues to be questioned. Ratees often see their supervisors as being negative about performance rather than constructively critical. On the other hand, administrators selecting from the applicants for vacancies have expressed doubts over the honesty and consistency of the appraisals. Merit (in terms of high ratings) has apparently been given greater weight at least since 1984 at least. Yet a widespread perception persists amongst the lower ranks that the promotion process is "a seniority and a numbers game" (*The Bulletin*, February 1986; *Newsletter*, April 1986; Heppleston, et al., 1987).

Such a perception has clearly shaped career expectations, causing a "loss of motivation for individuals to compete with their peers" (Hickson, 1982). With the police service seen as offering a job rather than a career, some staff (including noncommissioned officers and commissioned officers) have developed business interests outside it, and provide "low levels of productivity and contribution" as a result (Heppleston, et al., 1987). Ambitious graduates, especially those with law degrees, have left to pursue alternative careers (Working Party, 1985). But seniority is not the only influence shaping the desire to "get on." Eighty percent of the junior constables surveyed in 1980-81 intended to sit for promotional exams. Almost all were confident about long-term opportunities for future promotion—albeit to noncommissioned officer rank. Only a minority (roughly a fifth of the ex-recruits, and a third of the ex-cadets) aspired to commissioned rank, though the aspirations of these new constables increased with length of service (Robinson, 1982). Such career expectations were not reflected in the performance of female officers, nor that of older and more experienced staff. By 1986 only eight noncommissioned officers and two commissioned officers (an inspector and chief inspector) were women—3.3 percent of all women in the police. In the period

1975-86, the numbers of male and female candidates completing examination passes fell to their lowest point in 1983—in line with the opportunities for promotion. In 1979 it was estimated that over half of the constables aged 26 to 45 years had "decided to opt out of promotion" (New Zealand Police Association, 1979). Not merely a pessimistic view of the "numbers game" was involved. Also calculated were the financial and familial costs of promotion which, for sergeants in particular, is frequently accompanied by a transfer. Growing numbers of constables and noncommissioned officers who were qualified for promotion declined it. Increasingly since the mid-1980s, administrators have been prepared to give accelerated promotion to those prepared to transfer around the country. This, as well as substantial improvements in salary margins and the effects of a new early retirement scheme, may have recently altered the perception of opportunities and costs. Numbers completing their exams have risen sharply since 1984 (*The Bulletin,* February and June/July 1986; Duncan, 1987).

Generally speaking, the development of careers within the police has been haphazard, shaped largely by individual initiative, seniority, and a random pattern of vacancies. Not until 1983 (in establishing a Career Development Unit) did the administration begin to seek out more effectively the career aspirations of staff and "offer a sense of direction" (*The Bulletin,* October 1985). Nor had it systematically identified and developed those with potential for command and managerial positions. Since the 1960s some, but not all, in the senior ranks have been sent to training courses in New Zealand and overseas. However, executive development has been largely on a "please yourself" basis. Growing numbers of senior staff have acquired university qualifications and considerable expertise, while others have received little training in management (Hickson, et al., 1982; *Report of Police Personnel Policy Committee,* 1983). During 1984 and 1985 "total dissatisfaction with the career system and opportunities for personal development" was one of the major concerns identified during a wide-ranging review of police performance. Another stimulus to reexamine personnel policies came with the advent of earlier retirement (*The Bulletin,* December 1984, February and May 1985; *Newsletter,* January and

March 1985; McGill,1985). Reform of the career structure was also wanted by the Government, faced with a substantial increase in the police salary bill. In October 1986 an international firm of management consultants began "Project Blueprint"—a comprehensive human resources management review. Its interim report in April 1987 recommended far-reaching changes in organization and management. In particular, the consultants suggested that four ranks be removed. Ranks needed to be more closely related to command and management requirements and to job size. All police would hold a substantive rank, but appointments (promotions in effect) would be to position rather than rank. Payment would be determined both by job size and individual performance. To meet the needs of individual staff and the organization, "career development" plans and an "objective based performance appraisal system" should be developed (Heppleston, et al., 1987). The commissioner quickly declared himself "firmly committed to the introduction of needed change"—though the proposals had to be "carefully thought through before being implemented" (*Project Blueprint*, 29 April 1987). These recommendations have brought about many changes.

LEADERSHIP AND SUPERVISION

As we have seen, the formal goals or mission statement of the New Zealand police have not essentially changed since its inception. Nor has the broad structure of the organization, though major changes have been implemented by 1989. However, the management style and strategies in pursuit of the formal goals have changed, especially since the 1970s. And further changes have followed the recommendations of "Project Blueprint."

Though long divided into districts (16 in 1988) with an officer in charge, the New Zealand police organization has traditionally been highly centralized. Its administration has been shaped by an inherently autocratic style of leadership with a rank structure designed to preserve a line of command. Between 1951 and 1977 four new ranks were created doubling the number of commissioned officer ranks below the Commissioner. From the 1960s also, the proportion of police personnel in the supervisory ranks grew: that of commissioned officers rising from 2.2 percent to 4.6 percent, and noncommissioned officers from 14.5 percent to 21.0 percent between 1960 and 1987. In part this was to meet line of command requirements with a narrow span of control in a force that was rapidly growing, especially in the largest cities.

In the cities there was greater difficulty in coordinating the services of large groups of personnel. More detailed planning was needed to deal with major contingencies and day-to-day administration both in operational and personnel matters. Important decisions were seen to be made with greater frequency—hence the need for more officers to be on duty for the whole day, by contrast with smaller centers where noncommissioned officers were often left to make decisions or to consult off duty officers (Twentyman, 1970). But the growing numbers of officers and noncommissioned officers without direct supervisory or operational responsibilities also reflected the fact (noted earlier) that remuneration continues to be directly linked to rank. Increasingly, as management became more complex and specialized, rank was divorced from its traditional raison d'être of command.

Until 1955 at least, administration by supervisory ranks in the police was narrowly conceived in terms of control and supervision of personnel in operational matters, careful scrutiny of all expenditure, and routine attention to files and correspondence. In the police examinations for senior sergeants and commissioned officers, questions relating to administration focussed merely on the proper keeping of records (*Police Force Regulations*, 1919 and 1950).

The Commissioner, assisted by a small staff at national headquarters, approved all expenditure and made the final decision in personnel matters. Formal delegation of administrative decision making from higher to lower ranks was limited—though of course, in matters of law enforcement, it could be considerable in practice. Senior officers had little time to spare from routine administration to consider longer term strategies and plans, for which indeed they had not been formally trained. Rigid control and close monitoring of the conduct of subordinates was the emphasis of supervision at each level of rank. Noncommissioned officers were to report without delay to their superiors any irregularity. And the catalogue of disciplinary offenses was (and remains) long. The quality of supervision could depend on the size of station and the zeal of superiors. But strict adherence to rules and regulations was the norm, with caution rather than initiative in decision making being inculcated in noncommissioned officers.

Such attitudes have died hard. More than a third of Auckland constables and noncommissioned officers surveyed in 1983 saw commissioned officers as a major dislike in the job—and especially in their handling of complaints against the police (*South Auckland Police Development Plan,* 1984). Consultants reviewing the management of the police in 1986-87 often heard of the "Fitter"—an officer conducting an internal investigation. "A strong perception existed that people were rewarded for not getting it wrong, rather than for getting it right." They found that much effort went into seeing that "situations were well documented"; and the more senior an officer signing a document, the "safer you were." An unwillingness for mid-level and junior officers to accept accountability was observed (Heppleston et al., 1987).

During a brief period of civilian leadership (1955-58) the seeds were laid for a new style of management with emphasis on greater communication, delegation, specialization, and planning for future needs. Formal training of officers in administration began. With police headquarters now growing quickly in size and complexity, its first organization chart was published in 1961. From 1964 questions on the theory and principles of administration were introduced into police examinations for senior sergeants and commissioned officers. A textbook was prepared by two senior officers who drew on O. Wilson's *Police Administration* (1950) and earlier theorists of organization (Fitzpatrick and Kelly, 1964; Morgan, 1977). By the mid-1970s, would-be sergeants were being encouraged to begin studying the principles of administration: especially the "human relations aspect of supervision," organization of work, and decision making. Instead of control, the emphasis in supervision by sergeants was now on building morale, the effective induction of new constables, training, appraisal, counselling, and the development of discipline as a positive force rather than by the rigid enforcement of official rules. For their part, more senior officers were enjoined by one of their number to give sergeants room to move—a degree of autonomy which would allow them to exercise initiative (*New Zealand Police,* 1976; Rusbatch, 1976).

Analysis of officer training course syllabi suggests however that, until the mid-1970s at least, the police science of administration focused more on specific operational needs than on broader processes of management. Indeed, from the late 1960s, inspectors and more senior officers have received sophisticated command training in techniques of appreciations, planning, and organization for different types of operation. By the late 1970s, police preparedness for a major disaster or massive civil unrest was substantially greater than a decade earlier. The fruits of such training, planning, and experience can be seen in two remarkable operations: the recovery and successful identification of 83.7 percent of deceased victims of an Air New Zealand DC-10 crash in the Antarctic on 28 November 1979; and the largest ever mobilization of police personnel to contain widespread protests against the visit of the South African rugby team between July and September 1981 (Mitchell, 1978; *Bulletin*, November 1979; Morgan, 1980; Operation Overdue, 1980; Operation Rugby, 1982). More broadly, the major police contribution to the development of a national computer system for law enforcement agencies (in operation from September 1976) demonstrated its capacity for planning and implementation of new techniques and management support facilities (Hickson, et al., 1982).

Nonetheless, weaknesses have remained in the broader processes of managing the human resources of the police. Early in 1972 a review of national headquarters pointed out that only a few of its sections employed management by objectives. Such a systematic approach had been a part of organizational theory since Peter Drucker had popularized it in *The Practice of Management* (1955). But not until 1975 was it adopted by the New Zealand Police as policy at the instigation of a new commissioner. Formally at least a more participative style of management was introduced with fresh objectives. A Board of Management was established, comprising district commanders and senior administrators at headquarters. This met three times a year, becoming the Police Executives Conference (to more truly reflect its practice) under the next commissioner. A corporate planning section was also set up "as a magnet and a filter for ideas to improve the service administratively and operationally." It organized two seminars of police district representatives (including noncommissioned officers and junior commissioned officers) to discuss wide-ranging ideas from the lower ranks (Burnside, 1974 and 1975; *Report*, 1976; Trappitt, 1977). Where suggestions coincided with the thinking of senior administrators they gave an added impetus to the development of policy—notably in police-community relations and in the inspection of districts. Efficiency liaison teams were formed to monitor performance. But their demise within three years (along with corporate planning seminars) was symptomatic of a loss of impetus in the thrust toward a new style of management.

Superficially it might appear that changes in police leadership have, particularly since 1955, influenced the style of management. Certainly the new commissioner in 1978 brought a different personality and experience of leadership to his role. Since 1967, however, new commissioners have served as understudies to their predecessors and have been closely involved in policy making. And so the policy of participative management continued into the 1980s, with an increased emphasis on delegation in decision making. The commissioner urged all staff holding any supervisory role "to play their part in management," to exercise the responsibility that went with their position, and "not leave it to the person above as has been a habit in some quarters in the past."Those whose judgment erred "in good faith" could expect his support; but not those who acted illegally, or "without any foresight or through sheer stupidity" (*Bulletin*, May, June, and August 1978, November 1980). Symptomatic of the "more flexible attitude" (and of greater openness in public relations) was the authority now delegated to lower ranks to communicate directly with the media on matters they dealt with (Walton, 1978, 1980). More intangibly, a greater informality continued to develop in relationships between the ranks.

However, the practice of management by objectives remained limited. In part there was a lack of commitment—compounded by the lack of formal training and development of skills in such a systematic approach. Natural caution reinforced by experience suggested that a system devised for business was not necessarily appropriate for the police. In particular, the broad police goals could be seen as nebulous and conflicting, making it difficult if not impossible to specify overriding objectives that were susceptible of measurement. Without accurate measures of performance (to be discussed further below), a slavish adherence to a particular system of management seemed inappropriate. Moreover, to the police means were as important as the ends. Their actions had to be legal and public confidence had to be maintained (Trappitt, 1977; Rusbatch, 1985). By 1980 the setting and achievement of annual objectives was largely confined to headquarters, and then (as in the case of the Training Directorate) framed narrowly in terms of intraorganizational goals. In most districts, and for all front-line activities, there was no formal statement of operational objectives—apart from the broad national goals of the police. Evaluation of effectiveness and efficiency by police managers was (and still is) "largely informal and intuitive" (*Report of the Audit Office,* 1981). The allocation of personnel to the various facets of front-line policing continued to be determined by national headquarters, and remained essentially demand-led rather than goal-driven.

Ever tighter budgetary constraints in the face of mounting demands for service, and two external reviews of police administration in 1981-82, increased pressure to use resources, especially personnel, more effectively. From 1984 a new commissioner renewed the impetus for innovation in management style and strategies. A management workshop comprising most of the senior administrators critically examined existing policies and procedures. In particular, a strong desire was expressed for greater district autonomy and staff participation in decisions on the allocation of resources. In response, the commissioner issued a strategic management plan with a mission statement and national goals. Districts along with headquarters sections had to set measurable objectives and prepare action plans which contributed to the national goals (Thompson, 1984; 1985a). Implementation of strategic planning took time and was not by 1988 fully realized. Staff at all levels of management had to be educated to accept it and become involved in goal setting and evaluation of performance. Planning was still essentially learned on the job. To this end a booklet on the principles and methods of policing by objectives was issued, modeled on that used by the Northamptonshire police in England. Organizational change was also required as planning and evaluation achieved greater status at headquarters: a Management Audit section established in July 1983 became part of a Planning and Resource Management division in which corporate planning reappeared three years later. The need for more fundamental change in the organization was also recognized. This was addressed by management consultants in "Project Blueprint," mentioned earlier.

The consultants saw some significant barriers to the effective achievement of national police goals enunciated by the commissioner. Within the proliferating ranks, overlapping responsibilities between headquarters and district staff had developed—especially in personnel administration, provision of operational-support services, and in planning for major operations. Moreover, between subordinate and superior positions, a high degree of "accountability overlap" was observed, with "little effective delegation downward" of decision making apparently taking place. Senior officers surveyed in "Project Blueprint" reported spending between 60 to 80 percent of their time on "routine administration, and day to day operational matters" (Heppleston et al., 1987; Morgan, 1977; *South Auckland Police Development Plan*, 1984). Accordingly, a clearer division of functions between headquarters and districts—and a reduction of ranks—was recommended. Headquarters, with its key functions regrouped, would concentrate on strategic planning and policy development. Twenty-seven districts, grouped into six regions, would have greater authority to deal with operational matters and resources. In this way, it is believed, greater responsibility for decision making has been devolved to the districts and to lower ranks. The introduction of regions has been seen as strengthening the coordination of the districts and improving planning in the allocation of resources. With fewer ranks and increased district autonomy in operational matters, greater flexibility in staff deployment has been claimed. So too is a reduction in barriers to communication. Decentralization accords well with the renewed emphasis since 1984 on community policing (Heppleston et al., 1987; *Project Blueprint*, 29 April 1987; Thompson, 1985b).

The concepts of regionalization and headquarters restructuring were quickly accepted by the commissioner. In August 1987, six regional commanders were appointed to organize the new regional structures. This process, accompanied by a reorganizing of headquarters, was accomplished later. Rank restructuring has been a more extended process, involving delicate negotiations with the service organizations and a review of the salary structure. Such were its concerns with the effects of the process that the New Zealand Police Association withdrew in July 1988 from "an active role" in the "various discussion and evalution forums" of "Project Blueprint" (*Newsletter*, August 1988). Even so, the "managerial style" of the New Zealand police seems set to become (in the words of a commentator looking to the future of policing internationally) "more collegial, supplementing and even supplanting reliance on authoritative command" (Bayley, 1985).

STANDARDS USED IN EVALUATING INDIVIDUAL POLICE PERFORMANCE

To the degree that the broad goals of the New Zealand police have not changed through time, so too the absolute standards implicit in these goals remain unchanged. Clearly there will inevitably be a discernible gap between ideals and achievement in policing. Nonetheless public expectations of police performance may well have risen since the turn of the century—as the trend to a more orderly society (until the 1930s at least) became identified with a particular pattern of beat and suburban policing; as police behavior showed greater regularity and discipline; and as (from the 1950s) the police developed their capacity to respond to an ever growing volume of calls for service. Rising expectations probably faltered during the 1970s, particularly as the police increasingly emphasized the need for community self-help in the face of mounting reports of property crime and disorder. Yet the concept of police professionalism articulated in the 1970s implied an aspiration for improved performance. So, too, has evolution of management by objectives since the 1970s, accompanied by attempts to define standards and measure performance with ever greater precision. For 1987-89, the commissioner's main organizational goal was "to improve the quality of service to the public." To achieve this, three "key principles" were seen as necessary: the "efficient and effective" use of resources; "the highest personal and professional standards of performance"; and the "continuing growth of an effective community partnership determined to suppress crime and disorder" (*Annual Report*, 1987; Churches, 1987). Standards of performance in using resources and establishing a community partnership will be the focus of this section. The nature of personal and professional conduct is more appropriately left for a later discussion of public confidence, trust, and restraints on the police.

Only in the 1980s, in fact, have police administrators drawn a clear distinction between the concepts of efficiency and effectiveness. In this they have been influenced by growing pressure from recent governments, expressed through the various agencies that monitor departmental expenditure, for greater accountability of public service managers and better information on results achieved (*Report of the Government Administration Committee*, 1987). Particularly influential was a "pilot study" of police efficiency and effectiveness conducted by the government audit office during 1980-81. The audit office defined effectiveness as "the degree to which the objective...of a particular activity has been achieved when measured against the expected results"; and efficiency as "the maximizing of output, given a set level of input of resources (*Report of the Controller and Auditor-General*, 1981; *South Auckland Police Development Plan*, 1984). Hitherto police administrators' use of the term efficiency generally encompassed the concept of effectiveness.

Traditionally, the "efficiency" of the New Zealand police has been assessed in terms of a "rational/deterrent model" of policing inherited from the nineteenth century: its primary object was to prevent crime and maintain the peace by deterrence (Hough and Clarke, 1980). And like bureaucratic police elsewhere, details of "business" have been systematically kept. In particular, statistics of offenses reported and cleared up were seen, until the 1970s at least, as the chief index of police efficiency. Implementation of computerized records from 1976, gave police access to much more detailed offense and incident statistics. Indeed the "more efficient collection of statistics" had to be taken into account when interpreting the rapid increase in recorded offending during the 1970s (*Annual Report*, 1979, 1980). Even so, the massive increase of reported offenses against people and property during the last 30 years, despite an increase of police by more than a third in proportion to population, might suggest declining police efficiency when judged in traditional terms.

Police administrators have long been aware of the limitations of a simple rational/deterrent model of policing. Publicly they might claim credit when the level of reported crime fell, and point to lack of resources when it rose. But in their explanations for crime waves, factors other than a lack of police efficiency have generally been employed. Police point to a multiplicity of causes of crime. Other factors besides the police are seen as having a hand in shaping behavior—lack of religion, parental control, and effective penalties are commonly suggested. Increasingly from the early 1970s, police administrators emphasized (*Annual Report*, 1986) that "Police efforts alone to deter crime, no matter how effective, will prove insufficient to halt increases unless society as a whole commits itself to concerted action." A range of offenses (notably many involving violent behavior) can plausibly be seen as not susceptible to police control. Privately, police administrators have also expressed skepticism about their statistics, recognizing the effects of deficiencies and changes in recording procedures. More than this, some appreciate that reported offenses represent an unknown quantum of all offenses. Hence it is impossible to quantify police effectiveness. Yet the clearance rate is still seen as "some measure or an indicator of effectiveness" (*South Auckland Police Development Plan*, 1984; *Annual Report*, 1988). Though the 1985 clearance rate of 41.9 percent for all offenses was the lowest since 1956, the Commissioner declared it to be "a result better than most of our overseas counterparts (*Annual Report*, 1986). This bald figure encompassed a range of clearance rates typical of police performance in comparable societies: from 93 percent for murders and 80 percent for minor assaults, to 24 percent for theft and 17 percent for burglary. Moreover, as commentators elsewhere have recognized, clearance rates are flawed indicators of performance. They provide no evidence of police effectiveness in crime prevention, and only ambiguous evidence of effectiveness in detective work since the degree of assistance rendered by victims, offenders, and witnesses is not measured (Looi, 1976; Bottomley and Coleman, 1980; *South Auckland Police Development Plan*, 1984).

Apart from offense statistics, the other measure of efficiency employed by police administrators before the 1980s was the workload survey—to assess need for additional personnel or to reallocate them. Traditionally such surveys examined the workload of stations rather than of personnel and were essentially based on measurements of paperwork: files attended to; warrants, summonses and civil processes served; and arms certificates issued. Until the early 1980s, the standards used in determining acceptable workloads were essentially unchanged from those established in the national survey of the New Zealand police carried out between 1966 and 1970 (*Report of the Audit Office*, 1981). From 1973, workload studies of mobile incident patrols were conducted in Auckland to assess the optimum number of jobs that could be handled in responding to calls for service. The object was to improve response times; and assessment was based on reports submitted by field officers on duty. From 1976, analysis of preventive patrol activity was added to that of calls for service with the aim of improving the quality of service. With the introduction of computer-assisted despatch (in Wellington, Auckland, and Christchurch during 1977 and 1978) came new data on incident patrol work (*South Auckland Police*

Development Plan, 1984; *Annual Report*, 1978 and 1979). That front-line officers, aided by technology, now process a much greater volume of work than did their counterparts 30 years ago can be readily demonstrated. Yet police workload studies are limited measures of performance. They judge efficiency in the use of resources rather than effectiveness in achieving goals. They help to establish priorities, but give no evidence of public satisfaction with police work. They are (as the government audit office has commented) "input" rather than "output"-oriented (*Report of the Audit Office*, 1981).

The state of the art in measuring effectiveness and efficiency, as the Controller and Auditor-General acknowledged in 1981, is still in its infancy in New Zealand. The police then lacked (and still lacked in 1988) performance indicators necessary to objectively demonstrate their effective and efficient use of resources (*Report of the Controller and Auditor-General*, 1981). In a major review of the South Auckland police division undertaken in 1983-84, police administrators sought new means, besides the traditional measures, to evaluate police performance.

With the findings of the Rand Corporation study of criminal investigation in mind (Greenwood, et al., 1977), police researchers analyzed charge books of the South Auckland division to determine how effective different police units were in identifying and apprehending offenders. Results were in line with the Rand Report. Of the total arrests for serious crimes against person and property, patrol officers effected 58 percent, detectives 29.8 percent, uniformed enquiry staff 8.5 percent, and other staff 3.7 percent. Superficially it might seem that patrol officers were the most effective staff, and certainly the most efficient means of deployment when their response to calls for service is taken into account. However, as the authors of the South Auckland survey warned, such figures might be useful indicators but they were not absolute measures of effectiveness. Arrest rates may be too gross a measure to reflect the contribution of investigative units. No judgment could be formed of the contribution of the different units to crime prevention (*South Auckland Police Development Plan*, 1984; Greenwood, 1980). Nonetheless the South Auckland study added weight to a developing concern with the methods, workload, and organization of criminal investigation. The 1980s have seen the introduction of more systematic early case closure based on solvability factors, as well as experiments in integrating investigative and patrol staff. A major review of the police investigative function began in 1988 (*Report of Committee to Review the New Zealand Police*, 1978; Walton, 1981; *South Auckland Police Development Plan*, 1984; *C.I.B. Activity Survey*, 1985; *Annual Report*, 1988).

Greater technical efficiency does not necessarily bring greater public satisfaction, as New Zealand police administrators came to realize during the 1970s. Traditionally they had judged the level of public satisfaction intuitively through complaints against police and informal soundings of opinion-formers nationally and locally. In the review of South Auckland policing, administrators broke new ground by systematically surveying local public and police opinion. Recently completed research on the London and Victoria police provided the model. Since the findings are relevant also to a later discussion on public confidence and trust, they will be reported here only in so far as they relate to standards of performance. As a fundamental assumption for the review, the South Auckland police district was perceived as unique demographically and culturally: rapidly growing, relatively youthful, and dominated by working-class areas in which Maoris and people of Pacific Island origin were present in much higher proportions than the national average. These two ethnic groups were also disproportionately represented in the local unemployment and crime figures (*South Auckland Police Development Plan*, 1984). Whether the full pattern of public opinion in South Auckland regarding the police is unique remains largely untested. Comparable surveys have not been repeated elsewhere, though a variety of district statistics of public satisfaction with police performance in response to calls to service were reported (without comment) in 1988—showing broad levels of satisfaction ranging from 71 percent to 91 percent (*Annual Report*, 1988). Overall, the South Auckland findings paralleled those for London in many respects.

As in London, most people interviewed in South Auckland thought the traditional police roles of catching professional criminals and preventing crime to be of the highest importance. Conversely only a small minority saw settling family rows as very important—despite the frequent requests for police to intervene in domestic disputes. With such expectations, 75 percent of South Auckland respondents to a questionnaire felt the police service in their area to be adequate or excellent. However, this high level was based upon a population, nearly half of whom had had no contact with the police. A large majority of the teenagers surveyed showed little confidence in the police ability to perform their traditional roles. This was as much a reflection of police relationships with local youth as it was a perception of their effectiveness. When the responses of the three main ethnic groups were analyzed, Europeans were more likely to see the police service as inadequate (26 percent) than Maoris (23 percent) or Pacific Islanders (17 percent). But of those who actually requested police service, the pattern was reversed, broadly in line with the degree of contact: with 10 percent of Pacific Islanders being highly dissatisfied, 9.4 percent of Maoris, and only 6 percent of Europeans. Concern about accessibility to police when needed was highest among Maoris and lowest amongst Europeans. To police researchers, two conclusions were possible: the minority groups had higher expectations, or received an inferior service. There was a need for greater quality control of service (*South Auckland Police Development Plan*, 1984).

This was also suggested by a random telephone survey of those who had reported violence or property crimes (and who, in this survey, were disproportionately European males from the better-off section of the community). To a few of their calls, the police had arrived after a minute; but the general tendency was for the response time to be 30 minutes. Delay in attending incidents obviously influenced the level of public satisfaction. Yet the significance of response times has to be assessed in terms of the type of incident—which was not recorded in this survey. Conclusions as to the quality of service were thus not easily drawn. After arrival, police usually spent about 20 minutes at the scene. This length of time, and the rituals of investigation, clearly contributed to nearly two-thirds of the respondents expressing satisfaction with police performance. From this point, however, levels of satisfaction declined with less than half being satisfied with the result of the enquiry. While roughly a third had heard within a week about the progress of the enquiry, more than a third did not hear from the police after the first contact; and more than half never learned if enquiries were completed. Only a fifth knew that the police had caught an offender. Such a pattern of experience clearly shapes public perceptions of police effectiveness (*South Auckland Police Development Plan*, 1984).

Results from the South Auckland survey pointed in two directions. Overall there seemed to be general satisfaction with the police service. But viewed more closely, significant reservations about police accessibility, visibility, and quality of service could be discerned. Indeed there was, especially amongst Maori and Pacific Islander respondents, considerable doubt about the effectiveness of uniformed officers in their cars. These and similar findings from a less systematic study of opinion in a Wellington suburb underlined, for New Zealand police administrators, serious questions about the efficiency model of policing with its emphasis on mobility, communications and centralization. Greater efficiency in the use of resources had not necessarily increased effectiveness of service (Hamilton, 1984; *South Auckland Police Development Plan,* 1984).

Surveys of community opinion reemphasized for administrators in the early 1980s that prevention of crime should be the primary aim of the police. However such surveys also gave an impetus to the development of new strategies—in particular that of more decentralized community policing, echoing trends abroad. The rational/deterrent model of policing was not abandoned, but rather refurbished. Mobile incident patrols would remain. No longer however would the police raise expectations that they had the chief responsibility to protect life and property. Instead, as the commissioner put it in 1985, "there is a greater part to be played by the community in attending to its own policing needs.... The Police role becomes that of facilitation" (Thompson, 1985b). An effective community partnership had by then become a key principle of New Zealand policing (Bottomley and Coleman, 1980).

In fact the community policing strategy of the mid-1980s built on policies evolved over twenty years. Soon after the system of centralized radio-controlled incident and enquiry patrols was fully implemented, police administrators began to respond to community pressure for a more personal, visible style of local policing. The first suburban community liaison officers (later renamed community constables) were appointed in 1973. Their general responsibility was to reaffirm the traditional role of the police officer as a protector and friend by establishing direct communication with a particular community who can identify with that constable. This brief did not mean a return to the former pattern of individual suburban constables responsible for routine policing of their own patch. Instead, community constables were merely an adjunct to the predominant mode of reactive policing. Indeed they were but one element of a growing range of officers specializing in aspects of community relations. So the role of community constables was intended to be symbolic: to suggest the omnipresence of the police and generate feelings of security. How visible they were in reality depended on individual constables and the demands made of them. In the South Auckland police division, for example, there were six community constables by 1983 out of a total staff of 337. Four of these constables served as office attendants to small patrol bases, and two of them spent most of their time behind the desk rather than on the beat through shopping centers. Here as in other cities, the numbers of community constables (totalling 36 in 1983) were too small to have an effective symbolic role. Feelings of public safety continued to depend on how the effectiveness of mobile patrols was perceived. The potential of community constables to stimulate localities to attend to their own policing needs remained undeveloped before the 1980s (*South Auckland Police Development Plan*, 1984; Hamilton, 1984).

Educating the public in crime prevention began formally in 1965 with the appointment of a few specialized crime prevention officers. Encouraging the public to become "more security minded" also became a task for all frontline personnel. While community obligations were now being emphasized, the focus of prevention was narrow (on burglaries and certain types of theft) and the primary role of the police implicitly remained. Given the soaring rate of reported burglaries from the late 1960s, the effectiveness of this strategy was not apparent. Frontline personnel spent little time giving advice on protecting property—and then it was largely after the event. Yet it was not merely a question of the limited resources devoted to education in crime prevention: apathetic attitudes persisted despite media campaigns (*Annual Report*, 1978). And paradoxically, greater public precautions could greatly increase ineffective police work. This was particularly the case with burglar and raid alarms which were directly monitored by the police without cost to the user from 1962. By the early 1970s the percentage of genuine alarms was less than 0.5 percent of the total signals received. Commercial firms took over the job of monitoring alarms, though police continued to be called to attend the scene. Inefficient use of resources continued: activated alarms constitued a third of all incidents attended by the police in 1985; less than 4 percent were genuine alarms. In 1987 the police determined to attend only genuine alarms—private security firms or community support groups would have to respond in the first instance; users would be charged for police attendance if their alarms were false.

Demands for police service were also increased by organized community activity in the name of crime prevention. Late in 1974, a community service organization (Lions International) promoted a "speak up" campaign in one of the largest cities, encouraging the public to report anything suspicious to the police. Enthusiasm for a yearlong national campaign mounted and it was launched with police support in 1976. Simultaneously the service organization promoted Operation Identification in different cities, whereby householders could mark valuables in a way that could assist recovery should they be stolen (*Annual Report*, 1976). Such campaigns brought more incidents and offenses to police attention. They did little to develop community self-help in crime prevention. Rather they focused a myriad of individual expectations upon the police ability to respond effectively to calls for service, and especially for the protection and recovery of household property. Even so, techniques of organization, private sponsorship, and publicity were developed which the police adopted in a more sustained campaign to encourage neighborhood self-help. By 1979, computer-generated police statistics underlined the fact that domestic dwellings were second only to public places as the scene of recorded offenses (*Annual Report*, 1979).

The notion that families and neighbors should together take a more active role in crime prevention was formally espoused by the police when it launched a nationwide Neighborhood Watch program in October 1980 with considerable publicity through radio, television, and newspapers. Within four months more than 50,000 kits, with materials explaining how to better protect property and form Neighborhood Watch Groups, had been collected from police stations throughout the country. Police administrators estimated optimistically that over 300,000 householders were then participating in such groups (*Annual Report*, 1980; 1981). As with the "speakup" campaign, however, much neighborhood watch activity was by individuals rather than groups. Through sustained publicity demand for Neighorhood Watch kits continued. So too did reports from citizens of people or vehicles acting suspiciously.

Between 1979 and 1983 such reports rose from 12,146 to 36,541, making them the second largest category of incident dealt with by the police after burglar alarms (*Digest of Statistics*, 1986). Though in the first year of Neigborhood Watch there was a countrywide reduction in reported thefts from dwellings, house burglaries reported continued to increase (*Annual Report*, 1982, 1983, 1984). This implied that while there might be fewer insecure suburban houses, neighborhood surveillance had yet to become an effective deterrent in most areas. Apart from such crude measures there were few indicators of the program's effectiveness. Eighty-five percent of those surveyed in South Auckland in 1983-84 were aware of the aims of Neighborhood Watch; but only 11 percent were members of the scheme. Of those who were members, only 21 percent thought the scheme effective, suggesting that the cohesion of many groups was tenuous or not sustained. Of those who were not members, a quarter believed they already belonged to an informal mutual support system, a fifth thought the scheme would not work or was unnecessary in their area, and the remainder lacked sufficient information or motivation to become involved. "Publicity alone," the researchers concluded, "will not persuade people to become part of self help crime prevention schemes. Non-paid, non-professional volunteers have a role to play" (*South Auckland Police Development Plan*, 1984; Morgan, 1984).

Such a conclusion seems to have been confirmed by events since 1983. A savage attack on a woman in her Auckland inner-city home stimulated her neighbors to set up a close network to protect their physical safety rather than property. Its founders, women, were primarily concerned with violence, especially against women. They deliberately sought publicity to promote the concept of a Neighborhood Support Group (NSG) as a model of community initiative in fostering mutual support. With private sponsorship, they prepared a widely distributed kit and video on how to set up a NSG. Where the police-initiated Neighborhood Watch emphasized the need for people to be the "eyes and ears of *absent neighbors*," the promoters of neighborhood-initiated support groups looked to respond "to signals or cries for help." Where active watch groups aimed merely to protect their property with police advice and support, support groups were, in theory at least, to "empower" people whose lives have been severely limited or restricted by violence or the fear of violence and other crimes. Their feminist promoters believed it to be "critical for NSGs to continue to monitor, and challenge if necessary, the existing attitudes and policies of the police"—particularly regarding domestic and sexual violence (McNaughton and Woodhouse, 1986). Perhaps not surprisingly, the initial response of local police to such groups was less than cooperative. But police administrators proved more receptive when the concept of "neighbourhood support" flourished during 1984 with 2,000 groups being formed. For the first time since 1973, the overall rate of reported offending in Auckland fell in 1984. In particular, the number of house burglaries recorded fell by 9.4 percent—a decline widely attributed to "these community initiatives" (*Annual Report*, 1985).

Following a seminar convened by the commissioner to devise a new crime prevention strategy, district commanders were instructed in March 1985 to prepare and implement Community-Initiated Crime Prevention (CICP) programs. Neighborhood support groups now provided the model. Local police, especially community constables (who increased from 36 in 1984 to 176 in 1991), were expected to liaise with such groups and foster their development. Each district was to set objectives and report progress. By March 1988 there were 17,023 CICP groups throughout the country or 5.1 groups per 1,000 population (Cameron and Young, 1986; Dance, 1986; *Annual Report*, 1985; 1987; 1988). Though all the new groups were nominally NSGs, in reality there was a wide variety of types. Some conformed to the NSG model; many more were apparently little more than Neighborhood Watch Groups concerned to protect property rather than "becoming involved in domestic disputes, or taking action about incest or rape" (Mitchell, 1985). Most were probably somewhere in-between: being sponsored by local police or community organizations, and with members joining because of a generalized concern about "high crime rates," and wishing to reduce the risk of becoming a victim (Jonas, 1987a; 1987b; Dance, 1986).

However, the extent to which support groups have been effective in reducing crime and preventing victimization is not clear. Nationally, reported violence has continued to increase at a significant rate. A comparative study of two suburbs found that in one suburb, recorded violence decreased by 36 percent and dishonesty offenses by 27 percent during the first year following the formation of NSGs; in the other suburb, reports of these offenses continued to increase during the two years following their formation. The impact of NSGs on these statistics was not assessed in relation to other possible influences. Given the incomplete coverage of suburban support groups (and ignoring variations in their watchfulness), the question remains whether the existence of NSGs merely displaces certain types of criminal activity rather than effectively reduces them. Nor is it clear that NSGs have been an important influence on the increasing readiness to report domestic violence, incest, and child abuse (Jonas, 1987a, 1987b; Dance, 1986; Morgan, 1984).

Even so, by 1986 police administrators could point to a 16 percent decline in house burglaries reported in the Auckland police district since 1984. Nationally, for the year ending March 1987, recorded burglaries and thefts declined by over 6 percent; a trend which continued into the following year but not between 1989 and 1991. Clearly police could also point to other positive results from their point of view: they received "far better information" resulting in "many good catches" (though nationally, the clear-up rates have scarcely improved). In the perceptions of local police, "public relations" and confidence in them also seemed to be enhanced. True, only 38 percent of respondents in a national survey, reported in 1988, rated the police "excellent" or "very good" in terms of crime prevention (Mitchell, 1985; *Annual Report*, 1988). For their part, many members of support groups have apparently experienced a greater sense of security and a better relationship with their neighbors; fear of crime has been reduced for some.

Early in 1989 a new Commissioner of Police, following the initiatives of his predecessors in the 1980s, announced the decision to implement a community-oriented policing system by June 30, 1993. This was to be the principal police strategy for service delivery. The organizationally separate activities of patrol, crime investigation, and prevention were to be integrated at the local level. Each of the 28 new police districts was to develop a "COP" plan with a target date for full implementation by 1993. Community-oriented policing was thus married to the ongoing process of decentralization in decision making and location of police stations. The policing style now emphasized was problem-solving in consultation with the local community. At the level of both the police region and the police district sufficient consultation structures were to be established to assure community accountability (in the ambiguous phrasing of the police corporate plan). Patrolling was now to be flexible, with specific objectives and strategies shaped by local needs. Computer-assisted dispatch would be enhanced to better ration police resources by means of differential and delayed response according to circumstances. Where possible, crime investigators would become generalists again: working as part of larger teams focusing on communities rather than type of crime. The emphasis was on local innovations in policing strategies and using community resources as far as possible (*Police Corporate Plan, 1991-1992*). The new goals bore the imprint of concurrent developments in policing strategies overseas as well as a local trajectory of bureaucratic change since the mid-1980s.

Despite the rhetoric and new strategies of community policing many questions about its future development remain. The extent to which it will effectively reshape the centralized nature of New Zealand policing is yet undetermined. "What we are seeking," declared the Commissioner in 1985, "is an effective middle road that combines the efficiency of centralized command with a more intimate community relationship" (Thompson, 1985b; Workman, 1985). Yet, in the balance of reactive and preventive policing, the reactive style looks likely to remain predominant. "Without an efficient mobile response service Neighborhood Watch-Support is useless," a local police coordinator of support groups commented (Mitchell, 1985).

Indeed, after the rapid growth in their numbers during the mid-1980s, many neighborhood groups apparently existed only as a concept (signified by a street icon) rather than by activity in the early 1990s. The weakest groups, and the patchiest coverage, are found in the areas which are most victimized. Nor has the latent issue of acountability to the local population implicit in the strategy of community-oriented policing been effectively addressed. Greater decentralization of police decision making sought to be introduced by community policing does not necessarily mean greater responsiveness and accountability to community demands. In fact, the whole notion of local community to be consulted is problematic in many localities. Thus far the largely white, middle-class, male-dominated support groups have been the voice of local opinion; and they have tended to look to the police for advice and support rather than challenge their policies (Cameron and Young, 1986; Dance, 1986; Mitchell, 1986; and Jonas, 1987a; 1987b).

Insofar as issues of accountability have been raised publicly during the 1980s and early 1990s, they have focused on a third dimension of police performance, namely personal and professional conduct. In New Zealand, as has been observed of police elsewhere, such criteria as "adherence to law, absence of immoral behavior, generation of public trust, display of sympathy and concern,...and equitable treatment of persons" are important in judging performance (Bayley, 1985). Here the measures of performance are largely qualitative and will be considered in a later section.

PROFESSIONALIZATION

In 1978, a survey of members of the New Zealand police with more than 25 years service revealed that a small majority (54 percent) of the respondents thought that their occupation was a profession when they joined (between 1940 and 1956). An overwhelming majority of the respondents (83 percent) felt the police was a profession at the time of the survey. Clearly there was a widespread belief that during the 1960s and 1970s the New Zealand police had professionalized: become more recognizably a profession in occupational characteristics and status, or at least more professional than hitherto in terms of the degree of competence and skill with which policing tasks were performed. Comments in the survey revealed varied understandings of the concept of a profession and some ambivalence in applying it. Respondents often drew a distinction between professionalism in behavior and status. Some considered themselves professional but would not apply that to all police members. The general feeling was that the goal should be professionalism in police work but it was recognized that perhaps some members of the police who have gotten university degrees could be regarded as professionals, but not the general run-of-the-mill police officers.

An explicit ideology and language of professionalism gains currency in New Zealand policing only from the early 1970s, underpinning wide-ranging moves to enhance the image and social standing of the New Zealand police. This can be seen as symptomatic of a new phase in a longer term process of professionalization. In fact the impulse to professionalism, in terms of independence from civilian control and the pursuit of greater efficiency and consistency in police practice, has its roots in the late nineteenth century with the conscious adoption of the ethos of English policing. The absence of an explicit language of professionalism before the 1970s, and its ambiguities thereafter, is suggestive of some of the limitations of the process.

By 1920 the rudiments of professionalization had appeared in New Zealand policing. An ideal of service was articulated in a Commissioner's address published as part of a handbook (the so-called "Black Book") containing the disciplinary code for members of the force (O'Donovan, 1920). Efficiency was measured essentially by the absence of crime and was sought by the disposition and control of frontline staff rather than by technical innovations (before the late 1930s). Virtual autonomy in law enforcement had been established, as was a widely held image of police integrity and freedom from corruption. Discipline was the preserve of the police, as were the selection of recruits and the process of promotion. Standards (physical, moral, and mental) for recruitment had been adopted as well as basic training in law and practice at a police depot. Except for a few rural men, policing was a full-time occupation which most recruits saw as a career—with superannuation benefits for those who survived. A strong esprit de corps was evident in the pages of the *New Zealand Police Journal* from the late 1930s. Constables at the one-man stations in the small country towns and suburbs generally had considerable local standing.

In retrospect then, some long serving police could well view their occupation as being a profession in the 1940s and 1950s. Before the 1970s, however, the term is anachronistic. More commonly, policing would have been viewed as merely a job, or as a vocation by those with a strong sense of commitment. Competence, both in frontline policing and in administration of staff, was seen as coming from common sense and practical skills acquired through experience rather than formal training: practical professionalism in the parlance of the 1970s (Greenhill, 1981). The working class/farming background of most recruits, their limited technical training, the lack of a formal science of policing, and the level of pay all combined to make frontline policing an artisan occupation in New Zealand, as elsewhere. Indeed, as has been observed elsewhere, the means used to shape and control police practice were bureaucratic rather than professional (according to the popular models of law and medicine). The ideal of service was defined and enforced by a hierarchical military (and in New Zealand, centralized) structure of authority rather than by "a system of collegial control by peers" (Reiner, 1978; Walker, 1977). Personal autonomy, especially of the patrolmen in the cities, was in theory restricted. A "wise discretion" and a "discreet exercise of initiative" was enjoined, but also constrained: "Strict compliance with orders is the line of safety in normal conditions....Consistency and firmness without harshness should be the guiding principle...." (O'Donovan, 1920).

During the early 1950s, the limitations of "practical professionalism" became increasingly apparent in the face of mounting demands for service and strains within the police. A new phase in the process of professionalization (or from another perspective, bureaucratic change) began in the mid-1950s with the appointment of a civilian—a professional bureaucrat—to head the police. From the top, a new drive began for basic changes in police work-methods and organization: the shift began with policing by specialist units and personnel, as well as to the more general use of technology (especially cars and telecommunications). With the preparation of a *Handbook of Police Practice,* the formulation of standard police procedures was taken much further than the "Black Book" of 1920. And the process of making explicit and systematic a body of technical knowledge continued as formal police training developed. From 1956, as has been discussed earlier, emphasis was placed on raising the standards of recruitment and the quality of police training. Promotion strictly by merit (by-passing seniority) was sought but not achieved by the civilian administrator in the late 1950s. However, officer training began and became increasingly sophisticated: principles of police administration came to be studied; the work of the American authority, O. W. Wilson, became familiar. Thus was the basis laid for aspirations of managerial professionalism which became evident within the ranks of New Zealand police administrators during the 1960s. By developing expertise in administration, planning for change, seeking to respond positively to public demands and criticism, and (above all) claiming specialized knowledge and techniques, the police sought to maintain their independence from civilian control.

The ethos of managerial professionalism was evident in the national survey and major reorganization of policing carried out between 1966 and 1971 by the police themselves—generally without community consultation and with the retrospective sanction of the government. In similar fashion to trends abroad, the police administrators looked to increase the efficiency of their frontline staff by the application of technology and the principle of specialism in organization. Urban policing was centralized by the closure of suburban stations and redeployment of staff to radio-controlled cars. A newly formed management services section monitored the changes and planned further innovation—notably the introduction of a police computer system. By 1978 there was computer-assisted dispatch of mobile patrols in the three main urban areas. New Zealand policing, always essentially reactive, became much more clearly so.

The advent of the new system of policing coincided with (and in the longer term came to be seen as exacerbating) strains in the police relations with the public. Remedies were now couched explicitly in the ideology and language of professionalism which was not seen as the preserve of a managerial elite, but rather a necessity for the whole police service. As a police report put it in 1973: the service needed professional recognition to secure public approval and cooperation, but it was not now regarded as a profession because the essential ingredients upon which professionalism is traditionally based do not exist (Glynn, 1973). Thus again there was a renewed emphasis on training and on improving the police professional image. Smart modernized uniforms and new-look patrol cars were introduced in 1976. A booklet was issued to staff with advice on appropriate attitudes, communication skills, and public demeanor. In fact the common sense principles on what is a professional member of the police, though made more explicit, were essentially little different from those articulated by Commissioner O'Donovan in his "Address to the New Zealand Police Force" given fifty-five years earlier (O'Donovan, 1920; *New Zealand Police*, 1975). A review of professionalism in the police by its Board of Management concluded that all the criteria existed to some extent with the exception of a formal code of ethics. In view of the antipathy that followed the distribution of a police creed to every station in 1963, a formal code was not then adopted. Instead the salience of police ethics was increased in basic training.

By the early 1980s the moves to professionalize the New Zealand police had enhanced both public and self-images of the status and competence of its personnel. To most police, their occupation was now a profession, however conceived. Pay increases had brought constables into the ranks of the white-collar occupations. Attention to public image, a more highly educated and articulate personnel, the new skills demanded by specialization and technology, together with a strong sense of esprit de corps, deepened the sense of professionalism amongst the rank and file. Independence from civilian control had been preserved.

Yet, as will be apparent from the earlier sections, the pursuit of professionalism (in various forms) has not brought any nearer to solution some of the basic issues of policing—indeed it added to their complexity. For one thing, the goal of greater deterrence and order maintenance by mobile patrol and rapid response was not realized. True, the apparent deterioration in order by the early 1980s might have been worse if the old forms of policing (by foot patrol and one-man station) had been retained. However, this is conjecture. Certainly new policing made personnel more productive in terms of workload: more calls for service could be dealt with. In particular the police could and did enter more rapidly, and to a much greater extent than hitherto, the private domain of violence. Paradoxically then, the new image of professional policing seems to have contributed to rising expectations of order at a time when its maintenance was increasingly challenged by a variety of social processes. As demands for service grew, police managers had to establish priorities for dealing with them; public expectations had to be lowered to "accepting a level of police response commensurate with the incident reported" (*Annual Report*, 1979; 1984). Potentially, the application of technology might have brought reality closer to the myth of police omnipresence, but it could not stem the mounting fear of crime.

Police administrators claimed in 1970 to be learning from the experience of overseas forces where "too much accent (had been placed) on mobility and not enough on foot patrolling and getting to know the people. We have not made this mistake" ("The New System of Policing," 1970). Their optimism was not realized. Foot patrols did not disappear. A national survey in 1980-81 of the use of duty time by constables (with less than two years service) revealed that a national average of 13 percent of work hours was spent on foot patrol, with another third of the time spent in Incident cars, and the remainder on a variety of other duties (Robinson, 1982). Changes in policing may well have "increased the chances of police/citizen contact" (Young and Cameron, 1985). Yet the likelihood that urban frontline staff would have a local identity, or develop personal knowledge of their clients, was much reduced from the former pattern of much suburban policing. From the mid-1970s, there was a growing chorus of comment regarding the impersonality of centralized car-based policing.

Professionalization did not stem the flow of complaints against the police. Indeed by vaunting it, administrators raised public expectations of police practice. This continued to vary according to the style and context of policing. In fact specialization sharpened the differences in policing styles that had long been present in New Zealand policing. Youth aid and community constables (generally older than those on foot and mobile patrol) epitomized a social-service style with an emphasis on crime prevention and community assistance. At the other extreme, team policing exhibited a strongly legalistic, law-enforcement style in the large number of public order arrests that flowed from its activities. Personnel in Incident cars might adopt a social-service style in certain contexts. However, a law-enforcement style was probably more common amongst the youthful patrol personnel. This was partly a product of centralized control where violent incidents, potential threats to order, suspicious events or people take priority—and hence the prospects of confrontation and coercion are more likely. Signs of an action-oriented, crime-fighter, ethos can also be found amongst the rookie constables on foot and mobile patrols: turnovers (street questioning and searches) were the most frequent activity of such constables in 1980-81; and over half of those with less than two years service were assaulted while on Incident car patrol during a survey period in 1979-80 (Robinson, 1982; Pittams, 1980). Significantly perhaps, police administrators generally urged discretion on their frontline personnel rather than seeking to curb it. In the view of critics, nonetheless, a very legalistic style of policing has been experienced by Maoris seen to be disorderly in hotels and on the streets—to the extent that team policing tactics have been perceived to be harsh, and the police exercise of discretion (or the lack of it) to be biased (Jackson, 1988).

In theory, centralization has meant greater control of frontline personnel, and increased training implies better socialization of staff into norms of appropriate behavior. Since the 1970s the concept of professionalism has been conceived to be a universalist rather than an elite one in the New Zealand police (Cain, 1972). Even so there are clear tensions between the ethics of professional policing espoused by administrators and some of the long-enduring practices of street policing. While no systematic research exists to demonstrate the point, it is possible that the redefinition by subordinates of policy directives, that has been observed in Britain, is also present in New Zealand (James, 1979). Criminologists in New Zealand are certainly sceptical of the extent to which managerial concepts of professionalism have been routinely adopted by the rank and file (Cameron, 1986).

Finally, questions can be raised about the administrative outcomes of the new policing. Specialization and the growing complexity of administration led to the relative growth of non-frontline personnel. To the rank and file, the numbers of police at National Headquarters was indicative of the trend: the 203 in 1980 represented 4.1 percent of the total sworn staff, whereas in 1950 the ten police at Headquarters represented 0.65 percent of the total. Auckland Central division provides another extreme but nonetheless symptomatic example in the late 1970s: only a third of its sworn staff were then engaged in field operations, another third were in investigation units, and a final third were in support services (Parkes, 1978). That only a minority of police staff were (in this police division) on uniformed frontline duty marked a basic shift from the 1950s in the disposition of personnel. In part it reflected the desire for police autonomy. Despite growing numbers of civilians in administrative duties, sworn staff occupied all key roles whether in administration or technical support services. By the early 1980s, such a disposition of police personnel had come to be seen by governments as costly at a time of financial stringency. Given the salary loadings for overtime that all ranks below chief inspector received irrespective of their duties, and the continuing demand for more frontline police, pressure mounted for civilianization and a critical appraisal of the police administrative structure. An external functional review carried out at the behest of the government in 1982 recommended a growing measure of civilianization and changes in personnel policies. This challenge to police managerial professionalism was met (as has been discussed in an earlier section) by administrators embarking on "Operation Blueprint": police-controlled restructuring on advice of outside nongovernment consultants. Thus the mystique of police professionalism has helped to keep the department immune from some of the effects of state sector reform in the late 1980s. In particular, close control by outsiders has still been effectively resisted.

Ultimately, and probably inevitably, the New Zealand police continue to differ from the ideal-type professions of law and medicine in that, despite decentralization, the basic organization and ethos remains bureaucratic. By the late 1980s there was a broader band of policymakers in the hierarchy than in the early 1950s; decision making has become more collegial; but authoritative command remains. Thus the practical professionals of the frontline, whose daily decision making has the most influence on the welfare of their clients, still have (in theory) the least personal autonomy. With the further development of community-oriented policing during the 1990s, however, the practical professionals may become more clearly decision makers in the development of policing strategy.

POLICE WAGES, STATUS, SUBCULTURE, AND MORALE

Police wages clearly underpin status and influence morale. But whereas wage levels can be measured with some precision, the assessment of social status and morale is more problematic. Nonetheless improvements in training and pay have seen a rise in the police constable's socioeconomic status since the 1960s—at a time when public trust and confidence in the police has declined. Morale, inferred from a variety of indicators, appears to have fluctuated according to a changing sense of relative deprivation and levels of job satisfaction. Overall, morale seemed high now—possibly higher than thirty years earlier.

During the last few decades, the level of police incomes has risen significantly up the pecking order of New Zealand wages and salaries. In the early 1950s the total income (pay and allowances) of most constables was broadly equivalent to that of the most highly paid skilled manual workers, such as fitters (engineering) and engine-drivers. In 1955-56, the reform of police pay established new relativities: a constable's salary (at age 21) moved substantially above that of a skilled laborer and more than equalled the starting salary of graduates in the Public Service. From the 1970s the police gained further increases in salary that were "well ahead of those achieved by other public servants" (Butterworth, 1985). By 1987, a first-year constable began at a level of pay that was about a third higher than the top rates being paid in the public service for skilled tradespeople, and at the midpoint (supervisory level) in the salary scales for prison and road traffic law enforcement officers and for the executive/clerical grades of the public service. Constables' incomes were within the top 10 percent of male incomes and 1 percent of female incomes in 1986. A first-year sergeant, with generally less than ten years service in the police, received a salary that matched that of accountants and lawyers well-advanced up their public service scales. For their part, the commissioned officers were amongst the most highly paid civil servants and received incomes that rivalled those of senior academics and many in the medical profession in 1987.

By the early 1980s, the salaries of constables and sergeants were significantly higher than the basic salaries of their counterparts in most Australian forces (Remfrey, 1985). This reflects the different methods of remuneration for overtime, weekend work, public holidays, and night shifts. Where the penalty rates are paid according to hours worked in the Australian forces (Remfrey, 1985), the New Zealand police salaries (from the ranks of constable to inspector) incorporate a substantial loading for overtime and penal time—a loading which increased from 23.5 percent in 1966 to 41.5 percent in 1985. The overtime loading represents four hours paid overtime per member per week. Compensatory time off is credited for all overtime in excess of five hours per week. Such leave is clearly difficult to take: by March 1988 the value of time off owing in lieu of overtime in the New Zealand Police was estimated to be $3.3 million or 81 person-years (*Annual Report*, 1988).

Successive police administrators have resisted any union pressure for paid overtime. For their part, the rank and file have been divided on the issue: some might receive considerably greater incomes if all overtime was paid; most (if Australian experience was any guide) would not. Indeed a substantial minority would probably only receive the basic salary. Moreover, the higher comprehensive salaries have benefits in determining the level of pensions on retirement and the annual pay increases awarded (generally in percentage terms). A New Zealand Police Association survey of membership opinion in 1987 revealed overwhelming support for the present comprehensive salary (Ansley, 1986; *Newsletter*, April 1987; May 1987; July 1987).

Overall the New Zealand police have benefited from having a distinctive position within a national public service. As a result of a centralized wage-fixing system the police have received the annual general adjustments and improvements in working conditions awarded to the rest of the public service, keeping it in step with (and sometimes ahead of) the ruling rates of pay outside. Furthermore, in periodic reviews of police pay, the Police Association has also been able to win enhanced basic salaries for the special conditions of employment, as well as gain increased loadings for overtime and greater margins between the ranks. By the mid-1980s then, police salaries could be seen as highly attractive in securing "a better than average standard of recruit in terms of education and physical fitness" (Butterworth, 1985). And an improving economic position has apparently underpinned a long-term rise in the social standing of the New Zealand Police.

Police status is multifaceted issue. It involves both subjective perceptions of occupational prestige and objective measures of socioeconomic position. Also relevant as a determinant of social standing is the degree of public trust and confidence (which will be considered later). Evidence for the present social status of the New Zealand police is meager, and so it is useful to set it in the context of Australian research. Such conclusions as can be drawn must remain speculative.

A comprehensive status ranking of New Zealand occupations by university students, reported in 1954, placed police officers at 5.28 in a seven-point scale: at the top of the skilled manual wage-earners, but below self-employed tradespeople, bank clerks and primary school teachers; and roughly on a par (in occupational prestige) with minor government clerks and routine office workers (Congalton and Havighurst, 1954). Twenty years later, a revision of the seven-point scale to take account of wider range of occupations (but without resurveying public perceptions) saw no change in the social grading of the rank and file police (Davis, 1974).

Conventional wisdom that constables and sergeants have had a higher social standing in small country settlements than in the larger towns and cities is underscored in a ranking of 30 occupations by respondents in a small country town, a larger town, and Wellington (the capital) in the early 1950s. Police officers were ranked 12th out of 30 in the small town—above carpenter, fitter, newsagent, clerk, commercial traveller, news reporter, and insurance agent—and falling below these occupations to 17th in the larger town, and 19th in Wellington (Congalton, 1953).

Subjective ratings of social standing have placed Australian police officers amongst the elite of skilled manual workers (in 1968), or as lower middle class (in 1981). In Australia, as in New Zealand, police social status appears to have risen in public perceptions since the 1960s. However, occupational prestige may not have risen as fast as economic position. Furthermore, most rankings of status have made no distinction amongst the different ranks of police. When such a distinction was made, Australian university students surveyed in 1973 ranked police superintendents fifth (between accountants and sociologists) out of 23 in a scale of social prestige; police sergeants were ranked 14th, and police constables 17th (between carpenters and salespersons) (Swanton, Hannington, and Psaila, 1985; Swanton and Wilson, 1974). There is no comparable data for New Zealand police—and it is not evident that public evaluations of the police in New Zealand generally distinguish between ranks.

To the extent that the social prestige of the police depends on the degree of public confidence, their social origins, and the image they project of professionalism, the present social standing of the New Zealand police may well be higher than that of their counterparts in some of the Australian states. Historically, public trust in the police seems to have been greater in New Zealand than in most Australian states (Chappell and Wilson, 1969; Swanton, Hannington, and Psaila, 1985). This factor, when combined with the increasingly middle-class origins of New Zealand police recruits and improved training and income since the 1960s, makes it likely that at present New Zealand police would be ranked well within the white-collar occupations or middle-class. This view is reinforced to some extent by an objective socioeconomic index for males in the New Zealand labor force defined in terms of median educational and income levels reported for each occupation in the

1981 census. In this index, six socioeconomic levels are defined; police officers are placed in level 2, or broadly a lower professional-technical category. Here again there is evidence of an improvement in socioeconomic status: a similar index constructed on the basis of 1966 census data placed police officers in level 3, or amongst the clerical highly skilled workers (Elley and Irving, 1985; Elley and Irving, 1972). Since the 1950s then, the police have apparently moved in social ranking and ethos from being an artisan occupation to a subprofessional white-collar one.

There has been no systematic study of the New Zealand police as an occupational community or subculture. Much of the following discussion is thus impressionistic. Ostensibly, the New Zealand police share some of the salient characteristics of a police occupational culture that have been identified in American and British studies. Yet important qualifications have to be made (and some will be made below on the basis of an unpublished survey in 1978 of personnel who then had twenty-five years service or more in New Zealand police). Close observers will note that in the New Zealand police (as in their counterparts of countrywide forces overseas) the degree of uniformity of attitude and behavior can be exaggerated. Rank, specialism, size of station, nature of the local community, and point of career (especially the contrast between young unmarried rookies and older married men with children) may all underpin deviations from the stereotype. It has been well observed that the nature of police work and people doing it are historically and socially variable (Reiner, 1978).

Certainly the New Zealand police as an occupation has characteristics in common with forces elsewhere. It is an often adversarial occupation perceived to be increasingly fraught with danger and difficulty. In 1978, 70 percent of police surveyed (with more than 25 years service) had sought medical advice as a result of their job—mostly for minor injury, or illness arising from the hours of work or stress. Nearly two-thirds thought there was more stress in the job, not so much because of violence, but rather (reflecting perhaps their career position) because of the increased responsibilities that came with rank, paper work, the impact of the computer, and more generally the demands of the job—especially a more demanding public. In fact, a third of those surveyed could not recall being assaulted on duty; and many of those who had been were philosophical about it: luck still holding; all part of the job; although there is an escalation of violence in society, a large number of the police seem to attract violence toward themselves. Difficulties then came not so much from the prospect of physical danger, as from meeting the expectations for results within the constraints of legal and ethical behavior.

Typically, workers in potentially dangerous and difficult occupations develop strong norms of solidarity. The New Zealand police are no exception. Foundations for collective feelings are established in training, and hardened by the modern forms of urban policing that emphasize joint effort, team work, and back-up. The isolation of the one-man stations, and of individual urban foot patrol at night without radio, has all but gone. Pressures for conformity (albeit often conflicting) come from both departmental discipline and an informal code. "Jugging," a drinking ritual learned at Police College and carried over to the police canteens, has been a light-hearted way in which erring members of sections are penalized at the end of a shift. It's a time, according to one observer, for merriment and mirth. A time to wash from their memories the horrors of the job. The rituals, with their ambience of physicality and sexual innuendo, are redolent of a masculine culture "to the point of being uncouth to the uninitiated" (Sid, 1987). More than this, jugging reveals the sense of vocation, camaraderie, the links between work and leisure of many police—especially the young rookies who most commonly frequent the wet canteens. Such canteens appeared in the main stations from the mid-1960s. Like the police social clubs before them, they are a focus of an occupational community (though perhaps decreasingly so for married members who seek to divorce their leisure completely from work). Canteens provide a secure drinking place, free from being compromised in a public bar, and where outsiders could be invited on police terms. Understandably then, a majority of police surveyed in 1978 saw their canteens as having a good effect on both public and internal relations.

A wider sense of occupational community (in a workforce scattered throughout the country) has been maintained by national policing policies, the common experience of transfers, a headquarters monthly *Bulletin* distributed to all members, and especially by the activities and monthly journals of both the Police Association and the New Zealand section of the International Police Association. In sanctioning the formation of the Police Association, the

Minister recognized its value as a focus for collective feeling amongst a dispersed police, many of whom were then isolated in sole charge stations. Until the 1960s the Association's *Journal* provided extensive coverage of district and station news. From the late 1960s, this role has to some extent been taken over by the I.P.A. *Journal*, as the Association's *Newsletter* has focused more narrowly on industrial issues. Thus the triumphs and tribulations of one district engendered pride or a closing of ranks elsewhere.

Typical also of police elsewhere, there is a distinctive argot. In part it is a technical language for procedures, clients, and adversaries which binds together an occupational community, marking it off from outsiders. It also reveals an informal code, attitudes and practices which can shape frontline police work. Indeed "Disneyland" or "The Castle," as labels for police headquarters in Wellington, indicate the tensions within the occupational community—the perceived gap between the expectations of the bosses and the realities of street policing. Vocabulary and usage of slang is, of course, ever changing. Nonetheless, analysis of a recent compilation (*Copspeak 1*) suggests, speculatively, that the argot of the New South Wales and Victoria forces is comparatively richer than that of New Zealand, hinting at a more well-developed informal code, and possibly greater police deviance and social isolation.

Commonly observed of American and British police, a sense of social isolation is also felt amongst New Zealand police—though not universally. Just over half of the police surveyed in 1978 did not see their occupation as having had positive social effects on their spouses and families; rather the reverse. Shift work and irregular hours commonly disrupted family life, and restricted wider social activities. Some commented on the sense of isolation experienced by their wives, especially in country and small town stations. Others, by contrast, saw ready acceptance and a certain status as the policeman's wife, especially as higher ranks were achieved. Much depended on the husband's relationship with the local community. More commonly children of police faced some ostracism and harassment at school. Firm family friendships were disrupted by transfers to another station.

However, less than a third of those surveyed recalled being harassed off duty, or their family threatened. Again, some of those who had experienced such hostility were philosophical: harassment is the sort of thing one accepts; in a small town any policeman doing his job correctly has to face this sort of thing and grin and bear it, etc. Until the late 1970s, and then only in Wellington and Auckland, some of the new unmarried constables were housed in barracks. More usually, young unmarried rookies live in flats, often with nonmembers of the police. For their part, married personnel are scattered through the suburbs, seeking (like their neighbors) a private existence apart from work. Though often in police housing (until a change of policy in 1988), they are not concentrated in police colonies. Less than a fifth surveyed in 1978 felt that being a member of the police had had an adverse effect on their or their family's relationships with their neighbors.

Sporting activities, though difficult to pursue because of shift work and unpredictable hours, have served both to reinforce occupational consciousness and to break down social isolation. Before the relaxation of the liquor licensing laws from the 1970s, some sports clubs (notably golf with its 19th hole, and bowls) were avoided because of the prospect of illegal drinking. At some point in their careers, however, most of those surveyed in 1978 had participated in summer and winter sports, as well as in youth activities. Only a small minority (8 percent) had confined their sporting activities to police teams; 16 percent had been involved only in outside teams and two-thirds participated in both. Through their families, and in their leisure activities, most police become integrated into the community—increasingly seeking a world apart from the police. Nearly two-thirds of those surveyed with twenty-five years service (and hence generally aged 45 or older) had been involved in parent-teacher associations. A third had been members of working men's clubs. Many more were involved in a range of organizations, especially service clubs. As a consequence, a majority of New Zealand police (in the late 1970s at least) did not see themselves in conflict with the rest of society, despite the growth in public criticism.

It may be guessed that the balance of police attitudes in the recent years has probably altered from that revealed by a survey a decade earlier. In the face of continuing (if sectional) public criticism and greater workloads, increased pessimism seems likely. In 1978, 56 percent of those surveyed felt that public support had not changed or had improved during their service. The balance of opinion has probably reversed now. Moreover, attitudes towards the treatment of crime and offenders have probably hardened.

From this perspective, Association officials may find increasing rank and file support in their resolve to press their claims with positive action, if need be. Even so, the shift to shorter police careers through the advent of early retirement and optional disengagement, and the increasingly privatized nature of many police lives, may be tendencies that weaken police occupational cohesiveness in the future.

Rising status has not necessarily been accompanied by higher morale. Evidence for police morale is more ambiguous than that for social status. Pay and workload, while fundamental to morale, are not the only determinants. Perceptions of leadership, discipline, relationship with the media, and a sense of purpose and cohesion are all important influences. At any time the overall level of morale is a composite of a variety of attitudes to the job which are shaped by length of service, rank, type of work, and location (Chappell and Wilson, 1969). Ultimately, morale is "an observer's construct" (Reiner, 1978). It has to be inferred from a variety of indicators.

If an increasing stridency of police union rhetoric is indicative of declining morale, then the recent years could be viewed as a time of growing frustration and uncertainty for rank and file police personnel. Union advocates focused on the ever increasing workloads and need for more staff; the increased likelihood of assault and injury; the civilianization of police positions which had hitherto sheltered those who had lost fitness for the front line; a mounting sense of job insecurity with the reevaluation of ranks and positions in "Project Blueprint" (see above); and bosses who seemed less likely to support staff in the face of public complaints and the advent of an independent Police Complaints Authority in 1988. Symptomatic of the restiveness at some stations, police wives at Christchurch (the third largest city) formed a Police Families Action Group in May 1985 to press their husbands' claims for more staff and pay. In December 1985 a special conference of the New Zealand Police Association for the first time made preparations for industrial action to press its pay claim. Two years later the Auckland and Christchurch branches of the Police Association passed motions of no-confidence in the Minister of Police when she introduced legislation for a Police Complaints Authority. During the run-up to 1987 general election the Police Association pursued its campaign for more staff with hard-hitting advertisements and public meetings—thereby helping to make law and order a more prominent issue than ever before in New Zealand politics (Pratt, 1988; McLaughlin, 1987; *Newsletter*, June 1985, September and October 1987, May and August 1988). Yet the more outspoken rhetoric and overt lobbying since 1985 is a misleading guide to morale—it is more indicative of a new direction adopted by the New Zealand Police Association in pressing its claims.

Other evidence provides a different perspective on the level of police morale at the present time. Australian and New Zealand police attitudes surveyed in 1967-68 revealed that a majority of personnel in all the forces thought that the state of morale was no more than satisfactory. Only a minority thought it was poor. By comparison, New Zealand police seemed to be far more contented with their job than their counterparts in all the Australian forces, except for South Australia (Chappell and Wilson, 1969). There has been no comparable survey since. However, a survey of police attitudes in three Auckland divisions in 1983 concluded that almost half the respondents found their careers "meaningful and rewarding" and that officers generally showed "high self esteem." Though they grumbled about aspects of their work and their officers, the rank and file were not "suffering low morale, and giving grudging service to an ungrateful public" (*South Auckland Police Development Plan*, 1984).

That the level of morale in the early 1980s was no lower, but possibly higher, than it had been in the late 1960s is also suggested by the annual rate of voluntary resignations. This averaged 6.14 percent of the police between 1966 and 1969, but only 2.7 percent between 1981 and 1987. To some extent the lower rate of resignations in 1980s reflected the more attractive police pay and the greater difficulties of finding more satisfying jobs than twenty years earlier. Notably, in 1981—the year of civil turmoil accompanying the South African Rugby tour of New Zealand—the rate of resignations (3.30 percent) was lower than at any time since 1944. Absenteeism from work also fell sharply in 1981. Clearly, as a sense of purpose and camaraderie strengthened, morale rose—despite the profound divisions in the community and the stresses of policing. Absenteeism (as surveyed in the Auckland police) rose after 1981—especially amongst married men, and those over 44 years of age (*South Auckland Police Development Plan*, 1984). It may be that absenteeism is a better barometer of fluctuating morale than resignations. Though the ordinary resignation rate fell in the 1980s, the advent in 1985 of the Police Employment Rehabilitation Fund (PERF) opened the way for a growth in a new category of voluntary resignations. The PERF scheme provides for optional disengagement with generous lump sum payment for staff (with at least seven years service) whose health impairs their performance. The scheme is a concomitant of new physical and medical health standards for all ranks. But it was also envisaged that those who feel lagging enthusiasm for police work would henceforth be able to make an honorable and financially easier transition to civilian life (*Newsletter*, February 1985). Voluntary disengagements on physical, medical or psychological grounds rose sharply from 39 in 1985 to 199 in 1990. Nearly 70 percent of the 753 voluntary disengagements between 1985 and 1990 were primarily on psychological grounds (with a majority involving stress-related conditions). Most of the disengagements were sought by police aged in their mid-thirties, with an average of fourteen years service (Miller and Ford, 1991). However, the significance of this trend is ambiguous. Voluntary resignations by the traditional method decreased at a reciprocal rate to the increase of voluntary disengagements (by the new avenue). Thus, overall, the combined rate of resignations and disengagements (by the new avenue) between 1985 and 1990 (annually averaging 4.52 percent of police) was only a little higher than the average annual rate of voluntary resignations during 1970. If the discontented (as well as disabled) have been leaving more readily since 1985, the overall level of morale as well as mental and physical health of those remaining should have been higher. Yet the rising trend of optional disengagements can be seen as mirroring the growing stridency of union rhetoric from 1985, suggesting that morale may have continued to fall.

UNIONS AND ASSOCIATIONS

In 1988 there were three organizations representing most of the employees of the New Zealand Police Department. Virtually all the 5,100 constables and noncommissioned officers belonged to the New Zealand Police Association, formed in 1936. All commissioned officers, apart from the Commissioner, were members of the New Zealand Police Officers' Guild which was registered in 1955, but not effectively active until ten years later. (The Guild has no full-time paid officials, but rather has paid the Police Association for research and advocacy.) The unsworn civilian employees of the Department comprised 15.4 percent of the police workforce in 1987. They were then under the jurisdiction of the State Services Commission, and most were thus members of the monolithic Public Service Association (PSA)—the main union for public servants (including, for example, prison and traffic officers).

With the major reorganization of the public service under the State Sector Act (1988), the Commissioner became a Chief Executive with greater responsibility for his civilian staff who had a system of industrial relations differing from that of the sworn personnel. Consequently, he has sought to have his unsworn staff (now expanding with the process of civilianization) brought more directly under his control by making them members of police under the Police Act. Reluctantly the Police Association has agreed to open its membership to civilian staff holding positions equivalent to the rank of senior sergeant and below. (The Police Officers' Guild will accept civilians in positions equivalent to those held by commissioned officers.) This acceptance is symptomatic of a wider process of change in the Police Association from a service organization to an industrial union.

In New Zealand parlance (before major institutional changes in labor relations occurred in 1987-88), none of the organizations representing police staff were strictly unions. They were (and the Police Association and the Officers' Guild remain) incorporated societies whose membership was voluntary, and whose agreements with their state employers were (and for the police continue to be) not legally enforceable. By contrast, unions, registered under a succession of acts since 1894 (presently the Labor Relations Act 1987), secure compulsory membership and awards (collective agreements) enforceable by a Labor Court. This structure of industrial relations was completely overturned by the Employment Contract Act of 1991. Its consequences for police were not clear at the time of writing.

From the outset then, organizations representing the sworn staff have had an ambiguous status—like police unions elsewhere. Indeed, by comparison with British and Australian experience, police unionism came late to New Zealand. An attempt to form a police association was suppressed in 1913. Membership of the Public

Service Association was permitted in 1919 for constables and non-commissioned officers, but ended in 1922 when the PSA proved unwilling to make a special case for police exemption from public service pay cuts. Henceforth, until 1936, Commissioners were supported by Ministers in discountenancing any moves at rank and file organization (Holland, 1977; Meltzer, 1943). With the advent of the first Labor government in 1935 the climate changed: a deputation to the Minister in charge of Police secured ready approval for an association. Indeed the Minister urged all police (except the commissioned officers) to join so that an agreement regarding working conditions and remuneration could be arrived (*New Zealand Police Journal*, February, 1937).

That the Association was not a union was subsequently made explicit by the Minister. He spoke of the "vital difference"between members of the police and workers in "trade and industry," and that the formation of the Association could "only be justified up to the point that the Police Force differs from the Army" (Fraser, 1942). Not surprisingly then, other objects besides the improvement of working conditions and welfare of members were prominent in the rules of the Police Association (and later the Police Officers' Guild), namely: to maintain discipline, increase efficiency, and "foster a feeling of amity and good fellowship throughout the Police Service." The Association might aim to be the "official channel of communication" between its members and both the Minister and Commissioner. But it was so de facto rather than de jure. Until the definition in 1954 of a service organization to participate in a short-lived Police Council, there was no statutory recognition of the Association: it was simply approved by the Minister and police regulations were amended to make membership lawful. In fact, recognition and degree of consultation have continued to be on the Ministers' and Commissioners' terms which have varied. Until 1968, the rules of the Association prohibited it from affiliating with any other organization. And in practice it has acted independently of the other public service organizations, apart from the Officers' Guild.

From the outset until 1985 at least, a conception of the special status of police officers as public officers, not employees, shaped the ground rules of collective bargaining. Bound by an oath to uphold the law and maintain the peace, the police, as an Association guide asserted in 1984, have a special legal and constitutional responsibility that excludes direct industrial action. Conversely, their special importance to the community made them a special case in considering pay and other conditions of employment—entitled to the serious respect and attention of the most senior levels of Government. As a "service organization" rather than a union, the Association operates in defense of its interests on a political and public rather than on an industrial plane. Also implied was a larger conception of the Association's role: a professional concern with "policing policies" as well as protecting "the rights and welfare of its members" (*Welfare Guide,* 1984). How then has the role of the New Zealand police unions developed in practice?

Despite the hope that the Association would be a source of ideas to improve the "work and efficiency of the force" (Fraser, 1942), the Association has not been an advocate of administrative and operational innovation. Its primary role has been that of a union rather than of a professional association—with its emphasis on protecting and improving its members' welfare, rather than developing "standards of responsible performance" and strongly supporting "organisational efforts to enforce them" (Bayley, 1985). Thus the Association has opposed policies seen as adversely affecting its members, for example: changes in promotion criteria and procedures, civilianization, and station closures. In July 1988 it formally withdrew its cooperation with the major administrative changes associated with "Project Blueprint."

More broadly and publicly, the Association has voiced rank and file opposition to policies proposed or supported by Ministers, especially where the Commissioner has remained silent or acquiescent. In the mid-1980s, such policies included "user pays" for some police services, sponsorship of police vehicles, part-time policing, and the establishment of a Police Complaints Authority. Where the Government accepted the findings of the Royal Commission into the Thomas case (in 1980), and the Commissioner felt constraints in being openly critical, the Police Association and the Officers' Guild sought a judicial review. Most prominent between 1984 and 1987 was the campaign by the Association for a substantial increase in police staff. In 1986-87, the $99,960 spent on the staffing campaign amounted to 8.9 percent of the Association's expenditure. Its tactics emulated those of other pressure groups. Since the mid-1970s Association advocates have shown an increasing readiness to use the media as an instrument of pressure in opposing policies or pressing claims. Indeed, in 1985, the Minister of Police expressed "genuine anxiety over the airing of...domestic police issues in the media." To an Association branch which had shown a readiness to speak out, she expressed the hope that "the media is not and never will be your primary method of communication with your minister...or, for that matter, with the commissioner" (*Press*, Christchurch, 6 July 1985).

Defense of members' rights and welfare is not, of course, incompatible with the pursuit of efficiency, as the staffing campaign underlined. In fact, the Association's public perspective on staffing policies has generally emphasized issues of morale, the effective use of resources, and the need to maintain community support. More specifically, the Association has had a significant role to play in the maintenance of discipline, on which efficiency depends. From its earliest days the Management Committee of the Association has granted, at its discretion, legal assistance to members faced with either disciplinary or criminal charges rising out of their employment with the police. The degree of assistance depends on the "merits of the case and in particular, the conduct of the member" (*Welfare Guide*, 1984). Such assistance amounted to 12.6 percent of Association expenditure in 1986-87, and an exceptional 24.6 percent of expenditure in 1987-88 occasioned by the costly but successful defense of eight members who faced criminal charges of kidnap and assault (*New Zealand Police Association Annual Report*, 1988). In 1941 the Association secured (from the Minister) the right of the rank and file to elect their representative to the disciplinary Appeal Board. Such a move had been seen by the Commissioner as potentially subversive of discipline. The reverse was the case. What could be a harsh regime was mitigated somewhat by Association support for its members. Fears of its capriciousness were lessened by the participation of rank and file representatives. More than this, the mechanisms that the Association has provided for the airing and resolution of individual grievances have helped to maintain belief in "'the system,' especially in the absence of formal disputes procedures" (*Newsletter*, 1986). Above all, perhaps, has been the role of the Association leadership, until 1985 at least, in defusing the impulse to militancy which stirred more frequently amongst the rank and file from the mid-1970s (*Newsletter*, July 1982).

Such restiveness again parallels developments abroad amongst rank and file police, and the reasons are similar. Threats of militancy from the New Zealand police have accompanied protracted negotiations over pay demands (in 1976, 1979, and 1985-86). Where, in the buoyant 1950s and early 1960s, dissatisfaction with pay was underscored by a rising rate of resignations, such an individualistic response became less attractive with economic recession and growing unemployment from 1975. As in Britain, moreover, anxiety at the growing danger and difficulty of police work heightened the sense that the police should be a special case at a time of government belt-tightening—and be treated generously in terms of human resources and pay. To some extent, as in Britain, there has also been the demonstration effect of growing industrial and political militancy which has tended to erode commitment to institutionalized and established channels of negotiation, most clearly since 1975 (Reiner, 1978).

Until 1985, rank and file restiveness was constrained by successful Association advocacy. Indeed the decade from 1976 could be seen as the Association's heyday in its initiatives on pay and conditions. Significant pay increases, beyond the guidelines for the rest of the public service, were won in 1976 and 1986. A review of allowances in 1977 and 1978 was followed by an increase in salary margins in 1979. Surveys of hours of work in 1980 and 1985 brought substantial gains in salary loadings for overtime and penal time. By 1982 an hours of work agreement had been negotiated. In 1979, Association advocacy secured a government subsidized insurance scheme that then gave, for a nominal contribution, generous lump sum coverage for death or disability resulting from police work. A sick leave bank was achieved in the following year. During the same period, two organizations allied to the Police Association (the Benevolent and Welfare Fund and the Police and Families Credit Union) offered a developing range of services. The crowning achievement, persistently pressed for from 1981, was the early retirement and optional disengagement scheme implemented in 1985 (Butterworth, 1985; *Welfare Guide*, 1984).

Such success depended in only a small part on the occasional threat of militancy. Suggestions of police industrial action in 1984, for example, were publicly dismissed by the National Secretary of the Association as "not a police thing" and "not consistent with our responsibility to the public" (*Press*, Christchurch, 1 September,

1984). Self-denial of the right to strike was seen as strengthening the Association's hand in its negotiations. It looked for a special relationship with the police administration in settling changes to pay and conditions of service that would be pressed conjointly on the government (Moodie, 1988). Ultimately, also, the government would have to accept, and generally did, that the police were a special case. Such a position required advocacy that became increasingly sophisticated, epitomized by the growth in full-time Association staff (from three in 1976 to 25 by 1985) and in their budget for research and publicity.

Much, in fact, has depended on the personality and abilities of the Association's chief negotiator—its full-time National Secretary. Traditionally, this position had been filled by a person with legal training and from outside the police. During 1976-85, the National Secretary was a former police inspector who had become a university law lecturer: Dr. R. A. Moodie combined an insider's knowledge with wider political insights and a readiness to speak out. He was the chief architect of the Association's initiatives—especially those for early retirement and optional disengagement, and for appointing an examiner of police procedures and practices. In 1983 he secured Association participation in a government review of police personnel policy. When the National Government proved slow to implement its recommendations, Moodie exploited the opportunity of the 1984 snap election by getting the commitment of the Labour Party to do so. Equally important was the rapport he developed with two Commissioners (though not a third). From this flowed regular consultation and often joint action to secure government consent to agreed policies.

The close working relationship between the Association and the police administration began to weaken from about 1982. Partly it was a question of personalities and approach: the National Secretary found difficulties in working with a Deputy Commissioner who eventually headed the police administration. Partly also the deteriorating relationship reflected mounting pressure on the police administration to make cuts or act more parsimoniously at a time of economic stringency. And within the Association itself there were changing attitudes, apparent in a growing readiness to contemplate industrial action.

The effect of such tendencies on the established pattern of police industrial relations can be illustrated by events surrounding protracted pay negotiations in 1985-86. As was typical of pay negotiations from the 1960s, the Association was joined by the Guild as the junior partner. Their joint claim in September 1985 was for a basic salary increase of 26.8 percent together with improved payments for overtime and penal time. Such a claim was seen as necessary to reestablish relativities with other public servants eroded since 1976, as well as to more adequately compensate for the "demands and pressures of the job" (*New Zealand Herald*, 17 September 1985). Typically, it was scaled down after negotiations with the police administration which (in line with established practice) presented an agreed claim to the Government.

The first response from the Government's control departments of Treasury and the State Services Commission was severe: a nil increase in basic salary on the grounds that no recruitment or retention problems were apparent. Resentment that the unique position of the police had not been acknowledged led quickly to a special conference of National Councillors of the Police Association. In an unprecedented move, they decided upon a program of industrial action if negotiations failed (The Guild stood aloof from this). Significantly, the Association did not contemplate taking a case for arbitration to the Police Staff Tribunal, an avenue available since 1965, but rarely used. Instead the Commissioner was warned that if there was no reasonable response to the claim, the National Councillors' resolutions would be put before Association meetings in the Districts for endorsement. Nonetheless the Government responded with a 5 percent offer. This was rejected by the Association negotiators as totally inadequate, but accepted by the Commissioner who urged the rank and file (through a video) to do likewise. The united front of Commissioner and service organizations had broken down. Angry meetings followed in the Districts: motions of no confidence in the Commissioner and Minister were passed; and immediate industrial action was urged.

Here the role of Dr. Moodie, as chief negotiator, was significant. In the face of growing impatience and threats of wildcat action from some Districts, he postponed issuing a formal notice of industrial action until the Government had reconsidered its offer. With the Commissioner once again adopting the role as intermediary, an acceptable compromise was reached between the Minister and Moodie. Once again the government conceded that the police were a special case. But just in time, it seems. Association Councillors were insisting on action which would have blocked the police computer system (*Newsletter*, January 1986; Ansley, 1986; *New Zealand Times*, 22 December 1985; *Press*, Christchurch, 11, 20, 22, and 25 January 1986).

Throughout, the Association officials argued that their proposed industrial action did not breach the police oath. "We have to tip-toe around (it)," observed the Association president (*The Star*, Christchurch, 10 January 1986). Law and order would be maintained. However "all non-police and administrative duties" would be progressively shed. All work done by civilians would be refused, as would enforcement of the traffic laws, any work involving the computer, and filing reports. Naturally, this argument did not impress the Government. A blunt warning was given at the end of the negotiations. The Attorney-General issued a legal opinion which the Commissioner circulated to all sworn personnel. Given the police oath, any industrial action by the police "is plainly unlawful" and "imperils the rule of law itself," declared the Attorney-General. To which the Commissioner added that even limited police industrial action would have "serious consequences" for both the organization and individual members (Palmer, 1986b). The threat of legal sanctions has not, however, quashed the impulse to militancy.

Indeed the experience of the 1985-86 pay negotiations can be seen as signalling a new direction in the development of Association attitudes and their expression. So too did the appointment of an industrial advocate in 1985 to eventually take over this aspect of Dr. Moodie's role as National Secretary. The appointee was an experienced blue-collar trade unionist who believes the Association should be more of a union in its outlook and methods, and develop links with other unions (Harvey, 1988). To this end, he sees the primary goal of the Association as being the eventual negotiation and introduction of a police industrial award. Also important is the introduction of an independent disputes resolution procedure to hear complaints and hand down impartial decisions binding on both parties (*Newsletter*, October 1985). Despite the Attorney-General's warning against police industrial action, the Association's industrial advocate does not disavow it. Clearly, if they have to, the police workers will "bite with whatever industrial teeth they can find" (*Newsletter*, August 1986). Stronger links have been developed with the Australasian Police Federation, with the

New Zealand Police Association's industrial advocate becoming a member of the Federation's Industrial Planning Committee. This committee is to exchange ideas and "plan industrial initiatives" (*Newsletter*, December 1988). With the industrial advocate's prodding, the Association has made moves to affiliate with the New Zealand Council of Trade Unions, a federation of the main private and public sector unions. Most significantly perhaps, the Association has become more willing to exploit its political clout in the context of law and order politics. This was particularly the case with its vigorous "1000 More Police" campaign in the run-up to the 1987 election (In fact the re-elected Labour Government resented police politicking and made few concessions). The industrial advocate was more ready than his predecessors to articulate rank and file anxieties about "liberal views and their consequences for policing" (*Press*, Christchurch, 28 September 1988).

In the late 1980s it seemed likely that police industrial relations would become even more confrontational than hitherto. Certainly the police system of industrial relations remains institutionally distinctive. The Attorney-General's admonition against police militancy was used effectively by the Association to secure police exemption from those parts of the State Sector Act (1988) which brought public-sector industrial relations in line with those of the business world. Nonetheless the state sector reforms make the Commissioner, like other departmental heads, act more directly as the employer in determining pay and conditions within an allotted budget (Harvey, 1988). For the immediate future at least, the Commissioner will have to trade-off pay increases for staff numbers. Moreover the very privileged arrangements of leave for state sector union officials are no longer seen as justified by the State Services Commission (and implicitly, the Government). That police industrial action is indeed illegal "has never been tested," the industrial advocate has warned: "If police have to choose between some kind of blind oath and the destruction of the organization which protects them, they may see their options differently (*Press*, Christchurch, 5 and 25 November 1988). The future will thus reveal the extent to which union attitudes have indeed permeated the rank and file. The cohesiveness of police occupational consciousness remains to be fully tested.

PUBLIC CONFIDENCE, TRUST, AND RESTRAINTS ON THE POLICE

In a poll published early in 1988, 51.3 percent of the respondents said they had full trust and confidence in the New Zealand police. Indeed the police topped the poll, being the only institution which had the trust and confidence of more than half of the respondents. Even so the degree of esteem for the police, as for all other institutions surveyed, has fallen consistently and markedly from the 63.9 percent who expressed confidence in 1975 when regular polls began. Significantly the medical profession who had held first place in public esteem in 1975 were ranked second in 1988 (with 45 percent declaring their trust) (Swanton, Hannington, and Psaila, 1985; *Press*, Christchurch, 3 March 1988).

In an age when institutions of authority are apparently regarded much more critically than at any time in the recent past, the police might seem to have fared reasonably well in terms of public respect. Certainly police administrators in the 1970s and 1980s have drawn some comfort from the poll results, while noting the decline.

Even so, the regular surveys of faith in public institutions are implicitly comparative. And when viewed in abstraction from the reality of individual experience, the police rank relatively highly as could be expected of the most visible symbol of state authority. As an institution, it is the focus of less media criticism and popular cynicism than Parliament, trade unions, or indeed the media itself, which all ranked near the bottom of the poll of public confidence. The police are seen as more immediately relevant to most people's lives than Churches; apparently better able to maintain the mystique of professionalism, power, and service than doctors or lawyers; and (for Europeans at least) less the focus of those dissatisfied with outcomes in the justice system than the courts. The standing of the New Zealand police is also higher than the road traffic enforcement officers of the Ministry of Transport whose activities are more likely to be seen as irksome rather than helpful by many males. Indeed the minimal New Zealand police responsibility for traffic control has been seen as contributing to its relatively higher public standing than Australian police who suffer the resentment of motorists. Perhaps most importantly: by comparison with some forces across the Tasman, the New Zealand Police has maintained an image of freedom from corruption. So far as the suspicion of bribe-taking is concerned, there is little evidence that the high level of trust in this aspect of police integrity, revealed by a survey in 1968, has changed in the last 20 years (Chappell and Wilson, 1969).

Other recent surveys focusing on the New Zealand police in isolation from other institutions reveal a less positive expression of confidence: only 42 percent of respondents in 1987 (43 percent in 1980/81) had a "great deal of confidence" in the police, 42 percent had "only some confidence" (40 percent in 1980); nine percent had "hardly any" or no confidence (nine percent in 1980); seven percent did not know (eight percent in 1980) (The Royal Commission on Social Policy, April 1988; Department of Statistics, 1984). Quite a significant shift has occurred in the nature and degree of public confidence from the late 1960s. In a 1968 poll 72 percent of respondents expressed "great respect" for the police; 19 percent had "mixed feelings," and only six percent declared they had little respect (Chappell and Wilson, 1969). Not simply a decline of confidence had occurred by the 1980s; the large minority expressing only "some confidence" in the police indicated a much greater ambivalence than hitherto.

Of course, such bald statistics conceal a diversity of public feeling: not merely as between distinct social groups, but also within such groups and even within individual perceptions of the police. The broad patterns of esteem parallel those to be found in other similar societies. Typically, surveys since the 1960s show youth to have far less confidence in the police (only 25 percent of respondents under 30 years of age said they had a "great deal of confidence" in the 1987 poll). Typical also of ethnic minorities elsewhere, Maoris as a group are much less likely to express confidence in the police (31 percent having a "great deal" of confidence, 46 percent "only some"; and 18 percent "hardly any" or none—the percentages for Europeans being 43 percent, 42 percent, and eight percent respectively in 1987). Overall, males are less likely to express confidence than females, and city dwellers less trusting than those in medium-sized towns or in rural areas. Gender, geography, age, and race clearly influence the likelihood and nature of encounters with the police. Victims and defendants are less likely than others to show a "great deal" of confidence. However, the level of trust is not shaped merely by encounters with the police. In the 1987 survey, a third of the respondents in administrative and managerial occupations said they had been a victim of crime in the preceding 12 months. Yet they expressed noticeably more confidence in the police than did those in the professional/technical category of whom a quarter had been victims. Amongst the highly paid at least, the level of cynicism towards the police increases with the level of education (The Royal Commission on Social Policy, April 1988; Department of Statistics, 1984; Chappell and Wilson, 1969).

What then are the sources of this equivocal confidence? Police surveys in various districts during 1987-88 revealed that 71 percent to 91 percent of the respondents were satisfied with police performance in response to calls for service. Conversely, a substantial majority in a national survey were dissatisfied with police performance in terms of crime prevention—with dissatisfaction being greatest in Auckland (the largest city), amongst males, and those under 24 years of age (*Annual Report,* 1988). A broad pessimism about police performance of traditionally conceived roles thus underpins declining public confidence. More than this, various events "destroyed some of the old certainties about the police" (Palmer, 1986a). In particular the "on-going saga" of the A. A. Thomas case during the 1970s, culminating in a Royal Commission of Inquiry (1980) into the circumstances of his convictions for murder, "severely undermined" public confidence in the integrity of individual police and some of their practices (Wood, 1985). The Royal Commission found the arrest and prosecution of A. A. Thomas not justified; that some errors of practice had been made; and especially that evidence had been falsified (Report of the Royal Commission, 1980). Police shootings of three Maoris (in 1976, 1983, and 1986) also caused considerable disquiet.

Amongst youth and Maoris in particular, there is clearly a more general distrust of the police based on a variety of individual encounters and peer attitudes. Tensions and conflict between police and male youths have been longstanding (Chappell and Wilson, 1969) though probably becoming more evident from the 1950s as the behavior of rapidly growing numbers of teenagers increasingly challenged prevailing norms. Theft, property damage, rowdiness in the streets, underage (under 20-year-olds drinking in public bars, and (from the late 1960s) demonstrations, gang conflict, and drugs brought ever increasing numbers of young people to police attention. Between the late 1960s and the mid-1980s, people under 21 years of age comprised between 55 percent and 61 percent of those apprehended. A cohort study revealed that of those born in 1954-55, 13.3 percent of the boys (40.1 percent of Maori and 10.3 percent of non-Maori boys) and 4.3 percent of the girls (16.7 percent of Maori and 2.8 percent of non-Maori girls) had appeared in the Children's Court at least once by their seventeenth birthday. Many more were dealt informally with warnings or referral to other agencies by the Police Youth Aid Section. While children might well find Youth Aid personnel firm but fair, youths on the street more commonly found the uniformed patrol officers brusque and unfair—as a controversial legal comic, Streetwise, made clear (Mooney, 1971a; Department of Social Welfare, 1973; *Annual Report*, 1978; *Digest of Statistics*, 1985; Christchurch Community Law Centre, 1987). Youthful experience taught many that despite the professional image of policing, police behavior was, in fact, often shaped by one's status and demeanor. Youthful cynicism also shaped adult attitudes—especially those of Maoris and of the white liberal elite in the 1980s.

Between 1967 and 1972, student protests intensified against New Zealand's participation in the Vietnam War, American military presence in New Zealand, and rugby contacts with South Africa. Younger Maori in Nga Tamatoa (formed in 1970) initiated demonstrations against the annual celebration of the Treaty of Waitangi. Various incidents engendered a chorus of complaint from protestors. In particular, police dispersal of a demonstration against the visit of U. S. Vice President, Spiro Agnew, in 1970 became the focus of the Ombudsman's first major inquiry into police conduct (*Special Report of the Ombudsman*, 1970). In an attempt to forestall further severe criticism, new general instructions were issued shortly after the Ombudsman reported, emphasizing low-key police procedures in dealing with demonstrations. With some notable exceptions, this remained the police approach until the Springbok Rugby Tour of 1981. Then the appearance of escort groups (popularly known as riot squads) with visored helmets and long batons appeared to symbolize a "harder line" (Meyrick, 1984).

Experiences during the mass demonstrations against the Springbok rugby tour in 1981 changed the attitudes of many mature adults as well as youths in the white, liberal, well-educated middle class who had formerly had little contact with the police. As one demonstrator, a female teacher, typically put it: "Initially during the tour I was not anti-police but after finding myself in the middle of the Rintoul Street incident on 29 August, I began to see the police as dangerous and partisan...." (King and Phillips, 1982). In the long term, the experiences of the protest movement, especially in 1981, raised more publicly than hitherto issues of civil liberties and of police accountability.

So too did the experiences of Maori youth who, particularly in gangs (apparent in Auckland by 1970) or as street kids, were to be the focus of increasing media and police attention. By 1971, 60 percent of the Maori population was under 20 years of age, and was thus proportionately much more likely than the less youthful Pakeha (European) population to come in contact with the police. In fact 62 percent of the Maoris dealt with by the police were under 21 in 1984 (compared with 54 percent of Europeans (*Digest of Statistics*, 1985). During the 1960s and 1970s the disparity between the Maori and non-Maori rates of youth coming to official notice rose from 4:1 to nearly 6:1. And what was true of Maori youth was true also of adult rates of offending (Fifield and Donnell, 1980) Until the early 1970s, explanations to account for the racial difference focused on the impact of rapid urbanization, cultural conflict, socioeconomic factors, and the accuracy of racial classification in statistics (Department of Social Welfare, 1973).

Since the early 1970s Maori explanations of the disparities have increasingly emphasized the institutionally racist processes of a monocultural criminal justice system—seen especially in police decisions to prosecute (Race Relations Conciliator, 1982; Jackson, 1988). A sample of first offenders studied in Auckland in the early 1970s revealed that Maori youths were more likely to be prosecuted than non-Maori youths (Hampton, 1975). From 1974, the activities of the high profile Auckland Task Force sharpened the perception of selective policing amongst Maoris and Pacific Islanders who comprised two-thirds of those arrested in the first three months of its operations. Formed to deal firmly with an upsurge in street disorder and violence associated with hotels, the aggressive style of Team Policing (as the Task Force was renamed when similar units were formed in the other main centers) became the focus public criticism of police behavior, especially from Maoris (Dallow, 1974; Auckland Committee on Racism and Discrimination Task Force, 1975; Tait, 1978; *Report of the Ministerial Committee of Inquiry into Violence*, 1987). With minor public order offenses in particular, there is a widespread perception amongst Maoris that the police prosecute such charges against young Maori men in a prejudiced and racially-biased way (Jackson, 1988). Indeed, an Advisory Committee on Legal Services reported in 1986 that "frustration and anger about the police is very high within many Maori communities. Allegations were made of physical, verbal, and racial abuse, which resulted in Maori people being arrested and convicted" (*Te Whainga i Te Tika*, 1986; Jackson, 1988).

Ironically, a decline in public confidence has occurred, until the late 1980s at least, despite more concerted attempts by the police to enhance it by emphasizing greater professionalism and sensitivity to cultural differences in performance and by undertaking increasingly sophisticated efforts at public relations. From the mid-1950s, relationships with the media came to be seen as pivotal in maintaining public esteem. Hitherto police administrators had a long tradition of secretiveness, suspicion, and clumsy handling of the press. This began to change with the advent of a civilian Controller-General of Police. He quickly sought to encourage "open channels of communication" by appointing a civilian Public Relations Officer in 1955 (later renamed Press then Media Liaison to more accurately describe the role). Better publicity would, it was hoped, "bring the police closer to the people" (*Annual Report*, 1956). More frequent press conferences began in the main city police stations; an enhanced image of the police was now actively promoted through recruitment campaigns; newly established dog sections gave public displays; police personnel were encouraged to accept invitations to address groups; and talks in schools began. Epitomizing a softer image to be projected, the word "Force" was dropped from the formal title of the New Zealand Police.

From 1961 a new Commissioner gave public relations a high priority: being more accessible to the press than his predecessors; issuing a "policeman's creed" which emphasized good relations with the public; mounting "Operation Clean-up" to "weed out the bully" from police ranks; and establishing (short-lived) public relations committees at Headquarters and in the districts. Thus a majority of the police surveyed in 1968 felt that public opinion of them had improved in the preceding decade, and that "better public relations" was the main reason for the change (Chappell and Wilson, 1969).

From the late 1960s nonetheless, there were signs of increasing tensions in police public relations as public order seemed to deteriorate: in popular parlance, the "bobby" or "cops" became the "fuzz" or "pigs." Indeed, if there was a single dominant theme in the weekly current affairs program, *Gallery*, on New Zealand television during 1970, it was the relationship between the police and the public. All but one of the items was critical—especially those that dealt with police handling of demonstrators and Maori gangs in Auckland (Edwards, 1972). Significantly, the *Gallery* programs marked a new readiness amongst journalists and editors in the state-run broadcasting system to question police policies and behavior. Henceforth the television image of the New Zealand police became more ambiguous.

Awareness of growing strains in police public relations led to new initiatives on the part of the police. Paralleling developments in Britain and Australia, a pilot Juvenile Crime Prevention scheme had begun in 1957. This expanded into the Youth Aid Section (from 1968) in which community relations became an increasingly important aspect. *My Friend the Policeman*, for example, entitled both a book and record which summed up increased efforts from the late 1960s to both "keep ourselves safe" and to dispel the image of police as "bogeymen" amongst the young. Talks in schools and station tours were expanded from 1969 though their effectiveness was not evaluated. From 1976, after consultation with the Department of Education, a new Law Related Education Program was developed with more clearly defined objectives, a new curriculum, and specially trained police personnel. By 1986 the Law-Related Education Program had become a separate section within a recently created Public Affairs directorate. Though their effectiveness remains unevaluated, police education officers are now seen to play a key role in developing an understanding of law and policing amongst primary (elementary) school children.

In August 1970 Commissioner Sharp expressed concern at "the now regular accusations" of "unjustified force" used by police. "A good police service," he reminded his staff, "protects minorities, whether racial, religious, or social." To maintain the good name of police and earn public support, erring personnel would face charges in court if need be (*Bulletin*, August 1970). When a sergeant was indeed convicted of assaulting an insolent 14-year-old boy in 1973, the case proved controversial, with considerable public (but not press) support for police summary justice. However the "father figure of the old-time policeman who kicked bottoms and cuffed ears" had now gone (according to Commissioner Burnside) "because the society which accepted him no longer existed" (*Press*, Christchurch, 27 July 1973; 10 April 1975). Such a "softly, softly approach" was deprecated by some older policemen who took pride in "never backing down," and continued to be ignored by many rookies despite their training (Tait, 1978).

While referring explicitly to the handling of demonstrators, Commissioner Sharp's remarks also reflected an increased sensitivity about police relationships with Maoris and Pacific Islanders. Symptomatic was the formation, from 1971 in Auckland, of Joint ('J') Teams of Maori Affairs Department personnel, voluntary social workers, and police (generally Maori or Pacific Island in background). This was an attempt to avoid the authoritarian approach in dealing with mainly Maori gangs and street kids. The Teams looked to defuse conflict amongst gangs and initiate community action regarding "undesirable youth activity." In individual cases and specific gang confrontations, the Teams did effective work, especially in Wellington. Indeed some critics of the Auckland Task Force saw in the 'J' Teams a potential substitute in "genuinely preventive" policing (*Press*, Christchurch, 21 October 1974). Where the policing of gangs was concerned, however, a less "authoritarian" approach did not necessarily have majority support: 70 percent of Maoris surveyed in South Auckland in 1983 thought that the police were "not hard enough" on gangs (*South Auckland Police Development Plan*, 1984). In 1981 police involvement in 'J' Teams ceased: interdepartmental cooperation proved difficult to sustain; and (to police administrators at least) the six Teams seemed relatively ineffective when set against the broad canvas of mounting disorder and delinquency (*Bulletin*, September 1975; October 1976; February 1979; December 1981).

More enduring initiatives coincided with, or flowed eventually from, the visit abroad in 1972 by a Chief Inspector to study the relationships between police and ethnic minorities in the U.S.A., England, and the Netherlands. On his return he examined the employment of Maoris and Pacific Islanders in the New Zealand police and the attitudes held by police and ethnic minorities towards each other (Jamieson, 1973, and 1974). Simultaneously, police training began to place even greater emphasis on community/race relations and tackle more explicitly racial prejudice amongst recruits. From 1973 efforts were made to increase the representation of Maoris and Pacific Islanders: within three years they comprised 70 out of 1,100 police in the Auckland district. Achieving greater public cooperation and respect was the theme of a police corporate planning seminar held in March 1975. Again the need to inculcate professional attitudes and behavior was emphasized; to this end an information guide was issued to personnel in 1976. Also from the planning seminar's recommendations came the first Community Relations Coordinators who were appointed in the main centers in 1976. They had the broad brief to establish and maintain mutual trust and understanding between the police and the people.

Liaison was the chief function of the Community Relations Coordinators: not just with different social groups and organizations, but also with the specialized personnel within the police (especially Youth Aid, 'J' Teams, Crime Prevention, Press Liaison, and Community Constables) to ensure a concerted effort in securing public acceptance and cooperation. Thus police relations with the Maori and Pacific Island communities was not the sole focus of this increased community relations activity. Initially, however, it was a dominant focus, especially in Auckland where the first Community Relations Coordinator had been in charge of the controversial Task Force. He soon established contacts with Pacific Island community and church leaders and sought closer links with the local Maori communities by visiting *marae* (meeting places which are the centers of tribal life). However, a study of the South Auckland Community Relations Coordinator's activity in 1983 found that direct community liaison occupied very little of his time which was largely consumed by office work (*South Auckland Police Development Plan,* 1984). With the growing emphasis on more broadly based community crime prevention schemes by the mid-1980s, liaison with the Maori and Pacific Island communities was probably more reactive than close and continuing. Thus the extent to which effective relationships of mutual trust had been established is not clear. Much obviously depended on individuals.

An increasingly concerted effort at public relations failed to prevent an erosion in the overall level of public confidence in the police, especially amongst youth and Maoris. Sixty percent of Maoris surveyed in 1987 thought that police liaison with their communities was "inadequate"; a similar proportion thought police attitudes "prejudicial" towards Maori offenders. However a majority, even amongst Maori youth, thought that the police youth aid work was "adequate." Clearly the varied nature of their individual contacts with the police, together with "shared experiences and perceptions" of past events, shaped Maori attitudes much more profoundly than any public relations campaign (Jackson, 1988; *South Auckland Police Development Plan*, 1984). Until the beginning of a decentralized community policing scheme in a multicultural urban area in November 1988, police community relations was largely cosmetic and a one-way process, seeking to make centralized policing more effective by securing public cooperation with predetermined goals and strategies. Community liaison activity by a growing number of specialized staff did not necessarily bring greater sensitivity to cultural differences, either in police policy-making, or in the day-to-day behavior of frontline staff. Thus, in the late 1970s at least, the beneficial possibilities of closer contacts by community relations personnel could be, and indeed were, undermined by the impact of particular police operations. This was especially the case with a number of operations in Auckland soon after the first Community Relations Coordinator was appointed. In particular, the police tactics initially adopted (without community liaison) during an operation in October 1976 to round up illegal immigrants, together with the insensitive attitudes expressed, proved to be immediately controversial. So too was the fact that the Commissioner had acceded to a Ministerial "request" for "positive action" against "overstayers," and that the police focused on those of Pacific Island origin (Fleming and Silk, 1976). The policing of the "Overstayer issue" remained long in the collective memory of the Pacific Island communities and also of civil libertarians.

More than a decade of policy initiatives designed to improve police relationships with ethnic minorities had, it seemed, little real impact amongst the opinion-formers. In 1987 an influential Ministeral Committee of Inquiry accepted the reiterated complaint of ethnic insensitivity levelled at the police. It recommended that the Department set up a Cultural Perspective Advisory Group to develop "an appreciation of, and positive response to, different cultures" and especially Maori customs (*Report of the Ministerial Inquiry into Violence*, 1987).

This recommendation was but one aspect of the wider issue of police accountability which was rarely raised before the late 1970s, then spasmodically, before being given wider currency by the Springbok Rugby Tour of 1981. Questions about the control of police policies, and more particularly of the way police misconduct was investigated, were symptomatic of a changing climate of opinion (Young, 1986). What then are the restraints on the police?

As with forces elsewhere, restraints on New Zealand police behavior are applied through both external and internal mechanisms of control. Formed in the British tradition of policing, the pattern of control resembles the models of the London Metropolitan Police and the Australian forces but not completely. Accordingly, on a continuum posited by David Bayley, running from relatively "high external supervision" (experienced by the United States police forces) to a strong preference for internal regulation (exemplified by the Japanese police), the New Zealand police would occupy a middle position next to the British police perhaps on the "Japanese" side. Despite the Commissioner's complaint in 1977 of "the plethora of authority and interested groups" needing to be satisfied, the New Zealand police have maintained a significant degree of independence from outside control. Bayley's account of factors shaping the mixture of internal and external controls also offers insights into the changing climate of opinion regarding the pattern of control: since the 1960s New Zealand urban society has become less homogeneous, more individualistic in temper, and more skeptical of state benevolence. Calls for increased external supervision of the New Zealand police thus grew (Bayley, 1985; *Annual Report*, 1988).

In New Zealand the relative positions of the government Minister in Charge of the police and the Commissioner of Police are not clearly spelled out by statute. Rather they have been determined by convention, personality, and purse-strings. By statute, the Commissioner has "general control of the police." By regulation, he is "responsible to the Minister for the general administration and control of the police." By contrast with Australian forces, however, there is no legal provision clearly empowering the Minister to direct the Commissioner (Brown, 1985). Drawing on Australian and English case law, successive New Zealand Commissioners have established the conventional wisdom of police independence from ministerial direction in law enforcement and order maintenance. In such matters the police see themselves as possessing the initiative and being responsible to the law alone or more concretely, to the community through the courts (Kerr, 1977; Cull, 1975; Barton, 1978; Hodge, 1984; Orr, 1986). The "Overstayers issue" of 1976 revealed that the extent to which a Minister could instruct the police, and in turn be responsible for the Department's actions, remained cloudy. A call for his resignation was rejected by the Minister who declared that he was "responsible for the department," but "not responsible for the day-to-day running of it. That's for the commissioner" (*Press*, Christchurch, 24 December 1976). When, in 1983, a law professor suggested clarification by statute of the Ministerial power to direct the police on policies where the "public interest justifies political direction," the Commissioner responded that police independence of ministerial direction on operational matters was "strictly observed" and should be maintained (Orr, 1986; *Dominion*, 22 July 1983).

In matters of administration, however, Ministers can and do exercise control. Even so the dividing line between matters of administration and law enforcement is a moot point. Moreover, as Bayley has observed of the Japanese police, the New Zealand police are "virtually sovereign with respect to internal control" (Bayley, 1985). Appointments (below the rank of Chief Superintendents), transfers, promotions, and disciplinary matters, (including responsibility for investigating complaints of police misconduct) have remained essentially the preserve of the police.

In practice of course, police independence of the executive is a fiction albeit a powerful one. Certainly there is no recent evidence that Ministers have intervened in police investigation and prosecution of specific cases. When public and political pressure has demanded, however, governments have instituted major inquiries into the conduct and methods of the police in specific cases. This instrument of control has naturally been used sparingly (five times between 1953 and 1983) and has severe limitations as a form of ongoing restraint. More significant is the fact that Ministers have not been chary in raising privately with Commissioners wider policy issues, discussing the manner in which police performed their duties, calling for reports on specific cases, and sometimes requesting (not directing) police action to deal with specific offenses or patterns of disorder (Barton, 1978; Orr, 1986). For their part Commissioners have apparently found it expedient to comply (though the extent of compliance cannot be estimated). Ultimately the government holds the purse-strings and the power to dismiss (no Commissioners have been dismissed, though two of the twenty-one who held office during the last sixty years departed under threat of dismissal). "Sensible and reasonable cooperation must always exist" as one Commissioner put it (Hunter, 1985). When, for example, a Prime Minister carelessly suggested publicly in 1984 that there should be a crackdown on bookmakers ("it is time we had a chat to the new Commissioner"), convention was breached: the new Commissioner swiftly responded that police policy would be unchanged (*Press*, Christchurch, 30 January and 2 February, 1984). Thus "the fiction," as one commentator has observed, "is studiously maintained that the police are acting independently and hence the executive cannot be held responsible for their actions" (Orr, 1986).

To whom then is the Commissioner responsible? In an attempt to resolve the conundrum of ministerial control, a new government established in 1985 a Justice and Law Reform Select Committee of Parliament which, amongst other things, was empowered to examine police policy and administration. It is not yet clear how closely Committee members will scrutinize police policy and whether indeed Commissioners will take refuge in "vague notions of legal accountability" when called to account for operational practice. Certainly the Commissioner has already refused to give responses to Committee questions on staffing which might embarrass his Minister politically (Orr, 1986; Palmer, 1984; 1986a; *Press*, Christchurch, 8 May 1988).

What then of the role of the New Zealand courts? Not surprisingly an eminent Judge believes his peers "have not been timid in exercising their right to comment adversely if in their opinion a police officer has acted illegally, unfairly or even unwisely" (McCarthy, 1971). Certainly police activity leading to criminal prosecutions is shaped with an eye to close judicial scrutiny: police practice is constrained by procedural law and Judges' Rules formulated by courts, but not codified in a Bill of Rights (Hodge, 1984).

Nonetheless, it has been strongly argued that the legal accountability of the New Zealand police (as of police elsewhere) barely exists at a practical level in any significant sense. Much, indeed most, police activity does not result in charges brought before a court; it is thus not subject to judicial review. In particular, there is no judicial review of police decisions not to prosecute; nor of the police prosecutions diversion scheme for first offenders begun in

1988. When a case is brought into court "the actions of the individual police officer can be subjected to scrutiny; the tactical decision of the police hierarchy cannot." However the majority of criminal cases in the lower court are concluded by a guilty plea and thus a review of police conduct is not permitted. And in defended cases "courts at first instance frequently do not uphold due process principles" (Arnold, 1986). Critics of judicial scrutiny might also note that it was a Royal Commission of Inquiry which in 1980 found evidence of police malpractice in the case of A. A. Thomas, after two jury trials and two referrals to the Court of Appeal had failed to do so. This may be an unduly pessimistic view of the gap between the theory and practice of legal accountability. But that a significant gap exists is confirmed by the disquiet expressed by the President of the Court of Appeal in 1988. He echoed civil libertarians in seeing the need for legislation to define a suspect's rights under questioning: "otherwise there might be room for a suggestion that the police are stretching the limits of the law and that the courts are acquiescing" (*Press*, Christchurch, 23 August 1988; McBride, 1982). To enhance the credibility of confessions obtained by the police, the Commissioner accepted (late in 1988) that videotaping of interviews should begin on a trial basis (*Press*, Christchurch, 29 December 1988).

For aggrieved citizens with complaints of police misconduct, the courts provide an uncertain avenue of redress. Complaints of defendants in criminal cases are generally not entertained by the judiciary in the face of police denials. A private criminal prosecution of a particular police officer is theoretically possible, and very occasionally successful. But the "difficulties," the New Zealand Ombudsman has observed, "...are such as to make [it] of little practical value." A civil action for damages against police officers is also possible, but again difficult and expensive in practice. Between 1976-77 and 1979-80, civil claims against the police averaged (in total) one per week. But those considered justified (and settled out of court) by the police averaged only six per year. Most settlements were for claims of wrongful arrest. The effect of the Accident Compensation Act of 1982 (providing state compensation for personal injury by accident in lieu of the right to sue for damages) has apparently been to constrain an aggrieved citizen seeking civil action for assault (McMeekin, 1983; Hodge, 1984; Wiseman, 1980; Young, 1986; McBride, 1973). Overall, as a mechanism for control of the police, the courts provide only a limited measure of external restraint.

To what extent then has the gap in external supervision of the police, created by both the coyness of ministerial oversight and the restricted nature of judicial scrutiny, been filled by the Ombudsman? The first New Zealand Parliamentary Commissioner for Investigations (or Ombudsman) was appointed in 1962. His main function is to investigate complaints made by citizens against government departments, local authorities, and other public organizations (Robson, 1979; Hill, 1976). From the outset the police came under his purview, but did not figure prominently until the 1970s. By 1976 the Ombudsman had received 12,091 complaints, of which 457 had been against the police (who, perhaps unexpectedly, figured seventh in cumulative total after the Justice, Education, Inland Revenue, and Social Welfare Departments, the State Services Commission, and the Post Office). Only half of the complaints against the police were fully investigated and the remainder were either withdrawn, jurisdiction was declined, or investigation discontinued. Of the complaints fully investigated, only 16.2 percent were found to be justified. This is a significantly smaller proportion than for government departments as a whole (*Report of the Chief Ombudsman*, 1976). From the mid-1970s the number of complaints concerning the police grew in number, and the Ombudsman's annual reports began to express long-standing concern at the difficulties experienced in dealing with such complaints (Wood, 1985).

From the outset the Ombudsman's investigations were constrained by the Commissioner's determination to retain exclusive control of discipline. A practice evolved which was given legislative sanction in 1975: the Ombudsman's jurisdiction was excluded from any police action that might be the subject of a disciplinary inquiry unless a complaint made to the police had not been investigated or the complainant was dissatisfied with the final result. In effect, so far as the police were concerned, the Ombudsman could not initiate an investigation. And there was no external review of most complaints against the police: only 20 percent of the large number of complainants during the Springbok Tour of 1981 subsequently turned to the Ombudsman. In this situation "a more comprehensive review of police activity during the tour would have been preferable but I had no warrant to undertake it," the

Ombudsman observed. His conclusions on the complaints did not, he emphasized, "provide an adequate basis for a general assessment of police investigations of complaints made against them" (*Report of the Chief Ombudsman*, 1983). Moreover the lapse of time which occurred before the Ombudsman's inquiry could prevent an effective review and remedy: the reconstruction of events was made more difficult; police decisions as to appropriate action might preempt those of the Ombudsman whose recommendations were not binding anyway.

The ethos of police independence in law enforcement further circumscribes the Ombudsman's effective jurisdiction which is limited by statute to a "matter of administration." Commissioners have steadfastly maintained the view, supported by the Crown's (Government) legal advisers, that police decisions of whether or not to accept a complaint of an offense or to commence a criminal prosecution—and indeed the wider law enforcement operations, are not matters of administration. For their part, successive Ombudsmen refused to accept that their purview should be thus limited. None, however, were prepared to test the issue by seeking a declaratory order from the High Court. Potential problems were reduced by police willingness to make files available to the Ombudsman. In the mid-1980s most complaints investigated by the Ombudsman related to police misconduct; no more than 15 percent could be construed as "matters of administration" (including conditions of employment and management of resources). Nonetheless the effectiveness of this external oversight of police behavior (including pretrial decision making) was limited. For this reason successive Ombudsmen looked to extend their powers. Instead an independent Police Complaints Authority was established in 1988 (Robson, 1979; Wood, 1985; Young, 1986; Beattie, 1986).

The main force of the Ombudsman's recommendations has come through their publicity in annual or special reports. And to adverse publicity the New Zealand police have long been very sensitive. Hence the media, becoming more competitive and less conservative in editorial outlook since the 1960s, now provide perhaps the most significant external mechanism of restraint upon the police, indirectly as well as directly. Indirectly, in the sense that sustained adverse publicity can force the hand of the government to call for reports, set up inquiries, and shape police policy. The "Overstayers issue" of October 1976 illustrates this well. Newspapers and radio gave wide coverage to criticisms of police methods (labelled "excessively emotional news coverage" by the Prime Minister). By producing evidence of the controversial random checking that had been at first denied by Ministers on the basis of police reports, the Auckland press forced the Minister of Police to request a full (albeit internal) inquiry (*New Zealand Herald* and *Auckland Star*, 23 to 30 October 1976). Similarly, in 1983, the media was the crucial conduit for public pressure that compelled the government to appoint an independent examiner to oversee a police investigation of a police shooting (*Report re Paul Chase Shooting*, 1983).

More directly, adverse publicity can stimulate the police into close self-scrutiny. Again the "Overstayers issue" had this effect: a later Commissioner declaring confidently that "the lessons from 1976 have been well learned and applied" (*Evening Post*, Wellington, 21 November 1984). In 1977 Commissioner Burnside mounted a major internal inquiry (with results that were not publicized) following allegations of police malpractice on one television current affairs program (*Press*, Christchurch, 5, 6, and 8 July 1977). In part, the importance of the media as a mechanism of external restraint stems from the doctrine of legal accountability espoused by the police and that implies policing by consent. An apparent lack of police responsiveness to adverse publicity would (it might be anticipated) make consent more fragile, less freely given. A clear willingness to consider public criticism also buttressed police organizational autonomy; it forestalled public inquiries and greater external supervision. Adverse publicity thus stimulates the most important mechanisms of restraint—those within the New Zealand police.

Commissioners have been left to exercise control of their staff, and have done so. In particular, they have sought to maintain effective processes of discipline by means of a wide-ranging disciplinary code, close supervision, and a willingness to apply sanctions where necessary. Until the 1980s disciplinary procedures were little changed (Young, 1986). Essentially the mode of investigation and type of sanction still do not distinguish between complaints from outside the police or charges laid by supervising officers. Rather the processes vary according to the seriousness of the allegation of misconduct or neglect of duty. There is no special police investigation unit. Instead an investigating officer is appointed by the District Commander, with rank dependent on the seriousness of the allegation. Where allegations are denied, but are seen to have some foundation, then charges were likely to be preferred either before a police disciplinary tribunal or in open court in the case of criminal offending.

The New Zealand police have long believed their investigation of complaints against them to be rigorous; all the more so because of potential scrutiny by the Ombudsman. There is much truth in this belief, but judgments of rigor must be left to readers able to bring a comparative perspective to bear on the following data. Unpublished research indicates that 413 complaints against the police were recorded during 1978, of which a quarter were considered justified by District Commanders. In effect one complaint was received for every 11.6 police, and those justified equalled one to every 44 personnel (considerably lower ratios than for the London Metropolitan Police in 1977). The ratio varied markedly by police district, with the largest (urban) districts of Auckland and Wellington having, not surprisingly, the highest ratios. The bulk of the complaints were in four categories: a quarter concerned a lack of police action (including slow response and insufficient action); 41 percent were considered justified. Another quarter of the complaints alleged improper police methods; only 13 percent were deemed justifed. A fifth of the complaints were against police conduct (excluding driving offenses), mostly behavior seen as obnoxious or less than professional, but including a few allegations of theft; 25 percent were sustained. Allegations of assault comprised a further fifth of complaints, of which 18.9 percent were found to be justified. Two-thirds of the police subject to complaints thought justified by District Commanders were prosecuted; the remainder were presumably warned or counselled by superior officers. Of those prosecuted, half came before an internal disciplinary tribunal and 90 percent were convicted. The other half were tried in the District Court where 87 percent were found guilty. Those convicted in open court of theft or assault were later dismissed or resigned. However, not all charges of assault came before the District Court. Charges of unnecessary violence, used in circumstances where some force was considered justified, were heard by the internal tribunal. In 1978 there were five appeals against tribunal decisions; two were allowed by an Appeal Board chaired by a District Court Judge (Wiseman, 1980). The procedures and outcomes just described may well typify later police investigations that the Ombudsman found to be "in general, thorough and conscientious (*Report of the Chief Ombudsman*, 1983). Nonetheless, police practice remained essentially closed from public view except for the Ombudsman's published case notes and police charged in open court. Not until 1982 did the Annual Reports of the Department begin to provide some sparse statistics. These suggested that, on average, little over ten percent of the growing number of serious allegations were sustained.

In the aftermath of the 1981 Springbok Tour, public criticism mounted at the outcome of police investigations into allegations of misconduct. Of the 362 formal complaints arising from the tour, a quarter were deemed justified, but only six resulted in criminal or disciplinary charges, all of which were dismissed. Police procedures came increasingly to lack credibility. Calls for an independent "Examiner of Police Practices" to monitor police investigations of misconduct were taken up by the Labour Party in the 1984 election, and eventually realized after "a long and intense gestation" in a Police Complaints Authority. The Labour Government did not publicly dispute the high standard of police investigations into complaints. But the procedures and outcomes had to be seen to be fair. In the changed climate of community opinion, external supervision perceived as effective is crucial in maintaining public trust and confidence in the police (Palmer, 1984; 1987; 1988; Young, 1986).

The Police Complaints Authority which came into being on 1 April 1989, displaces the Ombudsman whose jurisdiction is now limited to complaints relating to conditions of service or industrial disputes concerning members of the police. From the police there was strong opposition to the Ombudsman assuming a wider jurisdiction over complaints against them; there was a lack of confidence in the Ombudsman's staff and perhaps resentment at his past readiness to criticize (Beattie, 1986; Young, 1986). In fact, however, the role of the Authority has been shaped by the Ombudsman's experience, as well as by the existence of similar authorities in Britain, Australia, and Canada.

The Authority is to be notified of all complaints against the police; and has considerable flexibility in dealing with them. As envisaged by the framers of the legislation, it will essentially supervise and monitor police investigations of complaints: "the great majority of complaints will continue to be investigated by the police themselves without the direct intervention of the Authority" (Beattie, 1986). However, it is empowered to do more than this. Any complaint can be investigated by the Authority itself as well as any misconduct, policy, or practice which relates to a complaint under investigation, even if the complainant did not refer to it. Moreover, it can investigate any incident where death or serious injury has apparently been caused by police. However, it cannot investigate of its own volition unless there are reasonable grounds that it is in the public interest to do so. Thus the independent initiative of the Authority is envisaged to be used only sparingly (Beattie, 1986) and this has proved to be the case.

After investigation, either by the police or itself, the Authority can recommend to the Commissioner such disciplinary or criminal proceedings deemed necessary. The Commissioner may refuse to implement any such recommendation. If, however, no action is taken which the Authority considers to be adequate and appropriate, the Attorney-General and the Minister of Police can be informed and a report tabled in Parliament. As with the Ombudsman, publicity is seen as the main sanction of the Authority. Altogether then, the jurisdiction given the Authority represents an attempt to secure a balance between preserving the Commissioner's responsibility for discipline (and police morale), and public confidence that police policies and behavior are effectively supervised. Only time will tell if this balance is achieved.

The Police Complaints Authority has sought to tread cautiously (as the first incumbent put it) in striking a balance between the formidable and frequently unpleasant task confronting the police and the occasions when individual members of police have gone too far or have failed to maintain a proper and professional standard. This can be seen in the Authority's handling of complaints regarding police use of force. Such complaints comprise the largest category received; some 27 percent of the 795 complaints accepted during the Authority's first year of operation. However, only eight percent of those where investigation was completed, were sustained: in the large majority of such cases, the Authority concluded that the use of force was no more than was necessary. Indeed, a large number of those who complain of excessive force are authors of their own injuries and have received more than they deserved (Police Complaints Authority, *Annual Report*, 1990). Not surprisingly, the leadership of the Police Association has been very satisfied with the practice of the Police Complaints Authority to date.

Given that the police have been left with the main responsibility to control the misconduct of their members, "the soft influences of culture, education, and conscience" (Bayley, 1985) remain as (as for forces elsewhere) perhaps the crucial constraints on New Zealand police behavior.

PROBLEMS OF THE POLICE

Much of the preceding discussion has dealt implicitly, if not explicitly, with police problems and attempts at resolution. What follows is thus an overview. Clearly there is little that is unique in the issues confronting the New Zealand police in the late 1980s and the early 1990s. Certainly police corruption is not a focus of concern as it has been elsewhere. But by and large, New Zealand police problems, and responses to them, may be seen as broadly similar to those identified for other forces in the Anglo-American tradition. Such distinctiveness as there is in the issues of policing in New Zealand stems from the specific political and economic climate of today, the national organization of the force, and the changing climate of race relations. Of course, the problems of the police are defined according to the perspective of the commentator. In particular it is necessary to distinguish between issues identified by the police and those perceived by commentators outside.

In fact, there is much common ground in police and popular concern regarding the role and effectiveness of the police in the face of an apparently massive growth in lawlessness and disorder since the mid-1960s. Popular pessimism of police efficacy in crime prevention has coincided with a mounting fear of crime and greater moves toward self-protection. By 1984 there were some 370 licensed security businesses with an estimated 10,000 employees outnumbering the police by two to one. Since the early 1970s, law and order has figured ever more prominently as a political issue, with an unprecedented salience in the run-up to the 1987 election. Forty-three per cent of respondents (especially women and the elderly) to a national survey in 1987 said their activities were restricted by fear of being a victim of crime (Royal Commission on Social Policy, April 1988; Department of Statistics, 1984). Much fear of crime could be seen as manufactured by media myths and by politicians for their own advantage. Nonetheless, fear of crime was (and is) seen by police administrators as deep-seated, socially debilitating, and a major problem to be addressed. So too was the growing evidence of intimidation, especially by gang members, of police officers and their families (particularly at rural and small town stations) and of witnesses (making them reluctant to take part in police inquiries and court proceedings). Reduction of such fears was one of the Commissioner's goals for 1987-88 (New Zealand Police, 1987a, 1987b; *Annual Report,* 1988).

Police pessimism at the current social trends has been reflected in changing organization and tactics and in a subtle redefinition of goals and role discussed in earlier sections. Where, in public rhetoric until the 1950s at least, the absence of crime was taken by successive Commissioners to be a sign of police efficiency, police administrators in the 1990s saw the removal of crime to be an unrealistic goal. Instead, as a senior officer put it, the modern police service can concentrate on the progressive management of crime in which the duty of maintaining public tranquillity lies with the community aided by the police (New Zealand Police, 1987a). Local initiatives and police responses have thus come together in the development of community policing with proliferating community constables and neighborhood support groups. Between 1985-86 and 1987-88 complaints of burglary and theft fell slightly, but those relating to violence have continued to increase. Widespread fears of lawlessness and especially of violence remain, as do the external pressures for enhanced police performance. In response, the Commissioner in 1992 reasserted the primary goal of the police to be reduction of crime rate to 1990 levels by the end of the decade.

For New Zealand police administrators then, the crucial problems are the strains both in police public relationships, and on the resources to meet the demands for service. Such problems are, of course, not new or unique. But they became ever more urgent in the particular economic, social, and political climate of the 1980s (*Annual Report,* 1988) and have remained unresolved. Major operations (linked to the growing demands of search and rescue, disasters, or of public order, notably the policing of the 1981 Springbok Tour, and the preparations of similar protests which did not eventuate in 1985) as well as the growth in major criminal investigations (associated especially with the growth in drug trafficking, the soaring number of homicides in the 1980s, and the advent of terrorism with the bombing of the Greenpeace vessel, *Rainbow Warrior*, by French agents in 1985) have combined with ever increasing reports of violence and property crime to place unprecedented strains on police resources. Even so, growing economic difficulties since 1974 have produced pressures to curb spending and a critique of the effectiveness of social services from which the police have not been immune. Thus politicians and their advisors have displayed a new keenness for more effective targeting of scarce state resources. During the 1990s a blanket increase in police numbers is no longer seen as a solution to law and order problems. Nevertheless, from 1991, a newly elected National government was faced with implementing an expensive election promise to provide 900 more police over three years at the expense of other police resources such as housing.

Since the late 1970s, successive governments have been ever less willing or able to meet police requests for increased resources, especially for sworn personnel whose salaries and allowances comprised more than two-thirds of annual police budgets in the 1980s. It may be added that governments have been more amenable to requests for spending on technology, training, and less expensive civilian laborers to make the existing police more productive. The number of reported offenses per individual police member rose from 57 in 1972 to 83 in 1983. In July 1984 the Commissioner asked the newly elected Labour Government for an increase of 489 sworn staff (of which 12 percent would be community constables) and 158 civilians. Four years later civilians had increased by about 130, and police numbers by some 170 (most of which were community constables). Government priorities, rather than the Commissioner's, shaped staffing increases. In fact, during the mid-1980s, the overall pattern of increased police expenditure was also shaped by police industrial relations and the desire to improve the quality of personnel: pay and early retirement took precedence over more sworn staff. Greater rank and file restiveness regarding workloads, civilianization, pay, and conditions has added a new dimension to the police administrators' problems in managing stretched resources. And from these resources, a greater police responsiveness is expected.

In the 1980s, critics of New Zealand policing outside the government have focused on issues of accountability and responsiveness

(Young and Cameron, 1985; Cameron and Young, 1986). For academic critics and civil libertarians, the issue of police accountability to the executive of government is unresolved; effective surveillance of police policies by a parliamentary select committee has yet to be realized and the efficacy of a new independent Police Complaints Authority remains to be tested. While such critics have been concerned about the degree of police autonomy, police administrators might well perceive increasing constraints on their independence in policy-making, arising from financial stringency and more clearly expressed political priorities (as seen, for example, in the "Overstayers issue" discussed above).

In the greater emphasis given to community policing from 1984, police administrators have responded to the patent weaknesses of fire-brigade policing, to local initiatives, and to government policy. Nonetheless, the concept and implementation of community policing has been shaped by the police themselves. Should the strategy of community-orientated policing be fully realized, there should be a fundamental shift in organization and methods. A measure of organizational decentralization has occurred with the creation of six police regions and more police districts in 1987-88. Thus in theory the "component units" will be given (as James Q. Wilson aptly commented regarding American policing twenty years earlier) "greater freedom, within well-defined general policies, to handle local situations in a manner appropriate to local conditions" (Wilson, 1971; New Zealand Police, 1987a). Functions and decision making may be decentralized to a degree, but the authority governing the police will not be dispersed. Indeed, control of the community policing initiatives remain with police administrators; such structures as have been established by police for local consultation are dominated by them, and new policing strategies can occur without local consultation. In September 1988, for example, the mayor of a country town (some 3,600 population) was a bit miffed when the local three-man police force announced a night curfew for young people without consulting him; but he was impressed with the results (*Dominion Sunday Times*, 4 September, 1988). Local communities within dominant pakeha (European) culture appear to remain largely content with the existing structure and ethos of policing and call merely for more resources and greater police powers.

However, a more profound challenge to police accountability and responsiveness is coming from Maori communities. It is part of a changing climate of race relations in which the Maori, the indigenous population, are more effectively than hitherto forcing the dominant European culture to confront the issues of monoculturalism and institutional racism. Since 1975, the Treaty of Waitangi (signed by Maori chiefs and a representative of the British Crown in 1840) has gained increased status in government legislation and policy-making. Indeed a landmark New Zealand Court of Appeal case (*New Zealand Maori Council v. Attorney-General*) in 1987 declared a leading principle of the Treaty to be one of partnership between the Maori people and the Crown, requiring the partners to act reasonably and in utmost good faith towards each other. Biculturalism has become official policy, though its meaning, implementation, and consequences are subject to considerable debate. Maori communities have long seen the Treaty as an affirmation of their right to self-determination: policies affecting them "should be determined by Maori people, in accord with their own values, systems and due resources but within the overall framework of a unified New Zealand" (*The Report of the Royal Commission on Social Policy,* April 1988).

Such a view has profound implications for the future of the hitherto monocultural criminal justice system, and (more specifically) the police. In 1988, a report, commissioned by the Department of Justice and based on wide consultation amongst Maori, advocated the establishment of a "parallel system of justice": a "distinct process to hear, sentence and dispose of charges against Maori offenders in which the authority to determine the procedure and the law is retained in Maori hands" (Jackson, 1988). The idea of a parallel Maori system of justice was quickly dismissed by the Minister of Justice (as well as by the parliamentary Opposition) as "a profoundly unacceptable development" because "it would shatter the cohesion of the law in our society." It could be argued, the Minister added, that "part of what Maori may have given up under the treaty arrangements and part of what they were surrendering themselves to was a system of British justice" (*Press,* Christchurch, 3 December 1988). Clearly the dominant culture will not readily relinquish its absolute control of the legal system. Yet the debate is far from over. The idea of a parallel Maori legal system was, according to a prominent Maori observer, "one of the most frequently-voiced issues at *hui* (Maori meetings) held all around New Zealand (cited by Stirling, 1988).

In the 1988 report, a parallel police system is apparently not advocated, but rather a more truly bicultural service. The recent police emphasis on multiculturalism (rather than biculturalism) in its training programs and community liaison, and the recruitment of more Maori into the police ranks has failed (according to the 1988 report) to "adequately address both the structural and cultural base of the systems they use to deal with Maori offenders, and the reality of those offenders' present lifestyles." Police training and policies have remained essentially monocultural, to the extent that Maori officers are "viewed with suspicion by their own people." Instead, a "permanent Maori support structure" should be developed within the police, composed of community as well as departmental personnel, to produce "more culturally aware officers" and a Maori perspective in the formulation of policing policies. There needed to be "an observable change in both the general operations of the police and the specific behavior of individual officers towards Maori offenders" (Jackson, 1988).

There is no sign that such a degree of change will occur within the organization and ethos of the New Zealand police despite further initiatives toward biculturalism. Policing policies will continue to be formulated within the perspective of the dominant culture. In part this is because police administrators share the view of the Minister of Justice that a legal system which produced "differences of treatment between similar people" would be "unacceptable" (*Press*, Christchurch, 3 December 1988). There is some police support for "Maori based tribunals," but strong opposition "to any suggestion that such tribunals would have any judicial or executive power" (New Zealand Police, 1987b). Fundamentally then, the police will resist any attempt to diminish their high degree of automony in determining how local communities are policed. In this tension between longstanding Maori aspirations and police professional ideals lies possibly the most difficult problem of New Zealand policing in the future.

CONCLUSIONS

Late in 1989 yet another report on the New Zealand Police was published by Strategos Consulting Ltd. This business consultancy was headed by a former National Government minister and had already reported to the current Labour Government on three other departments. Strategos was contracted to provide the Cabinet Expenditure Review Committee with an assessment of the police organization, taking into account past reviews, overseas research, and the "principles of State Sector reform" then underway in New Zealand . The relevant "principles" were:

(i) Policy and advisory roles as a general rule ought to be separate from administrative and operational roles;
(ii) Objectives should be stated in such a way that all parties providing public goods and services are absolutely clear as to their role;
(iii) Accountability should be maximized;
(iv) Competitive neutrality is needed to minimize costs and provide appropriate incentives and sanctions to enhance efficiency;
(v) Managers should be allowed to manage.

Essentially the Government was looking for greater effectiveness in its expenditure on the New Zealand police. Using the foregoing principles, Strategos sought "to relate a commercial analysis of policing activity to the more general thrust of reform."

Though controversial, the findings of the Strategos report sum up some of the major concerns regarding the New Zealand police as an organization in 1989, and point the possible direction for future developments. In its review of the current environment in which policing policies were made, Strategos noted that the continuing thrust of social and economic change was likely to "impact negatively on the level of crime," yet the police would face fiscal constraints for the foreseeable future. More police could not be afforded, nor (in the view of Strategos) did local experience or overseas research suggest this to be an effective strategy. Thus there was a need to analyze the extent to which resources could be reallocated from one strategy of policing (in this case vehicle-based patrolling and investigations after the crime) to another to achieve optimal results. The consultants recognized that a "new model of policing," "Community-oriented Policing," was currently being implemented. However the process of implementation could not be perfected until police activity moved "from being demand-driven to an output-oriented approach based on outputs which are derived from clearly defined objectives." Objectives needed to be more clearly defined; outputs prioritized. What had long been implicit, needed to be made explicit: "The legitimate objective for the police is neither to prevent all crime nor to enforce the law against all offenders. The funding and institutional arrangements should instead focus on achieving an optimal outcome in terms of enforcement."

Here then, the principles of state sector reform outlined above were seen to be applicable to the police. They suggested a new approach to the setting of objectives and outputs was needed, along with structural reform. Strategos criticized the prevailing notion that "the police are what they do." The current corporate plan was seen as too general to enable true management by objectives. Lacking adequate management and financial information systems, the police had not been able to properly specify outcomes and performance measurement criteria. The consultants suggested a more precise (and potentially narrower) definition of the police corporate objective, namely, to support the adjudication of the law and the imposition of sanctions in accordance with priorities determined by Government through:

- the exercise of coercive powers in pursuit of law enforcement;
- the exercise of persuasive powers to promote acceptance of and adherence to the law where vesting those powers in the police serves to reinforce the coercive function.

Framed in such a way, the objectives allowed a more rigorous appraisal of current New Zealand police activity, "outputs," a significant proportion of which was perceived to be "contestable"; it could in principle be performed by other agencies of the state or the private sector. Strategos saw only certain activities as "intrinsic to the police's coercive monopoly": jailing services to the point of court appearance, responding to offenses and emergencies, and responding to incidents where it could not be predicted whether coercive power would be required. Potentially contestable activities included: firearms licensing, vetting and validation, escorting, lost-and-found property, prosecutions, coronary services, custody of exhibits, checking jury lists, executing warrants and serving summonses, proactive policing, and public security services. The method of "contestability" might not necessarily mean withdrawal from the activity, but could also entail cost recovery, tendering, or the greater utilization of unsworn staff.

In the case of prosecutions, Strategos recognized that the police offered a "cost-effective service." Establishing an independent agency would be costly. Nonetheless there are strong constitutional and equity arguments for keeping the decisions to prosecute institutionally separate from the investigation of crime. Above all, the commercial perspective of the consultants led them to recommend that "prosecution be part of a stand-alone business entity within the police." Work could be contracted out by this agency, if it proved more cost-effective to do so.

Community programs, such as crime prevention campaigns and the law-related education program, were seen as inadequately targeted: less costly options than the use of highly trained police officers needed to be explored. Here again, contracting out to other providers or the greater use of unsworn staff was a possibility. Consistent with this pursuit of more cost-effectiveness in the use of resources was the consultants' view that the Commissioner should fully exploit current changes to the Police Act, allowing greater use of unsworn (civilian) staff and the employment of all sworn personnel on individual contracts.

Also consistent with the principles of current state sector reform was a controversial recommendation of structural reform: the creation of a Ministry of Police separate from the New Zealand police. Policy formation and implementation could be more clearly separated. From this, Strategos argued, various benefits would flow. The "constitutional ambiguity" in the relationship between Commissioner and the Government would be resolved: the Government was responsible for setting policy and monitoring results; the Commissioner was responsible for control of police operations and remained free from political interference in particular cases. This arrangement would allow a more rigorous focus on "core outputs" and maximize accountability. It would also mean that decisions as to the "contestable outputs" would not be left to the agency affected, namely the New Zealand police. A Ministry of Police would have the responsibility to develop a "strategic assessment of the overall criminal enviroment" in conjunction not only with the police but also other relevant Departments such as Customs, Immigration, Justice, and Inland Revenue.

More broadly, Strategos suggested that an amalgamation of services should be considered. The separation of traffic law enforcement from the police was perceived as an anomaly. While the amalgamation of these two law enforcement agencies could bring long-term gains in efficiency, the consultants did not see that this would be "the optimal answer in resource management terms." Significant efficiency gains could result from the amalgamation of all the emergency services (Traffic, Fire, Civil Defense, and Ambulance) with the police. Though "highly intractable political and industrial relations problems" could inhibit such a radical change, Strategos thought better policy formation and less resource duplication could be achieved by bringing all the emergency services within the ambit of a single Ministry of Safety and/or Emergency Services.

In the event, the major structural changes advocated by Strategos have not occurred with one exception: the merger of traffic enforcement officers (the Traffic Safety Service) with the police by July 1993. To a degree Strategos merely underlined the need for organizational changes already underway within the New Zealand police. From the late 1980s, the police corporate plan specified with greater precision priorities in policing which had been tacitly understood. Moreover, the continuing impetus for a narrowing of the police role, a differential response to calls for service, and the shedding of activities considered extraneous had begun long before the Strategos report. For the 1990-1991 financial year, police administrators recast the corporate plan to specify 13 policing "outputs," specifying the costs, the standards of performance, and the extent to which these standards were to be achieved. Notably, some of the activities that Strategos considered for constables were now specified as distinct outputs, such as responding to non-offense incidents; responding to emergencies and disaster; service provided to the court; prosecution; custodial services; coronary services; receiving and disposing of property; and licensing and vetting services. Potentially, to achieve some of these performance standards and obtain cost savings, some of these services could be privatized.

Even so, the approach and findings of the Stategos report are in some measure "contestable." In practice, the distinction drawn between the coercive persuasive (or deterrent) activity of the police is artificial: police power is "persuasive" because it is ultimately coercive. Moreover, the economic analysis of policy seeks a degree of precision which is in reality unavailable. Police effectiveness is ultimately impossible to measure in quantitative terms. While it is clear that police resources have to be rationed, policing in a democratic society is inevitably "demand-driven" especially for an organization whose credo now is "policing in and for communities" (Stategos Consulting Limited, 1989). In essence the approach of Strategos (for policies, priorities, and measures of effectiveness to be centrally determined by a new Ministry of Police) cuts across current moves within the New Zealand Police to devolve the management of resources to the regions. Thus the ultimate outcome of developments in community policing remains uncertain. Indeed, in 1989, the only certainty about the future of New Zealand policing was that it would continue to be in a state of flux, as it had been since the 1960s.

REFERENCES

Advisory Committee on Legal Services. *Te Whainga i Te Tika: In Search of Justice*. Wellington: Department of Justice, 1986.

Annual Reports of the New Zealand Police for the Years Ending 31 March 1956-88. *Appendices to the Journals of the House of Representatives*, Wellington, 1956-87, H16 (1956-72) and G6 (1973-88).

Ansley, B. "A Cop's Lot: Bargained Rates." *New Zealand Listener* (8 March 1986): 17-19.

__________. "The Cop in the House." *New Zealand Listener* (17 October 1987): 25-27.

Arnold, T. "Legal Accountability and the Police: The Role of the Courts." In Neil Cameron and Warren Young (eds.), *Policing at the Crossroads*. Wellington: Allen and Unwin, 1986.

Auckland Committee on Racism and Discrimination. *Task Force: A Failure in Law Enforcement, a Disaster in Community Relations*. Auckland: ACORD, 1975.

Auckland District Law Society, Public Issues Committee. *The Police and the Executive: The "Moyle Affair" Revisited.* (report for press release), 21 September 1977.

Australian Institute of Criminology. *Copspeak 1.* Unpublished, Australian Institute of Criminology, 1988.

Barber, L. W. "The Role of Women Police." Unpublished superintendents course opinion paper, July 1986.

Barton, B. J. "Control of the New Zealand Police." Unpublished L.LB (Hons) thesis, University of Auckland, 1978.

Bayley, D. H. *Patterns of Policing. A Comparative International Analysis.* New Brunswick, New Jersey: Rutgers University Press, 1985.

Bayley, D. H. and Bittner, E. "Learning the Skills of Policing." *Law and Contemporary Problems* 47 (4) (1984): 35-59.

Beattie, Sir David. "Report of the Committee on an Independent Examiner of Complaints Against the Police." Unpublished, 1986.

Bottomley, Keith A. and Coleman, Clive A. "Police Effectiveness and the Public: The Limitations of Official Crime Rates." In R. V. G. Clarke and J. M. Hough (eds.), *The Effectiveness of Policing.* Farnborough, England: Gower Publishing Company, 1980.

__________. *Understanding Crime Rates. Police and Public Roles in the Production of Official Statistics.* Farnborough, England: Gower Publishing Company, 1981.

Britannica Book of the Year. Chicago: Encyclopaedia Britannica Inc., 1988.

Brown, G. "Discipline and Accountability." In Bruce Swanton, Garry Hannington, and Trish Psaila (eds.), *Police Source Book 2.* Canberra, ACT: Australian Institute of Criminology, 1985.

Burnside, K. B. "The Future of the New Zealand Police." Unpublished memorandum. Wellington: New Zealand Police Headquarters, October 1974.

__________. "Delegation of Authority—Principles and Practice at the Commissioner Level." Unpublished report. Wellington: New Zealand Police Headquarters, n.d. [1975].

Butterworth, Graham. "The Dark Side of the Force: Personnel Problems in New Zealand Police and Their Solution." In Bruce Swanton, Garry Hannington, and Trish Psaila (eds.), *Police Source Book 2.* Canberra, ACT: Australian Institute of Criminology, 1985.

"C.I.B. Activity Survey, Part One." Unpublished report. New Zealand Police Headquareters, 1985.

Cain, M. "Police Professionalism: Its Meaning and Consequences." *Anglo-American Law Review* 1 (1972): 217-231.

Cameron, N. "Developments and Issues in Policing New Zealand." In Neil Cameron and Warren Young (eds.), *Policing at the Crossroads*. Wellington: Allen and Unwin, 1986.

Cameron, Neil and Young, Warren (eds.). *Policing at the Crossroads*. Wellington: Allen and Unwin, 1986.

Campbell, I. D. "Criminal Law." In J. L. Robson (ed.). *New Zealand: The Development of its Laws and Constitution*. London: Stevens and Sons, 1967.

Chappell, D. and Wilson, P. R. *The Police and Public in Australia and New Zealand*. St. Lucia, Queensland: University of Queensland Press, 1969.

Chapple, G. *1981: the Tour.* Wellington: A.H. & A.W. Reed, 1984.

Churches, M. T. "Corporate Planning." Unpublished Commissioner's Circular (1987/20), 24 December 1987.

Congalton, A. A. "Social Grading of Occupations in New Zealand." *British Journal of Sociology* 4(1) (1953): 45-59.

Congalton, Athol A. and Havighurst, Robert J. "Status Ranking of Occupations in New Zealand." *Australian Journal of Psychology* 6(1) (1954): 10-15.

Cull, H. A. "The Enigma of a Police Constable's Status." *Victoria University of Wellington Law Review* 8, (1975): 148-169.

Dallow, R. P. "Street Disorder and Violence" [in Auckland]. Unpublished. New Zealand Police, December 1974.

Dance, Owen. "The Police and Community Policing." In Neil Cameron and Warren Young (eds.). *Policing at the Crossroads*. Wellington: Allen and Unwin, 1986.

__________. "The Influence of Police Perceptions of Maoris on Decisions to Arrest or Prosecute." Unpublished Master of Public Policy research report, Victoria University of Wellington, 1987.

__________. "New Zealand Police, 1920-1980: An Isolated Occupational Community?" In S. Corcaran (ed.). *Law and History in Australia: A Collection of Papers at the 1987 Law and History Conference*. Adelaide: Adelaide Law Review Association, Law School, University of Adelaide, 1990.

Davis, Peter. *An Occupational Prestige Ranking Scale for New Zealand*. Christchurch, New Zealand: Department of Psychology and Sociology, University of Canterbury, 1974.

Department of Social Welfare, *Juvenile Crime in New Zealand*. Wellington: Government Printer, 1973.

Department of Statistics. *New Zealand Official Yearbook*. Wellington: Department of Statistics, 1984 and 1988.

_________. *Report on the Social Indicators Survey 1980-81*. Wellington: Department of Statistics, 1984.

Duncan, L. J. "Tertiary Education Should Be Compulsory For Aspiring Senior Police Officers. Unpublished Inspectors Management Course assignment, 1987.

Dunstall, G. "The Social Pattern." In W. H. Oliver (ed.). *The Oxford History of New Zealand*. Wellington: Oxford University Press, 1981.

Edwards, B. *The Public Eye*. Wellington: Alister Taylor, 1972.

Elley, W. B. and Irving, J. C. "A Socio-economic Index for New Zealand Based on Levels of Education and Income from the 1966 Census." *New Zealand Journal of Educational Studies* 7(2) (1972): 153-167.

_________. "The Elley-Irving Socio-economic Index: 1981 Census Revision." *New Zealand Journal of Educational Studies* 20(2) (1985): 115-128.

Farrow, J. D. "A Review of the Policy for the Employment and Promotion of Policewomen in New Zealand." Unpublished. New Zealand Police Headquarters, April 1973.

_________. "A Review of Uniformed Branch In-Service Training." Unpublished. New Zealand Police Headquarters, July 1975.

Fielding, N. "Police Socialisation and Police Competence." *British Journal of Sociology* 35(4) (1984): 568-590.

Fielding, N. G. "Evaluating the Role of Training in Police Socialization: A British Example." *Journal of Community Psychology* 14 (1986): 319-330.

Fifield, J. K. and Donnell, A. A. *Socio-Economic Status, Race, and Offending in New Zealand*. Wellington: Research Unit, Joint Committee on Young Offenders, 1980.

Fitzpatrick, J. G. J. and Kelly, G. E. S. *Outline of Administration*. Wellington: Government Printer, May 1964.

Fleming, W. R. and Silk, R. P. "Immigration Act 1964: Police Enforcement at Auckland, October-November 1976." Unpublished report. New Zealand Police Headquarters, December 1976.

Ford, G. W. "Research Report on Domestic Disputes: Final Report." Unpublished. New Zealand Police Headquarters, November 1986.

Fraser, P. "Conference Address." *New Zealand Police Journal* 6(1) (1942): 9-14.

Gallagher, R. C. "The Family, Personality-type and Motivation to Join the New Zealand Police. Unpublished student research exercise. Department of Sociology, University of Auckland [1971] (filed MB/11)

Glynn, J. F. "Report on Basic Assumptions, Philosophy and Objectives of Training/Education in New Zealand Police." Unpublished. New Zealand Police Headquarters, July 1973.

__________. *The New Zealand Policeman. The Developing Role of New Zealand Police*. Wellington: New Zealand Institute of Public Administration, 1975.

Glynn, J. F. and Watkins, T. K. "Report on Basic Training in the New Zealand Police." Unpublished. New Zealand Police Headquarters, October 1974.

Gordon, Margaret F. "Police Training in New Zealand: The Case For Organisational Change." Unpublished Master of Public Policy thesis, Victoria University of Wellington, 1984.

Government of New Zealand. "Regulations Under the Police Force Act, 1913." *The New Zealand Gazette*, 1919, 900-2933.

__________. "The Police Force Regulations 1950." *The New Zealand Gazette*, 1950: 338-366.

__________. *Police Regulations 1959*. Wellington: New Zealand Government Printer, 1959.

__________. *Crimes Act, 1961*. Wellington: Government Printer, reprinted with amendments, 1979.

Greenhill, N. J. "Professionalism in the Police Service." In D. W. Pope and N. L. Weiner (eds.). *Modern Policing*. London: Croom Helm, 1981.

Greenland, H. "Ethnicity as Ideology." In P. Spoonley, C. Macpherson, D. Pearson, and C. Sedgwick (eds.). *Tauiwi: Racism and Ethnicity in New Zealand*. Palmerston North: Dunmore Press, 1984.

Greenwood, P., Chaiken, J., and Petersilia, J. *The Criminal Investigation Process*. Lexington, Massachusetts: D. C. Heath, 1977.

Greenwood, Peter W. "The Rand Study of Criminal Investigation: the Findings and its Impact to Date." In R. V. G. Clarke and J. M. Hough (eds.). *The Effectiveness of Policing*. Farnborough, England: Gower Publishing Company, 1980.

Gurr, T. R. "Crime Trends in Modern Democracies Since 1945." *International Annals of Criminology* 16 (1977): 41-85.

Haldane, Robert. *The People's Force. A History of the Victoria Police*. Carlton, Victoria: Melbourne University Press, 1986.

Hamilton, Donald J. "Wainuiomata: Personal Policing." Unpublished. New Zealand Police Headquarters, 1984.

Hampton, R. E. *Sentencing in a Children's Court and Labelling Theory*. Wellington: Department of Justice, 1975.

Hartley, B. S. J. "Personalised System of Instruction." Unpublished Police Officers Course essay, October 1978.

Harvey, P. G. "The New Zealand Police System of Industrial Relations." Unpublished paper for Diploma of Industrial Relations, Victoria University of Wellington, 1988.

Heppleston, W. E., Cupples. J. L., and Mackmurdie, A. J. "Project Blueprint: An Interim Report on Progress, Findings and Recommendations. Unpublished. Hay Management Consultants Ltd, 1987.

Hesketh, B. L. "The Relationship of Self-concept and Occupational Stereotype to Job Satisfaction: Self-esteem and Conservatism Studied as Meta-dimensions." Unpublished research exercise, August 1974 (filed MC/12).

Hewson, V. A. and Singer, M. S. "Type A Behaviour in the New Zealand Police." *Police Studies* 8(2) (1985): 97-99.

Hickson, W. H., Saunders-Francis, N. P., and Bird, I. N. "New Zealand Police Functional Review." Unpublished. Wellington, August 1982.

Hill, L. B. *The Model Ombudsman*. Princeton, New Jersey: Princeton University Press, 1976.

Hill, Richard. "The First Police Association." *New Zealand Police Association Newsletter* 16 (12) (1984): 94-95.

__________. "Maori Policing in Nineteenth Century New Zealand." *Archifacts: Bulletin of the Archives and Records Association of New Zealand* 2, (1985): 54-60.

__________. *Policing the Colonial Frontier*. Parts 1 and 2. Wellington, New Zealand: Government Printer, 1986.

Hodge, W. C. *Doyle: Criminal Procedure in New Zealand*. Sydney: The Law Book Co., 1984.

Holland, K. J. "Police Unionism in New Zealand." Unpublished paper for Diploma of Industrial Relations, Victoria University of Wellington, 1977.

Holyoake, I. N. and Long, S. E. "Project Investigation: A Review of the Investigation Process in the New Zealand Police." Unpublished. New Zealand Police Headquarters, August 1988.

Hough, J. M. and Clarke, R. V. G. "Introduction." In R. V. G. Clarke and J. M. Hough (eds.). *The Effectiveness of Policing*. Farnborough, England: Gower Publishing Company, 1980.

Huang, M. S., Hewson, V. A., and Singer, A. E. "Type A Behaviour in the Police and General Population." *The Journal of Psychology* 115 (1983): 171-175.

Hunter, L. "The Relationship Between the Minister of Police and the Commissioner of Police in New Zealand." Unpublished Master of Arts thesis, University of Canterbury, 1985.

Jackson, M. *The Maori and the Criminal Justice System: A New Perspective*. Wellington: Department of Justice, February 1987.

__________. *The Maori and the Criminal Justice System, A New Perspective: He Whaipaanga Hou, Part* 2. Wellington: Department of Justice, 1988.

James, D. "Police-Black Relations: The Professional Solution." In S. Holdaway (ed.). *The British Police*. London: Edward Arnold, 1979.

Jamieson, J. A. "Employment of Maoris and Pacific Islanders in the New Zealand Police." Unpublished report. New Zealand Police Headquarters, June 1973.

__________. "The Police and Ethnic Minorities." In G. Vaughan (ed.). *Racial Issues in New Zealand*. Auckland: Akarana Press, 1974.

__________. "Police Training." Unpublished memorandum. New Zealand Police Headquarters, 15 February 1978.

Jonas, A. B. J. "The Neighbourhood Support Group Scheme—A Crime Prevention Strategy." 2 Parts. Unpublished. New Zealand Police Headquarters, May and August 1987.

Jones, S. *Policewomen and Equality. Formal Policy v Informal Practice?* London: The Macmillan Press, 1986.

Kerr, D. B. "Powers of Executive to Direct Police." Unpublished memorandum, Legal Section, New Zealand Police Headquarters, 16 November 1977.

King, P. and Phillips J. "A Social Analysis of the Springbok Tour Protestors." In D. MacKay, M. McKinnon, P.McPhee, and J. Phillips (eds.). *Counting the Cost. The 1981 Springbok Tour in Wellington*. Wellington: Victoria University History Department, Occasional Paper No. 1, 1982.

Lines, C. W. "A Review of Incident Car Patrolling." Unpublished. New Zealand Police Headquarters, November 1988.

Looi, C. F. "Methods of Detection Survey." Unpublished report. New Zealand Police Headquarters, 1976.

Lovell, R. and Stewart, A. *Patterns of Juvenile Offending in New Zealand: No. 1: Summary Statistics for 1978-81*. Wellington: Department of Social Welfare, 1983.

McBride, T. *New Zealand Handbook of Civil Liberties*. Wellington: Price Milburn, 1973.

__________. *Police Powers and the Rights of Suspects*. Auckland: Legal Research Foundation Inc., 1982.

McCarthy, T. "The Role of the Police in the Administration of Justice." In R. S. Clark (ed.). *Essays on Criminal Law in New Zealand*. Wellington: Sweet and Maxwell, 1971.

McCormick, I. A., Huang, M. S., and Walkey, F. H. "Repressive or Permissive: A Comparison of Police Recruit and Student Attitudes Towards Offenders." *Police Studies* 8(1) (1985): 54-57.

Macfie, R. "Women—an Untapped Resource." *New Zealand Police Association Newsletter* 17(4) (1985): 30-31.

McGill, I. "Organisation Development in the Police Department." *STEP* (10) (1985): 24-27.

McLaughlin, Murray. "Is the Force With Us?" *New Zealand Listener*, 5 September 1987.

McMeekin, P. "Police Accountability in New Zealand: A Comparative Evaluation." Unpublished paper, October 1983.

McTagget, S. "Changed Tune, Different Beat." *New Zealand Listener*, 28 September 1985, 17-18.

Mason, L. B. and Gordon, M. F. (eds.). *Trentham in Retrospect*. Wellington: New Zealand Police College, 1982.

Melrose, H. R. and Waitai, R. "Team Policing Survey." Unpublished. New Zealand Police Headquarters, 1987.

Meltzer, J. The New Zealand Police Association. *Journal of Public Administration* 6(1) (1943): 50-59.

Meurant, R. *The Red Squad Story*. Auckland: Harlen Publishing Company, 1982.

Meyrick, M. "Police and Protest: The Role of the New Zealand Police as Controllers of Public Order During the Period 1966-1973." Unpublished Master of Arts thesis, University of Auckland, 1984.

Miller, I. and Ford, G. "Patterns of Exit from the New Zealand Police: A Study of Disengagements, 1985-90." Unpublished report. New Zealand Police Headquarters, 30 July, 1991.

Mitchell, John. "Neighbourhood Watch—A Practical Evaluation. *New Zealand Police Association Newsletter* 17(7)(1985): 62-63.

Mitchell, R. S. "Disaster Preparedness Within the New Zealand Police." Unpublished report. New Zealand Police Headquarters, n.d. (1978).

Moodie, R. A. "Role of Police Service Organisations in Conditions of Service Negotiations." Unpublished Memorandum. New Zealand Police Association, 3 November 1988.

Mooney, B. S. "Youth Aid Perspectives and Principles—A Development Report. Unpublished. New Zealand Police Headquarters, January 1971a.

__________. "The History and Development of the Youth Aid Section of the New Zealand Police." Unpublished Diploma in Criminology thesis, University of Auckland, 1971b.

Morgan, J. "Police Sociology or a Sociology of Police: A Choice." Unpublished Master of Arts thesis, University of Auckland, 1977.

__________. Disaster: A Police Perspective on Air New Zealand Flight TE901 Which Crashed on Mt. Erebus, Antarctica, 28 November, 1979. Unpublished report. New Zealand Police Headquarters, 1980.

Morgan, James (ed.). *Community Policing.* Canberra, A.C.T.: Australian Institute of Criminology, 1984.

New Zealand Police. "The New System of Policing." Unpublished. Wellington: Police National Headquarters, 1970.

__________. *Survey of National Headquarters: Report on Recruiting and Training.* Unpublished, October 1971.

__________. *An Information Guide for Members of the Police.* Unpublished, 1975.

__________. "The Promotion System: Report of the Working Party." Unpublished. Wellington: Police National Headquarters, 1979.

__________. *Operation Overdue: The Police Role.* Wellington: Police National Headquarters, June 1980.

__________. *Operation Rugby: 19 July-13 September 1981.* Wellington: Police National Headquarters, February 1982.

__________. *South Auckland Police Development Plan.* 2 vols. Unpublished. Wellington: Police National Headquarters, July 1984.

__________. *Digest of Statistics.* Wellington: Police National Headquarters (published annually) 1985 to 1988.

__________. *Project Blueprint: A Message from the Commissioner.* Wellington: Police National Headquarters, 29 April 1987.

__________. *Submissions to the Royal Commission on Social Policy.* Unpublished, 17 June 1987a.

__________. *Final Submissions to the Royal Commission on Social Policy.* Unpublished, November 1987b.

New Zealand Police Association. *Newsletter,* March 1991, Wellington, 11-13. (See also *Newsletter* under *Newspapers, Newsletters, and Assorted Other Sources.)*

Norris, M., Devoy, S., and Lovell, R. *Patterns of Juvenile Offending in New Zealand: No. 4: Summary Statistics for 1980-81.* Wellington: Department of Social Welfare, 1986.

O'Donovan, J. "Address to the New Zealand Police Force." In *The Police Force Act 1913, Police Force Amendment Act 1919, and Regulations made thereunder for the guidance of the Police Force of New Zealand.* Wellington: Government Printer, 1920.

Orr, G. "Police Accountability to the Executive and Parliament." In Neil Cameron and Warren Young (eds.). *Policing at the Crossroads.* Wellington: Allen and Unwin, 1986.

Palmer, G. "The Accountability of the Police." Unpublished notes of speech to Police Executive Conference, New Zealand Police Heaquarters, 21 June 1984.

__________. "The Legislative Process and the Police." In Neil Cameron and Warren Young (eds.). *Policing at the Crossroads.* Wellington: Allen and Unwin, 1986a.

__________. "Implications of Industrial Action by Police for the Rule of Law." Unpublished memorandum, Attorney-General's Office, Wellington, 24 January 1986b.

__________. "The Police Complaints Authority: Help or Hindrance?" Unpublished notes of speech to the Executive Development Course, Royal New Zealand Police College, 17 November 1987.

__________. "Palmer on the PCA." *New Zealand Police Association Newsletter* 21 (11) (1988): 172-174.

Parkes, B. M. "Our Policing Methods: Time for Change." Unpublished. New Zealand Police College Officers' Course Research Paper, October 1978.

Paterson, A. I. H. "Tertiary Education for Policemen." Unpublished memorandum, New Zealand Police Headquarters, 20 December 1976.

__________. "Report on a New Zealand-United States Educational Foundation Study Tour of the United States." Unpublished, 1977.

Pittams, G. B. "A Study of Assaults on Members of the New Zealand Police During December to May 1979-1980." Unpublished, Management

Services Section, New Zealand Police Headquarters, September 1980.

Pratt, John. "Law and Order Politics in New Zealand 1986: A Comparison with the United Kingdom 1974-79." *International Journal of the Sociology of Law* 16 (1988): 103-126.

Race Relations Conciliator, *Race Against Time*. Wellington: Human Rights Commission, 1982.

Reiner, Robert. *The Blue-Coated Worker. A Sociological Study of Police Unionism*. Cambridge: Cambridge University Press, 1978.

Reith, C. *The Blind Eye of History*. London: Faber, 1952.

Remfrey, P.J. "Conditions of Service." In Bruce Swanton, Garry Hannington, and Trish Psaila (eds.). *Police Source Book 2*. Canberra, ACT: Australian Institute of Criminology, 1985.

Report for...Minister of Police from C. M. Nicholson Q.C. re: Paul Chase Shooting. Wellington: Department of Justice, 1983.

Report of the Audit Office on Effectiveness and Efficiency in the New Zealand Police for the year ended 31 March 1980. Unpublished, June 1981.

Report of the Chief Ombudsman for the Year Ending 31 March 1976. Wellington, New Zealand, 1976.

Report of the Chief Ombudsman on the Investigation of Complaints Against the Police Arising From the South African Rugby Tour of New Zealand in 1981. Wellington: Government Printer, 1983.

Report of the Committee to Inquire into the Training of the New Zealand Police Force. Unpublished, July 1955.

Report of Committee to Review the New Zealand Police. Unpublished, November 1978.

Reports of the Controller and Auditor-General for the Year Ending 31 March 1980 and 1981. Wellington, New Zealand, 1980 and 1981.

Report of the Government Administration Committee 1987. Wellington, New Zealand, 1987.

Report of the Inquiry into Departmental Annual Reporting Standards. Wellington, New Zealand, 1987, I.6c.

Report of the Ministerial Committee of Inquiry into Violence. Wellington, New Zealand: Department of Justice, 1987.

Report of Police Personnel Policy Committee. Unpublished. Wellington, December 1983.

Report of the Royal Commission to Inquire into the Circumstances of the Convictions of Arthur Allan Thomas for the Murders of David Harvey Crewe and Jeanette Lenore Crewe. Wellington: Government Printer, 1980.

Reports of the Select Committees on the Estimates of Expenditure and Supplementary Estimates for the Years Ending 31 March 1986 and 1987. Wellington, New Zealand, 1986 and 1987.

Robinson, M. "New Zealand Police Constables Job Analysis Survey." Unpublished. New Zealand Police Headquarters, May 1982.

Robson, J. *The Ombudsman in New Zealand.* Wellington, New Zealand: Victoria University, Institute of Criminology, 1979.

Royal Commission on Social Policy, The. *The April Report,* Volume I: New Zealand Today; Volume II: Future Directions; Volume IV: Social Perspectives. Wellington: The Royal Commission on Social Policy, 1988.

Royal New Zealand Police College. *Police Behavioral Science: Police History and Principles.* 1987a.

__________. *Police Behavioural Science: Police Ethics.* 1987b.

Rusbatch, S. A. "Sergeants Need Room To Move." *New South Wales Police News,* September 1976.

__________. "Management Models and Police Uniqueness." In *Project Blueprint.* Bramshill, England: Bramshill Police College, 1985.

Sherman, Lawrence W. "College Education for Police: The Reform that Failed?" *Police Studies* 1(1) (1978): 32-38.

Sid (pseud.). "To be a man in the NZ Police." *International Police Association (New Zealand Section) Journal* 21(4) (1987): 79-89.

Singer, M. S. H. and Singer, A. E. "Police Attitudes Towards Ethnic Groups in New Zealand." *Police Studies* 7(4) (1984a): 237-240.

Singer, M. S. H., Singer, A. E., and Burns, D. "Police Cynicism in New Zealand: A Comparison Between Police Officers and Recruits." *Police Studies* 7(2) (1984b): 77-83.

Social Monitoring Group. *From Birth to Death II: The Second Overview Report.* Wellington: New Zealand Planning Council, 1989.

"Special Report of the Ombudsman upon Complaints Against Police Conduct." Wellington, New Zealand, 1970.

Stace, M. "The Police as Prosecutors." In Neil Cameron and Warren Young (eds.). *Policing at the Crossroads.* Wellington: Allen and Unwin, 1986.

Stirling, P. "A Cop's Lot: Common Plight." *New Zealand Listener,* 8 March 1986, 19-20.

__________. "One Law for All?" *New Zealand Listener*, 3 December 1988, 18-20.

Strategos Consulting Limited. *New Zealand Police: Resource Management Review 1989*. Wellington: Strategos Consulting Limited, 1989.

Streetwize Comics No. 1. Christchurch: Christchurch Community Law Centre, December 1987.

Swanton, B., Hannington, G. and Biles, D. (eds.). *Police Source Book*. Canberra, ACT: Australian Institute of Criminology, 1983.

Swanton, B., Hannington, G., and Psaila, T. (eds.). *Police Source Book 2*. Canberra, ACT: Australian Institute of Criminology, 1985.

Swanton, B., and Wilson, P.R. "Police Occupational Standing—Prestige and Benefits." *Australian and New Zealand Journal of Criminology* 7(2) (1974): 95-98.

Tait, G. *Never Back Down*. Christchurch: Whitcoulls, 1978.

Te Whainga i Te Tika, see Advisory Committee on Legal Services.

The Police and the 1981 Tour. Wellington: Victoria University History Department, Occasional Papers No.2, 1985.

Thompson, K. O. "New Zealand Police Strategic Management Plan." Unpublished memorandum. Wellington: Police Headquarters, 21 December 1984.

__________. "In Search of a Better Police Service." Unpublished memorandum. Police National Headquarters, 19 June 1985a.

__________. "Community Policing: The Commissioner's View." *New Zealand Police Association Newsletter* 17(11) (1985b): 114.

Trappit, E. J. "Management by Objectives in the New Zealand Police—What Course Should It Follow?" Unpublished paper for Bramshill Police College, n.d.

Twentyman, G. E. "Status of District Commanders and a Review of Commissioned Rank." Unpublished report. New Zealand Police Headquarters, June 1970.

Walker, S. *A Critical History of Police Reform*. Lexington, Massachusetts: Lexington Books, 1977.

Walton, R. J. "Relationships with the Media." Unpublished Commissioner's Circular, 1978/27, 3 August 1978.

__________. "Comment to the Media in Criminal Cases." Unpublished Commissioner's Circular, 1980/16, 26 May 1980.

__________. "Serious Crime Investigation." Unpublished Commissioner's Circular, 1981/24, 22 September 1981.

Watkins, T. K. and Paterson, A. I. H. "Supplementary Report on Basic Training in the New Zealand Police." Unpublished. Wellington: Police National Headquarters, July 1975.

Welfare Guide. Wellington: New Zealand Police Staff Benevolent and Welfare Fund, 1984.

Wilson, J. Q. *Varieties of Police Behavior.* New York: Atheneum, 1971.

Wiseman, P. W. "Complaints Against the Police." Unpublished paper presented to Twentieth Officers Course, Australian Police College, 1980.

Wood, D. A. "The Ombudsman and the Police: An Historical Introduction." Unpublished Master of Arts extended essay, University of Canterbury, 1985.

"Working Party on Rationalisation of Tertiary Education in the Police." Unpublished. New Zealand Police Headquarters, March 1985.

Workman, Kim. "Community Policing—An Agent for Organisational Change?" *New Zealand Police Association Newsletter* 17(9) (1985): 84-85.

Young, S. "New Zealand." In Bruce Swanton, Garry Hannington, and Trish Psaila (eds.). *Police Source Book 2.* Canberra ACT: Australian Institute of Criminology, 1985.

Young, W. "Investigating Police Misconduct." In Neil Cameron and Warren Young (eds.). *Policing at the Crossroads.* Wellington: Allen and Unwin, 1986.

Young, Warren and Cameron, Neil. *Issues in Policing: The 1980's* Wellington: Radio New Zealand, 1985.

__________, (eds.). *Effectiveness and Change in Policing.* Wellington: Institute of Criminology, Victoria University of Wellington, 1989.

Newspapers, Newsletters, and Assorted Other Sources

Auckland Star:

23-30 October 1976

(The) Bulletin:

August 1967

October 1967

May 1968
August 1970

September 1975

October 1976
February 1979
December 1981
December 1984
October 1985
February 1986
June/July 1986
Dominion (Wellington):
22 July 1983
Dominion Sunday Times (Wellington):
4, 9 September 1988
Evening Post (Wellington):
21 November 1984
New Zealand Herald (Auckland):
23-30 October 1976
New Zealand Police Journal:
February 1937
New Zealand Times (Wellington):
22 December 1985
Newsletter (*see* also New Zealand Police Association):
July 1982
July 1985
October 1985
January 1986
April 1986
August 1986
January 1987
February 1987
April 1987
May 1987
July 1987

December 1988

December 1989

Press (Christchurch):

27 July 1973

10 April 1975

24 December 1976

5, 6, 8 July 1977

30 January 1984

2 February 1984

1 September 1984

6 July 1985

17 September 1985

11, 20, 22, 25 January 1986

3 March 1988

8 May 1988

23 August 1988

28 September 1988

5, 25 November 1988

3, 29 December 1988

SUMMARY AND OVERVIEW

by Dilip K. Das

The countries discussed in the book come from three different continents: Asia (India and Japan), Australia (Australia and New Zealand), and Europe (Finland). Geographically, Australia is a continental landmass in the southwest Pacific region. India is a peninsula with the Himalayan Mountains in the north, and surrounded by the seas including the Atlantic Ocean on the three other sides. Finland is one of the five Scandinavian countries. Japan is an island country with four large and numerous small islands. Situated in the southwest Pacific, New Zealand consists of two large islands and a number of smaller ones.

IMPACT OF HISTORY

In each chapter there is a reference to the history of the country reviewed. History helps in appreciating the contemporary developments of the police.

Australian law enforcement was initially in the hands of the military detachments primarily detailed for convict supervision. Military mounted police operated in the countryside, and they were modelled on the Royal Irish Constabulary. Later convicts were also selected for law enforcement role. These two factors were responsible for generating a climate of repression and coercion. According to the author of the chapter, namely, Stephen James (1994), so enormous have been the changes, that today the past appears indeed very distant. But he (James, 1994) adds that "the history of Australian policing plays a crucial analytical place in understanding contemporary policing." James traces several problems of Australian police to its historical legacy: hostile relations between the police and Aborigines; poor calibre of early recruits; brutality; and antagonism between the police and organized labor.

Finland's police also have inherited some problems from their history. In Finland the Czar established the first Chamber of Police in 1816 for policing of the ancient capital, Turku, and since then there has been considerable governmental authority over the police. In Finland the local or town police administration became the responsibility of the national government in 1904. Although rural policing was of lesser importance, it also became a national government responsibility by early twentieth century. While the Ministry of Justice has been the controlling authority over the police in other Scandinavian countries, the otherwise powerful and executive Ministry of the Interior has always exercised control over the police in Finland. There is also a stigma attached to the Finnish police as they were created by the Russian Czar to keep a strict control over citizens.

Centuries of foreign domination have created in India a condition of economic depression and a climate of social injustice. In this country, characterized by a mind-boggling diversity in language, religion, race and social practices, these factors have pushed the inherent diversities to fissiparous tendencies resulting in "regionalistic terrorism" (Diaz, 1994), endemic communal disharmony, sporadic violence with alarming frequencies, and a mood of national despair. That Indian police were a creation of a colonial power primarily for the purpose of their own imperial interests does not lend them enormous legitimacy in dealing with the nation's problems. According to the author of the chapter on Japan, in his country which is almost totally homogeneous, traditional wisdom stresses communal harmony. There is a belief that society cannot survive unless members "make mutual concessions to live together." They make major decisions by consensus in order to "appease...their opponents" (Ueno, 1994). The police have also a noble origin. Ueno says that the *Kebiishi,* the first formal uniform police in Japan, were manned by the sons of the powerful families in the countryside. He says that "the directors of the *Kebiishi* were appointed from the nobility." Dunstall (1994) comments that "the police in New Zealand is a fragment of an imported culture refashioned in a changing environment." Since 1840 when Britain acquired sovereignty over New Zealand, the colonial government adapted various British laws and modes of policing: small local forces supervised by magistrates, Armed Police modelled on the Irish Constabulary, nonmilitarized civil police, etc. It was again historical forces which, by the turn of the century, made the London Metropolitan Police the model for the police in New Zealand.

In none of these countries have the police been able to avoid the influence of history. History seems to have attached a stigma to the police in Australia, Finland, and India. That stigma continues to color the image of the police in these three countries. History is a major constraint on police reforms.

MANDATE AND PHILOSOPHY

In each of the societies, the police have a mandate and a philosophy. In Australia police commissioners enjoy considerable autonomy in the day-to-day administration. Individual officers are accountable to law and not their superiors although, as elsewhere, Australian police departments are designed hierarchically according to the classical principles of administration. It is part of police philosophy to accept "the essential reciprocality between the police and the policed" (James, 1994). Force is to be applied by the police only when its use is absolutely unavoidable. "Considerable governmental authority over the police" (Laitinen, 1994) as well as their Czarist connection tends to taint the police in Finland philosophically as an organ of the state. In 1973 the Police Act was amended to make room for advisory boards consisting of the members of the public for their input into police administration. The advice of such boards is not binding.

After the annexation of India's western region of Sind to British India in 1840, General Napier of the British Army organized the civil administration in the newly conquered territory and established a new brand of policing in India modelled on the Royal Irish Constabulary. This model spread to other parts of the British India, and in 1861 an act called the *Indian Police Act* was passed making policing a provincial (state) responsibility. In each province (state) the police were placed under the supervision of an Inspector

General of Police who was answerable to the provincial government. In the districts which are important administrative centers the police were placed under the general direction of the District magistrate who was the chief of civil administration. That arrangement continues to color the philosophy and mandate of the Indian police. In India, says Diaz (1994), "the Sind model spread everywhere...as a state-level organization serving the government of the state more directly as a ruler-appointed force" (Diaz, 1994).

In describing Japanese police philosophy and mandate, Ueno (1994) dwells on respect Japanese "reserve" for their police as they do "for the symbols of the state." He claims that the association of the nobility gave the police mandate and philosophy a moral fervor. Ueno adds:

> Young and ambitious countrymen gladly went to the imperial capital, Kyoto, to serve the guards for many years without pay. When they returned home with the honorable title of Kebiishi, their political power was guaranteed and they became influential in their region. They and their clan became Samurai who constituted the ruling class in the feudal age.

Later in the nineteenth century, the Samurai (aristocratic military class) became police officers "bringing with them the characteristics of the well-educated, ethical, self-sacrificing and responsible servants of the society." These officers were committed to the "ideals learned through Confucianism." According to Ueno, Confucianism became "the official ideology and subculture of the Japanese police." This is in sharp contrast with the situation in India where only the most backward and the poorer classes have traditionally supplied the rank and file personnel of the police.

In describing the mandate and philosophy of the police in Japan, Ueno (1994) also refers to the fact that Japan borrowed by 1874 a national model of policing as practised in France and Prussia. The political leaders under the Meiji government who introduced European culture and technology into Japan regarded the police as "an instrument for creating a new nation" (Ueno, 1994). The police are expected to act for the good of the public and use discretion which is regarded as "a product of wisdom and skill." According to Ueno, "the tradition of the Samurai and Confucianism continued to be the backbone of the police." After the war Japanese police were reorganized on the model of decentralized American police.

But decentralization did not work in Japan. In 1954 a new law brought about a new police system embodying the concepts of democracy and centralization.

According to the *Police Force Act* of 1913, the police mandate in New Zealand was "the preservation of peace and order, the prevention of crime, and the apprehension of offenders against the peace" (Dunstall, 1994). The mandate was apparently kept broad in order to honor the principle of constabulary independence. In 1984 the then Commissioner of New Zealand police issued a mission statement in which he called upon his personnel to work together with community and other agencies in order to provide a high quality of service for protecting life and property, preventing crime, maintaining the peace, and detecting offenders. He also urged police officers to adhere only to fair and legal means, exercise appropriate discretion, use the minimum degree of force, and to be committed to serving one and all regardless of race, color, or creed. In the 1988 *Annual Report*, the mandate and philosophy received a greater emphasis in the direction of community policing. Dunstall (1994) suggests that there is no clear mandate and philosophy, and to the severest critics it appears that the police mandate and philosophy is to be seen as "an instrument of government policy and of pakeha values: an inevitable defender of the status quo."

In the account of police mandate and philosophy presented above, one notes that use of minimum force, working with community, and constabulary independence are stressed in Australia and New Zealand. This is in the best tradition of English policing. In Finland the police are part of national government with a limited channel for citizen input into police activities. Japanese police, respected as a symbol of the state and for their moral qualities, are charged with a value-laden mandate. India's police have inherited the Royal Irish Constabulary mandate: to maintain law and order as an instrument of government.

FUNCTIONS

Legal requirements, expediency of administration, and social problems have thrust upon the police a variety of functions. Police work varies from country to country.

The police in Australia are responsible for such functions as: the preservation of the peace; prevention and detection of crime; protection and recovery of life and property; conflict resolution; the control of road traffic; the investigation of sudden deaths; enforcement of court orders; protection of fundamental freedoms; statutory duties such as supervision of the provisions of the Liquor Control Act; the provision of help to the needy; and miscellaneous services, such as search and rescue work.

The police in Finland are also engaged in the activities Australian police perform. Besides, they also carry out certain other functions regarding foreigners, administration of public licences, and recovery proceedings. Such functions are performed by Finnish police as an administrative agency of the state which is a tradition in the continental legal system. So they process foreigners, issue passports, exercise supervision over trade and business, as well as administer certain policies in regard to entertainment and games, social security, health and environmental affairs. Another notable task performed by Finnish police is picking up drunks from public places and bringing them to police stations where they are detained till they sober up. In Finland, like in other Scandinavian countries, public drunkenness is viewed as highly offensive and obnoxious. Laitinen says:

> A typical task of the Finnish police and, also, a problem, is the control and arrest of drunken persons for maintaining order. Annually, the number of arrested drunks is more than 2,000,000 which was high compared to the population of Finland consisting of 5,000,000 inhabitants.

The Security Police in Finland are involved in special tasks: prevention and investigation of anti-state activities.

Indian police are engaged in the functions that the police are required to perform in Australia as the police in both these countries were established by the British within the framework of the common law. The unique sociopolitical situation in India has bestowed upon the police certain unique tasks: promoting the nation's "integrity," resolving "conflicts," developing "amity," and collecting "intelligence on public peace and crime, especially affecting national integrity, security and economy" (Diaz, 1994). Communal disharmony, massive disturbances generated by religious fanaticism and intolerance, political squabbles, separatist tendencies in various regions of the country, and increasing violence in everyday life have made it imperative for the police to devote themselves to promoting national integrity, resolving communal conflicts, and preventing breach of public security. Political intelligence has been a police responsibility at local, state, and national levels since the colonial days.

Following the modification of the Police Law after World War II, Japanese police work today is broadly in conformity with American police functions which are similar to those enjoined upon the police in common-law countries. Like the *Police Judiciare* in France, and the *Kriminalpolizei* in Germany (Japan modelled on European police during the Meiji regime), the police in Japan have "ten special law enforcement agencies usually described as special judicial police" (Ueno, 1994). They are involved in investigation of certain offenses prescribed by special laws. Under the *Morality Business Act*, the police issue business licences to bars, cabarets, massage parlors, strip show theaters, adult shops, love hotels, gambling houses, and other entertainment establishments. The Security Division of the National Police Agency also conducts operations against terrorism and other subversive activities affecting national security.

The functions of police in New Zealand are similar to what the police do in Australia. Dunstall (1994) describes the police functions in New Zealand as "Corporate services" (administrative and other services used by the police as a whole); Community safety and security (motorized and beat patrol which constitutes the bulk of police activity); Investigative services (work done by criminal investigation branch including document examination, fingerprinting, witness protection, etc.); Drug enforcement and intelligence programs (including surveillance squads, undercover operations, and liaison officers in Bangkok, Australia, and Singapore); and Public affairs (community liaison, crime prevention, youth aid, and a law-related education program). Since the elimination of Special Branch in 1956, New Zealand police have not been concerned with political surveillance. There are units like the New Zealand Security Intelligence Service, the National Bomb Data Center, and the Terrorist Intelligence Unit with responsibility for national security.

According to the model of law (continental or common law, for example), police functions vary. The police are also entrusted with unique duties according to the problems a society confronts. Maintenance of order, prevention, and detection of crime, maintenance of national security, administration of political surveillance, civic administration, and various miscellaneous taks are performed by the police.

PERSONNEL PRACTICES

Included within personnel practices are recruitment, selection, training, and promotion. With a knowledge of the history, mandate, philosophy, and function of the police in the countries discussed in the book, it is useful to review how police departments acquire, acculture, and develop their personnel.

In Australia, and also in Finland and New Zealand, hiring takes place only at the level of a constable. A variety of recruitment efforts are made. The educational requirement is completion or near completion of secondary schooling (twelve years). Recruits must meet quantifiable standards in regard to education, height, weight, vision, and physical fitness. They are also subjected to qualitative criteria in communication skills, demeanor, maturity, and motivation. Nonacceptance rates for applicants is high. At the basic level training consists of months of classroom and drill instruction at an academy, field training under supervision, and a final period back at school. In spite of the fact that behavioral studies, management courses, police studies, and academic subjects like English have now been included in recruit training, it has remained generally vocational. Training is also provided for subofficers (sergeants and senior sergeants), commissioned officers, and specialists (especially criminal investigators). These courses for which officers become eligible on the basis of promotion are generally shorter in duration and more specifically aimed at developing skills as managers and specialists. James (1994) comments that Australian promotion system "comprises a mixture of seniority (period spent in the department) and merit" in terms of promotion examination success, experience and other relevant qualifications, and interviews. In the promotion process merit has been receiving increasing attention. External education, which is encouraged by incentive pay, is also given importance in promotion consideration.

Finland has national standards for police candidates in regard to education and physical criteria. Male candidates must have successfully completed compulsory military service with a limited experience as a supervisor. Previous work experience is considered an advantage for entry into police. Laitinen (1994) observes that recruits with high school diplomas, who are called "students" in Finland, are increasing all the time. It is hard to find Swedish-speaking and Helsinki area applicants to the police. Helsinki, like other major urban centers in the world, is not a rich source of police recruitment. In regard to paucity of Swedish-speaking candidates, Laitinen (1994) comments that "Maybe the Swedish-speaking people, who seem to maintain a strong identity of their own, regard the police as a symbol of Finnish power." More than 50 percent of the applicants are not accepted. Police training has been synchronized and blended with various stages of vocational education prevailing in the country. A police officer cannot jump one stage; he or she must complete one stage of training to go to the next. And, "formal qualifications acquired through training" (Laitinen, 1994) is one of the criteria for promotion, which involves education at Police Academy for prolonged periods. Laitinen also observes that professional and law-related topics "constitute the main bulk of police training." Success in examinations, potential for success in higher positions, and, perhaps, some amount of political consideration is necessary for promotion.

There are three levels of entry to police service in India: one can enter as a constable, a sub-inspector (subofficer), and a commissioned officer. But the national government, too, hires commissioned officers to serve as police executives in states. There has been in the recent years an increase in the number of constables with high school diplomas. Candidates who have a university degree with proper health qualifications are eligible to apply for the position of a sub-inspector or Deputy Superintendent of Police. The Indian Police Service members who must have a university degree are hired, trained, and deputed to states by the national government. Basic constable training is composed of "outdoor and indoor work;...with perhaps an extra emphasis on physical rigor, parade ground work such as footdrill, arms drill as well as weapon training" (Diaz, 1994). With considerable physical training, sub-inspectors and Deputy Superintendents receive instructions in criminal laws, criminological concepts, management principles and techniques including public relations. The Indian Police Service (IPS) officers are trained at the National Police Academy in criminal law, criminology, police science, maintenance of public order, community relations, and so on. Emphasis on physical training and unarmed combat exercises, parade ground work and weapon training is noticeable. Generally, those who join as constables tend to retire as constables. An important reason for this is that educational requirement for the position of a constable is very low, which makes promotions to higher posts almost impossible. Promotions from the positions of sub-inspectors and Deputy Superintendents are better. The Indian promotion system is based on merit and seniority (meritorious service record) at the junior levels of supervision.

In Japan the process of selection as police officers involves determination of potential as community leaders. Police officers are to be model citzens. A very thorough background investigation of the potential candidates, which is also an important step in the hiring process in New Zealand, is undertaken in order to assess their moral qualities. One out of ten applicants succeeds. The Executive Candidates Examination is utilized to recruit the members of the elite corps of Japanese officers who start their career as junior executives but rapidly advance in their careers like the members of the Indian Police Service. They are generally law graduates from the Universities of Tokyo and Kyoto which were established by the Meiji government "to produce high-class bureaucrats" (Ueno, 1994). University education is encouraged through the opportunity of shorter training and accelerated eligibility for taking promotional examinations. Ueno (1994) says that training is regarded as education (in Finland where training is thorough and long, it is called education) and about 10 percent of basic recruits drop out as they cannot cope with the educational demands in police schools. Education in general culture, traditional martial arts, and professional subjects are emphasized equally in all three kinds of police educational facilities, namely, Prefectural Police Schools, Regional Police Schools, and the National Police Academy. While there is a preference for police officers as instructors as they are regarded as role models, outsiders particularly at the National Police Academy are utilized for non-police topics. Promotions to the lower and middle supervisors' levels are based on competitive examinations designed to test professional as well as general knowledge. As a matter of fact, all eligible persons are encouraged to take promotion examinations, known as achievement tests, in order to motivate them to study new laws, regulations, and other relevant topics. In the cases of promotions to superintendent, senior superintendent, and above the recommendations of the prefectural chiefs of police are very important. The system also facilitates promotion from the lowest level: at the time of writing Ueno (1994) found four superintendent supervisors, and 39 chief superintendents, which are top-level management positions, coming from the positions of constables.

As indicated above, the character of the recruits is thoroughly investigated in New Zealand. Dunstall comments that "malpractice by staff is generally seen within the police as stemming from a deficiency of personal character rather than training and organization." One in five applicants succeeds in entering the police. New Zealand has been rather innovative to responding to recruiting shortages. In 1957 the police introduced hiring younger persons as police cadets (subsequently abolished) to bypass stiff competitions in the labor market for younger people. In 1990 the minimum age requirements were raised from thirty-one to forty to encourage police women who had left to have children to return. As in Finland where vocational education is considered sufficient to compensate for a lack of general high school education of police applicants, in New Zealand prior work experience and skills such as a trade can be substituted for formal education. Overall, the recruits' level of education has been rising and at present 25 percent of them are college graduates. In New Zealand police training is considered very important. The college combines models of army and general civilian education and seeks to develop a distinctive police culture based on professionalism. Civilian education officers work at the Police College and are responsible for what is known as liberal studies which include behavioral studies, community relations, community-oriented policing and so on. The Police College which is equipped with a first-class library represents centralized training within the department. Such nomenclature as "commandant" and "wing" (a group) display a military flavor. Overseas training, encouragement for part-time as well as full-time university education, and specialist training with "the ideal of training as an ongoing process" (Dunstall, 1994) characterize police training. According to Dunstall, included in the set of beliefs guiding police training in New Zealand, is that training must capture the "multi-faceted nature of policing in a rapidly changing society" and it is important for building professional prestige which "leads to public cooperation." Promotions at the junior levels are based on qualifying exams: merit, educational qualifications, physical fitness, and readiness to serve in any part of the country are important in earning promotions. A Promotion Board processes all promotions at the basic and middle levels of supervision and the Commissioner of New Zealand Police, after informal consultations, recommends all promotions at the senior level to the Police Minister. Dunstall (1994) notes that the promotion system is criticized by some as "seniority and numbers game." Although the number of promotion-seekers is growing, constables decline promotions because of transfers. Compared to Japan the promotion process in New Zealand is not as challenging: it is not viewed as an essential criterion for achievement.

In all the countries under review, the rate of nonacceptance of police applicants at the basic level is fairly high; it was the least severe in India with 50 percent rate of rejection. The educational level of police recruits is rising everywhere. In Japan and India there is a provision for hiring young people with university degrees as junior executives who rapidly move to senior positions. Among the countries included in this book, India is the only country with an additional level of entry as subofficers apparently because educational attainment of constables is very low. Training is generally vocational and, in Finland, stages of police training are made to correspond to various stages of vocational education in the country. At the basic level most instructors are police officers, but in New Zealand there are also civilian education officers at the basic training program due to historical reasons. Promotions are a combination of merit and seniority. For the lower-level supervisory positions, officers have to take examinations for promotion. At senior levels no promotion examinations are held; political considerations in promotions apparently play a role in Finland and India. University education enables officers to enjoy certain advantages particularly in Japan, Australia, and New Zealand.

LEADERSHIP AND SUPERVISORY CALIBRE

Logically, this can be considered part of the previous section on personnel practices as it also includes promotion. However, because of the importance of the subject in general, and particularly as leadership and supervision has a high profile because of semi-military, hierarchical, and people-intensive nature of police organizations, it is discussed separately.

As the accounts from various countries show, the authors had approached the issue of leadership and supervision in different ways. Australia's James (1994) discusses leadership and supervisory calibre by describing the qualifications of the leaders and supervisors. He mentions that most top police leaders in Australia have university degrees. They are most likely to be trained in professional schools in Australia and abroad on management skills in accordance with an "increasing concern to match the skills required of police executives to demands and complexities of modern police management." Laitinen (1994) comments that Finnish police have by and large a "flat hierarchy." Another important distinction in Finland is that, unlike the four other countries included in the book, there are two kinds of leaders and supervisors in police organizations. Professional police leaders are those who come up through the ranks by meeting various promotional requirements. Law graduates who do not receive professional training in police academies are the top leaders and, they join the force in most cases as city police chiefs or as sheriffs in rural areas. These lawyers are also the people who man the top positions in regional and national police establishments.

In regard to the Indian situation, Diaz (1994) comments that in a state police organization (the police in India are part of public bureaucracy in states) the police chief is "a person most acceptable to the party in power, and not the best person with the ability to perform well and to carry the whole team with him." In several states this has deprived police organizations at the present time of a sense of cohesiveness and shared purpose. A fact resented by the District Police Superintendent, the most important field police leader and supervisor, is that his autonomy is curtailed by the need to follow the general direction of the chief administrator of the district who is another government bureaucrat. At the cutting-edge level the officer-in-charge of the police station is the head of his area and legally he is the authority to decide whether a criminal case should be prosecuted or not. Unfortunately, at the levels of both District Superintendent and the Officer-in-Charge there is a suspicion of political interference.

Like effective leaders in other spheres of Japanese society, Ueno (1994) argues, police leaders must possess "understanding and sympathy," "ability to work efficiently in a group," and capacity for attracting "personal commitment" from subordinates. They also must be consensus builders. Police leaders accept the position, like leaders in other organizations, that they are responsible for good morale and moral behavior of their subordinates. Dunstall (1994) comments that despite many reforms New Zealand police leadership has remained highly centralized. Even today, as was the case in the past, supervisory tasks consist mainly of "control and supervision of personnel in operational matters, careful scrutiny of all expenditure, and routine attention to files and correspondence." He adds that the trend is toward greater delegation of authority and more collegiality among lower and higher levels of leadership and supervision. Gradual replacement of authoritative command by participative management style as well as management by objectives has also been noted.

In countries like Finland it is traditionally recognized that top police leaders must have university degrees in Law. In other countries university degrees for top leaders are becoming more and more popular. Police heads in some countries like Finland are nonpolice officers while professional police executives come from the bottom. Political influence is not unknown in the selection of police leaders. In homogeneous societies without major problems, like New Zealand, police leadership tends to be centralized.

STANDARDS USED IN EVALUATING INDIVIDUAL PERFORMANCE

The evaluation of individual performance could also have been included within personnel practices. It has been treated here separately as the practices in this sphere provide valuable insights into the style of management in a police department.

Referring to both subjective and objective methods among the variety of evaluation procedures used in Australia, James (1994) remarks that "adequately capturing the performance parameters of police work, that most complex and diverse set of rules, remains a considerable problem." In Finland the evaluation of officers' performance is almost exclusively "informal and subjective." In the case of highest-level appointments "general reputation, suitabilty and willingness to move to the new positions" are considered. In India three methods of evaluation are generally utilized. Evaluation may be performed by "a direct on-the-spot field check." Statistics in regard to the rates of arrests, convictions, and recovery of property, etc., are also used. Thirdly, public goodwill earned by an officer is also considered to be a measure of an officer's good performance. According to Ueno (1994), "kindness is more highly appraised than strength or perfection of law enforcement" in Japanese police leaders. Other attributes that are taken into account in evaluating performance are "team spirit, a sense of belonging and group activity." Groups are recognized more often than individuals. Dunstall (1994) comments that "the state of the art in measuring effectiveness and efficiency...is still in its infancy in New Zealand." He says that evaluation criteria are largely qualitative consisting of such factors as adherence to law, absence of immoral behavior, generation of public trust, and so on.

No foolproof procedure for evaluation of the individual officer seems to have been found. Both subjective and objective methods are popular. Statistics (the rate of arrests, convictions, and recovery of property, etc.), public opinion, and direct observations through inspections by superiors are utilized for officers' performance appraisals. Officers may also be asked to comment on their own performance.

PROFESSIONALIZATION

The previous sections throw light on the state of police professionalization in the countries under review and the topics that follow the present section are also connected with it. In other words professionalization is so fundamental that it cannot be isolated from police functions, recruitment, training, leadership, and so on. It is also not separable from subculture, unions and associations, and public relations, etc., which are discussed following the section on professionalization.

Echoing the arguments of Swanton, James (1994) comments that in Australia the model of police professionalism is a "modified classical model." Unlike the traditional professions of law and medicine, policing is an occupation "aspiring to professional status." Some of the major obstacles to professional status are: complex, militarized rank structure; greater power exercised by unions over the rank and file officers than their own professional leaders; directions by outside agencies like governments, legislatures, and Commissions of Inquiries, etc.; police propensity to seek results by ignoring the ethicality of means; engagement of police officers in manual jobs like chauffeuring; and, the emphasis of training programs on learning the procedural details than about the occupation of policing. James argues that the police executives of the higher level can be regarded as professionals in the usual sense of the term. Laitinen (1994) observes that changes in training and education have given the police in Finland "a better professional image," but there are several deficiencies including an absence of membership in professional associations on the part of common police officers. Such membership is enjoyed only by the lawyer members of police management. He also implies that police officers in top management positions can be accepted as professionals based on the traditional criteria.

Diaz (1994) comments that Indian police have generally achieved a fine degree of professionalization at the level of the Indian Police Service. A very highly competitive process of selection, the requirement of a university degree, and a comprehensive course of training are all reliable indicators of professionalism in this service. However, he adds that this is not even remotely so in regard to the field-level management, "the cutting-edge" level, as he puts it. Diaz deplores that professionalization is nonexistent at the lowest level of the police organization. According to Ueno (1994), professionalism as a remedy against police misconduct is not really something that is discussed much in Japan. The criterion of professionalism is rather simple: "a good police officer must be a good citizen" who has numerous qualities. The police are required to follow a very strict code of conduct. Further, he says that police professionalism consists of "efforts to develop complete support and cooperation of the public." Moreover, it calls for continued "efforts to uphold the dignity and importance of the service." Unlike the police in Japan, Dunstall (1994) explains, the police in New Zealand have been consciously trying to professionalize themselves in order to "secure public approval and cooperation." They have come a long way but still, compared to "the ideal-type professions of law and medicine," policing is "bureaucratic" with "authoritative command" which allows "the practical professionals of the frontline" in their daily decision making, "the least professional autonomy."

In all the countries, except apparently in Japan, the police are striving to achieve professionalization in order to serve the people better. In Japan the police are exhorted not so much to professionalize themselves, but to achieve the attributes of an ideal citizen. However, the objectives in Japan and elsewhere are the same, i.e., better service delivery. In Australia, Finland, India, and New Zealand professionalization movement has achieved partial success.

WAGES, STATUS, SUBCULTURE, AND MORALE

A knowledge about police wages and status is necessary in order to appreciate how important a role the police play in society. If their service is not recognized through appropriate wages and they are not given a proper status, the police are likely to develop a sense of alienation through a subculture that weakens morale.

James (1994) says that Australian police officers are "currently, relatively well-paid." Policemen are classified as "lower middle class." He agrees with several other researchers that status of a police officer varies according to the rank he or she occupies in the organization. James comments that "it is impossible to draw upon any coherent and comprehensive body of data on police subcultures in Australia." He is of the opinion that Australian police subculture generated by police cynicism, alienation, and occupational identity is not really so well marked as to be easily recognizable. James notes that "a much more confident, aggressive and publicly-located police solidarity" has emerged in the recent years. It appears from a number of surveys that the morale of Australian police is not uniformly high. True, James indicates that it is difficult to measure morale accurately. Laitinen (1994) observes "remarkable increase in salaries of police personnel." In a nine-level division of socioeconomic status, the police fell on level five. But the level varies according to the rank of a police officer. Laitinen indicates that a degree of subculture exists among Finnish police personnel. He also notes police support to the right-wing political forces. Morale is felt to be generally high.

Diaz (1994) remarks that "constables' pay is progressively increasing; they are doing better than the other higher ranks." He also notes that status differs according to the rank, and the lowest-ranking police personnel in India have poor status. Diaz talks about a strong subculture in Indian police and bad morale resulting from rampant politicalization. Ueno (1994) remarks categorically that "Japanese police officers enjoy good wages and high social status." According to him, police officers do not regard themselves as "blue-collar workers" because of public "reliance" and "high respect." Subculture is apparently nonexistent because of high wages and respectable status. Accordingly, morale is also good. Dunstall (1994) notes that "police income has risen significantly." Noting that status depends on ranks, and also on locations (Officers enjoy higher status in rural areas), Dunstall remarks that "New Zealand police would be ranked well within white collar occupations or middle class." "Strong norms of solidarity," "conformity" of behavior encouraged by departmental discipline and an informal code, "a distinctive argot," and "a sense of isolation" are cited by Dunstall in support of police subculture in New Zealand. He comments that morale is very complicated to measure. Based on a number of indicators—like satisfaction with greater educational achievement, greater training, and increasing pay—it can be said that "morale is higher" than before.

Police wages have increased remarkably in the recent decades. Accordingly, status of the police has also improved. In Japan police status has been traditionally high. A distinctive police subculture is confirmed in India, Finland, and New Zealand by the authors of these respective chapters. But Japanese police seem to be least affected by the negative traits of the occupational subculture and, in Australia, too, those traits are not abundant in the manner depicted in American police literature. In Japan and Finland police morale is high; it appears social support and cooperation from other agencies, including the courts, is responsible for this development. Morale is fluctuating in Australia and New Zealand. In India politicalization is the principal factor affecting police morale negatively in the recent years.

UNIONS AND ASSOCIATIONS

Police wages, status, subculture, and morale are affected by the state of their unions and associations. The virulence of union/associations' actions is likely to depend on the degree of officers' frustration with wages and status. Ineffectiveness or public disapproval of unions' militancy may affect morale which, in turn, may solidify subculture of the police.

James (1994) says that Australian police unions are "an influential variable in the context of police organization and development." Although police administration and government resisted police unionization vehemently, the police were forced to "organize" because of "profound industrial neglect and adverse conditions of employment and remuneration." Generally, Australian police unions are involved in six broad spheres of activity: economic, welfare, discipline/legal, resolution of grievances, defense of service and information. There are separate unions for commissioned and noncommissioned officers in all states except one. James notes that "a significant degree of militancy has been evident" on the part of the union in disputes with government. Unions are increasingly moving in the direction of "public lobbying" because public support and sympathy are considered as "critical factors in the nature and degrees of confrontation." There has been a tendency to resort to "muscle-flexing." In Finland, too, as Laitinen argues, "meagre" wages and "low" prestige have prompted police unionization. Finnish police union movement is splintered both at the local and central levels. Most prominent role played by police unions is collective bargaining with the management. Indian police are allowed to form "associations," but not unions. According to Diaz (1994), the police are entitled to "little or no collective bargaining," and strikes are not permitted. While they have many grievances, the police have "little or no public support." There are three different kinds of associations corresponding to the three categories of personnel in Indian police. Diaz says that associations play a useful role when pay commissions are instituted for determination of salary and allowances of police personnel. Japanese police are not unionized. There are associations which handle matters of mutual interests excluding salaries, working hours, and working conditions. Dunstall refers to the existence of three organizations representing the personnel in the police: rank and file police officers, commissioned officers, and civilian employees. To the Police Association with the bulk of the police personnel as members, its "primary role" is to "protect and improve members' welfare." Militancy has been used by the Association to achieve success in its negotiations with the government. Dunstall also notes that "the Association has become more willing to exploit its political clout in the context of law and order politics." The move to achieve the right to full industrial action by the Police Association is being pursued vigorously.

Police unionization, as it is seen in the cases of Australia and Finland, is police response to meagre wages, bad working conditions, and low prestige. Unions and associations' actions have been marked by militancy in Australia and New Zealand apparently because it has secured success. In spite of widespread grievances, government has been able to resist police demand for unionization in India. Low public support is one of the main reasons for government's ability to do so. Japanese police who are well-paid and respected are not allowed to unionize, but they are also not pressing for it.

POLICE PUBLIC RELATIONS, PUBLIC CONFIDENCE, TRUST, AND RESTRAINTS ON THE POLICE

Discussions concerning unions and associations, and those dealing with professionalization, functions, wages, etc., highlighted an undeniable fact, albeit mostly indirectly: public support and goodwill are an important asset for the police. Australian police unions, for example, are focusing on lobbying for public support as a way to win their battles against the governments. Notwithstanding many grievances, the police in India cannot unionize because governments can ignore their demands as public support for the police is poor.

James (1994) comments on various police efforts at public relations which even draw criticism as attempts to "improve public relations by negotiating the most favorable image of the police." In regard to public confidence and trust, James says that, according to opinion surveys, the police in Australia were regarded as "high or very high" in ethical standards. An overwhelming number of respondents "always found the police to be polite and helpful." It is also pointed out by the author of the Australian chapter that both formal (administrative hierarchy, courts, and ombudsmen, etc.) and informal restraints upon the police are "enormous." In Finland, as noted by Laitinen, public relations efforts are rather limited. In the last few years the police have "produced educational programs cocerning traffic conduct, crime prevention and certain other topics." Based on various surveys and opinion polls, he comments that the police enjoy a fair reputation. Public confidence and trust can be described as good. Only recently restraints on the police have become more noticeable.

Diaz (1994) remarks that in India public relations is a relatively new idea in the field of management, and "the police of India, except for a few individual exceptions, have not understood or practiced it at all." In accordance with a survey done some two decades back, "the image of the police was decidedly poor." Diaz is categorical that "there is a complete lack of mutual trust between the police and the public." A major restraint, resulting from the lack of public trust, is that confession before a police officer is not admissible. The police are also restrained in their innovative operations because of the fact the public cooperation is limited. Echoing American researchers, Ueno (1994), maintains that Japanese police have excellent public relations. But he admits that it does not mean that "all people are friendly and cooperative with the police." Mothers discipline children threatening that the police will be called "to take them away." Ueno remarks that Japanese police "practice restraint in the use of power. Self-restraint and patience are always emphasized." Based on regular public surveys, Dunstall (1994) remarks that New Zealand police, "as an institution...is the focus of less media criticism and popular cynicism than Parliament, trade unions, or indeed the media itself." Public relations efforts have been many and varied, including a Law-Related Education Program in the elementary schools. He also notes that policy initiatives designed to improve relations with ethnic minorities, the Maoris and the South Pacific Islanders, have had "little impact." The police in New Zealand, like their counterparts in Japan, have more internal than external restraints. The commissioner cannot be directed by the Minister of Police in operational matters. The police are subjected to only "a limited measure of external restraints" by the courts. There is also the Police Complaints Authority headed by a civilian. According to Dunstall, the authority of this civilian body is a "balance between preserving the commissioner's responsibility for discipline (and police morale), and public confidence that police policies and behavior are effectively supervised."

Public relations efforts vary from country to country. Such initiatives are considerable on the part of Australian and New Zealand police. In Finland, and also in India, public relations activities are minimal; it is more so in India. But the reasons are different. In the former country, the police occupy a good social position. It appears that there is no need felt by Finnish police to woo the public in view of public confidence they enjoy. It has been suggested that an attitude of apathy and indifference marks the police public relations in India. It appears that so secure is the foundation of police public relations in Japan that there was almost no need of special public relations initiatives on the part of the police. Restraints on the police depend on the trust and confidence of the public. James refers to enormous restraints on Australian police as the police have not been able to dissociate themselves from their shady past. But the police in New Zealand and Japan who seem to enjoy a great deal of public trust are subjected to less severe external controls. Finland also falls in the same category. However, in India public trust is so low that restraints on the police are almost debilitating.

PROBLEMS OF THE POLICE

Apart from the problems noted in the course of discussions on various aspects of policing, there are some more general police problems in each country under review. These problems are not specifically connected with one aspect or another of policing. These are broader organizational, operational, and social problems the police are confronting in each society. Perhaps it is useful to remember here that the problems discussed in this section are considered important by each author according to his own particular understanding and judgment.

According to James (1994), Australian police believe that crime, particularly several specific categories of crimes like white-collar and organized crime, drug trafficking, domestic violence, and child abuse are increasing and, the police are less able to prevent or solve them. Youth and aboriginals are problem populations for Australian police as both come into conflict with the latter for their disproportionately larger role in crime and disorder. Some other police problems highlighted by James are a lack of accountability, malpractice such as corruption, brutality, as well as criminal and disciplinary offenses. Police violence or threat of violence, abuse of power, corruption, perjury, breaches of criminal law, and other forms of misconduct have been regarded as "significant problems" by various commissions instituted by state governments. Recommendations of the commissions for tackling these problems, particularly the problem of corruption, have not generally been implemented. Besides, insufficient delegation of authority, inadequate decentralization, incomplete coordination of specialized units, and several other negative features of police administration are responsible for officers' perception that "departmental administration significantly lowered morale." Laitinen (1994) refers to a number of primarily organizational problems. These are: inadequate resources including personnel; a lack of proper police public relations; uneven allocation of police officers; bureaucratic, centralized, militaristic and law-oriented philosophy of policing; recent politicalization at the top of the police hierarchy; inadequate powers including a "blanket ban on all wiretapping" and, also, the presence of "certain semisecret units inside their organization."

Diaz (1994) says that one of the major problems in India is the near total deployment of the police for order maintenance. As a result of government concern for containing disorder, which erupts through ceaseless protests, demonstrations, riots, and other forms of mass actions, recent years have witnessed the massive expansion of armed police units at the cost of routine, preventive police. Thus, the police have been denuded of the ability to concentrate on routine tasks like preventive patrol, crime prevention initiatives, and criminal investigation. Diaz notes that lack of "technological support in regard to transportation, communications and scientific aids" has exacerbated the problem. People tempt the police to use force against suspects. There are instances of the police catering to the depraved taste of certain sections of the community by brutalizing those in custody. Third-degree methods have cast doubt on police professionalization. Public relations is bad. Professionalization at the lowest level is still a distant cry as constables are undereducated, ill-trained, and ill-paid.

According to Ueno (1994), a major problem in Japanese society is that there has been a general decline of "confidence in the authority of the government." This has made law-abiding behavior less attractive. As a result, Japanese police morale has been severely challenged. As required by American concept of democracy introduced after World War II, the police have not been able to totally accept the position of being public servants instead of being servants of the emperor. Dunstall (1994) opens his discussion on the problems of New Zealand police saying that "popular pessimism of police efficacy in crime prevention has coincided with mounting fear of crime and greater move toward self-protection." Police officers in rural and small town stations were also feeling intimidated by gang members. Dunstall (1994) also mentions that "the issue of police accountability to the executive of government is still unresolved." He adds that "a more profound challenge to police accountability and responsiveness is coming from Maori communities." Nevertheless, policing policies are likely to "be formulated within the perspective of the dominant culture." Dunstall considers this to continue as a dominant problem in the near future.

Frequent commissions of inquiries into alleged misconduct, reactionary organizational practices, as well as police inability to do much about rising crime and violence seem to have affected the morale of Australian police. Bureaucratic organizational practices, inadequate but also uneven distribution of resources, politicalization at the top, and a perception that police lack some essential powers apparently have affected Finnish police negatively. Indian police are bedevilled by their constant deployment for containing crises (primarily generated by demonstrations and protests), inadequate resources, a lack of professionalism, and insufficient or nonexistent public cooperation. In Japan the police, accustomed to being emperor's servants, are not yet totally attuned to being public servants in a democratic society. They are also somewhat demoralized by diminished respect accorded to the police by educated, affluent, and modern Japanese. Rising fear of crime coupled with erosion of public confidence in police capability to prevent it, and the unresolved problems of policing a multicultural society are worrying the police in New Zealand.

CONCLUSIONS

In international comparative police courses and study in the United States, there has been a tendency to highlight the shortcomings of the police in this country. This is perhaps demoralizing to innovative police leaders in the United States (Das, 1985). Such demoralizing spirit is not conducive to learning and experimenting with new ideas. Moreover, this defeats the purpose of international comparative study. It should not be judgmental; it should testify to the fact that international comparative police research is only a means of developing knowledge about the police and not for passing judgment (Banton, 1964; Das, 1985).

I do not propose to highlight here the shortcomings and failures of the U. S. police, contrasting them with attractive features of the police in Australia, Finland, India, Japan and New Zealand. A list of the unique features of the police included in the book can be made and perhaps it can be examined if there are features worth emulating. Instead, it is proposed to present in this section the basic issues highlighted by the respective authors in their own "conclusions." The issues raised by them constitute their recommendations to their police. They vary from country to country. My "conclusions" are a summary of the conclusions of the various contributors.

Contributors have highlighted some basic challenges faced by their police. Australian police have not been able to wash off the historical stigma. However, the police have made vigorous efforts for getting out of the constraints imposed by history. With better training, finer human qualities, and elements of professionalism, the police have earned a good social status. The police are displaying confidence in their competence and abilities. They even welcome public scrutiny.

Finnish police, unlike their Scandinavian partners, are more under the direct control of the government in Helsinki. Greater than Swedish perhaps is the extent of German influence upon Finnish policing. That may perhaps explain the legalistic attitude of the police in Finland. Uneven distribution of human resources has created problems in the new and fast-growing Finnish cities. However, the Finnish police, largely as a result of a benign environment, are successfully tackling the problems they are confronting. They have not been overwhelmed like the German police by a sense of alienation and public apathy (Das, 1994). They are in control.

India's problems are gigantic. The police have inherited a shady tradition. Independence has not changed their role as the strong arm of the government. Diaz sees a hope for the police in India if they can look upon themselves as the police of the poor. He seems to suggest that policing a nonaffluent society calls for a radical strategy. The police must help the poor more. This is very much unlike "equality before law" principle that forms a hallmark of the U. S. legal system. But, I believe, Diaz is stressing that the police in nonaffluent and technologically backward nations must be more humane toward the people, and most of them happen to be the economically depressed sections of the society.

In regard to how the police in Japan should be prepared for the future, Ueno suggests that Japanese police should remember that they are the best for Japan as U. S. police are the best for the United States. He implies that society deserves the police it gets. The police in Japan must bear in mind that the country must be perfect before they can achieve perfection. In other words, Ueno is perhaps emphasizing that not all initiatives are in the hands of the police. Society must practice the ideals it preaches. It can expect a perfect police if it adheres to perfect ideals.

The police in New Zealand have taken a more professional route to progress: "clearly defined objectives" and "prioritized outputs." There have been suggestions for "contracting out to other providers" services they can render more economically. More cost effectiveness in the use of resources was an important goal. Dunstall is not as philosophical in his conclusions as his counterparts from Australia, India, and Japan are. The Finnish countributor, too, mentions fair and even distribution of police resources as an important goal for future improvement of police service. He has also taken a management approach.

Is there something useful in the practices and experiences of the police in Australia, Finland, India, Japan, and New Zealand for the United States or any other countries? Perhaps there is. Can others borrow something from any of these countries and implement the same at home? The answer does not seem to be easy. Bayley (1976) says that "the most important reason for studying foreign experience is to learn to recognize the character of our own institutions." There can be no doubt that it is possible to do so through our present endeavor. Such an appreciation of one's own system is "essential for planning what we might become." True, "cultural and national traditions are powerful determinants of police activity in the community" (1983). Those who want to make changes must be able to decipher that reforms must conform to cultural beliefs and norms. Bayley seems to believe that the police can not change unless society changes. Police institutions have "unique compulsions and constraints." But comparative study of the police can provide us with "the knowledge needed to specify the limits to practicable action." Moreover, as Bayley says, the police are also capable of affecting social values and there exists a "reciprocal interaction" between a country's police, political system, and social environment. "Social change" may be brought about "by government instrumentalities, among them the police" (1977).

All the countries included in the book—Australia, Finland, India, Japan, and New Zealand—have worked with some forms of imported police models. They were brought in from the outside as there was a need felt for such an importation. In other words, the imported form of policing was found useful. Based on this experience of usefulness—which helped foreign models to succeed in Japan, India, or Australia—we can say that a society must correctly decide what must be changed in its police. If the changes desired are determined correctly, the implementation of a planned measure, an imported one at that, is likely to be successful.

REFERENCES

Banton, Michael. *The Police in the Community*. New York: Basic Books, Inc., Publishers, 1964.

Bayley, David H. "The Limits of Police Reform." In David H. Bayley (ed.). *Police and Society*. Beverly Hills, California: Sage Publications, 1977.

__________. "Knowledge of Police." In Maurice Punch (ed.). *Control in Police Organization*. Cambridge, Massachussetts: M.I.T. Press, 1983.

__________. *Forces of Order: Police Behavior in Japan and the United States*. Berkeley, California: University of California Press, 1976.

Das, Dilip K. "The Image of American Police in Comparative Literature." *Police Studies* 8 (2) (1985): 74-83.

NOTES ABOUT THE CONTRIBUTORS

This volume would have been impossible without the creative input and expertise of its contributing authors, who are listed below in the order in which their chapters appear in this work.

STEPHEN JAMES holds a Ph.D. and teaches in the Criminology Department at the University of Melbourne, Victoria, Australia. His research interests include police selection, training, and performance assessment, police organization and culture, police unions, and the policing of young people. He has published articles in the *Journal of Applied Psychology*, the *Australian and New Zealand Journal of Criminology*, and *Policing and Society*, and has written chapters in several volumes about the policing of Australian youth. Dr. James is currently working on police culture and violence.

AHTI LAITINEN is an Associate Professor of the Sociology of Law at the University of Turku and Docent of the Sociology of Law at the University of Helsinki, Finland. Dr. Laitinen holds a Master of Political Science (1972), Licentiate in Political Science (1974), and Doctor of Political Science (1977), all from the University of Turku, Finland. His published works include: *Sociology of Law* (with T. Kyntaja) (1983); *Biologism in Social Sciences* (1985); *The Crimes of Power* (1989); "Finnish Drug Control Policy, Change and Accommodation," in *Drugs, Law, and the State* (1992); and *Beyond the Law: Juvenile Delinquency and Crime Prevention* (1990).

S. M. DIAZ, Ph.D., IPS (Rtd), is a former Director of the National Police Academy of India, Hyderabad, and an Honorary Professor of Criminology at the University of Madras. He has written several books on police subjects and scores of articles published in national and international journals as well as chapters of collected editions. Currently he is the Director of the Institute of Criminological Research, Education, and Services, Madras, and is a member of the Advisory Committee of the National Institute of Criminology and Forensic Science, New Delhi (India).

HARUO UENO studied political science and law at Tokyo University before joining the police in 1965. After he served in the Criminal Investigation Division and Administrative Division in the prefecture police and the National Police Agency of Japan, he was assigned as First Secretary of the Japanese Embassy in Washington, DC (1977-80). He served as Private Secretary to Prime Minister Takeshita (1987-89), and Chief of the Gunma Prefecture Police (1991-1992). His major books, *Police in the World, Law Enforcement System of the United States* (1971; reprinted 1988) and *Police History of Japan* (1981), have been published in Japanese.

GRAEME DUNSTALL is a Lecturer in History, at the University of Canterbury, Christchurch, New Zealand. He contributed a chapter to the *Oxford History of New Zealand* (1981), and is presently completing Volume 4 of the *History of Policing in New Zealand* (1918-1945) and will write Volume 5 (1946-1990). He teaches a course on criminal justice history with special reference to New Zealand.

ABOUT THE EDITOR

Dr. Dilip K. Das is a professor at Western Illinois University, Macomb, Illinois. Before joining Michigan State University in 1979 for graduate studies in Criminal Justice, Dr. Das was Chief of Police in a department of 5,000 sworn officers in the Indian state of Assam. He became a member of the Indian Police Service, an elite national police service, in 1965 as an Assistant Superintendent of Police.

Over the years Das has extensively studied the police in various countries of the world. Besides numerous articles on comparative policing as well as other aspects of policing, he has written two books: *Policing in Six Countries Around the World: Organizational Perspectives* (OICI, 1993), and *Understanding Police Human Relations* (Scarecrow, 1987).